European Positivism
in the Nineteenth Century

An Essay in Intellectual History

EUROPEAN POSITIVISM
IN THE NINETEENTH
CENTURY

An Essay in Intellectual History

W. M. Simon
Cornell University

CORNELL UNIVERSITY PRESS
Ithaca, New York

CORNELL UNIVERSITY PRESS

First published 1963

Library of Congress Catalog Card Number: 63-16446

PRINTED IN THE UNITED STATES OF AMERICA
BY VAIL-BALLOU PRESS, INC.

To My Children

PREFACE

ACCORDING to orthodox doctrine the preface is the place where an author may bare his soul to the prospective reader and disarm the imminent reviewer. I have had to trespass for this purpose on Chapter I, since a preface would not offer enough scope. This procedure has the advantage that it leaves me space in which to acknowledge my debts, which are exceptionally many in number and heavy in nature, in a more than merely perfunctory way.

First of all I should like to give my best thanks publicly for the kindly personal help I received from private individuals in Europe. In England hospitality as well as advice was offered by the late T. S. Lascelles, Dr. C. Baier, Mr. D. G. Fincham, Mr. J. D. Marvin, Mr. F. O. Ellis, and Mr. M. T. Hindson. The first four, and Mrs. Mary Braunholtz, also allowed me to use MS materials in their possession. Help by correspondence came from Miss B. Descours, Sir Charles Tennyson, and the late Charles Singer. Similarly, in France, I received welcome hospitality and invaluable help in the use of the materials of the Musée Auguste Comte from M. Paul Carneiro, and through the courtesy of M. H. C. Corra, M. F. Fagnot, and Dr. M. A. Fagnot I was permitted to use the papers of Emile Corra at the Archives Nationales, where Mme. Gille offered me exceptional facilities. I also called upon the time and knowledge of M. M. Bouvier-Ajam, M. Pierre Ducassé, Professor Henri Gouhier, and MM. Pierre Grimanelli, Charles Jeannolle *fils,* J. Feliciano de Oliveira, and Fernand Rousseau, and spent an enjoyable day with Dr. Heinrich Molenaar in Munich.

I am grateful for professional advice from Professors H. B. Acton, W. H. G. Armytage, A. J. Ayer, H. Hale Bellot, A. V. Judges, and Joseph Lauwerys, Messrs. Cyril Bibby and Royden Harrison, and Miss Margaret Knight; also Mr. H. J. Blackham, Mr. Hector Hawton, and Mr. J. Hutton Hynd, and Messrs. Iliffe, Sweet & Co. and Field, Roscoe & Co., solicitors. Personal thanks are due to Mr. G. Woledge, librarian of the British Library of Political and Economic Science, and to Mr. J. Swift, librarian of the Public Library of the Borough of Holborn, and general thanks for the use of the facilities of the British Museum, the Bodleian Library, and the libraries of the University of London, University College London, the Ministry of Education, the Public Record Office, the Bishopsgate Institute, the London County Council, and Repton School, and the Bibliothèque Nationale and the Bibliothèque de l'Arsénal. In addition I enlisted the aid of a number of other private individuals, librarians, and officials whose resources did not yield positive information.

Here at home my thanks go to Mr. Sydney Eisen, now of City College, for letting me use his microfilms of the letters of Frederic Harrison; to Professors Walter Houghton of Wellesley College and Francis Mineka of Cornell University for specialized help; to a group of graduate students at Princeton University for criticism; and above all to Professor Carl Schorske of the University of California for reading an early draft and making many most helpful suggestions; but obviously neither he nor any others here named should thereby be regarded as implicated in my misdeeds. Indispensable financial support was provided by the John Simon Guggenheim Foundation, the American Council of Learned Societies, the Faculty Research Grants Committee of Cornell University, and the Institute for Advanced Study. The last-named also added its friendly hospitality. For endurance above and beyond the call of duty I pay tribute to Miss Frances Lauman of the Cornell University Library.

Finally, just a few words about the arrangement of the book.

Part One concerns Auguste Comte, his doctrine, and his principal disciples, providing a relatively condensed history of institutionalized Positivism. Part Two, the longer of the main divisions, deals with the fortunes of the doctrine in the world beyond the organizations of avowed disciples. A general Conclusion follows.

Existing English translations have been used except when textual accuracy was in doubt. Otherwise, translations from French and German are my own.

W. M. S.

Ithaca, New York
January 1963

CONTENTS

PART ONE

❧❊❧

The Founder
and His Disciples

Chapter I

AUGUSTE COMTE AND

POSITIVISM

AMONG the pleasures of Lewis Carroll's world, so Humpty-Dumpty informs us, is the privilege of making a word mean just what you choose it to mean. We on this side of the Looking-Glass are obliged to define our terms. The "defining of terms" is a necessary but also usually a dreary pastime, and I propose to be as brief about it as I can. By "Positivism" I mean the doctrine founded by Auguste Comte, not only because Comte himself gave the doctrine that name, but because other usages tend to impoverish the language. For an attitude of admiration for the natural sciences and the wish to extend their virtues to other disciplines we have the excellent word "scientism," while to apply the word "positivism" to an abstemious, empiricist refusal to philosophize is plausible but wasteful, as well as in danger of being self-stultifying.[1]

---

[1] See in this connection above all D. G. Charlton, *Positivist Thought in France during the Second Empire, 1852–1870* (Oxford, 1959), pp. 5–9, and my review in the *American Historical Review,* Vol. 65 (1959–60), pp. 169–170. I would like to emphasize that I think highly of the substance of Charlton's book but consider much of it vitiated by his definition. In particular I agree heartily with him when he says (pp. 19–20): "One cannot

3

Comte's own system was anything but abstemiously empiricist. Positivism was in fact more than a method: it was a system of affirmations, a "conception of the world and of man." Of course the method is fundamental, or, rather, what is fundamental is the assumption that the phenomena of human thought and of social life are continuous with the phenomena of the inorganic and organic world of nature and therefore susceptible of investigation by analogous methods which will yield comparably reliable results. But this assumption, common enough in the nineteenth century and the basis of all "scientistic" attitudes, was worked out by Comte in a highly individual manner, by way of two interlocking and interdependent propositions: the Law of the Three Stages and the Classification (or Hierarchy) of the Sciences. The human mind inevitably developed from a first, theological stage in which it explained the world in terms of the will of anthropomorphic gods, by way of a second in which it explained the world in terms of metaphysical abstractions, to a third and final, positive stage in which it explained the world in terms of scientific truth.[2] But the mind did not traverse these stages with respect to all knowledge simultaneously, but rather in one discipline at a time, in a definite order, the order of their decreasing generality and increasing interdependence and complexity, namely, mathematics, astronomy, physics, chemistry, biology, sociology.

---

assume that all the works after Comte which show a scientific bent or an acceptance of the scientific method must have been inspired by his philosophy." See also Noel Annan, *The Curious Strength of Positivism in English Political Thought* (London, 1959), which is interesting, though, it seems to me, likewise perverse in its definition. Cf. on the other hand G. Cantecor, *Comte* (Paris, [1930]), pp. 9–10.

[2] The stages, particularly the first, were subdivided (fetishism, polytheism, monotheism, and so on), but I am concerned here only with the bare outline. Nor am I concerned, here as elsewhere, with the originality or the sources of Comte's thought, which have been definitively studied by Henri Gouhier, *La jeunesse d'Auguste Comte et la formation du positivisme* (Paris, 1933–41).

4

Now, the whole point of Comte's work and of his life [3] was that the final phase of this entire development was about to occur: biology having recently reached the positive stage, it was now the turn of sociology, and Comte himself was to be the instrument. But this event would not only be the last phase of an old process; it would also bring with it the possibility of a new one, that of creating the philosophy of the various sciences and of science as a whole, and this is what "philosophy" was to Comte: a system, a doctrine derived from, based on, the "positive" sciences, hence "Positivism." This work, also, Comte himself would do; he was the founder both of the final science and of the philosophy based on the complete set of the sciences.

The sciences, then, did not exist for their own sake; Comte all his life berated scientific "specialists." Neither was philosophy itself to be cultivated for its own sake, but in the service of man. One reason why philosophy was impossible until the last science had become positive was that only this science, by virtue of its subject matter, enabled the philosopher to approach his work from the right point of view. To serve humanity it was necessary first to know humanity.

Equally with scientific specialists, philosophical monists were the objects of Comte's terrible condemnation. By dividing knowledge into six parts, each with its own peculiar problems and methods, Comte denied its unity. This denial applied, however, only to knowledge regarded "objectively." Knowledge regarded "subjectively," from the point of view of its sole use and purpose, the service of humanity, did possess unity; a "subjective synthesis"

[3] See for a penetrating and persuasive account and analysis of the interdependence of Comte's life and his work Henri Gouhier, *La vie d'Auguste Comte* (Paris, 1931); also Georges Dumas, *Psychologie de deux messies positivistes: Saint-Simon et Auguste Comte* (Paris, 1905), pp. 248, 250–254. For a general introduction, see now Frank E. Manuel, *The Prophets of Paris* (Cambridge, Mass., 1962). I have not attempted here to provide more on Comte himself than is necessary for an understanding of the later movement.

5

was possible and necessary—possible by the use of the "subjective method." Having worked his way up the ladder of the sciences by the appropriate objective methods, the philosopher, having scaled the heights of sociology, could then travel down the ladder again and construct a synthesis of them in the light of the unique and essential insight into the inferior sciences afforded by sociology and bearing in mind the requirements of humanity revealed by it.

The most urgent of these requirements was nothing less than the reorganization of society. From the very beginning this had been Comte's ultimate aim, and his whole immense, laborious excursion into the individual sciences represented by his *Cours de philosophie positive*[4] was merely the preamble to the redemption and regeneration of humanity (or at any rate of western Europe, or at a pinch maybe only of France), racked as it was by the upheavals of the Revolution for which there was no remedy save through positive philosophy. For only the philosopher, who alone had emerged at the top of the ladder into the full light of day, and who was animated by the *esprit d'ensemble,* was qualified to descend again into the cave, where ordinary mortals spent their time worrying at shadowy and useless fragments of information, to coalesce the meaningless assortment into a synthesis, and to diagnose the ills of society and prescribe the cure.

But because, from his analysis of history, Comte held that mental and moral change was logically and chronologically prior to social and political change, the philosopher was to become, not a king, but a priest, a member of the "spiritual power" to which Comte had devoted an essay before launching on the *Cours;* a spiritual power, a priesthood, serving not some theological fiction, but Humanity itself. Obviously Comte himself was to be the first High Priest of the Religion of Humanity, responsible for the mental and moral regeneration from which political regeneration would follow—for once the scientific diagnosis had been made it was as

[4] Paris, 1830–42 (hereafter *Cours*).

unthinkable that people should dissent from it in social matters as in any other. It was not necessary, of course, quite the contrary, that everyone should understand the whole of positive philosophy; for did not sailors every night entrust their lives to the assurances of astronomers?

It was a doctrine as amazing in its consistency as its founder was in his ambition. Once the premises of the *Cours* are granted, the conclusions of the *System of Positive Polity*[5] follow.[6] It was a doctrine which was all of a piece: it was in fact the last, half-heroic, half-desperate assertion of the *esprit de système*. The interlude of Comte's "incomparable year" of the companionship of Clotilde de Vaux inclined him more thoroughly in the direction of the cultivation of the sentiments, but it was a difference only in degree: the inclusion of the arts in the synthesis, the doctrine of subjective immortality, the superiority of the heart over the head, were all implicit in the *Cours* and in the youthful essays from the time of Comte's apprenticeship in "political messianism" with Saint-Simon. To be sure, his love for Clotilde de Vaux living, and his adoration of her dead, caused him to introduce some highly idiosyncratic ideas into his systematization of the public and private worship of the Religion of Humanity; and he became inclined to interpret the needs of Humanity, which determined the nature of the subjective synthesis, in terms of his own experiences and feelings and to elevate devices of the subjective method into established subjective truths.[7] But his detailed provisions for the regulation of public and private life were not essentially more absurd than those to be expected of any self-appointed savior

[5] Tr. Bridges and others, London, 1875–77 (first pub. 1851–54—hereafter *Polity*).

[6] On the unity of Comte's life and thought, see his own argument, *Polity,* IV, 460–461; Pierre Ducassé, *Essai sur les origines intuitives du positivisme* (Paris, 1939), pp. 4–5, 204, 208–209; and below, pp. 37–38.

[7] Above all in his last work, the *Synthèse subjective* . . . (2nd ed., Paris, 1900; first pub. 1856).

(compare, for example, his reform of the calendar with that of the French Revolution and his cult with that of the Supreme Being, which are not thought of as ridiculous), and to strain at the gnat of Comte's "guardian angels" ill becomes one who has swallowed the camel of his "spiritual power."

Nor did the "incomparable year" have the advantage, as often happens, of making Comte personally more amenable and genial; on the contrary, "the more he lived in Humanity, the less able he was to live among men." [8] His sacerdotal self extinguished any other, and if he had always seen himself *through* his work, he came to identify himself completely *with* his work. Thus he got into the habit of assuming that the world owed him a living and that willingness to contribute to his personal subsistence was a mark of the true disciple.[9] The formation of groups, or sects, or tabernacles of disciples is the fundamental fact of the history of the diffusion of Positivism, although it represents at the same time only one of the two principal strands in that diffusion which are studied in the following pages.

But that there should have been any diffusion, any history of Positivism at all, seems to me a circumstance which is not to be taken for granted. For Comte's system was *ab initio* a feat of sleight of hand. It was programmatic in its own behalf, announced its own necessity, and prescribed its own tests for its own truth. It was, in other words, a tissue of begged questions, a wholly circular argument, a dogma entirely uncritical of itself.[10] Moreover,

[8] Gouhier, *Vie,* p. 266.

[9] Comte, *Eight Circulars* (tr. Lobb and others, London, 1882), p. 6 (Second Circular, 1851); cf. *Polity,* I, xxvii, xxix. Likewise he "exaggerated the importance of each new convert and listed a man among the faithful as soon as he revealed the vaguest interest" (Manuel, *Prophets of Paris,* p. 273).

[10] For cogent brief critiques of the fundamentals of Positivism, see Louis Liard, *La science positive et la métaphysique* (3rd ed., Paris, 1893), pp. 41, 57, 72; Basil Willey, *Nineteenth Century Studies* . . . (London, 1949), p. 202; Svend Ranulf, "Methods of Sociology . . . ," *Acta Jutlandica, Aarskrift for Aarhus Universitet,* XXVII[1] (1955), 17–20, and see below, pp. 42–46.

it was presented, for the most part, in a repellent manner. Saviors must husband their energies. Just as he had no time (and, as he rationalized in his defense of "mental hygiene," no need) to read what other men wrote, Comte had no time for the niceties of literary style in what he wrote himself. He wrote his two major works (of six and four fat volumes respectively) without notes and without revision. The result is that they are to the last degree involuted, opaque, and repetitious, in fact unreadable without an effort almost as heroic as his devotion in writing them. Comte's is a German *esprit de système,* producing a *système* with absolutely no *esprit* at all. As one of my colleagues has remarked, Comte was the only French philosopher who wrote like a German one.[11]

That such a system so presented should have enlisted hundreds of full-fledged disciples and attracted partial assent from hundreds of others, including names both famous and unknown, is a matter that calls for explanation. Of course there are some obvious general explanations: the very atmosphere of "scientism" with which, I have argued, Positivism must not be confused; the anticlericalism of most "enlightened" opinion, especially in France, attracted to Comte's abolition of God; the growing dissatisfaction, in France, with the dominant "spiritualist" philosophy of Victor Cousin and the foundations laid, in England, by the secular and pragmatic outlook of Utilitarianism; the social unrest which was the original motive power behind Comte's own effort, the sense that the old organization of society was obsolete and that a new one was required; the hankering after a comprehensive conception of the universe characteristic of many who abandoned the traditional Christian conception. But these are really conditions for the success

[11] Cf. the trenchant annihilation of Comte's style (written, ironically enough, in German) by Alf Ross, *Kritik der sogenannten praktischen Erkenntnis* . . . (Copenhagen and Leipzig, 1933), p. 258: "One can read hundreds of pages in which the same phrases keep recurring and nevertheless be hard put to it to give an account of what has been said." The distinction between lucid French and obscure German philosophy seems at present, however, to have become somewhat blurred.

9

of Positivism rather than explanations of it. True explanations, accounting for the acceptance by particular individuals of this particular system, despite its grave faults of matter and manner as well as the quarrelsomeness of its founder, must be sought concretely in the specific lives, thoughts, and desires of those individuals. This is the time-honored method of historical research, which, it seems to me, has been insufficiently followed in the field of modern intellectual history, where "influences" have been a good deal bandied about on the sort of evidence that none of us would accept from a freshman on a topic in political history.

I have tried, then, to find out as much as I could about each individual association with Positivism. The first problem, obviously, is one of identification. In the case of the disciples this is easy: by joining the Positivist communities they identified themselves. In the case of partial adherents it can be difficult: the use of the word "positive" or "positivism" is no reliable guide; the attributions of others, whether in praise or in accusation, are even less reliable; and since by definition such people did not adopt the system in its entirety, but often only isolated portions of it (or pieces of debris, if one prefers [12]), one must be sure that the provenance is really Positivism. I have tended to be skeptical rather than credulous, to refrain from giving Positivism the benefit of the doubt. Of course I have not required someone to say "I got this from Comte" (although such affirmations were welcome!) before I would accredit him as an object of Comte's influence; the evidence, both positive and negative, was often indirect, and indeed Comte's influence itself could be indirect, or manifested otherwise than by agreement, without being the less real.

On the other hand, there is a sense in which the disciples were harder to handle than the attracted but unconverted, for the latter (or, rather, those with whom I could come to grips) were for the most part articulate, whereas the rank and file of the disciples

[12] See [L.] Dugas, "Auguste Comte: Etude critique et psychologique," *Revue philosophique*, XL (1895), 397–398.

were not (and some, indeed, remain anonymous), especially since Comte and the principal apostles made a point of trying to attract women and workmen, who enjoyed the advantage of not having had their common sense impaired by metaphysical philosophy. The evidence concerning them is therefore often scrappy, but there is nevertheless, I think, enough of it to be of some use and to escape from another bane of intellectual history (including most of my own treatment of the partial adherents), its exclusive concentration on intellectuals.

Two general points about Positivism should be made here before the problem of its diffusion is investigated specifically. The first is its amenability to different emphases and interpretations. It could appeal to the emotions as well as to the intellect, to the analytic as well as the synthetic mind, and Comte's shorter works, the *General View of Positivism*[13] and the *Catechism of Positive Religion*[14] particularly, could appeal to the merely literate as opposed to the philosophically sophisticated (and showed, as did his numerous aphorisms,[15] that he could use the language when he took the trouble). A potential borrower could pick out what he found true or useful and ignore the rest, but alternatively he might be scared away from what he could have adopted by his scorn for the rest. By the same token and as the obverse side of its comprehensiveness, which was one of its greatest claims to attention, the system confronted the potential disciple with a formidable amount of assorted ingredients to swallow.

And the second point is related: the mere existence of disciples and discipleship and of an organized, instituted religion presented an unusual situation. One who assented to the philosophical system of Descartes and might be called a Cartesian was nevertheless not

[13] Tr. Bridges (London, 1865) from Comte's *Discours sur l'ensemble du positivisme* (Paris, 1848), later the introductory portion of the *Polity*.

[14] Tr. Congreve, London, 1858 (first pub. 1852).

[15] These were collected and edited by Georges Deherme in Comte, *Pensées et préceptes* (Paris, 1924).

enrolled in an organized community, and one who agreed with Mill would scarcely even be called a Millite. But someone who, in England or France, gave his assent to Positivism did so in awareness of the existence of a Positivist Church. Again, though this might act as a deterrent to some or lead to a special anxiety to keep clear of membership in it, to others the prospect of "conversion" would constitute an added, perhaps the decisive, attraction. Which of these reactions took place usually depended to a greater or lesser extent on temperament, on a desire to "belong" or an aversion to it, although either one could be overcome by other considerations. In any event, one who did become a disciple was likely to become involved in the further diffusion of the doctrine, as a part of an organized group and not merely as an individual. But the energy and success with which the Positivist community could devote itself to this task depended, in turn, on its own institutional history.

Despite the impressive list of auditors of Comte's first oral presentation of his Course in Positive Philosophy in 1826, the written *Cours* was slow in gaining currency in France. Paradoxically enough, owing perhaps partly to the nature of periodical journalism in England, Comte's philosophy became known to a larger public earlier there than in its own country. The earliest English enthusiasts, however, either never became, in Comte's sense, full disciples or did not remain such.[16] The founder of organized Positivism in England was Richard Congreve, an Oxford don, "the best type of a college tutor," according to Frederic Harrison. "He taught history thoroughly, and with a broad mind. He inspired men with a taste for culture and thought. He worked hard, and was genial and good-natured." But he was without imagination and without any power of personal as opposed to intellectual attraction.[17] If this was so he would perhaps not

[16] For the following, see also John Edwin McGee, *A Crusade for Humanity: The History of Organized Positivism in England* (London, 1931), chap. ii.

[17] Frederic Harrison, *Autobiographic Memoirs* (London, 1911), I, 83–84.

have wielded any influence in favor of Comte and his system even if he had tried to do so, which apparently he did not. It was by sheer coincidence that three of his pupils at Wadham College in the early 1850's, E. S. Beesly, J. H. Bridges, and Harrison, became acquainted with Comte's philosophy, and that Harrison had an interview with Comte in Paris in 1854, the same year that Congreve himself met Comte for the second time.[18] But Congreve cannot have been totally without personal magnetism, for this trio, having each in his own way proceeded from study to acceptance of Comte, all some years later gravitated to Congreve and regarded him as leader and guide.

Congreve himself had declared his adherence to Positivism in 1853 and in the following year resigned his tutorship and left Oxford, but whether because of his intellectual conversion or because of his intended marriage, which would have been sufficient to disqualify him from his post, is not clear. But Comte did not settle on Congreve as the leader of English Positivism until Congreve's publication of a pamphlet urging the British government to return Gibraltar to Spain, a proposal which accorded with Comte's anticolonial teachings.[19] Even then Comte's lan-

[18] *Ibid.*, p. 87: "During our whole time at Oxford [i.e., 1849–1854], Congreve never once referred to Comte"; it must then have been in an entirely passive way that Congreve was "the apostle in Oxford of Comte's system of philosophy" (Susan Liveing, *A Nineteenth-Century Teacher: John Henry Bridges* . . . [London, 1926], p. 49). See also Harrison in M. A. B[ridges], ed., *Recollections of John Henry Bridges, M.B.* (London, 1908), pp. 74–76; *Autobiography*, I, 98–99. On the occasion of his first visit in 1849, according to Comte, Congreve had told him that all serious students at Oxford were reading the *Cours,* but this was probably one of Comte's hallucinations (Comte to Laffitte, 19 Sept. 1849, in *Correspondance inédite* [Paris, 1903–4], II, 84 [hereafter *C.I.*]).

[19] *Gibraltar* (London, 1856), also in his *Essays Political, Social, and Religious* (London, 1874–1900), I, 1–64; Comte to Fisher, 2 Jan. and 24 April 1857, in *Lettres à des positivistes anglais* (London, 1889), pp. 59, 72. Congreve wrote later: "I date English Positivism in the true sense, the complete sense, the religious sense from the publication of *Gibraltar*, undertaken as an act of discipleship to Auguste Comte or from the publication of

13

guage to Congreve remained, in his complicated way, equivocal: he called him "the spontaneous leader of the British Positivists, whose involuntary presidency I hope you will long retain." [20] Who these British Positivists were whom Congreve was supposed to lead is not clear, for although Comte thought that Congreve's house near London was becoming a Positivist center [21] this was, to say the least, an exaggeration.

Comte was congenitally optimistic: he looked forward to living to the age of Fontenelle and preaching Positivism from the pulpit of Notre Dame. But not only was his own career cut short prematurely, he had even greater trouble in finding leading disciples and a successor in France than in England; and the defections and schisms within the body of orthodox Positivism began during his lifetime. Originally the most likely candidate for the succession to Comte as High Priest of Humanity (the succession was a problem which Comte always had very much on his mind) was the man who, beginning in 1844, had first made Comte well known in France and had contributed to his reputation in England, Emile Littré.[22] Littré became one of the stalwarts of the Positivist Society

---

my Edinburgh lectures" (1855). Until then he had been "gravitating towards a complete acceptance of the political, social and religious construction of Auguste Comte" but without "avowed adhesion." Comte's recognition of *Gibraltar* as the work of a disciple marked "the beginning of my action as a complete Positivist" (undated fragment in the Congreve MSS at Wadham College, recently transferred to the Bodleian Library [hereafter cited as "Wadham"], MS c. 347 f. 103).

[20] Comte to Congreve, 9 July 1857, in *Lettres à Richard Congreve* (London, 1889), p. 61.

[21] Comte to Fisher, 24 April 1857, *Lettres à des positivistes anglais*, p. 72.

[22] Having first read Comte in 1840 and then met him, Littré published in his republican journal, the *National*, a series of articles skillfully summarizing the *Cours*, subsequently published separately under the title *De la philosophie positive* (Paris, 1845) and later reprinted in his *Fragments de philosophie positive et de sociologie contemporaine* (Paris, 1876). See also his *Analyse raisonnée du cours de philosophie positive de M. Auguste Comte* (Utrecht, 1845). For Comte's cordial reception of the *National*

organized by Comte in 1848, which, although ostensibly a political discussion and action group, found itself, in fact, mostly listening to interminable harangues from Comte. But the members' docility could not survive Comte's endorsement of Louis Napoleon's *coup d'état,* which led Positivism to its first schism. Littré, a republican before 1848, could not swallow Comte's willingness, in accord with his authoritarian philosophical principles, to sacrifice the political liberties of the Second Republic. Between 1848 and 1851, Littré wrote later, "I interpreted events . . . from a point of view which was no longer by any means my own," but Comte's, who had exercised a moral ascendancy over him as "an infallible master." It was only after breaking with Comte on the political issue that he began to free himself from this ascendancy and to see the necessity of "submitting to the control of the positive method all that he [Comte] had pronounced during the latter part of his life and that I had taken on trust." [23]

Although this account is based on Littré's subsequent recollections, there is no reason to doubt that the primary issue between Littré and Comte was political.[24] There is, however, a very revealing letter of Littré's to Comte which, though written before the rupture and while Littré was still doctrinally under Comte's spell, suggests that Littré had another motive as well, and that this first Positivist schism, like all the subsequent ones in both France and

---

articles, see his letters to J. S. Mill, 21 Oct. and 25 Dec. 1844, in L. Lévy-Bruhl, ed., *Lettres inédites de John Stuart Mill à Auguste Comte, publiées avec les réponses de Comte* (Paris, 1899), pp. 367, 374–375.

[23] Littré, *Auguste Comte et la philosophie positive* (2nd ed., Paris, 1864), pp. 592–602, 617 n., 618, and the second revised and enlarged edition of *Conservation, révolution et positivisme* (Paris, 1879; 1st ed. 1852), pp. ii–iii, v, vii, 78, 246, 266–267, 480–481; cf. also Maurice Wolff, "Auguste Comte: Deux sanctuaires du positivisme," *Larousse mensuel illustré,* VIII (1929), 150.

[24] Comte himself thought so: Comte to Hadery, 29 Jan. 1852, *C.I.,* II, 217–218; *Polity,* III, xv–xvi; but cf. *Lettres inédites à C. de Blignières* (ed. Arbousse-Bastide, Paris, 1932), p. 66.

England, was a compound of principles and personalities. The personalities involved here, besides Littré and Comte, were the latter's living but estranged wife and the dead woman whom, having tried in vain to make his mistress, he had sublimated into a saint, Clotilde de Vaux. Without going into the rights and wrongs of Comte's married life, suffice it to say that Comte had become increasingly venomous in his relations with his wife and that Littré considered the latter wronged.[25] In the letter to which I have referred, Littré was attempting to persuade Comte not to accompany his payment of his wife's allowance with such calumnies of her as would force her to refuse it, and he used significant language: "Your influence upon my mind is very great. . . . And yet my conscience objects. Whatever influence a man may have upon me, never shall he induce me to condemn an accused person [Mme. Comte] unheard." Neither the law nor his own teaching, Littré pointed out, permitted Comte to undo his marriage. "I know that this is a point on which you are particularly sensitive, and that you have given yourself to another lady [Clotilde de Vaux] to whom you want to evidence gratitude and affection." Comte's peremptory though as usual verbose refusal to accept Littré's advice on a matter on which the latter obviously also felt strongly may well have started him rethinking his entire relationship with his exigent master.[26] In any event, since Comte's involvement with

[25] On Littré's championship of Mme. Comte, see also his letter to Daniel Stern (the Comtesse d'Agoult) in P. Fleuriot de Langle, ed., "Deux lettres de Littré à propos de la femme d'Auguste Comte," *Mercure de France,* Vol. 227 (1931), p. 501; his "Circulaire positiviste," *Revue philosophique et religieuse,* VIII (1857), 156–159; and his obituary article on her in *La philosophie positive* (hereafter *P.P.*), XVIII (1877), 290–296. Comte, characteristically, thought that his wife's relationship with Littré was improper: *C.I.,* II, 7–8, IV, 31; *Lettres à divers* (Paris, 1902–5), I, 167–169; *Lettres à Blignières,* pp. 26–27, 57; and cf. Dr. Robinet, *Notice sur l'oeuvre et la vie d'Auguste Comte* (3rd ed., Paris, 1891), p. 403.

[26] See Littré's letter of 27 April 1851, in Albert Crompton, ed., *Confessions and Testament of Auguste Comte and His Correspondence with Clotilde de Vaux* (Liverpool, 1910), pp. 508–511, and Comte's refusal, *ibid.,* pp. 511–

Clotilde de Vaux affected not only his attitude to his wife but also his development in the direction of political and religious authoritarianism, Littré's motives even if mixed were not contradictory.[27]

Meanwhile Comte was obliged to cast about for another "principal disciple" and eventual successor, but his small circle of followers were for the most part not sufficiently docile, and his judgment of many of them fluctuated violently. Ultimately he declined to make any choice at all, though at the time of his death he was clearly beginning to have hopes of Dr. Georges Audiffrent, whose nature seemed to him "eminently priestly."[28] Despite his principle of "sociocracy," whereby a person in authority nominates his own successor, Auguste Comte therefore died (on 5 September 1857) sacerdotally intestate, having declared that he preferred to leave the future of Positivism to "the free exertions of my true disciples" rather than designate "an incompetent chief."[29] These free exertions turned into acrimonious and unseemly wrangling,[30]

518, esp. p. 517, where Comte rejects Littré's "vain pretention to preclude me from any worthy public expression of my just philosophical gratitude to my angelic Clotilde."

[27] Later interpretations of Littré's break with Comte are varied and sometimes inconsistent: see E. Caro, *M. Littré et le positivisme* (Paris, 1883), pp. 55–79, 103–106, 115–117 (this is altogether a curious book); Eugène Spuller, *Figures disparues: Portraits contemporains, politiques et littéraires,* I (3rd ed., Paris, 1884), 397–398; Hermann Gruber, *Der Positivismus vom Tode August Comte's bis auf unsere Tage (1857–1891)* (Freiburg im Breisgau, 1891), pp. 4–5; and most recently the unreliable book of Stanislas Aquarone, *The Life and Works of Emile Littré, 1801–1881* (Leyden, 1958), pp. 34, 36, 148, which dates the beginning of the break from 1845. A different motive altogether was suggested over fifty years after the event by a Positivist who as a young man had witnessed the events, namely, that Littré had been influenced by the views of the majority of Positivists in Lyon on Comte's religious development of his doctrine (René Faure in *Revue positiviste internationale,* III [1907], 353).

[28] Comte to Hadery, 27 Oct. 1856, 18 May 1857, *C.I.,* II, 355, 378–379.

[29] *Polity,* IV, 470–471. See also Comte's Testament, in *Confessions and Testament,* pp. 472–473.

[30] This may be followed in the reports of Audiffrent and Congreve, which, though written twenty years later, corroborate each other, are supported by

and the person who emerged from it victorious, Pierre Laffitte, was one whom Comte had gone out of his way to avoid mentioning with respect to the sacerdotal succession. Comte had valued Laffitte, one of his most devoted followers, very highly in some respects, appointing him to be president of the commission of thirteen executors of his will, but had considered him deficient in the qualities of character and energy required of a High Priest of Humanity.[31] Indeed, Laffitte did not believe himself qualified to give religious leadership and was therefore as reluctant to accept office as some of his colleagues were to offer it to him. In fact he became only the "president of the religious committee" and not High Priest, although the disciples clearly expected him to discharge some, at least, of the functions of sacerdotal office. Laffitte, however, began by moving in the opposite direction, renamed the "religious committee" simply "Positivist Committee," and in his official account of the proceedings said that he had been chosen its president only because he was already president of the commission of executors. He did, to be sure, go on to say that since parliamentarianism was contrary to Positivist principles the committee was merely advisory and he as president took full responsibility for all measures, but he specifically denied being Comte's "successor." In this respect there was an "interregnum."[32]

---

other evidence, and are nowhere contradicted: see G. Audiffrent and E. Sémérie, *Après la légende, l'histoire* . . . (Paris, 1878), p. 7; Congreve, *Essays,* II, 92–95; and cf. Robinet to Laffitte, 28 Sept. 1857, in the Positivist Archives of the Musée Auguste Comte at 10, rue Monsieur-le-Prince, Paris (hereafter M-le-P).

[31] See Comte's letters of encouragement and praise to Laffitte beginning in 1849, esp. 28 July, 29 Aug., 4, 12, and 19 Sept., and 2 Oct. 1849, 8 Aug. 1851, 4 Oct. 1855, *C.I.,* II, 36, 61, 71, 73, 80–81, 99–100, 114, 185; criticism, 22 Sept. 1851 and 8 Sept. 1852, *ibid.,* pp. 139, 143, 146, and to Blignières, 29 Nov. 1852, *Lettres à Blignières,* p. 70.

[32] 9th Positivist Annual Circular (for 1857—Annual Circulars of Pierre Laffitte and Charles Jeannolle, 1858–1913, M-le-P). Cf. also Laffitte's draft fragment of 16 Nov. 1857, M-le-P.

18

Chapter II

ORGANIZED POSITIVISM
SINCE COMTE'S DEATH

THERE is one testimony to the effect that Emile Littré was considered as a candidate for the succession in 1857,[1] but it is nowhere corroborated and seems on its face highly unlikely, in view of the degree of Littré's estrangement from Comte.[2] Littré in fact was becoming the focus of a rival group of Positivists,

[1] [H. Deroisin], *Notes sur Auguste Comte par un de ses disciples* (Paris, 1909), p. 182.

[2] Littré would have found himself virtually without support. Feeling among the loyal disciples ran particularly high just after Comte's death on the subject of Mme. Comte, who contested his will which favored them, and Littré was of course her champion. In any event, Comte himself had excommunicated Littré. These considerations, apart from any doctrinal ones, would have put Littré entirely out of the running. See Laffitte to Comte, 4 Sept. 1852, in *Revue occidentale* (hereafter *R.O.*), n.s. XXXVII (1908), 44, to Morlot, 13 Aug. 1864, M-le-P, and cf. his *Les grands types de l'Humanité*, III (Paris, 1897), 669–670; Lonchampt to Sauria, 1869, M-le-P; Robinet, *Notice*, pp. 154, 191 and n., 238–239, 279, 394–411, *M. Littré et le positivisme* (Paris, 1871), and even his obituary of him, "Le positivisme et M. Littré," *R.O.*, VII (1881), 80–104; Emile Laporte in Robinet, *M. Littré*, pp. 5–6; Emile Antoine, *Aperçu sommaire sur la vie et sur l'oeuvre de M. Pierre Laffitte* (Le Havre, 1880), pp. 52–58, 62–63, 65–66; Hadery to Laffitte, 20 Nov. 1857, M-le-P; but cf. Montègre to Laffitte, 2 April 1858, M-le-P.

consisting partly of those who had renounced Comte's leadership and left the Positivist Society in 1852, partly of those who did so later, and partly of new recruits to the "scientific" brand of Positivism that Littré dispensed.[3] Littré's fundamental proposition was that, partly as a result of his association with Clotilde de Vaux, Comte had forsaken his own positive method by adopting the "subjective" method, which radically vitiated all the work and activities of his later years; and Littré regarded it as the task of the true disciple, which to the end of his life he claimed to be, to cleanse Positivism of these "aberrations," which could only damage its reputation and that of its founder, and to propagate the doctrine in the pure, scientific form of the *Cours*.[4] Equally, of course, Littré rejected the argument of those who would throw out the Positivist baby with the bath water of Comte's later sentimentalities. It is particularly piquant that Littré should have engaged in a polemic in this connection with Mill, for the spokes-

[3] Littré's principal companions in the schism of 1852 were Charles Robin and L. A. Segond, both biologists. The most important recruit in the following years was Célestin de Blignières, an army officer, at one time one of Comte's favorites and later the author of an excellent summary of Positivism of the school of Littré with (despite the title) little emphasis on religion, the publication of which was thought by some of the loyal disciples to have hastened Comte's death: *Exposition abrégée et populaire de la philosophie et de la religion positives* (Paris, 1857). For the relations between him and Comte, see Comte, *Lettres à Blignières,* many published letters of Comte to others, and Blignières' letters to Laffitte at M-le-P. Whatever one may think of the medical aspects of Comte's fatal illness, the venomous fury lavished on Blignières was in all conscience sufficient to exhaust anyone's supply of bile.

[4] Let it be noted here, once for all, how most of the Positivist schisms turned at least in part on the question of "purifying" the doctrine, in this respect resembling, of course, many religious reform movements and particularly the Protestant Reformation. The fact that in this instance Littré came from a Protestant family was probably not relevant, though Comte (as he himself moved increasingly close to the Catholic Church and took to bracketing Protestantism with skepticism) tried to make it appear so.

men of the religious wing of Positivism lumped Littré and Mill together among those who attacked the "unity" of Comte's life and doctrine.[5] Littré, however, regarding himself as a "disciple" of Positivism and Mill as a critic, declared that Mill's critique left the system substantially unshaken because where it was correct it affected only those parts where Comte had departed from his own principles; and, just as Mill himself had once said that if he had to choose between Bentham and Coleridge he would still choose his old master Bentham, so Littré now wrote that, having to choose between Comte and Mill, he chose his old master Comte.[6]

In steering this delicate middle course Littré remained after his break with Comte, as he had been before it, the leading popularizer of the doctrines of the *Cours*.[7] In addition to his books on strictly Positivist subjects and to the references to Positivism inserted in his writings on other subjects (he was an amazingly

---

[5] See particularly the book of that title by J. H. Bridges and below, pp. 37–38; cf. also Ducassé, *Essai sur les origines*, p. 6.

[6] Littré, *Auguste Comte et Stuart Mill* (Paris, n.d.), esp. pp. iii, 2–3, 5–6, 8; see also the work of Littré's disciple G. Wyrouboff, printed with Littré's own: *Stuart Mill et la philosophie positive*, but cf. his generally favorable attitude toward Lewes in *P.P.*, XIII (1874), 94. (For Mill's critique, see below, pp. 192–193.) For Littré's conception of discipleship, see also *P.P.*, XXIV (1880), 32. Charlton, *Positivist Thought*, p. 63, thinks that in defending Comte against Mill Littré was in danger of falling from grace as a "true Positivist." Charlton's chapter on Littré (chap. iv) is very interesting.

[7] My estimate coincides with that of many others, see, e.g., the tributes of Gruber, *Positivismus*, pp. 5, 26–36 (who, however, considers Littré's performance as a philosopher "pitiful"); Spuller, *Figures disparues*, p. 396; Robert Flint, *History of the Philosophy of History* (New York, 1884), pp. 615–618; Emile Bréhier, *Histoire de la philosophie* (Paris, n.d.), II, 932; Th. Ribot, *English Psychology* (New York, 1874), pp. 78–79, but cf. Aquarone, *Littré*, pp. 68–69, 74. Some writers regard Littré's compromise as a tissue of contradictions: John A. Scott, *Republican Ideas and the Liberal Tradition in France 1870–1914* (New York, 1951), pp. 91–92; Caro, *Littré*, pp. iii, 133–138, 191, 193–195 (who nevertheless considers Littré's tradition the strongest, p. 197).

versatile scholar) and in the introductions that he contributed to the works of others, Littré's greatest achievement on behalf of the doctrine was his foundation in 1867, together with the young émigré Russian scientist G. Wyrouboff, of a journal entitled *La philosophie positive,* which compared very favorably in matters of interest, range, and style with the *Revue occidentale* started a decade later by the religious disciples. It contained many non-Positivist articles, reviewed non-Positivist and even anti-Positivist books charitably, and sought in general to cater not merely to a coterie but to a wider educated public. On the other hand, of course, it aimed to win its readers to Positivism (as Littré interpreted it), and most of its pages were accordingly devoted to discussions of aspects of the doctrine. Not surprisingly, these deteriorated in quality and especially in originality after about three years of publication, in many instances, despite the group's show of independence, merely echoing and even pandering to Comte. Nevertheless, when shortly after Littré's death Wyrouboff and his new coeditor, Charles Robin, stopped publication of the journal after sixteen years, they could write with some justification that it had fulfilled its purpose, Positivism having been extended beyond the limits of a school.[8]

During his lifetime Littré not only edited the journal but by his own contributions as well as his other writings defined its purpose and set its tone. In the current state of flux, he declared, "there is only one stable point and that is science." But Positivism was a philosophy and not merely a compendium of the sciences; indeed it was composed not of the several sciences but of the several philosophies of those sciences which Comte had founded before he had coordinated them all into a single system. This positive philosophy was "at the same time a system which comprehends everything that is known about the world, man, and societies, and a general method including within itself all the avenues by which these things have become known." Moreover, this philosophy in

[8] *P.P.,* XXXI (1883), 321–323.

turn had a further purpose and a practical one, to provide a "demonstrable rallying-point" and a "definite direction" for mankind, not only to "illuminate the intelligence" but to "warm the heart." In short, Positivism was a means of reconciling scientific speculation with the governing of mankind; philosophy was, in sum, the union of social with scientific development.[9]

Even after his break with Comte in 1852 Littré, then, did not abandon the belief that Positivism could and would become a universal philosophy and serve as a basis for social and political action.[10] What he rejected was Comte's insistence that this time was already at hand. The scientific and philosophical substructure, for which Comte himself had seen the need vis-à-vis Saint-Simon, was in Littré's opinion not completed by the *Cours*[11] and, above all, was very far from having been absorbed and digested even by the disciples, not to speak of the general public. Comte's attempts to draw from it rules for action (like his approval of Louis Napoleon's *coup d'état*) were therefore premature in principle as well as being wrong in detail.

While keeping the ultimate goal of regeneration in mind, therefore, Littré and his collaborators concentrated their immediate energies on discussion, elaboration, and completion of the doctrine of the *Cours,* disregarding the limitations that Comte had placed upon further research.[12] Indeed, they not infrequently allowed

---

[9] For this paragraph, see the following writings of Littré: "Etude sur les progrès du positivisme," Introduction to the fourth edition of Comte's *Cours de philosophie positive* (Paris, 1877), I, lxii, lxv; *Comte et la philosophie positive,* pp. 104–106, 519; *Paroles de philosophie positive* (2nd ed., Paris, 1863), p. 69. See, in similar vein, e.g., Wyrouboff in *P.P.,* XXII (1879), 27; Louis André-Nuytz, *Le positivisme pour tous: Exposé élémentaire des principes de la philosophie positive* (Paris, 1868), pp. 19, 33.

[10] For Littré's optimism, see more specifically *P.P.,* XX (1878), 314.

[11] Specifically, Littré believed that Comte had left gaps in the fields of political economy, psychology, aesthetics, and ethics (*Comte et la philosophie positive,* pp. 674–678).

[12] On this last point see, e.g., Ch. Mismer in *P.P.,* XX (1878), 317–318.

themselves to suggest that what was preeminently important about Positivism was not its results, still less its ultimate effects, but its method.[13] This tendency was of course connected with Littré's contention that Comte had been led into error and had relapsed into metaphysics by abandoning the positive and adopting the subjective method, and with the corollary that the first thing to be done was to restore the positive method, the method of the sciences, to all investigation and particularly to philosophy itself.[14]

Although agreed on the necessity of keeping clear of anything which would allow the late religious, "subjective" Comte to get his foot in the door, Littré and his collaborators were nevertheless not sure just how unfettered the use of pure experimental scientific method should be.[15] They were similarly uncertain about just how unquestionable the two basic principles of Positivism, the Law of the Three Stages and the Classification of the Sciences, could claim to be. Comte had declared that he had derived them empirically. If so, they might in theory be overthrown by further scientific investigation, but in that case whatever was distinctive about Positivism would be fatally undermined. If on the other hand they were abstract, deductive laws, they required proof.[16]

[13] See perhaps most radically Wyrouboff in *P.P.*, V (1869–70), 310: "The real originality of Comte's philosophy is in its method far more than in its doctrine."

[14] "The method having been perverted everything was perverted, even what was good and true" about Comte's later notions. See Littré, *Comte et la philosophie positive*, pp. 533–534, *P.P.*, II (1868), 187–188; Wyrouboff, *ibid.*, XXI (1878), 464–465.

[15] See for various formulations Littré, *Comte et la philosophie positive*, pp. ii–iv, *Fragments*, pp. 475–476, and editorial note, *P.P.*, XI (1873), 208; Robin, *ibid.*, I (1867), 78–79; E. de Roberty, *ibid.*, XXI (1878), 147; Paul Lacombe, *ibid.*, XIX (1877), 150, 212; and Wyrouboff in a number of places in *P.P.*: I (1867), 181, II (1868), 246–249, XXI (1878), 461–462, XXIII (1879), 183, XXIV (1880), 345–346, XXV (1880), 157, 169–184.

[16] For discussion of these questions, see Littré, *Comte et la philosophie positive*, pp. 289–295, *Paroles*, pp. 71–74, and in *P.P.*: VII (1870), 392, X (1873), 322–323, XI (1873), 29, 32–33; Wyrouboff, *ibid.*, I (1867), 37–38,

Finally and consequently, Littré and his circle were undecided on the larger general problem of the relationship between science and philosophy. Their basic position was that philosophy could only coordinate the findings of the sciences, and in doing so must employ the method of the sciences. Philosophy, therefore, could be allowed a life of its own only within very strict limits. But this position presented a number of difficulties in the light of their acceptance of the philosophical framework (including the Law of the Three Stages and the Classification) supplied by Comte in the *Cours*. What if new scientific discoveries, for example, undermined this framework? Littré's labeling of positive philosophy variously as the daughter, the servant, and the prolongation of the sciences is symptomatic of his own and *a fortiori* of his followers' uncertainty on this point.[17]

The most illuminating illustration of the Littréists' view of science in general and of scientific method in particular is furnished by the uniform suspicion, if not hostility, with which they (and indeed all Positivists) greeted Darwin's theory of Natural Selection. It was nothing more than a hypothesis, Littré wrote repeatedly, rationalistic and not experimental, ingenious but lacking sufficient evidence. He protested (too much?) that he had "no dogmatic repugnance" against it and that it was plausible enough to be accepted as a hypothesis, but he insisted that it was

---

49 n. 1, XXIV (1880), 352; and other writers *ibid.*, XVII (1876), 219, XIX (1877), 403–404, XX (1878), 261–264, 415–416, XXVI (1881), 222–223, XXVIII (1882), 335–336, XXXI (1883), 243–247, 273.

[17] See Littré, *Comte et la philosophie positive*, pp. 671, 673, Preface to Prosper Pichard, *Doctrine du réel* (Paris, 1873), p. xii, "Préface d'un disciple" in Comte, *Cours de philosophie positive*, 4th ed., I, vi–vii, *Comte et Mill*, p. 33, and in *P.P.*, VI (1870), 5 n. 1, XIII (1874), 165–167, XIX (1877), 302; Wyrouboff, *ibid.*, VI (1870), 239, VII (1870), 342, XXII (1879), 394, XXIII (1879), 196–199; L. André-Nuytz, *ibid.*, XI (1873), 169, 174, 176–183; Eugene Bourdet, *Principes d'éducation positive* (2nd ed., Paris, 1877), p. v, André Sanson, *Science sans préjugés* (1st series, Paris, 1865), p. 14, and *Semaines scientifiques (première année)* (Paris, 1866), pp. iii–iv, vi.

too insecurely founded to have any conclusions based on it.[18] He preferred, he said, to maintain a completely agnostic position on the matter of the origin of species, but at the same time he avowed himself "provisionally" in favor of "the primordial multiplicity of species and their appearance in time"; to accept this was not to accept polygeny, it was "to state a fact, not to declare one's adherence to either natural or supernatural creation." This theory also had the advantage that it did not presume a process different from the one that could at present be observed. In any event, Littré wrote, the matter was of purely biological and not of philosophical interest; even if Darwin's hypothesis were proved, it would carry no philosophical implications.[19] The fact remained, however, that the biological part of the *Cours* had, of course, been written without benefit of Darwin, and Littré must have been aware that if a theory which had acquired such notoriety as Darwin's were to be generally accepted many people would become dubious about a self-styled scientific philosophy that took no account of it. That he was so aware may be indicated by a passing remark of his that French as opposed to English Positivism supported Comte's favorable view of Lamarck and therefore took the view that Darwin had contributed nothing essentially new.[20] Littré and his group, anxious to avoid the label of "Comtist," were far less outspoken

[18] *Fragments*, p. 508, *Conservation*, 2nd ed., p. 49, in *P.P.*, XV (1875), 441, XXII (1879), 165, and in L. Gensoul, *La république au-dessus du suffrage universel . . . avec une lettre et des remarques de M. E. Littré* (Paris, 1871), p. 35 n. 1.

[19] *P.P.*, XV (1875), 441–448, XX (1878), 161, 164–165, 169, XXIII (1879), 169–172, 176.

[20] *Fragments*, p. xiii. Comte had endorsed Lamarck's insistence on the connection between organism and environment, but had rejected Lamarck's specifically evolutionary ideas as purely speculative. Littré and Comte's other early followers regarded Darwin's evolutionism as no more and no less speculative than Lamarck's and could therefore argue that Darwin had not improved on Lamarck and that Comte had recognized what was valuable in Lamarck as in other scientific pioneers of the turn of the century, such as Gall (see text below).

on this point than the orthodox wing of Positivists,[21] but their eagerness to man the barricades against Darwin (from no theological bias, certainly) does not look entirely disinterested.[22]

Another key problem for all Positivists concerned the nature of psychology and its place in the hierarchy of the sciences. Littré and his colleagues were much exercised about the central place occupied by psychology in the theory of knowledge of "English positivists." Actually they were not referring to the English disciples of Comte, whose views were little different from theirs, but to Mill and to the Scottish school of Alexander Bain who, contrary to Comte's Classification, made of psychology an independent science and their epistemological point of departure. Littré was unable to throw Comte into the breach against these opponents because this was one of the subjects on which, he asserted, Comte spoke with two voices:

Mental phenomena have their seat . . . in the nervous system; consequently they belong to physiology; here I am of M. Comte's opinion. But, being part of physiology from this point of view, they are not necessarily a part of it from all points of view. . . . Comte prostrates psychology before phrenology. . . . The physiological conditions of thought unquestionably belong to physiology; but the laws of thought do not. . . . Nevertheless, given that these laws can only be studied directly by their manifestation and, as Mr. Mill says, by observation and experiment, it remains true that there is a science of thought, of the mind, . . . a science in its own right.

[21] See below, pp. 46–47 and 67.

[22] Of particular interest is the contribution of Clémence Royer, "Lamarck: Sa vie, ses travaux, et son système," *P.P.,* III–IV (1868–69), who in praising Lamarck mentions, among other things, that his system was essentially French (IV, 29). See also Wyrouboff, *ibid.,* IV (1869), 52–53, XXIV (1880), 343; Robin, *Anatomie et physiologie cellulaire* (Paris, 1873), p. xxxii; Sanson in *P.P.,* II (1868), 50–51, X (1873), 65; E. Jourdy, *ibid.,* VIII (1873), 66, XIV (1875), 25–41 *passim*. Contrast, finally, the much friendlier way in which the atomic "hypothesis" was treated by A. Naquet, *ibid.,* II (1868), 85–86, 88, 107.

Thus defined, psychology was "the integrating [*intégrante*] part of a general theory of man, which comes only after all the other sciences and to which biology furnishes only one very important element." Now all this is rather curious, not only in the broad concessions made to Mill and his school, but particularly because Comte, having dismissed psychology from his hierarchy of six abstract sciences in the *Cours,* which Littré accepted, may be said to have brought it back in the *Polity,* which Littré rejected, under the label "ethics" as the seventh and culminating science, drawing on both biology and sociology, just as Littré is here advocating. But Comte of course did more than this in the *Polity* with respect to psychology. Littré has already referred to phrenology. In adapting the phrenological theories of Gall, he goes on, and attempting to construct a theory of the mental faculties, Comte proved inadequate to the task: his theory (of the correspondence of organs and faculties) has been empirically proved wrong. Comte was misled into this wholly unscientific and metaphysical attempt by his adoption of the subjective method and especially by his desire to exalt the affective faculties. Littré insisted, on the contrary, that if the affections are allowed to dominate, egoism will dominate, since egoism is, on Comte's own admission, dominant among the affections. (Comte taught that altruism could be made dominant by social pressure.) Egoism can be subordinated only by subordinating the affections to reason and intelligence: reason must rule the passions, the mind must not be subordinated to the heart, as Comte taught. Finally, Comte had compounded the felony by building his whole sociological construction on these worthless foundations; he had tried to unite the principles of a positive regime with the consequences of a theological regime. Why, Littré countered, should the mind be subordinated to the faith which it has demonstrated? [23]

[23] *Comte et la philosophie positive,* pp. 270–272, 538–550, 554–561; see also his "De la méthode en psychologie," *P.P.,* I (1867), esp. pp. 274–280, 364, and *ibid.,* I, 21–22, and VI (1870), 19–20, where some of these points

And here we come to the real gravamen of Littré's charges against Comte's "second career." Comte's error had been to believe that, beyond "finding the principles, tracing the outlines, furnishing the method," he had also "anticipated the work of future generations and drawn the consequences by constructing the religious and social edifice of the future." [24] The causes of this error were psychological. His meeting with Clotilde de Vaux had coincided with the crisis of his reflections on the projected *Polity* and had caused him "to regard the subjective method as a clear guide by the light of which he could discern the distant future of a mankind entirely given over to love." This nervous crisis which had plunged him into the subjective method had been aggravated after Mme. de Vaux's death by his turn toward mysticism, so that some parts of his subsequent work were expressions of entirely personal needs and had no relation to the system. All this had not been helped by his maintenance of "mental hygiene." [25]

Still, since sociology had formed an integral, in fact the culminating and largest, part of the *Cours*, Littré could not, of course, ignore it or take an entirely negative stand on it, and did not want to. But it proved difficult to find and steer a middle course which would neither give too many hostages to the Comte of the *Polity* nor leave nothing substantial of the Comte of the *Cours*. This difficulty did not apply to the treatment of Comte's interpretation

---

are sharpened. H. Stupuy, "M. Cousin et l'éclectisme," *ibid.*, II (1868), 208–245, drives another nail into the coffin of Comte's *bête noire* in the field of psychology. The two Russian émigrés Roberty and Wyrouboff carried on a polite argument in the pages of Littré's journal as to whether psychology was closer to biology or to sociology: Roberty, XXI, 130–131, 141–142; Wyrouboff, XXVI (1881), 24. (This controversy also extended to other matters.)

[24] *Paroles*, pp. 92–93. Note here again, when it comes to criticizing Comte, the tendency to stress the method (cf. above, p. 20). See also Wyrouboff in *P.P.*, XXVI, 154.

[25] *Comte et la philosophie positive*, pp. 580–584, 587. See also C. de Blignières, *Lettre sur la morale à M. l'évêque d'Orléans* (Paris, 1863), p. vi.

of history, the descriptive preliminary to his sociology, built up around the Law of the Three Stages and closely resembling that of Saint-Simon. Here Littré and his collaborators could reproduce the master's voice faithfully, so much so that Littré praised Comte's work as the first philosophical appreciation of history and claimed that it was in this field (not in mathematics!) that he had been an accomplished specialist, apart from his synthesizing achievements in philosophy.[26] But complications appeared as soon as the transition from a descriptive historiography to an analytical and normative sociology was attempted. The first requirement, and Comte's fundamental assumption, for the latter discipline was the possibility of extrapolating from the past to the future, the susceptibility of human and social activity to analysis and hence to prediction by the application of scientific method. The total historical process must be deterministic and determinable: the Law of the Three Stages was only the most basic of the laws governing this process.

On the whole Littré and his collaborators subscribed to this view (indeed, if they had not, the Law of the Three Stages itself would have come tumbling down, and Comte's method as well as his findings would have been fatally undermined). Littré, in the inaugural and only lecture he gave from the chair of history at the Ecole Polytechnique in 1871 before being interrupted by the consequences of war, said:

History . . . means research into the conditions which bring about the succession of one social state after another in a determined order. Events, therefore, play only a secondary role; being products of the passions and interests driving peoples and their leaders, they sometimes serve the spontaneous movement of mankind and sometimes obstruct it; but, taken all in all, . . . they are dominated by this movement.

This was a progressive movement, which brought societies "from an inferior to a superior state."

[26] *Comte et la philosophie positive*, pp. 181–182.

30

When I speak of evolution and progress, I affirm a natural phenomenon; I am not merely spellbound by optimism. . . . And since it
is a natural phenomenon, chance must be excluded.

Peoples, like the Moslems and the Chinese, who underwent no
progress could have no history written about them but only annals
devoid of interest. History was immune from arbitrary interference, but "modifiable by wise, judicious, and far-sighted intervention." Social phenomena being (according to Comte's corollary
to the Classification) the most complex are therefore the most
modifiable, "but only on condition that their essence, which is
invulnerable to all our assaults, is respected." [27]

This declaration, itself shot through with begged questions and
other questionable logical devices, and already ambiguous, was
further confused by amplifications offered by Littré elsewhere
on the problem of chance and determinism and of the influence
of men upon events. He clearly allowed chance an important role
when he wrote that "the accidental follows from the intervention
in social events of biological, chemical, and cosmic conditions,"
while "the necessary follows from the nature of societies and from
the law of their development." The Franco-Prussian War could
have been avoided by a wiser policy, yet the Positivist recognizes
that "civilization follows the course traced out for it by history."
If Bonaparte had died and Hoche lived, "the immediate consequences of the French Revolution would have been quite different
although, in the long run, the progressive forces of Europe triumphed." Turgot failed, although he was on the side of progress,
because Louis XVI did not see where his own interest lay.[28] One
of Littré's colleagues elaborated on this judgment in a special study
on Turgot.[29]

[27] "Ecole Polytechnique: Cours d'histoire," *P.P.*, VII (1870), 385–391.
[28] See *P.P.*, IV (1869), 51, VII (1870), 199, IX (1872), 160, XX (1878),
12, 15.
[29] See H. Stupuy, "Turgot était-il un homme d'état?" *P.P.*, XIX (1877),
esp. pp. 453–455, 466, 468, also *P.P.*, X (1873), 366, and the following: Em-

Now it is admittedly an easy game to catch even the great philosophers in inconsistencies, perhaps more cheaply on the question of freedom and determinism than on any other. But it still does not augur well for the Littréists' attempt to construct a Positivist sociology free from the aberrations of the *Polity* to find them so uncertain in their grasp of what ought to have been for them a methodological *sine qua non*. Comte's own proposition that the course of events is modifiable as regards its speed and its secondary manifestations certainly challenged exegesis but scarcely benefited from it. That sociology was the "queen of the sciences" and, though coming last chronologically, the key to all the others, was not in dispute.[30] What was in dispute was the degree of its completion, the state of its advancement. Littré took the position that it was as yet in its infancy, "instituted," in terms of Comte's own jargon, but not "constituted." In the first place he stressed the principle which Comte had stated in connection with his Classification, that while each higher science was dependent on the lower ones, and especially on the one immediately preceding, it was not identical with any of them; sociological laws, therefore, could not be deduced from biological ones but must be based on observation and experience with sociological materials (i.e., history).[31] But sociology still existed only in general outline; moreover, being the most complex of the sciences, it would even when

---

manuel Lemoyne, *P.P.,* XI (1873), 130; Ch. Mismer, *P.P.,* XXIII (1879), 255, XXV (1880), 458–459, XXX (1883), 452 (contradicting Littré concerning the lack of progress among the Moslems); Achille Mercier, *P.P.,* XI (1873), 56; E. de Pompéry, *P.P.,* XXVI (1881), 145–150; J. de Bagnaux, *P.P.,* VII (1870), 221. Guarin de Vitry, *P.P.,* XVII (1876), 355, specifically declared the question to be an open one which sociology was not yet in a position to answer.

[30] Littré, *Paroles,* p. 75, and, as one instance of many, André-Nuytz in *P.P.,* VI (1870), 177. The slippery slope of the hierarchy of the sciences in reverse order, ending up in the subjective method, again seems not far distant.

[31] *P.P.,* II (1868), 188–190.

completed require great care in the formulation of hypotheses and permit only short-run deductions and predictions: "the future is too complex for us to penetrate very far." Comte's mistake, which he himself had briefly shared, was to think that history had already been absorbed into the domain of natural phenomena and that the time had therefore come to constitute a Positivist society according to formulas deduced from it, whereas in fact the period of transition to a Positivist society had not yet begun.[32]

Yet, at the same time, none of the Littréists could forget that sociology was the "queen of the sciences" not only in the sense that its place was at the top of the hierarchy, and that knowledge of it shed a flood of new light on the inferior sciences, but also that the ultimate purpose of the Positivist philosophy was to alter society according to the laws discovered by sociology. In spite of reiterated statements regarding the impropriety of specific political applications at the present stage of development of sociology, and the impropriety of those made by Comte,[33] neither the co-editors of the journal nor many of their collaborators avoided political prognostication and prescription, even disagreeing among themselves on the Positivist teaching on some of the most important issues. In fact the journal began to place a greater emphasis not only on sociological but also on political questions after the outbreak of the Franco-Prussian War, seeking often to explain or to answer current problems by the use of historical examples. The central issue was the degree of toleration or acceptance to be

---

[32] *Conservation,* 2nd ed., pp. 232–233, 250, 481; *P.P.,* IV (1869), pp. 32–34. Caro, in his very critical book on Littré, concludes that with him Positivist sociology, "so full of magnificent promises," amounted only to a theory of progress without adding substantially to previous ones (pp. 131–132). This seems to me to miss completely Littré's point that sociology was potentially a science yielding certain, though limited, predictions, but that it was still incomplete.

[33] Littré, *Comte et la philosophie positive,* pp. 667–668, *Conservation,* 2nd ed., pp. 218–220, 248, 268–272, 365–366, and in *P.P.,* XXIII (1879), 140–144; Wyrouboff, *ibid.,* V (1869–70), 465.

accorded the Third Republic, and this issue in turn was epitomized by the question of universal suffrage. This was a dubious institution, not only because it had brought Napoleon III to power in the first place, but on the other hand also because Comte, who unlike Littré had accepted the plebiscitarian regime of Napoleon III, had nevertheless taught that democracy and universal suffrage were worthless and harmful. Littré reluctantly came to the conclusion, however, that universal suffrage was for the time being a necessary evil and must be supported, both because it was in the deck dealt by history and in order to save the Republic, which could be replaced only by worse alternatives.[34] Littré could point, too, to the welcome fact that the Republic was turning toward an increasingly anticlerical policy.[35] Littré's coeditor, while resigning himself to universal suffrage as a *fait accompli* against which it was useless, for the moment, to rail, nevertheless took a markedly stronger tone against it than did Littré.[36]

What shows through very clearly in the Littréists' political writings [37] is Comte's *idée maîtresse* of a spiritual power, a body whose function it was to persuade the people of the rightness of the findings of science, particularly of sociology, and of the Positivist solutions to social problems. The existence of objective social and political truth was incompatible with the principle of free

[34] *Conservation,* 2nd ed., pp. 64–65, in *P.P.,* XIX (1877), 277, letter of 8 July 1871 in Gensoul, *La république au-dessus du suffrage universel,* and review of the book in *P.P.,* VII (1870), 495–497.

[35] *P.P.,* XX (1878), 121. Littré also wrote in his journal comments on a variety of other political issues, the most important probably being those advocating Positivist support for a modest and piecemeal kind of socialism.

[36] Wyrouboff, "La politique qualitative et la politique quantitative," *ibid.,* VIII (1872), 5–23 and esp. pp. 6, 15–18, also *P.P.,* XXVIII (1882), 8. He was holding to this position as late as 1908; see *Coopération des idées,* n.s. II, 129–137.

[37] In addition to those mentioned, see also, in *P.P.,* the articles by Antonin Dubost (a future president of the Senate!), XIII (1874), 257, 386–389, Stupuy, VI (1870), 482–484, XVII (1876), 403, 405–406, and others.

majority decision. This idea of a spiritual power, in Littré as in Comte, derived from the even more fundamental idea that social improvement must depend in the first instance on a prior mental and especially moral regeneration, on a replacement of arguments and divisions by harmony based on agreement on the truths revealed by science and coordinated by Positivism.[38] Since sociology was a science, Littré deduced with entire logic, "the time will come when the decisions formulated by it will be carried out without the need for consulting the crowd, any more than the crowd is consulted on decisions in astronomy, physics, or chemistry"; and it was for this reason that universal suffrage was to be regarded as no more than a "revolutionary device." [39] Still, Littré did accept universal suffrage for the time being, and his claims on behalf of a spiritual power lay in the future. Wyrouboff brought it considerably closer to home (note the use of the present tense):

As M. Comte said, there is no freedom of conscience in the sciences, in the sense that the mind is not free to refuse assent to what has been proved. Therefore, as that which has been proved grows in scope, society undertakes to teach it, without worrying whether it violates private and subjective freedom of conscience. I protest against a freedom of conscience which permits error except as an individual whim. In philosophy, evil is called error.[40]

This discussion illustrates clearly the connection between Comte's sociological and religious constructions, in that science was given a religious or quasi-religious authority and Positivism itself became a "demonstrable faith"; and it illustrates also the problem facing the scientific Positivists of accepting these premises, and in particular the central notion of a spiritual power, without adopting or accepting Comte's attempts to institutionalize the spiritual power. They wished to construct a religion without

[38] *Conservation,* 2nd ed., pp. 192–195, *P.P.,* VII (1870), 185.
[39] *P.P.,* IV (1869), 39.
[40] *Ibid.,* III (1868), 476–477; see also Stupuy, *ibid.,* X (1873), 32, 61.

theology, but not a "Catholicism without Christianity." [41] Littré, although his ardor toward Comte's religion had cooled,[42] nevertheless remained committed to the Religion of Humanity. He accepted Humanity as a religious symbol and believed that men would rally around it as they abandoned the theological religions. What he doubted was that the conception of Humanity should be transformed into a worship, and Comte's semi-Catholic ecclesiastical organization built around such a worship "exceeded the power of sociology to predict." [43] While it had been legitimate for Comte to invest positive philosophy with a role equivalent to that of the historic religions, it was illegitimate to go further by postulating Humanity as "a collective personality which could be worshipped." It was not necessary to worship or adore Humanity, or any other part of the universe or the universe as a whole, as distinct from a love of Humanity which was inculcated by Positivist ethics.[44]

Yet given the notion of a "demonstrable faith" and an "act of philosophic faith," [45] the word religion, and the reality of Humanity as a collective being,[46] it is hard to see why in principle its worship should be objectionable, whatever the status of sociological prediction.[47] This was indeed the view of some members of Littré's circle, who accepted Comte's Religion of Humanity more literally.[48] Wyrouboff, adopting a significantly defensive posture, even accepted at least one part of Comte's institutionalization of

[41] This term was invented by T. H. Huxley (see below, p. 222).

[42] See *Conservation,* 2nd ed., pp. 386–387, 410, 425.

[43] *Fragments,* pp. 473–474, *P.P.,* XII (1874), 312–313.

[44] *Comte et la philosophie positive,* pp. 524–526.

[45] *Conservation,* 2nd ed., p. 496.

[46] See also Stupuy in *P.P.,* XVI (1876), 444–445.

[47] Cf. Caro, *Littré,* pp. 154–163, who maintains that Littré's religion stultifies his philosophy.

[48] See in particular E. de Pompéry, *La morale naturelle et la religion de l'humanité* (Paris, 1891) (dedicated to Littré), pp. 75, 79, 109, and E. Bourdet, *Vocabulaire des principaux termes de la philosophie positive avec no-*

it, the Calendar of Great Men. Admitting that this was a product of Comte's "second phase," Wyrouboff declared that "even among M. Comte's errors, even among the strangest of his conceptions there are things to be considered seriously," though they must be carefully and minutely examined. The Calendar, though defective in some details, was one of these, and fulfilled a present need of society. It should, he thought, replace the Christian calendar.[49] Littré, however, endorsed the Calendar only as a medium of historical instruction.[50]

Still, none of the Littréists accepted Comte's religious construction integrally; if they had they would have been left with little if any reason not to rejoin the "theocratic Positivists." From many aspects of Comte's speculations and prescriptions they dissented unanimously and sometimes violently.[51] But on the whole it cannot be said that the group's effort to perpetuate the science and philosophy of the *Cours* while at most picking the religion and the religious sociology of the *Polity* over in a gingerly fashion was, intellectually speaking, markedly successful (which did not prevent them, of course, from being successful as propagandists among their contemporaries). It is very possible that Comte, being Professor Berlin's hedgehog *par excellence,* had logically (if I may make use of an unattractive metaphor) to be swallowed whole or not at all. An exception may be made for those of his latter-day ideas (most conspicuously, for example, the "utopia" of a Virgin-

---

tices biographiques appartenant au calendrier positiviste (Paris, 1875), p. 229, who refers to Humanity as the "great being."

[49] "Remarques sur le calendrier de M. Comte," *P.P.,* XVII (1876), esp. pp. 49–50. See also his review of Bourdet's book cited above (n. 48), *ibid.,* XVI (1876), 148.

[50] *Comte et la philosophie positive,* pp. 436, 590–591.

[51] Thus, for example, on the subject of "fetishism" and Comte's attempt to "incorporate" it into Positivism, which for them epitomized Comte's relapse into the subjective method if not into the first (or theological stage) of the three stages, see Littré, *Comte et la philosophie positive,* pp. 569, 573–578, and cf. Lesigne in *P.P.,* XXII (1879), 188.

Mother [parthenogenesis]) which can clearly be seen to stem from his personal life rather than from his theoretical speculations; but apart from these "the unity of Comte's life and doctrine" appears to me to withstand attack successfully.[52] This is to the credit of Comte's life more than of his doctrine, and it was entirely reasonable that Littré, to some extent (and partly for personal reasons) disenchanted by the late Comte, should have attempted in all sincerity to rescue what he continued to regard as sound by removing it from contamination, in the public's view, by association with what he considered unsound. But it was difficult to hold the line in such an operation, and Littré's group very understandably fell to disagreeing among themselves at various points on just how much, if any, of the product of Comte's last ten years was to be accepted.[53] The group in any event had little if any *esprit de corps,* and Littré never tried to impose any discipline. They never con-

[52] These were indeed the opinions expressed in extreme old age by a former associate of Littré who had also been a direct disciple of Comte (Deroisin, *Notes,* pp. 12–17). Comte himself gave, it seems to me, the unanswerable argument that even the religious outlines of the *Polity* had been given in one of his youthful essays, "On the Spiritual Power." Comte reprinted a number of these essays as an Appendix to Vol. IV of the *Polity* specifically in order to show the continuity of his thought. Cf., for that matter, the concluding sections of the *Cours* (which Harriet Martineau, significantly, omitted from her condensed translation). See also above, pp. 6–7, and below, p. 59.

[53] Omitted from consideration is the whole topic of Positivist morality and its sanctions, which probably caused more disagreement than any other, because the point that the Littréists had their internal dissensions has been sufficiently illustrated and because their discussion of the subject has little intrinsic interest and few if any implications of wider interest, except for the question whether altruism could and should be inculcated by society. It need hardly be said that none of them accepted ethics as the seventh and highest science of the hierarchy, as Comte's revised Classification of the Sciences had it. Also omitted is the whole rather sordid subject of Littré's alleged deathbed conversion to Catholicism, which seems to me irrelevant to my discussion.

stituted themselves into a "school," much less a formal society. They had no corporate existence except in relation to the journal.[54] They were not, therefore, interested in recruitment or conversion in any formal sense, and the journal itself was intended not as a "house organ" but to ventilate and introduce scientific Positivism among the educated general public. When the journal was closed down, the group dispersed. Only a very few of them joined or had anything to do with the closely knit and intellectually rather inbred school of orthodox disciples who under the leadership of Laffitte had been devoting themselves since Comte's death to carrying on the master's teaching integrally.

Reluctantly Laffitte had yielded in part to the pressure of the other disciples in giving to his direction an increasingly religious character.[55] But despite continued pressure he declined to make himself dependent on the very precarious finances of the movement by giving up his teaching of mathematics and becoming a full-time Director, although he showed a marked eagerness for all Positivist property to be in his name. Moreover, while acknowledging the importance, even sometimes the supreme importance, of the religious aspect of Positivism,[56] he insisted that it was not the

[54] A Sociological Society was, indeed, founded in 1872 with Littré as its first president (for details see *P.P.*, VIII [1872], 298–301) but soon disintegrated; cf. Wyrouboff, *ibid.*, XXVI (1881), 5–6.

[55] For the pressure, see letters to Laffitte from Dr. Robinet, 9 Oct. 1857, and from Audiffrent and Joseph Lonchampt throughout late 1857 and early 1858, M-le-P; also Lonchampt to Sémérie, 28 Dec. 1857, Richard Congreve Papers, British Museum, Add. MS 45240 f. 178 (hereafter cited as BM, followed by MS and folio numbers). For Laffitte's response see Laffitte to Foleÿ, 18 and 28 Oct. 1857, his Notes of 8 Nov. 1877, and the Positivist Sacrament books, all M-le-P.

[56] "What is more important than anything else is to consolidate and increase the religious nucleus, without which Positivism would tend to degenerate into purely academic digressions" (to Sauria, 11 July 1859, M-le-P). "Worship [*le culte*] is the ultimate end of any Religion, and it is the last sphere of which the positive spirit must take hold. . . . Worship alone can

39

only one: "The propagation of Positivism must have for its aim not only the formation of the nucleus of regeneration [i.e., a priesthood and disciples] but also the modification of the opinions on a large number of issues of those who will never become Positivists," aims which he said were complementary. Positivism must show "the most extreme tolerance for all the possible degrees of Positivist adherence." [57] In 1868 he formally set out the aims of the movement as follows:

1) the establishment of a general system of universal education for all;

2) the establishment of a "culte," "that is to say a set of meetings and ceremonies at which each one of us shall be periodically brought back to that general point of view which our everyday life, profoundly dispersive as it is, tends to make us lose sight of";

3) the establishment of a political direction by the enlightenment of public opinion through periodical publications.[58]

All told, one cannot avoid the very definite impression that Laffitte was considerably less enthusiastic about the Religion of Humanity, above all about its actual manifestations, than were those whom he was supposed to lead in it. With his equal or greater interest in infiltrating the doctrine among the general public, as distinct from building up the group of disciples and creating a priesthood, it seems possible that, had it not been for his personal loyalty to Comte and hence to the memory of Clotilde de Vaux, and Littré's espousal of the cause of Mme. Comte, Laffitte might, despite important shades of difference, have joined forces with

---

make the dogma popular, it alone can make it effective by touching the heart. . . . By placing worship above dogma we place moral culture above intellectual culture" (Annual Circular for 1858). See also the Circular for 1875 where he discusses the "three laws of our nature" on which worship is based. In all his early Circulars much is made of the Positivist Sacraments.

[57] Minutes of the meetings of the Positivist Committee, 1860–62, M-le-P. Cf. also: "The very relativism of Positivism admits of different degrees of cooperation, from a very partial sympathy to the full acceptance of our Religion" (Circular for 1870).

[58] Circular for 1868.

Littré. At any rate their intellectual positions were sometimes closer to each other than were those of Laffitte and most of his flock. If they had joined forces, the joint propaganda effect might have been considerable. As it was, Laffitte was hampered in his own exposition by being driven to incorporating more of the Religion of Humanity than he really wanted, as well as by the activities in this direction of some of the others.

Nevertheless Laffitte's capacity for lucid explanation even of Comte's more obscure and esoteric doctrines went far to overcome those obstacles. He had a powerful and encyclopedic mind; he was, in fact, the only man who thought Comte's system through for himself in its entirety. As a result he did not content himself with summaries of the doctrine and exegesis of particular points; he made the doctrine relatively more intelligible by rearrangement, illustration, and other means. He relieved it of the intolerable burden of Comte's dense, verbose, repetitive, and awkward style. A few excerpts will both suggest the flavor of Laffitte's writing, as different from Littré's as it is from Comte's, and give the general tenor of the method and content of his argument:

The state of reason . . . consists in harmony between our conceptions and external reality. Reason is present when the evolution and development of our thoughts reproduce external reality in such a way that we can predict the latter by the course of our meditations themselves. . . . The state of reason . . . consists in harmony between our conceptions degree of approximation permitted by the [scientific] results obtained and by the needs of our modifying action on the world, man, or society.

Practical reason consists of conceptions connected directly, so to speak, with the modification of things. The characteristic of practical reason, therefore, is its profound reality. . . . It is connected with cases entirely particular in nature, such that new reflection and new observations are required in order to pass from one case to a very similar case. . . . Theoretical reason [by contrast] consists of a general appreciation of the fundamental conditions of the existence of things, without any purpose of immediate practical application. . . . Theoretical reason constructs . . . a picture of reality reduced to its essential conditions. Its most distinctive characteristic is coordination.

Theoretical reason in turn is divided into abstract reason, "relating to the laws governing various orders of phenomena," and concrete reason, which is "the sum of general theories about phenomena [*êtres*] themselves." These propositions are stated in the preface to two volumes devoted to "the first philosophy," consisting of the most general laws, laws of the understanding and of the world (fifteen in number, outlined but never discussed systematically by Comte) governing the discovery and the existence of laws relating to phenomena. The "first philosophy" therefore codifies the laws of laws, "the totality of general abstract laws independent of the nature of phenomena." [59]

Now all this, and *a fortiori* Laffitte's system generally, may not be acceptable philosophy, and especially not acceptable epistemology; in places, in fact, it is egregious. But it has at least the appearance of being within the normal philosophical universe of discourse, as opposed to being a nightmarishly prolonged soliloquy by someone obsessed, which is often the impression made by Comte's own exposition. Still, Laffitte of course could not get away from the defects of Comte's original, most of which stem from the basic defect of circularity. Laffitte, like Comte, made a practice of referring the reader for proof of an assumption underlying a statement occurring early in his book to a later, more appropriate moment for discussing the proposition constituting that assumption; then at some later point the original statement itself would be used in its turn as an assumption for something else; the first assumption was sometimes never proved, sometimes proved only by the use of another unproved assumption, sometimes indeed by using the statement originally supported by the assumption. It would be tedious, depressing, and unprofitable to give instances of this practice; it would lead far afield and into philosophical technicalities of no interest or importance, and we are concerned with the contents and the merits and demerits of Positivism only to the extent that they explain its history. Its cir-

[59] *Cours de philosophie première* (Paris, 1928, 1894), I, v, xxxi–xxxiv.

cularity was undoubtedly indirectly, when it was not directly, the single most frequently charge made against it by people (professional philosophers and others) rejecting it as a total system. It was often phrased as an objection to the absence in Comte of any serious attempt at an epistemology. Laffitte, particularly in his "First Philosophy," tried to remedy this state of affairs. But actually his laws of "first philosophy" were in the main assumptions about "human nature" [60] (frequently, as already said, buttressing each other) which in the guise of "laws" then led to the discovery of other more specific "laws," the most important of which, in Positivism, were those describing and prescribing human behavior. Laffitte was always talking about the connection of everything with everything else, about the world being "a vast, fundamentally indivisible system all of whose parts reciprocally act and react" according to regular laws.[61] Above all he, like Comte himself and almost all other Positivists including Littré, took undue advantage of the "relativity" which was all that Comte had claimed for the truth of his system (this is what he later expressed in the phrase "subjective synthesis"). This proposition

[60] Laffitte summarized the Positivist theory of "human nature" as follows: "1. Irrespective of their origin, of which we can have no knowledge, there exists among men perfect identity as to the fundamental characteristics which constitute them. . . . 2. Mentally and morally the human race is mediocre; it is in general capable neither of very great virtues nor of very great vices. . . . 3. All progress [*perfectionnement*] is transmitted and established by heredity, and the long sequence of generations produces the evident profound differences among peoples. This is the origin of *races,* that purely sociological phenomenon. . . . 4. The result of all mental effort is prevision, on which action depends" (*Grands types,* I, 123). Laffitte completed and elaborated on Comte's physiological theory of the mind, with its "table of cerebral functions" and the consequent views on the feelings, altruism, mental harmony and pathology, and the complex emotional as well as rational processes involved in acquiring knowledge (*Grands types,* III, 58, 288–289, 603–604, *Philosophie première,* I, 245–247, 249, 256–257, 268, 271–274, 277–283, 298–300, 302, 304–309).

[61] *Ibid.,* II, 251, 280.

might mean, on occasion and given a suitable temperament, that the system was literally "relative" to the time and place of its origin and liable to change. Comte, whose temperament was not suitable, usually meant that it was relative, not to himself or even to Paris in the early nineteenth century, but to "human nature" generally, or rather to any human being anywhere who had reached the third or positive stage. This was a system, Comte said and Laffitte agreed and elaborated, which to be sure did not necessarily describe an objective reality (this men could never know and was a "metaphysical notion") but did describe the only reality and the only relations among the elements of reality which were true, relevant, and valuable (useful) for human individuals and especially human society as they happened to be constituted. But ultimately the trouble with the Positivist "conception of the universe" was that, though they insisted that its laws were rigorously derived and necessary laws, it corresponded more with what Comte and his followers thought was relevant for people to know in the sense of what it was useful for them to know than with any other criterion of truth, subjective or objective. This is the explanation for, among other things, the curious parallelism suggested by Laffitte between the operations of the mind and the operations of the universe which collaborated, so to speak, in the construction of the Positivist synthesis.[62] For to the Positivist all knowledge served only one purpose, the betterment of society, one of whose primary elements was the achievement of mental harmony, first of all within each individual member of the society and then among them. Mental harmony, however, was not only intellectual but above all emotional in nature. The Positivist synthesis was designed, therefore, not only to convince but to kindle enthusiasm.[63]

[62] See above, pp. 41–43, and also *Philosophie première,* I, 317–318, 336, 338, 400, II, 2, 89, 210–211, 231–232; and I, 349, where he seems to suggest that the purpose of formulating the "law" of three stages is to ensure its observance, which is surely to confuse two meanings of the word "law."

[63] See, e.g., *ibid.,* I, 406. This view of "mental harmony" was in turn

This attribute of drumming up trade on its own behalf is peculiarly repellent when used by a doctrine built up by circular argument. The ulterior purpose of Positivism was stated by Laffitte, as by Comte and all other Positivists, quite frankly:

This course is designed to be a demonstration of the superiority of our doctrine, the only one capable of doing justice to all and of assigning to everyone his place in Humanity. All others are powerless to do this: only our own, from its relative point of view, can properly appreciate its predecessors . . . and at the same time explain the necessary advent of a new doctrine.[64]

Positivism, Laffitte said, was

a general doctrine providing common and universal rules for the direction of the world, man, and society, . . . a doctrine which comprehends all that it is given to us to know, and which in its totality contains parts so well connected and so consonant with each other, and so complete, that nothing is left to chance, no problem is left without solution, and everyone knows in all circumstances what he must think.

In this way Positivism produces a "consensus of opinions" which "must express [*résumer*] itself in one individual who assumes both direction and responsibility." [65]

After this conspectus of the general nature of Positivism as expressed by its most lucid philosophical spokesman, it may not be

---

connected back to the axiom that the "cerebral functions" leading to scientific knowledge were emotional as well as intellectual in nature (see n. 60 above). The "subjective synthesis" was justified, then, by kindred assumptions as to the character of human nature and as to the requirements of human life. The circularity of this whole complex of arguments needs no further emphasis, but see, in addition to other references, *Philosophie première*, I, 125 and n., 134, 137, 148, 151–152, 157–158, 167 and n., 183–184, 191–192, 194–196, 210.

[64] *Grands types,* I, 22.

[65] *Ibid.,* I, 6–7. On the ulterior purpose of Positivism, see also, particularly, Laffitte's *General View of Chinese Civilization* . . . (tr. Hall, London, etc., 1887), p. iii.

illegitimate to suggest that Positivism managed to combine many of the worst and weakest aspects, often in exacerbated form, of the eighteenth-century *esprit de système,* Kantian phenomenalism, the Hegelian coherence theory of truth, scientism and garbled scientific method, pseudo-Romantic evangelical sentimentality, and totalitarian notions of social engineering.

Of these it was some aspects of the last two, an organized Religion of Humanity and political authoritarianism, that Littré rejected, and though he is perhaps to be admired for this rejection it did not rescue his version of Positivism from the damning element of circularity while on the other hand making it internally less consistent. Conversely, the orthodox disciples, pushing their sometimes reluctant leader Laffitte ahead of them, by accepting the social and religious prescriptions that followed from the Positivist analysis offended many outsiders who had not noticed the circularity of the analysis itself. Laffitte considered it his achievement to have explicated and completed those parts of Comte's system which the master, owing to his premature death, had done no more than outline,[66] chiefly the sociology (including politics) and the religion and ethics (including "psychology"). But his powers of lucid exposition [67] could not rescue Laffitte from the palpable absurdities of Comte's lucubrations on these subjects in general and in particular (e.g., fetishism, the utopia of the Virgin-Mother, number mysticism, the nature of historical determinism, the proposal for a "Religious League" between Positivism and the Roman Catholic Church). Moreover, he and the majority of his followers attempted to combine their acceptance of the *corpus* of Comte's writings as the true and saving doctrine with an insistence that Positivism as the scientific philosophy must maintain intimate connections with work in the sciences (so long as it was

---

[66] See the estimate of Robinet in *R.O.,* I (1878), 78–79. Laffitte, who was genuinely modest, sometimes reduced the importance of his own work by exaggerating Comte's, e.g., *ibid.,* 10–12.

[67] Above all in his *Philosophie première.*

socially useful) [68] and must never depart from the scientific method (so long as it was aimed at producing a "subjective synthesis").[69] This feat was even harder for them than for the Littréists, since they would only with the greatest reluctance admit that any of

[68] *Ibid.*, II, 178, and Annual Circular for 1881; see also Emile Antoine in *R.O.*, VII (1881), 393–394, and Paul Dubuisson, *ibid.*, I (1878), 145, and to Rhétoré, 28 Dec. 1879, in the Papers of Emile Corra, Archives Nationales, Catalogue No. 17 (hereafter cited as A.N.), AS 2; but cf. A. M. de Lombrail, *Aperçus généraux sur la doctrine positiviste* (Paris, 1858), p. 160, who thinks that the Religion of Humanity without any scientific preamble is enough to convince people of the truth of Positivism. Laffitte and his circle, like Littré's, rejected Darwinian evolution (e.g., Laffitte, *Philosophie première*, I, 215–216, II, 175); they also followed Comte in rejecting vivisection on the ground that the method proper to biology was observation, not experiment (Laffitte, *R.O.*, XI (1883), 226–227). On strictly scientific questions, in fact, the "orthodox" Positivists differed little from the "scientific" ones, for both could follow Comte. See for a good general summary of the "orthodox" approach to scientific questions Dr. Bazalgette, "Les sociétés animales," *R.O.*, III (1879), 260–276. On the necessity for science to be "useful," see *inter alia* Laffitte, *Philosophie première*, I, 16–17, 40, 83–84, *Grands types*, I, 12.

[69] For various statements on "scientific method" (observation of properties leading to induction of laws, dependence of hypotheses on the external world as well as on the intelligence, objectivity in the formulation of abstract hypotheses, danger of excessive subjectivity, and so forth), see *Philosophie première*, I, vi, 130–132, 143–144, 237 and n., *Grands types*, III, 459–460. On the inescapability, nevertheless, of the "subjective method" and the corresponding desirability of the "subjective synthesis," see *Grands types*, II, 123, *Philosophie première*, I, 137–147, 193–194 ("Since we cannot avoid having inclinations, we must regulate them. . . . To adopt the most sympathetic hypothesis is to choose, of two hypotheses of equal simplicity, the one which presents men in the most favorable light" [pp. 144–145]). Despite the subjectivity or "relativity" of the Positivist synthesis, however, Laffitte claimed for the teacher the right to lay down unchallenged dogma: "He is not talking to his equals" (*Grands types*, II, 226). For sheer methodological muddleheadedness, probably nothing surpassed E. Husson, "Encore l'Incognoscible," *R.O.*, n.s. XV (1897), 273–311, XVI (1897), 1–51, 166–208, 337–397.

Comte's teachings was in need of correction, as opposed to completion.[70] They were content to quote, paraphrase, summarize, and explicate Comte. Nevertheless a revolt arose within the body of these orthodox Positivists—a revolt, however, not against but for Comte, a revolt against Laffitte's directorship on the ground that he was not energetic enough on behalf of the master's doctrine. Agreement with Comte was not enough, the rebels argued; action was necessary, political action or religious action or both. Motives, as usual, were mixed; and an important additional complication stemmed from the fact that the origins and leadership of the revolt were to be found in England as much as in France.

Organized Positivism in England had taken a different turn from that in France very soon after Comte's death.[71] Its course, indeed its very existence, was almost entirely the result of the efforts of Richard Congreve. Recognized by Comte, shortly before his death, as the leader of English Positivism, Congreve had in fact no challenger. The obstacles in his way were financial rather than personal. His private income was adequate to maintain his family and to enable him to devote his entire time to Positivism, but he could not subsidize the movement as well (of course he sent his contribution to Paris). For financial reasons, therefore, and also because he had undertaken an arduous medical course of study himself, he was confined in the beginning to giving free lectures and courses and holding meetings; but even these early efforts had a markedly religious tendency, and as early as 1859 he considered

[70] Some of Laffitte's elaborations on the fifteen laws of the "First Philosophy" have the appearance of correcting Comte, but Laffitte went out of his way to minimize Comte's errors while pointing out his own improvements: *Philosophie première,* I, 302, 315–316, 334, 394, and cf. particularly *R.O.,* XVII (1886), 96, 110–112. There is scarcely a single real criticism of Comte on fundamental matters (as opposed to specific application of political principles) in the entire output of Laffitte and his school, but see Laffitte, *Philosophie prèmiere,* I, 343; Méhay in *R.O.,* XIII (1884), 431, Dubuisson to Congreve, 30 Aug. 1876, BM Add. MS 45237 f. 1.

[71] For the rest of this chapter, cf. throughout McGee, *Crusade,* chap. ii.

the "Positivist Church" in England to have been founded.[72] He aimed from the start at a formal religious organization and at a Positivist religious community; in 1867 he founded the London Positivist Society, and in 1870 he was able, through the financial backing of two followers, to take the essential step. He moved from Wandsworth (at that time still rural and difficult of access) to Bloomsbury and rented a room in Chapel Street, near his new house, as a permanent headquarters.

It cannot have been easy to persist for a whole decade virtually single-handed in behalf of an unfamiliar doctrine, to dedicate one's life and inheritance to an unpopular and apparently hopeless cause; but Congreve had the true evangelical spirit and an iron determination. "Positivism," he wrote truly, "is the one idea of my life." He admitted discouragement, but he never considered defeat, and he never lowered his sights: "To rally all possible elements of a new Society is my object," he wrote, and by that he meant not "a mere scientific society" but a church organization. "It is a new Religion I am engaged in putting forward and . . . I claim as much as the ministers of the existing faiths. Not an eclectic movement—no—it is the complete system of Comte which I aim at spreading—nothing less." [73] The constitution of "a strictly Positivist society" took unquestioned precedence with him over cooperation with outsiders who sympathized with individual Positivist aims or doctrines.[74] He conceded very early in his career that Positivism as a "demonstrable religion" "must never lose sight of the basis on which the demonstration rests, never shrink from

---

[72] *Essays,* I, 279. See in general his early essays and lectures in that volume, and cf. Sydney Eisen, "Frederic Harrison: The Life and Thought of an English Positivist" (Ph.D. thesis, The Johns Hopkins University, 1957), p. 195.

[73] To Henry Edger (an American Positivist), 2 March 1858, BM Add. MS 45232 f. 25; to Sulman, 3 Aug. 1870, MS 45234 f. 2.

[74] To Edger, 4 Oct. 1867, *ibid.,* MS 45232 f. 159. In a later letter he observed that a body of firm believers was necessary if only for financial reasons (27 Feb. 1868, f. 176).

any demand of verification." [75] He did not want to frighten away adherents by making his definitions too sharp.[76] But even before 1867, when he was not expecting to make converts (though he rejoiced when he did),[77] he never saw his ultimate goal as any other than religious. The religious aspects were, moreover, the most promising for the purpose of bringing people over; the doctrine was to be used only defensively, and where intellectual propaganda was required appeals on social subjects would be the most suitable.[78] After 1867, despite continued private discouragement, Congreve became in public increasingly confident and rejected even more explicitly any idea of a Littréist appeal in order to secure "partial" adhesions. On the contrary, a complete scientific education (such as he had given himself) was not necessary and was often impossible for the convert: it was enough if he obeyed "the logic of the feelings, which is a more powerful, and often a surer, guide than the mere intellect."

If we stand conspicuous by the offer of a system of great comprehensiveness and consistency, adherents will flock to that system without waiting to inquire whether in all points it is justifiable by the strictly reasoning faculties.

Comte's *General View* and his *Catechism*

offer a sufficient exposition of the subject for them to make up their minds whether the system is one which satisfies them or not. In many cases even this amount of labour would be superfluous, for their keen

[75] Same, 23 Oct. 1857, *ibid.*, f. 14.

[76] Same, 13 Sept. 1860, *ibid.*, f. 68. See his criticism of one of his followers: "He is too full of the advantages of discussion, of upsetting old superstitions, encouraging free thought etc. to be quite adapted for our views. However we must take what we can get, and if he would to any extent cooperate it would be a gain" (to his wife, 21 April 1860, Wadham MS e. 51 f. 18).

[77] To Edger, 18 April 1861, 19 June 1860, 21 March 1862, BM Add. MS 45232 ff. 81, 63, 91.

[78] "Culte des morts" (1862), in *Essays*, I, 334–335.

interest in social well-being, acting in conjunction with distrust and dislike of existing beliefs, will lead them into the support of our cause.[79]

It is in the religion and as the heart of the religion—as that which most powerfully appeals to and acts upon the feelings—in the worship, that lies our greatest strength, our best hope of influencing those around us whom it is most wished that we should influence, viz. the minds of a religious stamp which have ceased to find satisfaction in the older organizations.[80]

And privately: "The one essential point is to get the Religion accepted and the life-giving stimulus it will supply will do what we want." [81]

This outlook (which he may understandably have derived in part from his own experience) was reflected in the conditions that Congreve required of an applicant for membership of the Positivist Society. He exacted temperamental submission rather than intellectual conviction: "In general terms I should say that membership should imply a complete acceptance or at least that attitude of mind which is ready for acceptance of the leading principle, to make no difficulty with the fair deductions and applications." [82] And in practice Congreve tended increasingly to demand, and to enforce when he could, acquiescence in his own interpretations of Comte on matters of faith and morals.

Congreve's decided emphasis on the Religion of Humanity, and his inclination to set himself up as its English High Priest, had the most far-reaching consequences for the future of organized Positivism in England. In the first place, they made for difficult relations when men as independent-minded as three of his former Wadham pupils joined him in the propagation of Positivism; in the second place, they caused him to become dissatisfied with Laffitte as Director of Positivism and brought him into sympathetic

[79] "Education" (1870), *ibid.*, 388–389.
[80] "The Combination between France and England" (1873), *ibid.*, 478.
[81] To Edger, 5 Aug. 1874, BM Add. MS 45232 f. 246.
[82] To Oliver, 15 June 1872, *ibid.*, MS 45235 ff. 3–4.

contact with Laffitte's disaffected French disciples; and in due course these two sets of consequences intertwined.

Beesly, Bridges, and Harrison all found themselves, for different reasons, in London during the 1860's. Beesly was appointed to the chair of history in University College in 1860 (a position which he never used to propagate Positivism).[83] Bridges was in London briefly before setting out for Australia with a new wife to a new medical practice. During this period "my close friendship with him [Congreve] was resumed, and our joint fellowship in the social and religious movement of Positivism was fully and irrevocably established." His young wife died tragically after only a few months in Australia; on the voyage back with her body Bridges kept himself occupied by translating Comte's *General View,* and Positivism became his "dominant interest." [84] He received the Sacrament of Destination from Laffitte in 1864, and in 1866 Congreve was still calling him his only active disciple.[85] By 1868, however, he was gravely disturbing Congreve by proposing to remarry in violation of Comte's injunction of perpetual widowhood, and Congreve complained that "others who call themselves,

[83] Beesly's academic career was, in fact, not distinguished in any way: "He held the chair for 32 years, and left the subject, as he had found it, one of little importance. . . . He contented himself with appearing in college once or twice a week to deliver his lectures and walking away" (H. Hale Bellot, *University College London, 1826–1926* [London, 1929], pp. 332–333). His main interest during this period was in social questions, especially the nascent trade-union movement; see his letters to Congreve, 15 May 1867, BM Add. MS 45227 f. 27, and to Laffitte, 10 Oct. 1876, M-le-P, and especially two articles by Royden Harrison (who is engaged in a general study of the Positivists and the English labor movement): "E. S. Beesly and Karl Marx," *International Review of Social History,* IV (1959), 22–58, 208–238, and "Professor Beesly and the Working-Class Movement," in *Essays in Labour History,* ed. Asa Briggs and John Saville (London and New York, 1960), pp. 205–241.

[84] *Recollections of Bridges,* pp. 79–83; Liveing, *Bridges,* p. 82.

[85] See Bridges to Laffitte, 4 Aug. 1864, M-le-P; Congreve to Edger, 17 Aug. 1866, BM Add. MS 45232 f. 130. Cf. Eisen, "Harrison," p. 195.

and to a certain extent are, Positivists" sympathized with Bridges.[86]

The most prominent of these partial and *soi-disant* Positivists was undoubtedly Frederic Harrison. Having, like Congreve, undertaken a course of scientific training after graduation from Oxford, he had come to London to practice law. There he found his friends all converging toward Positivism, and under the influence of Congreve added the *Polity* and Comte's other late works to his previous reading. In 1860 he began the translation of Volume II of the *Polity;* by 1861 he "entirely accepted and adopted in practice" the Classification of the Sciences and proposed to himself as his "agenda for life":

1) "to clear up the mind on the question of religion . . . If it is to be permanent it must rest on scientific proof."
2) "Knowledge of the working classes."
3) "Popular Education."
4) "Social Improvement."

A year later he wrote in his diary:

The more I work at Comte the less dogmatic he becomes to me. I find him full of broad practical tolerance. . . . I believe his disciples . . . ought to seek to make his *principles* actively felt in society. . . . They ought to found a school, not a sect. At least that only is the limit to which I can go.

He was therefore repelled by the sectarian form in which Congreve was presenting Positivism, even though he was steadily assimilating "the whole scheme of Auguste Comte." He went to Paris and met Laffitte, "but I did not seek affiliation to the body in Paris, which still seemed to me premature, nor did I make any attempt to take part in a propaganda of Positivism as a religious system." [87]

[86] Congreve to Edger, 22 May 1868, BM Add. MS 45232 ff. 179–180; and see below, pp. 56–60.

[87] *Autobiography,* I, 150–151 (on the role of F. D. Maurice in undermining his Christian orthodoxy), 247–249, 280–282, II, 253–255, *The Creed of a Layman* . . . (New York and London, 1907), pp. 26–27, 34–35.

In 1869, still not a member of the English Positivist Society founded two years earlier, Harrison published an important essay in the *Fortnightly Review,* then edited by John Morley, entitled

---

The remarkable analysis of Harrison written after his death by his son, who was not sympathetic to Positivism, is worth quoting at length: "To a man so deeply religious, so naturally philosophical, so temperamentally impulsive, yet so mentally deliberate, the historical intellectualism of Comte appealed almost irresistibly, for it provided him not only with a faith but with a vocation. . . . He was not a fanatic, or an ascetic; he was the passionate type of moral enthusiast. . . . He lacked the quiet of the philosopher. To a man so scrupulous and ardent, religion was the only career. . . . To an emotional ethicist such as my father, rationalism provides no consolation. Both mind and soul had to be requisitioned. . . . Thus, my father turned resolutely and instinctively towards the synthetic social science of Comte, which offered him emotional application. . . . With him, religion meant example, a living morality, and it was this ascetic call of individualization that so attracted him to Comte. . . . Here was no metaphysic, no ruling absolute, no condemnation. It left the whole play of his faculties free. . . . Even the imagination had an historical perspective, and there was a due regard for tradition. . . . A religion without theology—that was the attraction; a religion which revealed and connected history, thought, science and the arts with the living present, and left the sum of a man's intelligence unafraid and open. . . . It . . . gave him what his nature longed for—an intelligent and conscientious relation to life, a purpose and a mission. . . . For my father needed direction. . . . Always moral purpose bound him. . . . From the hour that he had convinced himself of the social justice of a religion which embraced and implemented all man's higher faculties, he never looked back and he drew from it increasing solace. . . . It always seemed a little strange to me that so fierce an individualist and so profound a thinker as my father should have merged his personality so completely in the thought of Comte, and I can only account for it on the ground of Faith, which happened to synchronize with his intellectual equipment" (Austin Harrison, *Frederic Harrison: Thoughts and Memories* [London, 1926], pp. 37, 96, 123, 124, 129, 133–136, 178. Orig. pub. 1926 by Heinemann, London; pub. 1927 by Putnam's, New York; quoted by permission of Putnam's & Coward-McCann.) Perhaps the rarity of this particular temperament goes far to explain the exiguity of Positivist disciples and especially leaders.

"The Positivist Problem."[88] The purpose of Positivism, he wrote, was "to harmonise our conceptions and to systematise human life; and . . . to do the first *only for the sake of the second.*" Consequently Positivism was not comparable with any existing philosophy; it was in fact not a philosophy, nor was it a religion or a polity, but nevertheless professed "to comprehend them all, and that in their fullest sense." Positivism had to be judged as a whole. The charge, for example, that Positivism "might check the discovery of some curious facts" was irrelevant: "The problem of human life is not to secure the greatest accumulation of knowledge, or the vastest body of truth, but that which is most valuable to man." Criticism of the system on the ground that it was a system was question-begging. "The idea that thought and life may some day on this earth be reduced to organic order and harmony may be Utopian, but is it one so grotesque that it need arouse the horseplay of every literary trifler?" The range of possible objections of detail was infinite, but "there is no reason why men, positive in spirit and in general aim, should feel bound to defend every point in turn in a vast body of philosophy for which they are not responsible and which in its entirety they do not pretend to teach." As to the religious aspect: "The real point in issue is whether it be possible to direct mankind by a religion of social duty, if humanity as a whole . . . can inspire a living devotion . . . ; whether it be possible to maintain such a religion by appropriate observances and an organised education." And as to politics, the "leading conception is to subordinate politics to morals by bringing the practical life into accord with the intellectual and the emotional." Positivism was the only "systematic attempt to conciliate progress and order."

One would think that any objective observer would regard this essay, published in one of England's leading magazines, as a powerful boost for Positivism. Harrison did not and could not escape from the internal contradictions of the system (it is surely ironical

[88] *Fortnightly Review,* XXXV (1869), 469–493.

to read a Positivist accusing others of question-begging!), but his essay was skillfully argued and well written, and it was certainly not halfhearted in the Littréist sense. Yet Congreve was not enthusiastic. He wrote in a disgruntled fashion that the article was "calculated in some respects to do us service, in others not. It is meant in some degree as a statement of the writer's own position in reference to the organisation which he has never definitely consented to join." [89] For Congreve, he who was not for him was against him, and what he resented was precisely that Harrison had not "consented to join" and thus to put himself under Congreve's discipline. But Harrison was a man of independent mind and of a will almost as strong as Congreve's, and relations between them were likely to become strained as soon as Congreve

[89] To Edger, 5 Nov. 1869, BM Add. MS 45232 f. 198. Eisen, "Harrison," p. 212, adduces the mildness of this passage as evidence that Congreve was not always intolerant. But what Congreve wrote was no more than the truth, for Harrison had specifically dissociated himself, in the article, from those who, like Congreve, "definitely accept Positivism as a religion, and regard themselves as a community" (p. 491), and the article could therefore not be considered suitable for recruiting converts, which was what Congreve wanted. It might be said that Congreve imposed a kind of stoical forbearance on himself at this time, but only as a temporary expedient; cf.: "All differences here are tolerated. I ask no questions for convenience' sake. But we must wait for real unity" (to Edger, 5 Feb. 1874, BM Add. MS 45232 f. 238). At any rate Harrison himself had the impression that because of this article Congreve withdrew his confidence and friendship from him (*Autobiography,* I, 352 n.). But cf. also Congreve's more tolerant attitude to Harrison and Beesly elsewhere (to Lobb, 11 Nov. 1870 and 21 Feb. 1872, Wadham MSS c. 183 f. 281, c. 184 f. 2) and his unnaturally restrained comment on Littré's activities: "There is good in this, if largely mixed with evil" ("Human Catholicism II" [1876], *Essays,* II, 259). Privately Congreve had added that Littré's success tended "to distract attention from our movement and to lead new inquirers often to unsatisfactory results" (to Edger, 9 Oct. 1868, BM Add. MS 45232 f. 184).

attempted to impose discipline. As early as 1861 Harrison had privately written of Congreve: "He was a different man when we first knew him [i.e., at Oxford]. . . . I can honour, admire, support, but I am not attracted farther." And in 1864: "I feel indeed only more bound to respect his purpose, that I cannot say that I share his special convictions." Much later, he wrote in retrospect: "For many years after ceasing to be his pupil at Oxford, I received most valued instruction and inspiration from him, and felt towards him sincere respect and regard, though I never could submit myself to his control or to his principles." [90]

"When in 1870," Harrison recorded, "Dr. Congreve resolved to open a small hall in Chapel Street, . . . I thought it to be quite premature, as no sufficient body of persons definitely committed to the active Positivist propaganda and cult was yet collected. I did what I could to postpone this step, but I did not choose to secede from it." [91] Finally he made his feelings quite clear to Congreve himself:

The real task before those who adopt Comte's conceptions is to work for the spread of Positivist convictions and Positivist life, and to leave the formation of a formal Church . . . to the spontaneous and natural result of a considerable society finding itself permeated with the same sentiments and faith. To form a Church without such an existing body of members is to form a sect, from which public opinion—the life of Positivism—is excluded, or is only faintly represented. And it is to form a group which are wholly taken out of the practical society in which they must live. . . . Hence I hold that to form a Church without members adequate for the working of a Church is premature and must end in abortion. . . . I shall hold my tongue about the hierarchical and sacramental machinery taught by Comte, because though looking on it favourably, I feel no kind of enthusiasm for it, and wait to see how a sufficiently large body of opinion might show any disposition to adopt it. I am therefore in no sense a member of any religious organi-

[90] *Autobiography*, I, 350–352.   [91] *Creed of a Layman*, p. 47.

sation. . . . My object and interest is the spread of the sentiments and convictions systematized by Comte, and I know of no conscious dissent in me from any of them.[92]

Congreve's cry was restrained but came from the heart: "I think I felt stronger when I stood more alone." [93] Two years later he chafed: "We are governed . . . by the most lukewarm Positivist among us. F. Harrison." [94]

It is clear that this growing antagonism between Congreve and Harrison was based far more on a difference of tactical appreciations than on a difference of doctrines, though certainly Congreve's insistence on founding a Church and on treating his audience as a congregation was traceable to a much greater emphasis on his part on the religious practices prescribed by Comte in the *Polity*.[95] But Harrison was not being disingenuous when he professed agreement with all Comte's teachings; he was no Littréist, thinking to divide Comte in half; he simply disliked what might be called the small-town pettiness of sects, and he disliked Congreve's evident aspirations to sacerdotal functions. Thus he could sarcastically refer to the Positivist Society as "the brethren," [96] and yet write with as much passion as Congreve about Positivism to George Eliot, whom he was trying to encourage in pursuing the "Faith of the Future." [97]

Congreve meanwhile was busy lecturing and writing on a variety

[92] Harrison to Congreve, 21 March [1872], BM Add. MS 45228 ff. 239–245.

[93] To J. Geddes, 21 July 1872, *ibid.*, MS 45231 f. 187.

[94] Same, 10 April 1874, *ibid.*, f. 203.

[95] See Congreve on the meaning of discipleship and on Positivist proselytization in "Religion of Humanity" (1871) in *Essays*, I, 394.

[96] To Morley, Dec. 1871, in F. W. Hirst, *Early Life & Letters of John Morley* (London, 1927), I, 201.

[97] Letters of 19 July 1866 and 11 Nov. 1868, in *The George Eliot Letters*, ed. Gordon S. Haight (New Haven and London, 1954–55), IV, 286–289, 484. To his own son Harrison said that intellectually Comte had "released the springs of the modern world" (Austin Harrison, *Harrison*, p. 137).

of subjects, but mostly on aspects of the Religion of Humanity and with an increasing inclination toward Roman Catholicism. He gave a series of three lectures entitled "Human Catholicism" in which he said, among other things, that Roman Catholicism had been "the first attempt at a Religion of Humanity," [98] and he retorted to Huxley that Positivism was not Catholicism *minus* Christianity but "Catholicism *plus* Science." [99] Science and reason were portrayed, however, as subservient to faith:

We have properly speaking no controversy with science[!] . . . ; we only wish it to work its full work—to accept in all its difficulty the task that devolves on it of contributing, by its own self-completion, to the social and moral growth of Humanity, to renounce all other and vaguer aspirations.[100]

One subject, at least, on which Congreve and his refractory associates could agree was on the rejection (and the confusion) of the views of Mill and Littré as "incomplete Positivism," though even here there were differences of emphasis. The main effort in this direction was made by Bridges in a long reply to Mill's book on Comte, written more in sorrow than in anger, in which he argued for the inconsistency of Mill by adducing the consistency of Comte and defended Comte on every point raised by Mill, including the social and religious applications.[101] Bridges, who had himself called Harrison a "semi-Positivist," [102] appeared to be

[98] "Human Catholicism III" (1877), *Essays*, II, 302. All three lectures are printed in this volume and are largely devoted to the theme of the similarities between the two religions.

[99] "Mr. Huxley on M. Comte" (1869), *Essays*, I, 265 (reprinted from the *Fortnightly Review*).

[100] "Human Catholicism I" (1875), *ibid.*, II, 233–234. Cf. also "Human Catholicism II" (1876), *ibid.*, 279.

[101] J. H. Bridges, *The Unity of Comte's Life and Doctrine: A Reply to Strictures on Comte's Later Writings Addressed to J. S. Mill* (London, 1866).

[102] Bridges to Laffitte, 4 Aug. 1864, M-le-P.

closer to Congreve's position than to Harrison's, and it does not seem surprising that Bridges expressed "cordial thankfulness" to Congreve when the latter took the step in 1877 of introducing a prayer to Humanity into his "service." [103] But this was the last sign of harmony. From this time on organized Positivism in both England and France was racked by repeated schisms, which weakened the movement as a whole not only internally but also in its relations with the world outside.

The Positivist schism of 1877–1878 was a joint Anglo-French affair and was caused by a complex combination of doctrinal convictions and personal inadequacies, misunderstandings, and incompatibilities.[104] In England, as we have seen, Congreve tended increasingly to stress the religious aspects of Positivism, Comte's infallibility, and his own autocracy as its English High Priest, while most of his more prominent colleagues, and particularly the triumvirate of his former Wadham pupils, resented his personal arrogance, regarded Comte as an ordinary mortal, and feared that the emphasis on the Religion of Humanity was tactically premature (though avoiding—particularly Bridges—any bifurcation of Comte's life and work *à la* Littré). At the same time Congreve

[103] Bridges to Congreve, 5 Nov. 1877, BM Add. MS 45227 f. 150, quoted by Congreve in *Essays,* II, 85. Note also Congreve's introduction in 1875, as a preamble to his Annual Addresses on the Festival of Humanity (New Year's Day), of an invocation to Comte, his companions, and the symbols of the Religion of Humanity, full of capital letters and extravagantly phrased (*ibid.,* II, 225–226).

[104] The remainder of this chapter provides only an outline of the history of organized Positivism in France and England after the schism of 1877. Generally speaking, the account given here is based chiefly on the papers in the Musée Auguste Comte, the Archives Nationales, and the British Museum already cited, as well as on numerous published Positivist writings; I have given specific references only for direct quotations and at other key points. I hope to present substantive details and full documentation elsewhere. For England, cf. throughout McGee, *Crusade,* offering a fuller account than is provided here but writing without most of the unpublished materials.

became involved with some of the French Positivists who for a variety of partly contradictory reasons chafed at Laffitte's directorship: some were still dissatisfied with his restrained approach to religious activities; others were more interested in political propaganda and action; almost all agreed that Laffitte was intolerably dilatory in correspondence and other practical matters of his stewardship. This discontent by 1877 grew into insurrection and an attempt to depose Laffitte from office; some thought of replacing him with Congreve. The latter, lured by this prospect, seized the opportunity to break with the English triumvirate who, for their part, sympathized far more with Laffitte's "intellectual deviation" [105] than with the assorted religious or political desires of Congreve and his French allies. But the latter fell out among themselves and were outmaneuvered by Laffitte, whose only major concession was the founding of a journal, the *Revue occidentale*. The great majority of his followers subsided and acquiesced in his continued leadership. Two of the leaders of the revolt declined to make their peace and set up a rival group in the rue Jacob with financial support from Congreve; but even this splinter sect fell prey to internal discord and within a few years dissolved.

On his home ground, however, Congreve, though opposed by the majority of his followers, was able in virtue of the provisions of the lease to eject them from the Positivist headquarters in Chapel Street and to maintain himself there as the head of an entirely independent group, while the others, under the leadership of Harrison and Beesly but acknowledging the paramountcy of Laffitte, set up a new meeting place at Newton Hall. For almost forty years the two groups went their separate ways and even succeeded in establishing satellites in the provinces (Manchester, Liverpool, and Newcastle-on-Tyne were the most important). Congreve became ever more overbearing in his priestly pretensions and concentrated on consolidating his small flock into a full-fledged religious con-

[105] The phrase occurs in the letter which touched off the whole imbroglio, Sémérie to Congreve, 1 Sept. 1877, BM Add. MS 45239 ff. 230–250.

gregation; Newton Hall, through the medium of the oral and written efforts of Harrison and others and, beginning in 1893, of a journal, the *Positivist Review,* edited by Beesly, paid more attention to propagation among the general public and had some success. Around the turn of the century, however, both groups lost their leaders through death or retirement, becoming in consequence both weaker and less intransigent, and reunification took place in 1916. Nevertheless the numbers of the faithful continued to dwindle, causing financial difficulties, which in turn hampered the movement in its efforts to attract a new generation. Even the varied gifts of F. S. Marvin did not avail to give the movement new life. The *Positivist Review,* after an abortive attempt at reorganization, ceased publication in 1925, Chapel Street was abandoned in 1931, and the remaining London adherents were forced to turn to various secularist and humanist societies as second best. Their memory is perpetuated, however, in the annual Auguste Comte Memorial Lectures at the London School of Economics, which were endowed in 1951 with most of the remaining funds and which have already become a distinguished series. The satellites faded out one after the other too, though the Liverpool church, whose early leaders had had their troubles with the imperious Congreve, maintained itself longer than any other English center and finally succumbed only before the onslaught of another world war.

In France, although the Congrevian dissident faction in the rue Jacob soon disappeared, Positivism after 1878 was no more united than it was in England. Eruptions, quarrels, and recriminations were the rule rather than the exception, and there were even two further outright schisms, again the result of a mingling of principles and personalities. Laffitte had by no means emerged from the events of 1877–1878 chastened; in his personally unobtrusive way he continued to discharge his responsibilities very much according to his own lights. Like the English Positivists of Newton Hall he set more store by making an impression on the general public than on preaching to the converted; and he was inclined to dilute the Positivist gospel with generous doses of common sense. He was therefore vulnerable to attack by those of a stricter Comtist persuasion who objected to his acquiescence in the "Opportunist" Republic of Gambetta, Freycinet, and Ferry (including the latter's colonial policy in Tunisia) and to his continued reticence on the religious aspects of Positivism. He even went so far as to denounce the "sectarian spirits" who indulged in "servile imitation of Catholicism" by dwelling on "the most questionable conceptions of Auguste Comte." [106]

The superorthodox targets of such remonstrances had meanwhile been furnished with a new collective grievance by Laffitte, this time in his capacity as president of the commission of executors of Comte's will. In brief, Laffitte proposed to abolish the commission and to concentrate all Positivist functions, including the management of the house at 10, rue Monsieur-le-Prince, where Comte had lived and taught and which was now the headquarters of French and of international Positivism, in his own hands. The majority of the other executors, including some of the oldest and most respected disciples who, like Dr. Robinet, had finally rallied to Laffitte in 1878, could not stomach this idea. The issue came to a climax in 1892, when Laffitte realized one of his life's ambitions by being appointed, partly through the good offices of Ernest Renan, to the newly created chair of the history of science at the Collège de France, a step which seemed to Robinet and to many orthodox disciples to compromise fatally the "spiritual independence" of the Director of Positivism.[107] But, as regards the house, Laffitte had the law on his side (like Congreve in Chapel Street, ironically!) and prevailed; the other executors, according to Positivist form, fell out among themselves, the dissident faction turning from being merely advocates of the inviolability of Comte's

[106] Annual Circular for 1885 and Laffitte to Deuillin, 19 May 1888, M-le-P.

[107] Robinet to Laffitte, 2 Feb. and 20 July, 1892, M-le-P.

will into what Laffitte called "sectarian Comtists," intent among other things upon literally applying forty years later Comte's most reactionary political prescriptions.[108]

Again, questions of fundamental Positivist dogma had become intertwined with questions of practical Positivist policy and with Laffitte's personal conduct of his office. Meanwhile, having held that office for nearly forty years, Laffitte finally yielded to insistent demands, especially from Newton Hall, that he designate a successor in order to avoid even worse confusion than had attended his own elevation, but his long hesitation as well as the identity of the nominee, Charles Jeannolle, gave rise to further dissatisfaction. A great display of unity was put on when Laffitte, in his eightieth year, in a sense achieved the climax of his career in leading organized Positivism at the ceremony unveiling the statue of Auguste Comte that still stands in the Place de la Sorbonne. But when early in the next year, 1903, Pierre Laffitte died, having been Director of Positivism for forty-five years and having accomplished a heroic task in his propagation of Positivism by teaching and writing, even the last tributes to him allowed doctrinal dissension past and still to come to be read between the lines. Nowhere was this clearer than in the speech of Emile Corra,[109] who within three years was to displace Jeannolle in the minds of most French and international Positivists as their Director.

If in recent Positivist dissensions matters of principle, of property, and of personality had been mixed about equally, in this second major schism the last two factors appear to have far outweighed the first. Jeannolle defended no novel doctrine; indeed, one aspect of the objections to him was that he defended no doctrine very vigorously. Content to follow Laffitte's pragmatic lead, he did not capitalize on this attitude as Laffitte had done by popu-

---

[108] See particularly the volume edited by one of the younger executors, Léon Kun: *Auguste Comte méconnu, Auguste Comte conservateur: Extraits de son oeuvre finale* (Paris, 1898).

[109] See Corra in *R.O.,* n.s. XXVII (1903), 164–165.

larizing the system: "Let us leave to those who have the public's ear more than we do the task of making Positivism more widely known."[110] Jeannolle, partly for financial reasons, appeared to be launched on a holding and even a retrenching operation, and Emile Corra emerged as the leader of those who opposed this stand and who believed that, with suitable adjustments, Comte's doctrine could still be made palatable and attractive to the young generation and that the best means of consolidation was aggression. To this extent the old question of Comte's infallibility reared its head again; on the other hand the sordid and petty personal intrigue into which the French Positivists on both sides plunged for three years has to be read to be believed[111] (and probably a great deal was never even recorded on paper). It involved jealousy, financial skulduggery, jockeying for position, and procedural and even legal wrangling such as one would expect from the affairs of a shady gambling enterprise, not from persons dedicated to the propagation of truth. Significantly enough, what finally set in motion the process at the end of which Corra emerged as the leader of a dissident but majority faction was the absurd circumstance that Jeannolle had no speech prepared for the traditional ceremonies on the anniversary of Comte's death on 5 September 1905. With the active support of Bridges and Harrison the highest councils of international Positivism declared the office of Director vacant and then proceeded to invest Corra with it. Jeannolle died in 1914, brokenhearted at the outbreak of war; the *Revue occidentale* disappeared altogether, and his small group of loyalists, though still in possession of Comte's house and of most Positivist property, including the archives and library, sank into oblivion.

[110] Jeannolle, *ibid.*, n.s. XXI (1900), 182.

[111] The melancholy record is preserved in Corra's papers in the Archives Nationales and to a lesser extent in the rue Monsieur-le-Prince; selected portions were published in the *Revue occidentale* and in the new organ founded by the rebels in 1906, the *Revue positiviste internationale* (hereafter *R.P.I.*).

Organized Positivism as a whole had, of course, suffered another serious setback as a result of the energy and time absorbed, the manifold suspicions aroused, and the material disadvantages caused by this second schism; but the dissident group, with international backing and under the energetic leadership of Corra, did their best to minimize the damage. Corra, although he believed in the popularization of Positivism and hence in its adaptation to current needs, was very far from being a Littréist. He did not believe that a sharp line could be drawn between an earlier and a later Comte; indeed, while repudiating mysticism and some of Comte's more extravagant rituals, he went out of his way to introduce more religious ceremony and teaching into the life of organized Positivism. Even before he became Director he laid down the line from which he never substantially departed during his twenty-five years' tenure:

Auguste Comte is, for us, neither a god, nor an infallible prophet, nor an oracle; we are in no way opposed to a discussion of his conceptions before they are adopted. . . . We take inspiration far more from the spirit than from the letter of his work. . . . We bring to the public . . . not an absolute *credo*, . . . but ideas which we believe to be scientific and which are, therefore, veriafible, demonstrable, and open to examination by all men of good sense and good faith.[112]

Apart from the subjective and personal aberrations which he regarded as due to Comte's involvement with Clotilde de Vaux, Corra believed in the Religion of Humanity as an integral and indeed the culminating part of Positivism:

Positivism is not merely a philosophical doctrine; it is also a system of popular education. It does not aim to satisfy only the needs of the mind, by scientific procedures; it is concerned no less intimately with the aspirations of the human heart.[113]

[112] Corra in *R.O.*, n.s. XXXI (1905), 70–71.
[113] Corra in *R.P.I.*, VIII (1910), 113.

He insisted that the establishment of the Religion of Humanity was not a utopia; but the question of the kind and degree of emphasis to be placed on the religious aspect of Positivism was, as in the time of Laffitte, largely a matter of tactics:

Personally I do not believe that at this time the popularization of our religion would be advanced by giving it a more precise organization. It is very probable . . . that its ultimate organization will differ markedly from the one conceived by Comte which savors too much of a transposition of Catholicism. After all, one can organize only what exists. Well, the public is not yet converted to the Positivist doctrine, and the task of persuading it of the superiority and of the inevitable triumph of the positive spirit, of positive morality, and of peaceful activity, is a more urgent necessity.[114]

It can be imagined that Corra, like Laffitte before him, was troubled by assaults from more militant and more fundamentalist colleagues who rejected such an order of priorities and who at one point formed an auxiliary grouping devoted specifically to worship. What was new was a campaign in the opposite sense, for closer touch and collaboration with thought and research in the universities and particularly for adaptation to the findings of what was now almost a century of work in the natural sciences since Comte had stopped reading. The most important instance was biological evolution, rejected by Comte in its Lamarckian form and obediently rejected ever since by official Positivism, despite the intervention of Darwin, as both speculative and materialistic. Pressure gradually built up within the Positivist group, led by a physician, Dr. Hillemand, to abandon this anachronistic stand, and finally Corra himself declared that it had become unreasonable to reject evolution.[115] But there were limits to Positivist toleration

[114] Corra, *ibid.* (1927), p. 211.

[115] See Hillemand in *R.O.,* n.s. III (1891), 389, VI (1892), 149, XV (1897), 371, XXXI (1905), 424–428, *R.P.I.,* V (1908), 100–105, and Corra, *ibid.,* V, 279–280, VI (1909), 19–22, 37.

of unorthodox views, and such a prominent scientific scholar as Marcel Boll was driven out of the Positivist circle.[116]

It was not on scientific questions only that dissension persisted within the ranks. In fact the twin rocks on which Positivism was built, the Law of the Three Stages and the Classification of the Sciences, were no longer entirely secure, and even the founder's private life came in for attack. Finally, the social and political interpretation of the doctrine continued to be disputed. Corra himself in general followed Laffitte's lead in this respect, tolerating the democracy of the Third Republic but demanding strong leaders and disciplined subjects. Some of Corra's followers, however, including Dr. Hillemand, inclined to a more pronounced authoritarianism; and an extreme manifestation of this tendency arose among the dissident Positivist group formed at the end of Laffitte's reign by some of the members of the commission of executors of Comte's will which Laffitte had purported to abolish. In the first decade of the twentieth century, four out of twelve of them were members of the Action Française, adding monarchism as a gloss to Comte's pro-Catholic and conservative authoritarian views and achieving some success in making Comte known and admired in Action Française circles.

All attempts to reintegrate this faction with the group led by Corra and, after his retirement in 1931, by Maurice Ajam failed. A measure of cooperation was resumed, on the other hand, between Corra's group in the rue de Seine and Jeannolle's successors, who were still in possession of the house in the rue Monsieur-le-Prince nearby. The Second World War broke up the organization in the rue de Seine entirely (it had been declining in numbers and consequently in finances for twenty years), and since then organized Positivism in Paris has been represented mainly by Brazilians (reexporting the doctrine which was the official philosophy of the Brazilian republican revolution) and chiefly concentrated

[116] See Boll's letters to Corra of 3 Jan., 24 June, and 18 Oct. 1924, A.N., AS 5. He had been contributing to the *R.P.I.* for over a decade.

in the library and archives of the rue Monsieur-le-Prince, although Brazilian money also still preserves the Church of Humanity constructed early in the century in Clotilde de Vaux's house in the rue Payenne. M. Paul Carneiro, lately Brazilian delegate to UNESCO, has been the moving spirit in attempts, which have met with some success particularly in connection with the centenary of Comte's death in 1957, to promote the Positivist cause in scientific and academic circles.

To this extent the movement in France has retained its separate identity, in contrast to England, where it has merged altogether in newer humanist organizations. The possession and preservation of Comte's house, in contrast to the "sordid hole," as Harrison once called it, of Chapel Street and rented quarters in Newton Hall or elsewhere in London, obviously constituted a source of strength, and the mere fact that Comte was a Frenchman worked to some extent in favor of French relative to English Positivism. In fact, that organized Positivism and the Religion of Humanity should have flourished in France for two generations, even on a small scale, is astonishing enough; that it did so in England amounts to a *tour de force*. In both countries, although some external circumstances helped, the success of the movement was above all due to the energy of a few devoted leaders with the gift of attracting others.

With regard to the principal leaders, some information is provided in the Biographical Appendix. What of the less prominent leaders and the rank and file? They never exceeded a few hundred at any given time, though a grand total of two thousand may not be far off. Many of these of course remain entirely unknown, but certain interesting correlations emerge from the available data. The Positivist groups, as one would expect, were not an average cross section of the population in either England or France. In France an analysis by occupation yields the following breakdown: 51 manual workers and craftsmen, 49 doctors, 26 civil servants, 23 army officers, 20 lawyers, 17 engineers, 12 teachers. Among the

69

strikingly large number of doctors, several were specialists in mental pathology; this is probably due to the fact that Comte, though railing at doctors both in his books and in person, had some very remarkable things to say about the nature and treatment of mental illness.[117] The recruitment of army officers and engineers is likely to have resulted in most cases from a penchant for authoritarianism and "technocracy" absorbed during attendance at the Ecole Polytechnique; and a similar inclination may account for a good many of the civil servants. It is worth noting that 23 members were sons or other near relatives of Positivists, and in 16 further cases conversion resulted from personal friendship or contact with Positivists. The general impression one forms of the membership is of a serious, middlebrow, rather inbred group, making up in zeal what they lacked in the way of finances and facilities.

In England the proportion of doctors was only slightly smaller, and the professional class in general was relatively prominent. Positivist intermarriage and other family relationships were again high. Probably the most striking element is the number of known cases of religious disorientation prior to contact with Positivism, in other words the degree to which Positivism played the role of a substitute religion. The element which most clearly differentiates the English from the French disciples is the extent to which writers like G. H. Lewes and John Stuart Mill, and even H. T. Buckle with his merely passing references, could lead other men to embrace the orthodox Positivism which they themselves rejected and the extent to which Comte's doctrine, having interested though not converted a number of prominent intellectual leaders, was integrally adopted through their mediation.[118] The process by which it interested such figures, in both England and France, is the subject of the following chapters.

[117] See below, pp. 117–118 and 122–123.

[118] I have the detailed biographical data on the Positivist rank and file on which the preceding summary is based and should be glad to communicate with anyone who wants further information.

PART TWO

The Diffusion of Positivism
in Partes Infidelium

Chapter III

THE MEANS OF DIFFUSION

ALTHOUGH there can, of course, be no reliable statistical estimate of the number of definite subscribers to one doctrine of Positivism or another, as opposed to disciples,[1] we can get some perspective on the matter by knowing something about the scale on which Positivism was diffused to the general public. It can be said with confidence that many of the disciples made very great efforts to spread the gospel, in the hope of attracting to it sympathizers and partial adherents if not necessarily additions to the membership. It is true that some of the disciples—generally the more orthodox and "Comtist" ones—did not value such recruits, deeming it important only to augment the actual membership and to consolidate the nucleus of the future priesthood and resenting any diversion of energies from this task. As some of the disciples interested in a general propaganda effort pointed out, recruitment to integral Positivism, even the very use of the phrase "integral Positivism," might conversely in themselves constitute obstacles to success in the wider arena.[2] Nevertheless, by about 1880, and owing above all to the efforts of Laffitte and Littré in France and of Har-

[1] For definitions, see above, pp. 10–12.

[2] See, for example, the observations of P. Grimanelli, Boll, and Swinny, in response to a questionnaire of Corra's, recorded in Corra's Annual Circular for 1921, pp. 24–35, 39–43, 62, and Boll, Desch, and Massy in the Circular for 1922, pp. 22–36.

rison in England, Comte's system was undeniably in the domain of public acquaintance. The "conspiracy of silence" of which Comte in his querulous way had accused the intellectual Establishment certainly no longer existed, if it ever had.[3]

The process of diffusion took several forms.[4] The widest audiences were perhaps reached by the courses of lectures and individual lectures given by Positivists both within the framework of the organized movement and, more importantly for this purpose, beyond it. Comte himself began this practice, first of all with the ill-fated oral presentation of the *Cours* and later with a number of other lecture series. None of the distinguished auditors of the first few lessons of the *Cours,* mostly scientists, are recorded as having been persuaded by it.[5] The closest to it was the famous biologist Blainville, by some years older than Comte and introduced to him by Saint-Simon. Insofar as what they had in common did not derive from common sources, Comte seems to have learned from Blainville more than he taught him, but Blainville

[3] The matter was referred to in specific terms by Harrison to Hillemand, 23 Sept. 1891, M-le-P, but cf. Mrs. Harrison to Marvin, 13 Dec. 1897, Papers of F. S. Marvin (in the possession of Mr. J. D. Marvin; hereafter FSM), still referring to the "conspiracy of silence."

[4] It goes without saying that those who subsequently became full-fledged disciples were also, for the most part, beneficiaries of one sort or another of this general diffusion.

[5] They included Alexander von Humboldt, Blainville (discussed below), the mathematicians Binet, Fourier, and Poinsot, the physicians Broussais and Esquirol, the economist Dunoyer, the Saint-Simonian Gustave d'Eichthal (cf. below, pp. 175–178), and the engineer Navier (Comte, *Cours,* I, v; Hermann Gruber, *August Comte, der Begründer des Positivismus* [Freiburg, 1889], pp. 25–26). Gruber, *ibid.,* and Comte, to d'Eichthal, 1 May 1824, *Lettres à divers,* II, 38–39, claimed approval of Comte's early opuscules by a number of men other than those listed above, but I can find no corroboration. The men were Guizot (cf. below, p. 153 n. 1), Lamennais, J.-B. Say, Carnot, the physicist Flourens, four others identified as Lenoir, Delessert, Laborde, Broglie, and a German historian, Buchholz.

was the only eminent and influential man in France before Littré who referred to Comte's work in public, though only in passing, as an important philosophical event. Later, however, Blainville declined to contribute to Comte's financial support, and Comte, who was always inclined to mix personality with philosophy, subsequently made a special pontifical speech at Blainville's funeral condemning him for having failed to draw the proper philosophical and moral consequences from his scientific knowledge.[6]

Comte never recaptured his eminent audiences of 1826 and 1829. When he gave a course of lectures on popular astronomy in the 1840's, which, as an extended introduction, contained a "Discourse on the Positive Spirit," [7] his large audience was composed to a considerable extent of workers. At another course of lectures given from 1849 to 1852 at the Palais Royal, the remote room with a capacity of 100 was usually half empty, the audience consisting mostly of various publicists, alumni of the École Polytechnique, some professors, and only a few workers.[8] In 1848 one of his disciples had written to Comte that even among highly educated people he had not met a single person "who had a real knowledge of your work and was in a position to pass a truly informed judgment on it." [9]

[6] In his *Histoires des sciences de l'organisation et de leurs progrès, comme base de philosophie* (Paris and Lyon, 1845), first given as lectures in 1839–1841; cf. Henri Gouhier, "La philosophie 'positiviste' et 'chrétienne' de D. de Blainville," *Revue philosophique,* Vol. 131 (1941), pp. 38–69, esp. pp. 65–66; correspondence between Blainville and Comte, 1826–1846, *C.I.,* I, 17–62; Pol Nicard, *Etude sur la vie et les travaux de M. Ducrotay de Blainville* (Paris, 1890), pp. 10–12, 190–192; *Polity,* I, 462–463, 595–601.

[7] English ed. by Beesly, London, 1903.

[8] See Deroisin, *Notes,* pp. 5–6; Joseph Ageorges, "Souvenirs inédits sur Auguste Comte," *La Revue,* 6th series, Vol. 108 (1914), p. 21. The room was made available to Comte through the good offices of his estranged wife and of his one friend in high places, Senator Vieillard, the degree of whose agreement with him Comte, as usual, overestimated (*Polity,* I, xxiv; to Fisher, 21 May 1857, *Lettres à des positivistes anglais,* p. 75).

[9] C. Jundzill to Comte, 1 Feb. 1848, quoted by Comte, *Synthèse*

This was certainly no longer the case in France a generation later, after Pierre Laffitte had begun to lecture. From all accounts Laffitte was a gifted lecturer, charming and witty, with a great talent for popularization. All of his books were first given to the public in the form of lectures, and several courses were not published or appeared in outline only. He lectured, chiefly in Paris but also elsewhere, beginning in 1869. He was increasingly successful until by 1888 he had overflow audiences in the largest auditorium of the Collège de France.[10] Finally, from the new chair of the history of science, Laffitte lectured on that subject from an avowedly Positivist point of view.[11] Others of Laffitte's school likewise lectured wholly or partially on Positivist subjects on the most various occasions up and down the country, though none matched him either in activity or in drawing power.[12] Oral propaganda was

---

subjective, p. xlix. The value judgment must be taken with due reserve, since the early disciples expected a high degree of acceptance and devotion before they were willing to acknowledge anyone as even a sympathizer.

[10] See Gruber, *Positivismus,* pp. 54–65; *R.O.,* X (1883), 393–404, XI (1883), 473–478, n.s. I (1890), 37–42, V (1892), 106. Cf. also above, pp. 40–41, and the tribute to Laffitte's teaching by Lionel Dauriac, *Croyance et réalité* (Paris, 1889), p. v. See Laffitte's own arrogant comment on the original permission given him to lecture in the Collège de France, in his Annual Circular for 1881.

[11] Laffitte, "Cours sur l'histoire générale des sciences: Discours d'ouverture," *R.O.,* n.s. V (1892), esp. pp. 298–305, 309–310, 320, 326, 333–334, and the recollections of his successor, Paul Tannery, to Karl Sudhoff, 14 Oct. 1903, and to H.-G. Zeuthen, Oct. 1903 and 10 Jan. 1904, in Tannery, *Mémoires scientifiques* (Toulouse and Paris, 1912–1950), X, 410, 668, 675, but cf. Pierre Louis, *ibid.,* XVII, 35.

[12] The *R.O.* and *R.P.I.* recorded over 70 lectures or courses of lectures given by twenty Positivists, adding explicitly that they could not attempt to attain complete coverage. Some of these lectures were given to audiences of 500 and 600. Positivists took advantage when they could of any positions that they held (civil service, labor, and the like) in order to further the propagation of Positivism. Many of these lectures, especially in the provinces, reached an even wider public by being reported in the press.

also furthered by other devices, such as discussion groups like the "Cercle d'études sociales des prolétaires positivistes de Paris,"[13] but attempts to infiltrate Positivist social doctrine into labor circles did not on the whole meet with much success.[14]

Perhaps the most important step in the propagation of Positivism next to Laffitte's lectures and until the campaign for Comte's statue was the opening of a Positivist lending library in Paris in 1880, containing the books prescribed by Comte.[15] But his doctrine had by this time begun to be propagated in a variety of other written forms. In addition to specifically Positivist books and to articles in the several Positivist journals, some of the disciples were in a position to introduce references to Comte or to one or another of his teachings in books on other subjects, or had access to non-Positivist periodicals for articles either wholly or partially Positivist in nature, and the latter two categories were, in general, most apt to come to the attention of those not already converted. It was almost certainly Littré who made the greatest impression this way. In the well-known and widely used medical dictionary which he edited with Charles Robin opportunity was found here and there to suggest Positivist viewpoints.[16] The same is true of some of the

---

For example, there was a Positivist center for "study, propaganda, and action" in Le Havre (record in A.N., AS 2).

[13] Founded in 1880; see Laffitte's Annual Circular for that year. For a similar group, see *R.O.*, IX (1882), 143–149.

[14] See, e.g., A. Keüfer, "Le huitième congrès du parti ouvrier," *R.O.*, XX (1888), 106–115; cf. also Gruber, *Positivismus*, pp. 66–68.

[15] This at any rate was the opinion of Robinet in a letter to Rhétoré, 8 Sept. 1880, A.N., AS 2. The Paris municipal council lacked one vote to decide to subsidize this library in the rue Réaumur (*R.O.*, XII [1884], 142–149). A similar library was later opened in St. Etienne (G. Grimanelli to Antoine, 13 May 1900, A.N., AS 3).

[16] *Dictionnaire de médecine, de chirurgie, de pharmacie, de l'art vétérinaire et des sciences qui s'y rapportent* (13th ed., Paris, 1873), e.g., pp. 1171 (Law of the Three Stages), 1246 (on Comte himself), 1277 (on psychology), 1387–1388 (the Classification of the Sciences).

prefaces that Littré wrote for his own general books and for the books of others,[17] and even more so of half a dozen articles which appeared in the very popular *Revue des deux mondes* between 1846 and 1859 and of one in the *Revue du xixe siècle*.[18] Perhaps a second person who should be singled out in this connection is Maurice Ajam, a prolific journalist who found occasional opportunity to insert Positivist references.[19] Altogether, and excluding newspaper articles, one may count in the vicinity of a hundred items of this nature written by French Positivists, including at least two poems.[20] This impresses one, to be sure, as a fairly modest total —fewer than two per year. But it must be remembered that Positivist activity was all carried on in spare time, that many members lacked the gift of tongues, and that in any event most of this sort of activity went into the specifically Positivist journals, meetings, and lectures, the latter of which were sometimes attended by many outsiders. We cannot even guess how many disciples laced their conversation, consciously or unconsciously, with Positivist refer-

[17] See the Prefaces to his own *Etudes sur les barbares et le moyen âge* (2nd ed., Paris, 1869), pp. ii–iii, xxxii, and to Eugène Noël, *Mémoires d'un imbécile écrits par lui-même* (Paris, 1875), pp. ix–x, xx–xxi, xxvii–xxviii, and Eusèbe Salverte, *Des sciences occultes . . .* (3rd ed., Paris, 1856), pp. vi–ix.

[18] For three of these, see the Bibliography; the others are identified in Littré's *La science au point de vue philosophique* (4th ed., Paris, 1876), where they are reprinted. One might also add a book review in the *Journal des débats* of 21 and 22 April 1861; note of course his original popularization of the *Cours* in the *National* (see above, p. 14 n. 22).

[19] Clippings of many of his articles were collected and are in the possession of M. Maurice Bouvier-Ajam.

[20] All books and pamphlets of this nature that have come to my notice are listed in the Bibliography, likewise almost all articles in non-Positivist journals (not newspapers), i.e., all except those few that I have not been able to identify accurately enough to find. Of course the Positivist references in many of them are only brief. This total must be regarded as conservative since many miscellaneous items may have escaped my attention. The activity, for example, of the Positivist Gaston Prunières as a publisher's editor is impossible to assess.

ences or ideas. It was perhaps only the Littréists who could be considered as having neglected their Positivist duty once Littré's journal had ceased, for only two or three of them ever thereafter made any public reference to the doctrine at all.[21]

The general situation with regard to the diffusion of Positivism in England was similar, although less well documented except in the case of Harrison. In his autobiography Harrison listed about seventy lectures or courses of lectures to non-Positivist audiences, but most of these cannot be regarded as having had any Positivist impact, though they might be, as Harrison stated, "all constituent elements of an organic scheme of general education as understood by Positivism."[22] Some of these lectures were later published either separately or in one or another of Harrison's books, many of which had a wide appeal. *The New Calendar of Great Men,*[23] edited and partly written by Harrison, was of course planned according to Comte's prescription, had a large sale, and went into a second printing, but was in fact only remotely Positivist in its possible impact. Much more important, however, were about fifteen articles in periodicals (mostly the *Fortnightly Review*) which can be considered directly Positivist. Harrison also played a part in the publication of the joint volume *International Policy,*[24] which, though again not obviously Positivist in character, was as a result

---

[21] It should be noted that the efforts of the disciples in behalf of the doctrine were augumented by some 65 recorded instances of casual references more or less favorable to Positivism in the press. These are in addition to reports of lectures by Positivists. Positivist-sponsored meetings could draw audiences many times greater than the total number of disciples.

[22] *Autobiography,* II, 301–307.

[23] London, 1892, 2nd ed., 1920, ed. Harrison, Swinny, and Marvin; cf. Liveing, *Bridges,* p. 226. There were references to Comte in the Preface and scattered throughout, and the volume as a whole perpetuated Comte's values, e.g., as regards Protestantism.

[24] *International Policy: Essays on the Foreign Relations of England* (London, 1866), including essays by Congreve, Harrison, Beesly, Bridges, and others. The anonymous Preface attributes the book's guiding principles to Comte and Positivism.

of its radicalism likely to call attention to its authors.[25] The same is true of the activity of Harrison, Beesly, and others in the early labor movement and then in the Fabian movement, although most trade-unionists and Fabians were not prepared to proceed from such of Comte's economic and social ideas as suited them to his ideas in other areas.[26] "It is difficult," the historian and quondam secretary of the Fabian Society wrote, "for the present generation to realize how large a space in the minds of the young men of the eighties was occupied by the religion invented by Auguste Comte."

The "Religion of Humanity" offered solutions for all the problems that faced us. It suggested a new heaven of a sort, and it proposed a new

[25] The book was "so far as I know the first composite volume in which a number of writers laid down an ideal foreign policy" (A. J. P. Taylor, *The Trouble Makers: Dissent over Foreign Policy, 1792–1939* [London, 1957], pp. 67–68).

[26] See R. Harrison, "Beesly," in *Essays in Labour History, passim;* Edward R. Pease, *The History of the Fabian Society* (London, 1916), pp. 14, 18–19, 263; Eugene Oswald, *Reminiscences of a Busy Life* (London, 1911), pp. 455–456 (met Harrison at a lecture at the Working Men's College and subsequently attended Positivist functions). Gerhart von Schulze-Gaevernitz, *Zum socialen Frieden . . .* (Leipzig, 1880), II, 8, considers Thomas Carlyle partly responsible for the reception of Positivism in radical circles, but this seems very doubtful to me; cf. *ibid.,* I, 246, Carlyle's Journal, 8 June 1868, quoted by James Anthony Froude, *Thomas Carlyle* (New York, 1904), II, 315 ("Poor 'Comtism,' ghastliest of algebraic spectralities"), his conversation with G. H. Lewes, July 1852, quoted by David Alec Wilson, *Carlyle at His Zenith* (London and New York, 1927), p. 418; Hill Shine, *Carlyle and the Saint-Simonians . . .* (Baltimore, 1941), p. 169 n. 30a. See also Thomas Burt, a trade-union Liberal M.P., "Working Men and War," *Fortnightly Review,* XXXVIII (1882), 722, and cf. McGee, *Crusade,* pp. 39–42; but see above all [Sir] Sydney Olivier, *Letters and Selected Writings* (ed. Margaret Olivier, London, 1948), pp. 9, 60–62, 144–145, 175, 180, 182. Olivier introduced Positivism into the Fabian movement, and Comte, despite criticism, was for him "very much the most comprehensive thinker we have had since Aristotle."

earth. . . . At any rate, it was worth examination, and most of the free-thinking men of that period read the "Positive Polity" and the other writings of the founder and attended either Chapel Street or Newton Hall. Few could long endure the absurdities of a made-up theology and a make-believe religion; and the Utopia designed by Comte was as impracticable and unattractive as Utopias generally are. But the critical and destructive part of the case was sound enough.[27]

Harrison also participated in the increasing Positivist practice of lecturing to the Humanist and Ethical societies, and although only half a dozen occasions are on record there were certainly many more, especially after the turn of the century.[28] Altogether, in addition to Harrison's individual contributions and to the various essays in the bulky *New Calendar,* one can count about forty "independent" lectures, articles, and books by Positivists. These do not include the activities of Congreve between 1860 and 1870, when he was lecturing but not yet under a specifically Positivist banner,[29] or such enterprises as those of Marvin, who as an Oxford under-

[27] Pease, *History of the Fabian Society,* pp. 14, 18–19.

[28] Cf. above, p. 62.

[29] Cf. Eisen, "Harrison," pp. 195–196, on Congreve's various activities and on the "astonishing stir" that he and his exiguous group managed to make. Congreve's audiences in the '60's are reported as ranging between 11 and 75 (Congreve to his wife, 23 April 1860, 11 March 1861, to Lobb, 21 April, 16 May, and 11 Nov. 1870, Wadham MSS e. 51 f. 19, e. 52 f. 87, c. 184 ff. 1–2; J. W. Cross, *George Eliot's Life* . . . [Boston and New York, 1909], II, 349–350; George Eliot to Mrs. Congreve, 5 May 1860, her journal, 5–7 May 1867, Haight, ed., *George Eliot Letters,* III, 293, IV, 360). "Curiosity brings some, interest in the subject others, and the rest go with the wish to express adhesion more or less thorough" (to Sara Hennell, 13 May 1867, *ibid.,* IV, 363). There seemed to be a considerable turnover among the audience (journal, 19 May 1867, *ibid.,* IV, 363 n. 8). Beesly and Bridges were drawing audiences of 60–65 and 90, respectively (Congreve to Lobb, 11 Nov. 1870, 17 April 1872, Wadham MS c. 184 ff. 2–3). At a later date Congreve once lectured to an audience of 400 in Liverpool (Congreve to Geddes, 7 Oct. 1879, BM Add. MS 45231 f. 287).

graduate founded a Comte discussion group [30] and later in life ran adult education courses at which an odd Positivist remark might be made. It must also be borne in mind that the *Positivist Review,* probably more than the French journals, reached beyond avowedly Positivist circles,[31] not, of course, necessarily eliciting approval.[32] Nor is there any way of estimating, on the other hand, how many other works may have offended readers as did Bridges' edition of a text of Francis Bacon by its inaccuracies.[33] At any rate, Harrison was delighted to report at least a hundred press notices of one of his Newton Hall addresses on the anniversary of Comte's death.[34]

From this brief and necessarily incomplete survey of the means used for the diffusion of Positivism among the general public in both France and England one very important element has so far (with the exception of Laffitte's professorship) been omitted, namely, the infiltration of Positivism into, and influence by way of, institutions of formal education. Comte and his disciples had, in fact, a detailed educational philosophy and a plan of educational reform based on it; indeed, it has recently been argued at length that Comte's entire system should properly be regarded as a vast educational enterprise.[35] Granting the fruitfulness or even the

[30] Among the members were Sidney Ball, his own tutor, and Gilbert Murray, for whom see below, pp. 226 and 231 (Bridges to Laffitte, 30 Nov. and 15 Dec. 1889, M-le-P).

[31] Cf. Liveing, *Bridges,* p. 228.

[32] One protest at least is on record, from a friend of Marvin's whom he introduced to Positivism (A.J.H. (?) to Marvin, 17 Nov. 1895, 19 Dec. 1896, FSM).

[33] The incident is bemoaned by Harrison to Hillemand, 27 May 1898, M-le-P.

[34] Same, 23 Sept. 1891, M-le-P. Cf. also for this whole section the general remarks of McGee, *Crusade,* pp. 56–92.

[35] Paul Arbousse-Bastide, *La doctrine de l'éducation universelle dans la philosophie d'Auguste Comte* . . . (Paris, 1957); cf. also Georg Friedrich Sterzel, *A. Comte als Pädagog* . . . (Leipzig, 1886).

justice of such a view, we can nevertheless confine ourselves to the specific proposals concerning the actual educational process of children and adolescents as commonly defined. The Positivist ideal, very briefly, was for education in the home until age fourteen, followed by an encyclopedic training at school, and in some cases at the university, based upon the Classification of the Sciences—implying, of course, in the conditions of the time, a great increase in emphasis on the teaching of the natural sciences at the expense of the humanities. The goal was attainment of a philosophical perspective of the whole range of human knowledge rather than immersion in specialties, which was one of Comte's many *bêtes noires*. Owing, no doubt, partly to his resentment at the treatment meted out to him personally by the educational authorities, Comte insisted on educational as well as religious "disestablishment," i.e., complete separation between School and State as well as between Church and State, as implied by his separation between the spiritual and the temporal powers. Education should be a function first of the mother and then of the priesthood, which must be financially independent of the state.

This educational ideal of Comte's received perhaps less than its due share of attention on the part of the disciples. It is to be noted, however, that Laffitte as well as Littré welcomed the Ferry proposals for secularization of schools even though they substituted the State for the Catholic Church as a supervising agency, and it was over this more than any other educational issue that controversy arose in Positivist circles, even across the Channel.[36]

[36] Littré above all in *Conservation, révolution et positivisme*, 2nd ed., pp. 27–28, 271–272, 353–355, 377; also in *P.P.*, XVI (1876), 7–8, 161, and XXIII (1879), 309. Of Littré's school, see in *P.P.* Wyrouboff, II (1868), 456, XII (1874), 417–418, XVII (1876), 274–285 (agreeing with Littré on the necessary role of the state but wishing to preserve a place for language and literature), and some half-dozen other articles dealing specifically with education also in agreement. Two are in disagreement in important respects: Paul Robin, *ibid.*, VII (1870), 109; Lucien Arréat, *ibid.*, XXIX (1882), see p. 34 n. See also Charles Robin, *L'instruction et l'éduca-*

Two rather separate questions need to be asked, then, in connection with Positivist influence on and through education: first, to what extent did these Positivist views on the educational process itself gain currency in pedagogical circles; secondly, to what extent were Positivist views on other subjects given currency in the schools and universities.

As to the first question, once the leaders of the two Positivist schools in France had both endorsed the Ferry proposals and acquiesced in state control of education, Positivism might be thought to have had a chance to provide a source of secular ethics in primary education to supplant the Christian basis of ethics withdrawn by Ferry, and to play some part in the reorganization of higher education as well, especially as the two officials responsible under Ferry for educational reform were both acquainted with Posi-

---

tion (Paris, 1877); Eug. Bourdet, *Principes d'éducation positive* (2nd ed., Paris, 1877), esp. pp. 244–252; Emile Rigolage, preface to his edition of *La sociologie par Auguste Comte* (Paris, 1897); references by Antonin Dubost, *Des conditions de gouvernement en France* (Paris, 1875), pp. 475–500. Orthodox elaboration by Laffitte occurs above all in "Morale pratique," *R.O., XVII and XVIII* (1886 and 1887), *passim;* cf. also Alfred Sabatier, *Programme d'éducation positive: Les écoles communales* (Paris, 1872), esp. pp. 7–12; Corra, *Les devoirs naturels de l'homme* (Paris, 1905), pp. 74–79; Hillemand, "Education intellectuelle" (1908) and "Education positive de l'adolescence" (1911), MSS, M-le-P. Controversy over the competence of the state in education is found in the *R.O.* in articles by Emile Antoine, "De l'instruction primaire obligatoire," II (1879), 319–365 *passim;* Jules Mahy, "La liberté de l'enseignement supérieur et la loi Ferry," III (1879), 131–144 *passim;* and Jeannolle, IV (1880), 233–234; see also P. Grimanelli, "Le monopole scolaire," *R.P.I.,* VII (1909), 337–362 *passim;* and scattered references elsewhere. For a compendious orthodox English statement on education generally, see Congreve, "Education" (1870), *Essays,* I, 365–385; cf. also Harrison in *Positivist Review* (hereafter *P.R.*), V (1897), 163–166; Marvin, *ibid.,* III (1895), 6–10, 84–88; C. H. Desch, *ibid.,* XII (1904), 133–136; and the rather eccentric (from a Positivist point of view) statements of F. J. Gould in almost all of his writings.

tivism: Felix Pécaut, who was inspector-general of primary education, and Louis Liard, director of higher education.[37] Pécaut, many
years later to be sure, described Comte as a genius and himself
as an "old lover of Comtism" and published an edition of Comte's
Catechism, but his introduction to the latter, though sympathetic,
was reserved, and in his own independent writings (he was by
profession a philosopher) he displayed at best a rather cool respect
for Comte.[38] Liard, though believing that Littré had improved on
Comte, held that even Littré's version was radically false; that the
Law of the Three Stages and the Classification of the Sciences
both begged questions, that the critique of metaphysics was self-
contradictory, and that Positivism lacked an epistemology and relied on mere assertion rather than proof.[39] Clearly little favor was
to be expected by Positivism from these two even though the
secularization left a gap; in fact there is some reason to believe
that Positivist—especially Littréist—ideas, as a radical form of
secularism, were at a greater premium in the secondary schools,
at least, before the Ferry law than after.[40] It even comes as some-

[37] I owe this formulation of the problem in part to a conversation with
Prof. Henri Gouhier.

[38] Pécaut in discussion of E. Gilson's "La spécificité de la philosophie
d'après Auguste Comte," in *Communications et discussions* . . . (Paris,
n.d.), p. 380; Comte, *Catéchisme positiviste* (ed. Pécaut, Paris, 1909), pp.
ii, xxxv; Pécaut, "Un spiritualisme scientifique: La philosophie d'Emile
Durkheim," *Revue de l'enseignement français hors de France,* 1920, no. 2,
p. 50; and remarks on Comte and Positivism in Pécaut's other writings
listed in the Bibliographical Appendix.

[39] Liard, *La science positive et la métaphysique,* pp. 41–47, 57, 60–64,
69–72; cf. Lionel Dauriac, *Contingence et rationalisme* (Paris, 1924), pp.
64–65.

[40] See Georges Weill, *Histoire de l'idée laïque en France au xixe siècle*
(Paris, 1925), pp. 176–178, and the view (before Ferry) of Gambetta,
"Discours de M. Gambetta," *P.P.,* XXVI (1881), 447, but on Gambetta cf.
below, pp. 154–155. Cf. the dubious claim of Positivist influence on the
Imperial minister of education, Duruy, made by Ant. Ritti, *ibid.,* VI (1870),
547.

what of a surprise that Liard helped to make a lecture hall available to Laffitte.[41]

He seems not to have been involved in Laffitte's appointment to the new chair of the history of science at the Collège de France.[42] The idea for such a chair (the first of its kind in France) had first been hatched in the fertile brain of Auguste Comte, who had not always been hostile to state control of education and had, indeed, pestered the government of the day with his own candidacy.[43] The idea was then revived at the time of Ferry by a Littréist, Stupuy, and sustained by another, Dubost, who was a deputy, and received the support of Léon Bourgeois, who was minister of education in 1890 when the chair was decided on and to whom the name of Laffitte had been suggested by Charles Dupuy, who himself became minister of education in 1892.[44] In the Senate, Bourgeois cited Laffitte's scientific qualifications and urged tolerance of Positivism, and the appointment was approved by a large majority on the motion of the scientist Berthelot.[45] In retrospect an official of the Collège de France said:

His faith was not our concern. The Collège de France is not a church; it is a school, a great school which does not fear novelties, which indeed fosters them when they are important in literature or science. The Collège welcomed with pleasure the freethinker . . . who represented a scientific method widely practiced nowadays, that of precise observavation in the social sciences, and a fruitful doctrine when discerningly applied, that of evolution.[46]

[41] See above, p. 76.   [42] See above, p. 63.

[43] See below, p. 153 n. 1.

[44] Stupuy in *P.P.*, XXIII (1879), 6–7; Laffitte in *R.O.*, n.s. V (1892), 301, VI (1892), 182–183, Edouard Pelletan, "La nomination de M. Pierre Laffitte à la chaire d'histoire générale des sciences et la presse," *R.O.*, n.s. V (1892), 365.

[45] Pelletan, *ibid.*, pp. 409–415. The remainder of the article is devoted to showing the approval of the appointment given by various organs of the republican press.

[46] Pierre Levasseur (administrator of the Collège de France) in *R.O.*, n.s. XXVII (1903), 161.

Laffitte's appointment can fairly be attributed to a benevolent neutrality on the part of the educational authorities toward Positivism, but no more.

Laffitte's replacement on his death by Wyrouboff appears to have been a first-class academic scandal:

For the historians of science at that time, the answer was simple enough and perhaps unanimous: there was but one man in France fitted for that chair—[Paul] Tannery. He was nominated as first choice by the professors of the Collège de France and that nomination was confirmed by the Académie des Sciences. . . . In spite of that, the second candidate, Wyrouboff, was appointed. . . . Tannery's qualifications were generally acknowledged by every competent person at home and abroad; Wyrouboff's were unknown outside of the positivist chapel (and still are).

Tannery himself attributed his defeat to the ministry's preference for someone with more scientific and contemporary interests, such as Wyrouboff claimed for himself in disavowing his Positivist past, as opposed to Tannery's historical ones; his biographer speculated that the ministry may have wanted to keep Tannery out as a Catholic.[47] In either case, this appointment even less than Laffitte's appears to have been a triumph for Positivism.

But by this time the familiarization of students, at any rate at the university level, with Comte's doctrine no longer had to depend on the appointment of Positivists to academic posts or on other educational activity on the part of the disciples. Indeed, such activity was surprisingly limited. Emile Corra, who was inspector-general for technical education, seems to have done very little on behalf of Positivism.[48] The most significant step was the opening in Paris in the '90s of the Collège Libre des Sciences Sociales under the direction of the disciple Ernest Delbet, where Positivist courses

[47] George Sarton, "Paul, Jules, and Marie Tannery," *Isis,* XXXVIII (1947–48), 35–36; cf. Tannery, *Mémoires scientifiques,* X, 38–39, 161, 677–678.

[48] See his program as reported in *R.P.I.* [XIII] (1912), 126–128, but cf. *ibid.,* 1921², pp. 168–172.

were given among others.[49] Delbet and others also took part in various other educational activities, but these tended more and more to merge into the normal academic routine and curriculum.[50] Comte and Positivism by the turn of the century had begun to be the objects of regular academic study in such fields as sociology and political science,[51] although of course not always in a manner approved of by the orthodox disciples. More than that, even the pedagogical principles themselves began to find support. The most conspicuous advocate was a professor of philosophy at Lyon, Alexis Bertrand, who declared that Comte's general plan of popular education was both desirable and practical, and "wonderfully suited as a basis for reforms." "I am no disciple of the Positivist church, but I am sure that the general plan of education proposed by Comte is destined sooner or later to conquer France and the world." He thought particularly highly of the Classification of the Sciences as a pedagogical device and of the priority of broad perspective over specialization and of the sciences over the humanities. Of course it was necessary to avoid Comte's inanities, but the educational reforms that he proposed, to a parliamentary commission and elsewhere, need not, Bertrand said, commit anyone to Posi-

[49] See in general *R.O.*, n.s. XIV (1896), 269–270, but cf. Jacques Bertillon in *R.P.I.*, VI (1909), 92, where the school is described as neutral. In Le Havre a public course in Positivism was given by a professor of philosophy at the lycée who, though a member of the Positivist Society, did not regard himself as a complete Positivist (Corra, Annual Circular for 1907, p. 18; V. Gignoux to Corra, 5 March 1908, A.N., AS 6).

[50] See *R.P.I.*, VI (1909), 97, and also *ibid.*, X (1911), 38, XI (1911), 447.

[51] Among the well-known professors who gave special courses on Comte were Henri Michel at the Sorbonne and René Worms at the Ecole des Hautes Etudes Sociales and the Collège de France; for Worms, cf. below, pp. 147–149. For further signs of acceptance of Comte into academic instruction, see Oscar d'Araujo in *R.O.*, n.s. VII (1893), 103–104. A special number of the *Bulletin* de la Société Française de Philosophie in 1958 gives an account of a centenary commemorative meeting under the auspices of a number of academic bodies on the initiative of André Lalande.

tivist doctrine as a whole.[52] There were also others who spoke in such terms,[53] and although it would be going much too far to say that these ideas were explicitly adopted, there was emerging a more open-minded attitude toward them.[54]

In England, where the anticlerical incentive for educational reform was less strong or relevant, Positivist educational ideas as such made almost no discernible impact at all. Neither the early disciple A. W. Williamson nor even Beesly, in their academic capacity, did anything to promote them,[55] and T. H. Huxley, the moving spirit behind the promotion of scientific education, was

[52] Bertrand, "Un réformateur de l'éducation," *Nouvelle Revue*, 15 Jan. 1898, pp. 286–304 *passim*, *Les études dans la démocratie* (Paris, 1900), pp. 4–5, 14–16, 44–48, 226, 245, 252–253, 264–267, 272, *L'égalité devant l'instruction: Crise de l'enseignement* (Paris, [1904]), pp. 68–72, 89, 99, 128; cf. *R.O.*, n.s. XVI (1897), 444–446, and an orthodox Positivist appreciation of Bertrand by Daniel Brunet, *ibid.*, XIX (1899), 297–301, 308.

[53] See L. Dugas, *Le problème de l'éducation* . . . (Paris, 1909), pp. 2–8, 21–22, 26–27, 297, 315, 329–330, 335–336; R. Thamin, *Education et positivisme* (3rd ed., Paris, 1910), which though a critique of Littréist educational ideas yet pays considerable tribute to both Littré and Comte (esp. pp. vi, 8); W. M. Kozlowski, "La réforme de l'enseignement philosophique à l'Université," *Revue philosophique*, Vol. 93 (1922), p. 100; Ch. M. Moreau in *R.P.I.*, 1937, p. 38; André Cresson, *ibid.*, 1938, pp. 6, 49–53, 55; and cf. Lucien Momenheim in *R.O.*, n.s. XI (1895), 335–338.

[54] One objective critic of Positivist doctrine in general found, indeed, that one trend in French moral teaching was "to base ethics on the certainty and authority of the positive sciences," although he attributed this achievement to Durkheim rather than to Comte and his direct disciples (J. Delvolvé, "Examen critique des conditions d'efficacité d'une doctrine morale éducative," *Revue de métaphysique et de morale*, XVI [1908], 385–388); cf. above, pp. 6–7. For Durkheim, see below, pp. 144–147.

[55] The minutes neither of University College London nor of the Senate of the University itself disclose any activity of this sort. Williamson, who was professor of chemistry, in giving evidence before the Royal Commission on Scientific Instruction and the Advancement of Science (Devonshire Commission) expressed himself, indeed, in terms by implication opposed to Positivist ideas (*Reports* of the Commission [London, 1872–75], I, pars. 1172, 1225). For Beesly, see also above, p. 52 and n. 83.

notoriously hostile to Positivism.[56] Spot checks conducted at both privately and publicly operated schools in England failed to reveal any motives behind the increase in scientific instruction which could be called even remotely Positivist. Marvin's position as staff inspector to the Board of Education appears not to have produced any results of this sort either.[57]

In France more than in England, owing partly, no doubt, to obvious differences in the intellectual life of the two countries, academic circles were more prone than other parts of the "pagan" world to receive Positivist doctrines sympathetically from the beginning; and the most significant measure of the effectiveness of the various means of diffusion employed (or in some cases not employed) by the disciples is, of course, the results obtained. These results have been variously estimated, both in general and in particular areas and both from within and from without. Among the objective appraisals there are to be found on the one hand phrases like: "Positivism . . . has become nowadays the dominant philosophy";[58] "he [Comte] more than any other thinker is the powerful image of his century," "we are all impregnated with his spirit," "Comte dominates our age," "his vast doctrine nourishes the various currents of modern thought";[59] "By his philosophy properly so-called he is a 'representative man' of his entire century," "the point of extreme diffusion which has been

[56] See Cyril Bibby, *T. H. Huxley: Scientist, Humanist and Educator* (London, 1959), p. 38 and *passim,* and Huxley's evidence before the Devonshire Commission (see n. 55 above), I, par. 354, the Select Committee on Scientific Instruction (*Report,* London, 1868, par. 7988), and other bodies, where, however, he pleaded for the training of scientists in social science.

[57] There are, however, some scattered tributes to Marvin's own educational methods by some of his correspondents, most explicitly by Margaret McMillan, of the Rachel McMillan Training Centre, Deptford, to Marvin, 7 Oct. 1919, FSM.

[58] M. Ferraz, *Socialisme, naturalisme et positivisme* (4th ed., Paris, n.d.; first pub. 1882), p. 313.

[59] Dugas, "Auguste Comte," pp. 397–398, but cf. above, p. 10 and n. 12.

reached by the positive spirit"; [60] "He has constituted an integral part of French thought for the last half century," "everything is more or less suffused with the positive spirit [*souffle*]"; [61] "the most powerful doctrine of the century," "the majority of thinking men either declared themselves *Positivists* or acted as such without knowing that they were"; [62] "Comte was one of the seminal minds of the nineteenth century." [63] At the other end of the spectrum: "In France . . . his reputation has not assigned him to the first rank of thinkers"; [64] "few people in France bothered about him then [ca. 1900] and everyone makes fun of him now [1926]"; [65]

[60] L. Lévy-Bruhl, *The Philosophy of Auguste Comte* (tr. Klein, London, 1903), pp. 17, 19.

[61] J. Benrubi, *Les sources et les courants de la philosophie contemporaine en France* (Paris, 1933), I, 286–287.

[62] Jacques Barzun, *Darwin, Marx, Wagner: Critique of a Heritage* (2nd ed., Garden City, N.Y., 1958), p. 49.

[63] Eisen, "Harrison," p. 256. Eisen continues: "His attempt to base an organized system of thought on science . . . was a source of inspiration. . . . His attempt to employ the historical method to discover [the laws of human society], and his insistence that he had in the Law of the Three Stages a formula by which he could predict the behaviour of man, intrigued even those who felt that he had overreached himself and taken science beyond her legitimate boundaries. Those who thought his religion and polity the products of an unbalanced mind could not disregard the possibilities held out by a reconstruction of religion and society on the basis of science. . . . Even if Comte's vision of the future was repugnant, he was giving voice to feelings that lay in many hearts." Cf. also D. Parodi, *La philosophie contemporaine en France* . . . (Paris, 1919), pp. 23–24, interesting because he regards Positivism as dominant during the 1860's (but not later), but it is clear that he means "the positivist spirit" only, as diffused not only by Littré but also by Taine, Renan, Sainte-Beuve, and Claude Bernard (q.v. below); cf. his *Du positivisme à l'idéalisme: Etudes critiques* (Paris, 1930), p. 90. In contrast, Charlton, *Positivist Thought,* pp. 228–229, finds Positivism (in his definition) more influential after 1870 than before.

[64] James Martineau, *Types of Ethical Theory* (3rd ed., Oxford and New York, 1891), I, 398.

[65] Louis Dimier, *Vingt ans d'Action Française et autres souvenirs* (Paris, 1926), p. 18.

"it is very difficult to attribute any philosophical efficacy to [his work]"; [66] "orthodox Positivism is not part of the history of knowledge [*Wissenschaftsgeschichte*] at all and comes into general intellectual history [*Geistesgeschichte*] only as a pathological phenomenon." [67] With respect to England specifically, judgments vary somewhat less radically but still significantly: "met with little esteem among professional philosophers" but "fertilized . . . the general intellectual life of the time," "comparatively wide sphere of influence"; [68] "possible to regard Comte as the central figure of his century. . . . Comte is, in a sense, the century in epitome"; [69] "if his works are today seldom mentioned . . . that is partly due to the fact that he has done his work too well. For Comte's views have affected the categories of our thought . . . deeply." [70] On the other hand: "Positivism was dead by the nineties. . . ." [71] The disciples themselves, with few exceptions, understandably entertained very optimistic views as to the penetration of the doctrine *in partes infidelium.*[72]

---

[66] Cantecor, *Comte,* p. 164. Cantecor continues: "One can, if one wishes, grant Comte the honor of having contributed to the power of the positive spirit to the extent that his books were read. One may or should also recognize that he may have suggested specific ideas here and there, even stimulated in others interesting work in sociology which diverged more and more from his own views. But when all is said and done Comtism was no more than one episode among many others in the development of the positive spirit, and if it had not existed the general shape of the century would not have been noticeably different" (pp. 168–169).

[67] Alexander Marcuse, *Die Geschichtsphilosophie Auguste Comtes* (Stuttgart, 1932), p. 20.

[68] Rudolf Metz, *A Hundred Years of British Philosophy* (tr. Harvey *et al.,* London and New York, 1938), p. 172.

[69] Basil Willey, *Nineteenth Century Studies,* p. 188.

[70] Isaiah Berlin, *Historical Inevitability* (London, 1954), p. 3.

[71] D. W. Crowley, "The Origins of the Revolt of the British Labour Movement from Liberalism, 1875–1906" (Ph.D. thesis, University of London, 1952), p. 200.

[72] E.g.: Littré in *P.P.,* XX (1878), 314; Corra in *R.P.I.,* 1920^2, p. 205;

These widely divergent appraisals are undoubtedly due in part to explicit or implicit differences in definition and interest, but in part also, I think, to a predominantly intuitive approach to the subject. An examination of the available evidence may provide a sounder basis for judgment.

Ajam, *ibid.,* II (1907), 202; Marcel Boll, *La science et l'esprit positif chez les penseurs contemporains* (Paris, 1921), esp. p. 256; Georges Deherme, *Aux jeunes gens* (Paris, 1921), pp. 38–50; Ducassé, *Essai sur les origines,* p. 6, and *Les grands philosophes* (Paris, 1941), p. 109; but cf. Emile Delivet, *Le positivisme et le mouvement social* (Paris, 1907), p. 7. For Positivist penetration in England, see Marvin, *Comte: The Founder of Sociology* (London, 1936), pp. 188–212; Harrison, "The Positivist Problem," p. 471, but cf. letter, n.d. (late), to Matilda Betham-Edwards quoted in her *Mid-Victorian Memories* (London, 1919), pp. 19–20. See, finally, the *Positivist Year Book 141 (1929): Annuaire Positiviste* (ed. W. Hartley Bolton, Paris, 1929), which lists about 750 people all over the world who were Positivists or "interested in Positivism."

Chapter IV

FRANCE: PHILOSOPHY, SCIENCE, AND PSYCHOLOGY

IN marshaling evidence, necessarily of a fragmented nature, as to the diffusion of the doctrine, any order imposed on it will be to some extent arbitrary.[1] It has seemed to me most useful to classify it, in the first place, as regards France by subject matter and as regards England by individuals, with other subsidiary groupings in both instances. Whereas in England Positivism was seriously considered most strikingly by a few well-known public figures of broad intellectual interests, in France it gained currency principally in academic circles, where topical compartmentalization is at its notorious best. It will be as well to make clear at the outset, however, that in neither country have I been able to find evidence to support claims made by and on behalf of Positivism for extensive influence outside its own ranks. These excessive claims are often results of the confusion between Positivism and scientism.[2] In any event much of the following chapters will have to be

[1] The evidence offered in this and the following chapters is supplemented in the Bibliographical Appendix, to which the reader's attention is called. Cf. also the methodological discussion, above, pp. 9–12.

[2] See above, p. 3.

94

devoted to the somewhat melancholy task of whittling them down to more nearly correct proportions.

Among French professors it was the philosophers who on the whole offered (or withheld) hospitality to Comtian ideas in the widest range of ways, and among French philosophers the earliest and at the same time the most protean figure who enters upon the scene was Ernest Renan, who, the great historian of French religion writes, "derived . . . from Auguste Comte a religious cult of science."[3] The chief item of evidence called in behalf of this contention is almost always Renan's early work *L'avenir de la science,* written in 1848 but not published until 1890.[4]

This book contains several specific references to Comte (i.e., to the Comte of the *Cours* only). Renan explicitly disavowed Comte:

To philosophize means to know things. . . . Philology is the *exact science* of the things of the mind. It is to the humanistic sciences what physics and chemistry are to the philosophic science of bodies. This is what has not been sufficiently understood by a mind otherwise distinguished by its originality and its creditable independence, that of M. Auguste Comte. It is odd that a man concerned above all with the method of the physical sciences and aspiring to apply this method to the other branches of human knowledge should have conceived the science of man and of the human mind in the narrowest fashion and applied to it the crudest kind of method. M. Comte has not grasped the infinite variety of . . . human nature. Psychology, for him, is a science without objects, the distinction between psychological and physiological facts and the mind's contemplation of itself is a chimera. M. Comte's method in the humanistic sciences is . . . pure *a priori.*

[3] Adrien Dansette, *Histoire religieuse de la France contemporaine* (Paris, 1948–51), I, 425.

[4] In his *Oeuvres complètes,* III, 712–1151. Although in a preface written at the time of publication he indicated that his views had moderated somewhat, in general he stood by them (see esp. pp. 719–720), and for my purposes we can take the text at face value. Cf. also Maxime Leroy, *Histoire des idées sociales en France* (Paris, 1946–54), III, 226.

Comte wants to reduce everything, Renan says, to simple laws, and this flies in the face of reality. He leaves no place for ethics, poetry, religion, or mythology.

> M. Comte thinks that man lives entirely by science. . . . M. Auguste Comte's misfortune is to have a system and to fail to immerse himself sufficiently in the human mind in all its variety [*dans le plein milieu*]. . . . To write the history of the human mind requires wide culture.

The "geometric spirit" is inappropriate: "In a word, M. Comte understands nothing about the humanistic sciences because he is no philologist." He "proposes to remedy the dispersive effect of specialization by creating one more specialty, that of the scientists who, without specializing in any branch, would concern themselves with the generalities of all the sciences." The Law of the Three Stages, finally, is "a formula which contains a very large amount of truth, but how can we believe that it explains everything?" [5]

It has been argued that despite his low opinion of Comte and his rejection of all his generalizations Renan may "be numbered among the positivists. He discarded theology and metaphysics as entirely as Comte. Only positive science, he held, could supply men with the truths without which life would be insupportable and science impossible." [6] Now advocacy of the merits of "positive science" does not suffice to make of Renan a Positivist in the sense here defined, and to assert a partial parallelism or similarity is not to prove either derivation from or propagation of Comte's ideas. But let us inquire further into the substance of Renan's

[5] *Oeuvres complètes,* III, 780, 847–849, 1137–1140. It need scarcely be said that I am not concerned, as to Renan or anyone else, with the correctness of judgments passed on Comte and Positivism.

[6] Flint, *History of the Philosophy of History,* pp. 623–627. Cf. also Gabriel Séailles, *Ernest Renan: Essai de biographie psychologique* (2nd ed., Paris, 1895), pp. 59, 338, in whose judgment Renan was not a Positivist but placed all his faith in positive science and its methods.

position. It should in the first place be noted that Renan was a very good friend of Littré and considered himself as sharing his ideas,[7] but thought it Littré's greatest weakness to have "confined himself in a school bearing a definite name and acknowledged as his master a man who, though in many respects remarkable, did not merit such homage." Comte seemed to Renan to have "repeated in a bad style what had been thought before him and said in a very good style by Descartes, d'Alembert, Condorcet, and Laplace." Renan believed, and regretted, that Comte would become famous one day. Because of Comte's influence "the great Littré spent his life in prohibiting himself from thinking about the important problems."[8] What Renan abhorred was sectarianism, even in so mild a form as Littré's.[9] In *L'avenir,* Renan made a few allusions which recall formulations of Comte's—to a tripartite division of history (or alternatively the more Saint-Simonian division into critical and organic periods), to the association of order with progress, to the possibility of moral science, to humanism as a religion, to mankind as an "organic being," to government by scientists[10]—but none of these in the form and context in which they appear can, it seems to me, be regarded as deriving from or owing any debt to Comte. Renan's faith in "the future of science" concerns a science which has become philosophy and whose results are derived from "the most scrupu-

[7] Renan to Littré, 25 May 1876, printed in Aquarone, *Littré,* p. 190.

[8] "Réponse au discours de réception de M. Pasteur (27 avril 1882)," in *Oeuvres complètes,* I, 766–768 (Pasteur succeeded Littré as a member of the Académie Française). Cf. George Eliot's remark on Renan: "He interested me by what he said of Littré; of Comte he talked the usual nonsense" (Journal, 29–31 Dec. 1866, Haight, ed., *George Eliot Letters,* IV, 328).

[9] "There's a very delicate line beyond which a philosophical school becomes a sect: woe unto him who crosses it!" (*Re* the Saint-Simonians, *Oeuvres complètes,* III, 811.)

[10] *Ibid.,* III, 968, 982, 935, 1070–1071, 1082, 809, 1007–1008, 1012–1013, 747.

lous analysis of details." The scientific history of the human mind "is possible only by way of patient and philological study." [11] "Science" is equated with "reason" and "criticism" and is held to have an intrinsic value independent of results.[12] He talked about "positive and experimental science," but also about the perpetual novelty of philosophical problems: if a set of assertions were ever accepted as absolute and immutable, that would be the end of philosophy.[13] What was required above all and more than ever was specialization and monographs.[14] "Religion" for him consisted in "beauty of a moral order"; a religious man was one who "takes life seriously and believes in the holiness of things": "The need for religion, the religious faculty to which the greatest systematic and ceremonial doctrines have corresponded hitherto, is a part of mankind and therefore, like it, eternal, but it will be adequately satisfied by the cult of good and beautiful things." [15]

Under the most benevolent interpretation, it is impossible to establish more than a parallelism between Renan's youthful and ambitious dream of the future progress of science and Comte's chicanery of science into a systematization of all knowledge; and how can it be said that, although no Positivist, Renan together with Taine did more "for the diffusion of the ideas and method of Comte than Littré and all the other positivists together"? [16] An admiration of and faith in science were not necessarily acquired from or even indirectly due to Comte. At the time of the writing of *L'avenir* these qualities of Renan's cannot be attributed to the influence of any particular individual more than of any other, and later on his "faith in positive knowledge" is as likely to have been confirmed by Darwin or such a French scientist as Marcelin Berthelot as by Comte; even his historicism is more likely to have come from Germany than from French or English Positivism. His measured praise of Comte personally is outweighed by his specific

[11] *Ibid.*, 731–732. [12] *Ibid.*, 745, 752, 762, 780.
[13] *Ibid.*, 766, 776–777. [14] *Ibid.*, 913.
[15] *Ibid.*, 1107, 1113–1114. [16] Lévy-Bruhl, *Philosophy of Comte*, p. 17.

criticisms, and substantive references capable of a Positivist interpretation are balanced by others demanding a contrary one. Renan was fundamentally a skeptic and certainly did nothing consciously and probably little or nothing unconsciously for "the diffusion of the ideas and method of Comte." Skepticism, empiricism, and scientism are not to be equated with positivism in any sense, and still less with Comte.[17]

A few years after Renan's *L'avenir* was written, another work, by a man of a rather earlier generation, appeared whose principal thesis has been attributed in part directly to the influence of Comte and whose effect has been diagnosed as a "continuation of the most orthodox kind of positivism." This was the *Essai sur les fondements de la connaissance et sur les caractères de la critique philosophiques* (1851) of Augustin Cournot,[18] who, it is claimed, "unquestionably contributed with all the force of his great intelligence to the diffusion of scientific positivism."[19] The most detailed study of the relationship between Cournot and Comte of which I know argues that though Cournot made no direct references to Comte there was nevertheless a direct influence, and though their minds were "profoundly different in complexion and aim, united only by a common point of view which they owe to the similarity of their

[17] Cf. Benrubi, *Sources et courants,* pp. 34–39; Cantecor, *Comte,* p. 168; and further André Cresson, *Ernest Renan* . . . (Paris, 1949), p. 39 ("The very idea of sociology in the manner of A. Comte caused Renan to smile, not without irony"), and Leroy, *Histoire des idées sociales,* III, 11, 104, 221. Gabriel Monod, *Renan, Taine, Michelet* (3rd ed., Paris, 1896), pp. xii, 43–44, uses the word "positive" in relation to Renan in a general way only. Charlton, *Positivist Thought,* chap. vi, in showing Renan to have been no "true positivist" also differentiates him in various respects from Comte; see esp. pp. 100–106.

[18] Translated as *An Essay on the Foundations of Our Knowledge* (New York, 1956), to which reference is here made.

[19] Bréhier, *Histoire de la philosophie,* pp. 986–989; Georges Batault, "Le positivisme scientifique et son critique M. Emile Meyerson," *Mercure de France,* Vol. 94 (1911), p. 450. See also the claim of Littré in *P.P.,* XXIV (1880), 35.

essentially scientific upbringing," Cournot's epistemology "was an extension of Comte's, in those very directions in which the latter appears to be drawn by the internal logic of his thought." There follows an analysis of their relationship which is excellent, but which does not justify these assertions.[20] In the *Polity,* most of which appeared after Cournot's essay, Comte certainly did not extend his ideas in a direction in any way resembling Cournot's; whether "the internal logic of his thought" should have led him to do so is moot, but unlikely if the unity of Comte's thought from the beginning of his career is accepted. It should, further, be added that in his essay Cournot gave definitions of "positive history," "positive science," and "positive facts" which agree ill with Comte's, that he insisted on a sharp distinction being maintained

[20] Jean Delvolvé, *Réflexions sur la pensée comtienne* (Paris, 1932), pp. 257–268. The analysis runs as follows: In contrast to Comte (who knew Kant very little), Cournot took Kant consciously as a point of departure in directing his attention to the problem of the relationship of mental activity to its materials, but nevertheless there was a precise correlation between Comte's notion of construction as a function of the subjective method and Cournot's logic, which aimed at "a *raison des choses* which can alone offer the mind a valid approximation of intelligible reality." Both of them "imply a rational activity which goes beyond experimental and deductive connections," though Cournot's determining principle was theoretical, while Comte's was practical. Cournot's reflections on mathematical probability led him to an analysis of the objects of science in general, "which he undertook after Comte and along lines analogous to those of the *Cours,*" namely, that "the task of philosophy is always to orient theory toward fundamental reason," ending in hypotheses of pure philosophy beyond the possibility of experimental control. This analysis of the theoretical function of rational activity, "neglected by Comte," reestablishes in a sense different from that of Kant as well as of Comte "the continuous connection between the scientific and the properly philosophical use of the reason." Whereas Comte's ontological agnosticism was tendentious, Cournot's speculation on the nature of reality was disinterested. Cournot like Comte preferred a hierachy of sciences to the idea of a single homogeneous science, but for different reasons, with different results, and with greater consistency, and the hierarchy itself is in any case different from though congruent with Comte's.

between philosophy and science;[21] and that very generally the epistemological emphasis and purpose of Cournot's essay are radically different from those of the *Cours,* which was epistemologically very unsophisticated. Moreover, such resemblances or, better, analogies as there are between Cournot and Comte are not necessarily to be attributed to influence of the latter on the former, direct or indirect; although this would be the simplest explanation, "the facts oblige us to reject it." Cournot habitually cited his authorities and never cited Comte; in fact he probably read Comte only in the '60s and then refuted him summarily, indeed so superficially that only a shallow acquaintance is suggested.[22] In short, in temperament and in philosophic purpose they were opposed; on a few specific matters they agreed more or less, but often merely negatively and on the evidence independently. What is above all interesting to note is that whereas the claim of Comtian influence on Renan rests on the empirical side of Comte's scientism, his alleged influence on Cournot is made to rest on his rationalism.[23]

A far more likely example of Comte's influence on French philosophy at the mid-century was Charles Renouvier, who had

[21] Cournot, *Essay,* pp. 462, 466, 471; cf. also pp. 472, 503. In another work (*Considérations sur la marche des idées et des événements dans les temps modernes* [Paris, n.d.]) Cournot calls "positive philosophy" a contradiction in terms; in his *Souvenirs* (Paris, 1913) he makes no mention of Comte.

[22] F. Mentré, *Cournot et la renaissance du probabilisme au xixᵉ siècle* (Paris, 1908), pp. 633, 639–643; cf. also Gabriel Tarde, "L'accident et le rationnel en histoire d'après Cournot," *Revue de métaphysique et de morale,* XIII (1905), 324–325, R. Audierne, "Note sur la classification des connaissances humaines dans Comte et dans Cournot," *ibid.,* 509, 514–519, and the introduction to the *Essay* by the translator, Merritt H. Moore, pp. xxi–xxv. (Some of Mentré's points [pp. 636–639] must, I think, be rejected.) See also Raphaël Lévêque, *L'élément historique dans la connaissance humaine d'après Cournot* (Paris, 1938), pp. 34–36, 268–278.

[23] Incidentally, to the extent that Delvolvé's argument rests on the supposition of Cournot's acquaintance with the *Cours,* it cannot explain the latter's consideration of Comte's subjective method which first appeared (and then only in outline) in 1848 in his *General View.*

been a pupil of Comte's at the Ecole Polytechnique and who adopted Comte's phenomenalism and the reduction of phenomena to laws. If Renouvier as the pioneer of what became known as the neocriticist movement in France, i.e., of criticism of metaphysics and the *esprit de système,* popularized Kant rather than Comte, it can plausibly be maintained that the initial impetus of his philosophical position came from his teacher of mathematics, whose personal or literary influence caused Renouvier to place a greater stress on science than many of the contemporary neo-Kantians in Germany. If Renouvier produced a classification of the sciences totally different from Comte's, the notion of classifying them at all may well have come from Comte. For the rest, Renouvier accused Comte of gross errors in historiography and in ethics and poured scorn on the Comte of the "second phase." Renouvier was quite certainly no Positivist and almost certainly did nothing to spread Comte's doctrine, but very probably his own philosophic career was given its fundamental orientation by Comte even though he later found a better master.[24]

A follower of Renouvier's of the next generation, in a book dedicated to Renouvier, explained very interestingly how he also, while still in school in the late 1860's, had come under the sway of Comte (having been taught about him at third hand) by way of the conversational teaching of Laffitte in the rue Monsieur-le-Prince. Lionel Dauriac recalled how he had been repelled by the skepticism enjoined by the dominant eclectic philosophy of Victor Cousin and had been drawn to Positivism as its opposite, as a philosophy in which meditation was not purposeless, in which

---

[24] Renouvier, *Traité de psychologie rationnelle d'après les principes du criticisme* (2nd ed., Paris, 1875), III, 43, *Les principes de la nature* (Paris, 1864), pp. 4, 126, *Introduction à la philosophie analytique de l'histoire* (Paris, 1864), pp. 163, 165, 167–172; Bréhier, *Histoire de la philosophie,* pp. 970–976; Benrubi, *Sources et courants,* I, 298–303; Lionel Dauriac, "Les sources néocriticistes de la dialectique synthétique," *Revue de métaphysique et de morale,* XVII (1909), 487–489, 492–493.

uncertainty was banished, and in which account was taken of science. Later, however, at the Ecole Normale, he was disabused of this penchant by the teaching of the Kantian Jules Lachelier, who without professing hostility to Comte got his students to realize that there were truths beyond science, and henceforth Dauriac declined to be "imprisoned" within the results of experimental science or to accept the "dogmatic infallibility" of the rue Monsieur-le-Prince.[25] But much later he still praised Positivism for having dissipated the aura surrounding Cousin and particularly for the foundation of sociology in the fourth volume of the *Cours.*[26] With Dauriac as with Renouvier we may confidently assert a demonstrable, historical modifying influence by Comte on thinkers who did not become his disciples.

A philosopher of the same generation as Dauriac, Alfred Fouillée, remained even in maturity far more conscious of Comte than Dauriac or Renouvier and attempted nothing less than a

[25] Dauriac, *Croyance et réalité,* pp. v–vi, xii–xv, "La philosophie au collège," *Critique philosophique,* n.s. I (1885), 17. Cf. also the very early remark of Paul Janet, *La crise philosophique* . . . (Paris, 1865), pp. 98–99: Positivism "could render very important services if it contented itself with being a philosophy of the sciences, instead of trying . . . to be all of philosophy."

[26] Dauriac, *Contingence et rationalisme,* pp. ix, xviii; cf. also pp. 8, 25, 71. Dauriac also gives us valuable information concerning Emile Boutroux, another follower of Renouvier but of the next generation and closer to the critical philosophy of science of the twentieth century. According to Dauriac (*ibid.,* p. 26), Boutroux had not read Comte when he wrote his fundamental work (*The Contingency of the Laws of Nature,* tr. Rothwell, Chicago and London, 1916, first pub. 1874). Nevertheless attempts are made (e.g., Höffding, *Modern Philosophers,* pp. 88–91, 99–100; Delvolvé, *Réflexions,* pp. 269–278) to establish Positivist parentage for Boutroux's insistence on the mutual irreducibility of the various fields of knowledge. It is true that Boutroux subsequently became interested in Positivism, but he was never an *aficionado.* See also his (much later) historical estimate of Positivism in "La philosophie en France depuis 1867," *Revue de métaphysique et de morale,* XVI (1908), 684, 711.

103

deliberate reconciliation of philosophical idealism and historical naturalism by means of his original concept of "idées-forces."[27] Fouillée approached the problem definitely from the point of view of idealism, seeking to distinguish and absorb what was acceptable in naturalism and Positivism, and not the other way around, but his persistent effort to be fair to Positivism is very notable:

> Whatever opinion may be held of the positive philosophy which, as has been noted, is never either sufficiently positive or sufficiently philosophical, nobody can deny its importance and its influence. . . . A conception which claims to embrace the whole world and all mankind, to organize the sciences and to formulate the laws of scientific progress; which provides the foundations for the new social science and sees in this science the best vantage point on the universe—this is without doubt a vast enterprise, the most systematic one that there has been in France for a century and a half.

Despite Comte's own errors and those of his disciples, he deserved to be well and accurately known, for Positivism had given rise "to the three great streams of our age: agnosticism, evolutionism, monism. . . . Whatever one may think," Fouillée concluded, "of the ideas of this reformer, the generous inspiration by which he was moved is incontestable. . . . In order to understand his various doctrines . . . one must sympathize with the truth and nobility of their contents."[28] Undoubtedly such an

[27] Perhaps we should be mindful of the neo-idealism of someone like Wilhelm von Humboldt, but Fouillée's "idées-forces" are almost certainly not dependent on Humboldt.

[28] Fouillée, *Le mouvement positiviste et la conception sociologique du monde* (Paris, 1896), pp. 345–347; Gruber, *Positivismus*, p. 137; Heinrich Waentig, *Auguste Comte und seine Bedeutung für die Entwicklung der Socialwissenschaft* (Leipzig, 1894), pp. 194–197. In his general history of philosophy Fouillée chiefly criticizes Comte but calls him a "universal scholar, profound thinker, and great innovator. . . . In reading his works it is astonishing to find how many ideas which are now taken for granted . . . are expressed there." (*Histoire de la philosophie* [13th ed., Paris,

admonition from an eminent member of the enemy camp did arouse sympathy for Comte's doctrines if not for his person, and helped to dissipate the "conspiracy of silence."

The first philosopher not himself a Positivist to express real enthusiasm for Comte and his doctrines was the author of a rival classification of the sciences, Louis Bourdeau, who acknowledged that Comte was his most powerful competitor. Comte's classification was superior to all others on the score of its clarity. It was to be criticized, however, for various specific and general reasons, so that "none of the sections established by Auguste Comte seems to us to deserve a place in a definitive classification without considerable modifications." Moreover, Comte had made the mistake of wishing to go on from science to the philosophy of science (this was of course the whole *raison d'être* of Comte's system) and had lapsed into metaphysics and sectarianism. The improved classification proposed by Bourdeau need not detain us except that the principle on which he set out to construct it bears great affinity with Comte's and may in view of the author's familiarity with Comte be thought to derive from him. Bourdeau wished to replace "agreed groups of things by rational classes of phenomena, and a multitude of particular sciences which resist any coordination by a small number of [abstract] general sciences which are susceptible of being arranged in a fixed order and are systematically connected to each other." [29] In a later, more substantive work Bourdeau showed familiarity with Comte (apparently by way of Littré) in other respects, quoting him in general with approval on the subject of ethics and subscribing to gratitude and veneration toward the "great being" Humanity, though not in the "fetishistic

---

n.d.], pp. 424–428, 550 n. 2). See, finally, Fouillée's *La science sociale contemporaine* (6th ed., Paris, 1922, first pub. 1880), pp. 67–71, where he attempts to reconcile Comte with both Darwin and Spencer and finds a place for Comte's sociological method.

[29] Bourdeau, *Théorie des sciences: Plan de science intégrale* (Paris, 1882), I, xi, xvi–xviii, 5, 18, 45, II, 304, 309–311, 458, 463–464.

form" proposed by the French Revolution and by Comte.[30] Another participant in the popular pastime of classifying the sciences paid tribute to Comte as the first man to have conceived a hierarchical classification but dissented from it in every detail and judged that Comte had confused the theoretical problem of arrangement of the sciences with the practical problem of the division of labor among scientists.[31]

After the turn of the century, however, sympathetic appraisals of Comte by professional philosophers became more frequent. Gustave Belot, in a special article on the subject, while disagreeing with most of Comte's specific views, considered his contribution in the field of ethics to be of great importance and to have been underestimated by all except his direct disciples. He saw the strength of Comte's ethics in his disinterestedness and in his historical approach by way of the growth of altruism. He dissented from Comte's application of his ethics in the *Polity* but regarded it as irrelevant to their merits; even so, he attributed the excesses of the *Polity* more to optimism than to intolerance.[32]

As an example of the important negative influence exercised by Comte (perhaps analogous to Hume's role in awakening Kant

[30] *Le problème de la vie: Essai de sociologie générale* (Paris, 1901), pp. 3–5, 17, 124–125, 128, 253, 326, 341. In his *L'histoire et les historiens* (Paris, 1888) Bourdeau endorsed the Law of the Three Stages and the notion of historical providence and prediction but regarded Comte's definition of sociology as unsatisfactory (pp. 5, 289, 327, 356, 375, 413–414).

[31] Edmond Goblot, *Essai sur la classification des sciences* (Paris, 1898), pp. 2, 5, 7–9, 293. His *Traité de logique* (4th ed., Paris, 1925) discusses the "scientific spirit" without mentioning Comte.

[32] Belot, "Les principes de la morale positiviste et la conscience contemporaine," *Revue philosophique,* Vol. 56 (1903), pp. 561–591 *passim.* In a general work on ethics Belot went out of his way, however, to point out Comte's error in regarding individuals as passive rather than active vis-à-vis society, i.e., in advocating a socially oriented ethics (*Etudes de morale positive* [2nd ed., Paris, 1921], I, viii–ix). His "L'idée et la méthode de la philosophie scientifique chez Aug. Comte," in *Histoire de la philosophie* (Paris, 1902), pp. 413–472, was entirely critical. Cf. Benrubi, *Sources et courants,* I, 236–241.

"from his philosophic slumbers") we may take the case of Emile Meyerson. Meyerson also saw Comte's fundamental merit in connection with the Classification, in his insistence that each science was methodologically *sui generis,* and in his denial of the possibility of deduction across their borders, and many of Comte's excesses were to be explained by the circumstance of pressing these points in a hostile environment. On the other hand, the Positivist view of science was radically and totally false in that it ignored ontology or, rather, adopted the unconscious ontological assumptions of common sense and to that end, when necessary, prohibited certain lines of research. But it was only historically that the scientific "problems concerning common sense" could be solved, by "a procedure somewhat analogous to that extolled by Auguste Comte," who had stressed the importance of the history of science (although he had preached it better than he had practiced) and who "merits great praise for proclaiming the fertility of the *a posteriori* method to discover the laws which rule the human mind," i.e., the method of "penetrating the functioning of thought by analysing its action in science." Meyerson maintained against Comte, however, that explanation was not necessarily prediction, and he objected to the extent to which Comte's science was governed by his ultimate social purposes.[33] Quite evidently, however, Meyerson found Comte's view of the nature and function of science stimulating.

The utilitarian approach to the whole activity of science and scholarship and the unsophisticated acceptance of common sense to which Meyerson objected were also the grounds alleged against traditional Positivism by the author of a so-called "new positivism," "more realistic and more confident of the powers of the human

---

[33] Meyerson, *De l'explication dans les sciences* (Paris, 1927), pp. 7, 19–20, 31, 42–44, 48, 57–60, 96, 100, 105–106, 112–113, 589–590, 690, *Identity & Reality* (tr. Loewenberg, London and New York, 1930), pp. 7–10, 20–21, 23, 41–42, 109 n. 105, 111 n. 127, 384, 412, 416, 439; Batault, "Le positivisme scientifique," p. 458. Georges Mourélos, *L'épistémologie positive et la critique meyersonienne* (Paris, 1962), stresses Meyerson's opposition to Positivism.

mind," which however amounted in fact to a revival of intuition-ism: "the free activity of the mind intervenes as an essential prin-ciple in the genesis of the most positive kind of knowledge, and laws are necessary only if we persist in maintaining certain atti-tudes relative to the usages of practice." In this new philosophy,

science and metaphysics are reconciled in the midst of life. Not only, therefore, does the criticism [of traditional Positivism] with which we started not end in skepticism, but the new positivism which it sustains no longer even acknowledges those insuperable boundaries which separated the old positivism from access to absolute truth. . . . Philosophic intuition is . . . the creative form of thought.[34]

What can be made of this inversion of Positivism under the guise of a "new positivism"? The author is clearly, it seems to me, not in the same category as Meyerson, who was deeply affected by Comte and felt himself obliged to struggle with and overcome the partial truth in Comte before he could reach the whole truth. Edouard Le Roy, the creator of the "new positivism," had no need to struggle with Comte or "old positivism" at all because he could reject it entirely. One of his colleagues makes the point clearer. The "positive spirit" means a respect for facts and is the obverse, not the contrary, of the "critical spirit." Scientific facts do not speak for themselves, but are

relative to a whole collection of prior points of view. *The positive spirit is a spirit of relativism.* . . . Positive truth is not buried in the earth like a treasure; it is . . . a living treasure, . . . a spirit of life. . . . *Any criticism, if it is oriented toward life, sooner or later becomes a new positivism.* . . . *To criticize means to look for a new life; to be positive means to vivify experience.*

In physics, for example, "the positive spirit is the spirit of inven-tion." [35] What this view amounts to is an acceptance of a scientific

[34] Edouard Le Roy, "Un positivisme nouveau," *Revue de métaphysique et de morale,* IX (1901), 140–141, 146, 152–153.

[35] Joseph Wilbois, "L'esprit positif," *ibid.,* 154–160, 644.

approach, but only in the context of science defined as a series of intuitive principles as part of "life." Nevertheless the author traced one line of his ancestry back to the metaphysics of Comte's "subjective synthesis." Comte had been a metaphysician, and a great one, in that he had sought for all past and present manifestations of the human conscience, but he had been too much of a mathematician and had lacked a proper "critique of science." Moreover, he had lacked an "evolutionary notion of mankind." But Comte's successors had labored to construct logic and sociology as he had envisaged them and from two different directions had largely supplied these two deficiencies: the criticism of science in the work, among others, of Le Roy and the historical point of view in the work, above all, of Henri Bergson. "Comte's idea, incomplete and misunderstood, has vivified these two series of immense researches." [36]

It appears that these two are disciples of Bergson seeking to appropriate the words "positive" and "positivism" for a version of Bergson's scientific and evolutionary intuitionism. Shall we take them at their word about the influence of Comte? We have, it seems to me, two choices: we can admit that Comte's subjective synthesis was capable of interpretation and exegesis along these lines—we may even suspect that Comte himself, had he lived longer, might have developed it along these lines—in which case, and it is plausible, Comte's philosophical influence can be attributed not only to its empiricist and rationalist but also to its mystical aspects; or we can draw the line at intellectual "influence" of this perverse sort and disallow the author's own claim to the words and teachings of Comte. It might help us to decide if we looked at Bergson's own views. Bergson recommended the *Cours* quite straightforwardly as "one of the great works of modern philosophy," the idea of a hierarchical order among the sciences as one of genius which could be regarded as a definitive truth, and Comte as the founder of sociology. Equally straightforwardly he accused

[36] *Ibid.*, X (1902), 587–589, 604.

Comte of being "a metaphysician at heart" and of trying to deify mankind.[37] I should prefer, therefore, to regard the statements of the "new positivism" as a cautionary tale in the tracing of intellectual influences, even when they are claimed by the subject himself. Certainly we should be historically on much shakier ground than with Renouvier, who did not claim the word "positivism" for himself. What is, of course, of very great significance (apart from the warning that the mysticism of the Comte of the *Polity* and of the *Synthèse subjective* should not be ruled out as philosophically unimportant) is that Le Roy should have thought it worth while to claim both Comte's word and his influence, since it constitutes very strong evidence of the esteem in which Comte and his doctrine were held even by their adversaries among professional philosophers at the turn of the century, if only as representative of the prestige of natural science, which is, I think, all that Le Roy was really affected by.

Probably the French philosopher of the twentieth century who, without becoming a Positivist, was both most influenced by Comte and himself most influential in spreading knowledge of Positivism farther afield was the man who as Emile Chartier taught at one of the famous Paris *lycées* and under the pseudonym Alain wrote many semipopular books and articles on a variety of subjects. Corra, indeed, apparently approached him on behalf of organized Positivism, for Chartier assured him that he esteemed Comte's disciples highly and would always do his best to help them; that, furthermore, he never let a year go by without giving considerable time to Comte's philosophy; and that if he did not become a disciple himself it was not for doctrinal reasons but because he was temperamentally and intellectually opposed to meetings and

[37] Bergson, "La philosophie française," *Revue de Paris,* 15 May 1915, pp. 244–245. Cf., however, Delvolvé, *Réflexions,* pp. 281–282, who represents Bergson himself as working "along the axis of development of Comte's thought" (what is that?) and as excessively affected by Comte's sentimentalism.

discussions.[38] In fact Chartier paid comprehensive but discriminating homage to Comte, to whom he said he owed much and to whom he would always refer anyone "on all human and cosmological problems." "This is not to say that I am all that fond of this author. I find him a little too serious for my taste; there is too little *élan,* too little venturesomeness." But he had been taught by Comte that there was such a thing as social statics, "that is to say, permanent conditions resulting from human structure." [39] From Comte he had also learned "a thousand other things," for instance, that "the words of the common language contain common thought" and the importance of the difference between love and hate.[40] In general "there is no system so conducive to reflection and even to invention" as Positivism, which it was a mistake to regard as dogmatic; "the positive spirit is still the best guide for grateful humanity." [41] Humanity, indeed, as conceived by Comte, was real, Chartier affirmed, and was the proper subject of sociology, and he was always particularly interested in the social bearing of Positivism. If he were to teach sociology he would first of all reread the *Cours* (the *Polity* he remembered sufficiently) and recommend to his charges Comte's preliminary historical survey, the Law of the Three Stages, the Classification of the Sciences, the Calendar, and the "esprit d'ensemble" which was identical with the "esprit sociologique." Above all it was necessary to read Comte at first hand, "which comes to only ten volumes in which everything is put in its place, even true mysticism, by dint of an encyclopedic knowledge." [42] Chartier insisted on the unity of Comte's thought, defended his view of fetishism and even the idea of the

[38] Chartier to Corra, 14 April and 8 May 1929, A.N., AS 5.

[39] Unpublished notes of Chartier (1946) in *Hommage à Alain* (Paris, 1952), pp. 302, 305–306.

[40] *Lettres au docteur Henri Mondor sur le sujet du coeur et de l'esprit* (Paris, 1924), pp. 15, 67.

[41] *Idées: Introduction à la philosophie. Platon, Descartes, Hegel, Comte* (7th ed., Paris, 1939), p. 7, *Propos sur l'éducation* (Paris, 1932), p. 295.

[42] *Ibid.,* pp. 266, 287–289, 293–294.

Virgin-Mother, and expressed admiration for Clotilde de Vaux. At the same time Positivism was "far more accessible on all sides than is commonly thought" and had a civilizing effect by its "immense and unforeseeable implications which correspond completely to our urgent needs." [43] In fact scarcely any adverse criticism of Comte's doctrine is to be found in Chartier's writings.

After this survey of the various directions of Comte's philosophical influence and of some of the problems raised thereby [44] it will be instructive to consider the judgment of the principal recent student of Comte's philosophy not a member of the "school," Jean Delvolvé: [45] Comte had from the beginning been a metaphysician with a passion for unity and system and without real scientific experience or talent. His uniqueness lay in his attempt to achieve a total philosophy by science, i.e., objective analysis,

[43] *Ibid.,* p. 295; *Hommage à Alain,* p. 324; *Idées,* pp. 291–294 *et seq.* See also his *Humanités* (Paris, 1946), pp. 276–277, and *Correspondance avec Elie et Florence Halévy* (2nd ed., Paris, 1958), pp. 54, 67; comment by Daniel Halévy in *Hommage à Alain,* p. 69; and Lubac, *Drama,* p. 103.

[44] Reference to other individuals will be found in the Bibliographical Appendix, but mention should be made here of the author of the first important objective analysis of Comte's philosophy, Lucien Lévy-Bruhl, who, though of a predominantly empirical turn of mind, undoubtedly did Positivism a service by his sympathetic treatment of it. See also Maurice Leenhardt in Lévy-Bruhl, *Carnets* (Paris, 1949), p. vii, and cf. Benrubi's unconvincing argument in *Sources et courants,* I, 204–208. See also, for what it may be worth, the results of a poll conducted among professors of philosophy between ca. 1895 and 1907, in A. Binet, "Une enquête sur l'évolution de l'enseignement de la philosophie," *Année psychologique,* XIV (1908), 152–231.

[45] Note that Delvolvé did give a lecture under the auspices of the Société des Amis d'Auguste Comte, under the title "Auguste Comte et la religion," printed in the *Revue d'histoire de la philosophie et d'histoire générale de la civilisation,* n.s. V (1937), 343–368. It was a fair, sympathetic, but penetrating critique: Comte had seen the social value of religion and had tried to satisfy spiritual aspirations by science; the problem was valid but Comte's solution of it idolatrous and full of difficulties, though fruitful; nevertheless he was a great mind deserving of the respect and gratitude of philosophers.

alone, but he had proposed an oversimplified and premature solution to a problem faced by all philosophers. Taken not as a final synthesis but as a preliminary sketch, however, it was impressive. His weaknesses were accentuated during his later years, as Littré had seen without seeing that they had always existed. The principal philosophic interest of Comte's work was its internal tension expressed by the contradictions in which he had entangled himself. Summing up: "Comte's positivism is a vast poem on the destiny of man," and "Comte survives as the great propagator of the positive prejudice." [46]

It is of this "prejudice" in its specifically Comtian form that we have, more than of anything else, seen the influence on succeeding generations of philosophers, the "prejudice" that a total philosophy or "conception of the world" could and should be derived from science and from science alone. Of at least equal interest, therefore, is the question of the extent of Comte's influence on the scientists themselves; to Comte himself, certainly, it would have been of far greater interest, despising philosophers—for reasons both good and bad—as he did, and scientists were the first occupational group to which (still in Comte's lifetime) the propaganda was directed. This was done through a "Biological Society" founded in 1848 on the initiative, among others, of two Positivists, L. A. Segond and Charles Robin, who became one of its vice-presidents and proceeded to expound before it such Positivist principles as the Classification of the Sciences and the superior importance of physiology to anatomy, which became one of the accepted doctrines of the society. Others were the preference given to synthesis over analysis and the insistence on arranging and not merely collecting facts. Although the Classification, which was Robin's philosophical point of departure, did not make much headway, Comte's fundamental idea that one of the principal problems of biology was to find a few general laws concerning the relation of the organism

[46] Delvolvé, *Réflexions*, pp. v, 22–23, 26–27, 32–37, 54, 67–68, 122, 181, 185, 200, 252.

with its environment became generally accepted in and partly through the society.[47] An eminent contemporary biologist affirms that

there was no biologist or physician in France between 1840 and 1880 who, in defining the place of his researches . . . , the meaning and importance of his work, did not have to deal either directly with the themes of Comte's biological philosophy [the dualism of life and matter, the correlation of organism and environment] or indirectly with that philosophy through the themes which developed from it.[48]

If not precisely a test case, then certainly the *locus classicus* of this statement would be the eminent physiologist Claude Bernard. He has been claimed as a signal instance of Comte's influence because of his rigorous and comprehensive physiological determinism and experimentalism, despite his avoidance of any philosophical commitment; or, alternatively, because of this very avoidance.[49] On the other hand, there were those who thought from the beginning that, even though Bernard's famous *Introduction to the Study of Experimental Medicine*[50] might "faithfully summarize all the essentials of Comte's positivism," there was no

[47] E. Gley, *Essais de philosophie et d'histoire de la biologie* (Paris, 1900), pp. 186–192, 198, "Les sciences biologiques et la biologie générale," *Revue scientifique*, Vol. 47^1 (1909), p. 6. Against Littré, see *P.P.*, I (1867), 490 and X (1873), 41; also Raoul Caveribert, *La vie et l'oeuvre de Rayer (1793–1867)* (Paris, 1931), p. 38.

[48] Georges Canguilhem, "La philosophie biologique d'Auguste Comte et son influence en France au xixe siècle," *Bulletin* de la Société Française de Philosophie, special number (1958), pp. 22–23. Canguilhem calls Comte's biological philosophy "knowledgeable and well informed" and refers to Comte as "the last and the greatest representative in the 19th century of the Medical School of Montpellier [Comte's birthplace]" (pp. 24, 25).

[49] On the one hand, Mathias Duval in *P.P.*, XX (1878), 443, and Lucy Prenant, "Karl Marx et Auguste Comte," in *A la lumière du marxisme: Essais*, Vol. II: *Karl Marx et la pensée moderne*, Part I (Paris, 1939), pp. 69–70; on the other hand, Georges Canguilhem, *La connaissance de la vie* (Paris, 1952), pp. 25–26.

[50] Tr. Greene, [New York,] 1949; first pub. 1865.

influence of one on the other: "There is no cause-and-effect relationship between the positivism [of Comte] and the experimental
method [of Bernard]: there is identity." If Bernard had not ruined
Comte's Positivism, he had at least broken through its boundaries
by enlarging the field of sensible reality beyond science and restoring reason to its proper role: "In short, Cl. Bernard had . . .
reopened the perspectives which Aug. Comte had . . . closed." [51]

Such a judgment received considerable reinforcement with the
subsequent publication of some philosophical manuscripts of
Bernard's. These afford an insight into the historical development
of Bernard's thought, so that the editor of one of these publications
could say: "Before 1865 it would have been possible without too
much distortion . . . to place him among the disciples of Auguste
Comte. . . . The position at which he arrived in 1865 [the date
of the *Introduction*] was quite different: a clearly and resolutely
anti-positivist position which leaves room for metaphysics." [52] The
manuscripts included, in fact, Bernard's notes and annotations on
the *Cours,* in which Bernard, though recognizing "some truth"
(elsewhere, however, he described it as "banal") in the Law of
the Three Stages, on the whole decisively rejected it and, moreover, diagnosed it as the source of Comte's fundamental error:

[51] Pierre Lamy, *L'Introduction à l'étude de la médecine expérimentale:
Claude Bernard, le naturalisme et le positivisme* (Paris, 1928), pp. 2, 36, 78,
and cf. also pp. 35, 40–42, 45, 77. The author added that Bernard's was indeed the only "integral positivism" (p. 5), but like Charlton, *Positivist
Thought,* chap. v, attributed this distinction not to his following Comte but
to his diverging from him. This is a consistent position, but cf. my discussion
above, p. 3 and n. 1.

[52] Bernard, *Philosophie: Manuscrit inédit* (ed. Chevalier, Paris, [1938]),
p. 50. See also A.-D. Sertillanges, *La philosophie de Claude Bernard* (n.p.,
[1943]), pp. 26–28, 31, 40–41; J. M. D. Olmsted and E. Harris Olmsted,
Claude Bernard and the Experimental Method in Science (New York, 1952),
pp. 143, 231 n., 246; Reino Virtanen, *Claude Bernard and His Place in the
History of Ideas* (Lincoln, Neb., 1960), pp. 4, 19, 47, 49–53, 57, 61, 63; and
Paul Foulquié, *Claude Bernard* (Paris, n.d.), pp. 114–118.

the supposition, basically sentimental, that because science was self-sufficient it was sufficient for human nature. Comte's religion was as mystical and absurd as all the others, just as his philosophy was as metaphysical as all the others. But above all, perhaps, Bernard objected to Comte's view of philosophers as those who specialized in generalization: "Clearly, only specialization is capable of reaching general conclusions. . . . Comte's idea of considering positive philosophy as the generalities of science is bad. There is no way of avoiding getting down to details." And he rejected the approach to social science via natural science and the idea of a social consensus.[53] It will scarcely do to accuse a man who has come so firmly to grips with Comte of underrating or suppressing his own debt to him; the debt to the *Cours* of the whole intellectual climate in which he grew up is, of course, another question and one on which Bernard was not in a good position to judge.[54]

Even if Claude Bernard can be dragooned within the range of Comte's influence only with great difficulty, there is other evidence, though necessarily scattered, which seems to warrant the belief that Comte's biology (Vol. III of the *Cours*) exercised a considerable and specific influence, above all through the teaching of Charles Robin and through Littré's and Robin's medical dictionary.[55] Among the most significant testimonies are those of

[53] Bernard, *Philosophie*, pp. 25–34, cf. also pp. 35–39, *Introduction*, p. 221, and *Pensées: Notes détachées* (Paris, 1937), pp. 63–64, 66–67.

[54] Cf. Sertillanges, *Philosophie de C. Bernard*, p. 41, with Virtanen, *Claude Bernard*, pp. 50–51.

[55] See in general the following writings: Eugène Dally, *De l'état présent des doctrines médicales dans leurs rapports avec la philosophie des sciences* (Paris, 1860—dedicated to Littré), Preface; Edouard Bourdet, *L'évolution de la médecine* (Paris, 1875—dedicated to Robin), pp. 10–11, 15, 19, 34, 36–38, 45, 54, 66–67, 77; C. Pagès, "Auguste Comte et la vétérinaire," *R.O.*, IX (1882), 365–372, reprinted from a veterinary journal; Alexandre Calas, *Auguste Comte médecin* (Paris, 1889), esp. pp. 4–5, 90, distinguishing sharply between Comte's "two phases" but highly praising the importance

Charles Bouchard and Georges Pennetier. Bouchard, a physician, wrote that he had drawn from Comte "habits of mind and a kind of intellectual discipline" useful for study and research, and his biographer added: "Comte and his disciples without any doubt rendered a great service to those who wished to advance medical science." [56] Pennetier, director of the museum of natural history, recalled: "Dazzled amid the numerous brilliant doctrines whose principles are not susceptible of verification [especially Cousin's], anyone seeking truth found a refuge in the philosophy of Auguste Comte, which served as a rallying-point for minds freed from metaphysical influence." [57] Perhaps most interesting of all is the statement of another physician, who declared that he, like all cultivated men in France, accepted Positivism in part but not *in toto:* it represented to him the noblest effort of the French mind since Descartes to coordinate all human thought. Feeling as he did he asked a friend to explain to him the role of organized Positivism, but the friend complied by talking mostly in political and social terms.[58]

To this evidence must be added the undoubted originality and influence of Comte's doctrine (however overlaid with both scien-

of the first; Gley, "Les sciences biologiques," p. 7, concerning Félix Le Dantec (q.v. in the Bibliographical Appendix); C. Lefebvre de Rieux, *De la méthode comparative dans les sciences médicales* (Paris, 1926), pp. 13–15, 19–20, 23, 27, 29–34, 86–87; and cf. Louis Pasteur, "Discours de réception," *P.P.,* XXIX (1882), 128–139, seeking to counter the "illusion" (which therefore evidently existed) that Positivism rested on scientific method.

[56] Paul Le Gendre, *Un médecin philosophe: Charles Bouchard, son oeuvre et son temps (1837–1915)* (Paris, 1924), pp. 29–30, 452; cf. Const. Hillemand, *La vie et l'oeuvre de Auguste Comte et de Pierre Laffitte* (Paris, 1908), p. 9.

[57] Georges Pennetier, *Discours sur l'évolution des connaissances en histoire naturelle* (Actes du Muséum d'Histoire Naturelle de Rouen, Rouen, 1911–1924), XVII, 29; cf. also pp. 33–35, 40.

[58] F. Helme, "L'opinion d'un médecin sur la Société Positiviste Internationale," *Revue moderne de médecine et de chirurgie,* July, 1912, pp. 246–251.

tific and philosophical nonsense) of the totality of an organism as regards its health or illness, derived from the more general idea, not of course original with him, of the continuous relationship between the organism and its environment. This was a doctrine which anticipated what is now called psychosomatic medicine and which appealed to many medical practitioners, especially those who had to deal with mental pathology.[59] From this evidence must be subtracted the effect of the disciples' obstinacy regarding Darwin and evolution,[60] but this is hard to assess.

On the other natural sciences Comte's influence was certainly smaller.[61] The famous chemist Marcelin Berthelot, whom the disciples claimed for Positivist inspiration,[62] did define positive science as consisting of the chain of relations among facts and spoke of the possibility and the importance of extending positive method to ethics and consequently of solving social problems, though he qualified this by saying that such a moral science could achieve only very general knowledge and would be an "ideal" and not a "positive" science.[63] On the other hand, Clémence Royer, though an occasional contributor to Littré's journal, declared explicitly that "the world has already gone beyond Kant, Fichte, Hegel, Comte and is looking for something better in Stuart Mill,

[59] See, e.g., E. Dally, *Remarques sur les aliénés et les criminels au point de vue de la responsabilité morale et légale* (Paris, 1864); above, pp. 69–70, and below, the Bibliographical Appendix.

[60] See above, pp. 25–27, 46–47, and 67.

[61] But cf. the claim of Ducassé, *Essai sur les origines,* pp. 252–253, 257, on behalf of Comte's mathematical pedagogy.

[62] *R.P.I.,* II (1907), 327.

[63] "La science idéale et la science positive: A M. Renan," in his *Science et philosophie* (Paris, 1886), pp. 4, 13–14, 37, 39–40; see also his "Le rôle de la science dans les progrès des sociétés modernes," *Revue scientifique,* series 4, VII (1897), 641–643, and cf. Charlton, *Positivist Thought,* pp. 59–60. On Comte and chemistry generally, see G. Urbain, "La valeur des idées d'A. Comte sur la chimie," *Revue de métaphysique et de morale,* XXVII (1920), esp. pp. 162, 174, 179, who gives a very low evaluation. On Berthelot, see also Emile Picard, *La science moderne et son état actuel* (Paris, 1914), p. 13.

Herbert Spencer, Bain and the whole English school." [64] Scattered tributes to Comte or to his doctrine can indeed be found, even extravagant ones as in the case of the historian of the Ecole Polytechnique, of which Comte was "the most influential [*puissante*] product" as he was "the greatest thinker of the 19th century" and the *Cours* "the most considerable, the most powerful, and the most fruitful work that philosophical genius has ever brought forth." [65] By 1914 a historian of science could write in retrospect of Comte's shortcomings as a scientist and the oversimplifications of his doctrine but nevertheless conclude: "Despite his narrowness he exactly represented the opinion of the majority of scientists during the second half of the last century, particularly of those who, being mainly experimenters, distrusted theories." [66] This analysis implies the paradox that, being a bad scientist, Comte evolved a philosophy which enabled good scientists to dispense with philosophy. But this appears to be exactly what happened. Among scientists, even more perhaps than among philosophers, Comte was felt (rightly, of course) to be on the side of science,

[64] C. Royer, *Deux hypothèses sur l'hérédité* (Paris, 1877), p. 17 (however, she opposes Darwin and quotes a few times from Charles Robin); cf. her "Lamarck: Sa vie, ses travaux, et son système," *P.P.*, III (1868), 173–205, 333–372, IV (1869), 5–30, "Attraction et gravitation d'après Newton," *ibid.*, XXXI (1883), 206–226, and the Bibliographical Appendix.

[65] Gaston Pinet, *Ecrivains et penseurs polytechniciens* (2nd ed., Paris, 1902), p. 203, also pp. 205, 208–209 (based to a considerable extent on Audiffrent, p. 203 n. 1), *Auguste Comte: Notice biographique* (n.p., n.d.), pp. 3, 12; cf. his "L'ensemble de la science mathématique: Résumé des idées d'Auguste Comte," *P.P.*, XXVII (1881), 165–186. See further Charles Boysset, *Catéchisme du xixᵉ siècle* (Paris, [1868]), cf. his "Considérations générales sur la moralité scientifique," *P.P.*, VIII (1872), 402–427 (some signs of fellow traveling); Louis Olivier, "Alexandre Etard, sa vie et ses travaux (1852–1910)," *Revue générale des sciences pures et appliquées*, XXI (1910), 605 (Etard influenced by Comte); Roger in Ch. Bouchard and G.-H. Roger, ed., *Nouveau traité de pathologie générale* (Paris, 1912–14), I, 7–8 (Positivism as a means of avoiding philosophy).

[66] Picard, *La science moderne*, p. 13.

and nonphilosophical scientists could (wrongly, of course) jump to the conclusion that they need not bother their heads any more about philosophy, "philosophy" representing to them the inconclusive speculations of Victor Cousin. Thus Comte came to stand for science *against* philosophy rather than for a scientific philosophy, and we might well say that Comte therefore benefited from the prestige of natural science more than he contributed to that prestige by supplying it with a philosophy and a purpose, which was his ambition.[67] To a modern philosopher-scientist Comte fell between two stools:

the theory of the sciences in the *Cours* . . . is still only *philosophy,* . . . [going on] above the sciences properly speaking. . . . His philosophy of science, infinitely richer, more complete, and more scientific than the logic of the old philosophy, eliminates all speculation on the method of knowledge. Only the Law of the Three Stages is of this order of ideas. That is very little.

Comte's attempt, Abel Rey continues, at a philosophy

freed from all conjecture about the unknowable, . . . nevertheless still corresponds . . . to a sort of aesthetics of science, to a release from the specialization that had oppressed the mind. [But] it is specialization which increasingly, in theory as well as practice, will make for progress. . . . By the side of positive science and technology there is room for philosophical study. . . . This study cannot be positive in the sense in which the sciences and technologies must be; its conclusions will be

[67] Sir Isaiah Berlin represents the situation as a forerunner of that of twentieth-century logical positivism: Comte "understood the role of natural science and the true reasons for its prestige better than most contemporary thinkers. . . . He demanded evidence; he denounced intellectual impressionism. . . . Above all he grasped the central issue of all philosophy—the distinction between words . . . that are about words, and words . . . that are about things, and thereby helped to lay the foundation of what is best and most illuminating in modern empiricism" (*Historical Inevitability,* p. 4). Cf. also Batault, "Positivisme scientifique," p. 450 (most scientists are materialists, not positivists).

neither verified by experience nor demonstrated by reason. . . . It will afford us, as the fruit of reflection, only hypothetical glimpses of the future.

Philosophy must be the servant of science, but at the same time it will in its turn react on science and its application: "That is its *raison d'être.*" [68] In other words: Comte was right "to envisage philosophy as a new specialty by the side of science," but he was wrong in the definition he then gave of it which confused the philosophy of science with the popularization of science and therefore condemned philosophy to being always behind science and thus useless. Positive philosophy could only be "the system of positive science," not, as Comte thought, "the systematization of scientific knowledge," and it must be constructed from the bottom up "by applying historical and critical method to contemporary scientific thought." This would be modern, that is to say "absolute," positivism.[69] "When I speak of contemporary positivism, when I profess adherence to positivism I do not mean that I subscribe to Comte's doctrine, but only that I accept . . . all the teachings of positive science and nothing but those teachings." [70] Nevertheless Rey approved of Comte's Classification of the Sciences (though he thought it should be supplemented by Spencer's) and of the Law of the Three Stages, and readily conceded that Comte was "the greatest of the successors of Descartes." Only, he insisted, Comte must be treated as a point of departure, by applying his method and developing his doctrine, and not as the author of final solutions. Hypotheses, in particular, must be allotted a larger place in science and above all in philosophy, and would lead to a "vue d'ensemble" which would "link up with sociology . . . in a sense very close to that given to the word in Comte's

[68] Abel Rey, "Ce que devient la logique," *Revue philosophique,* Vol. 57 (1904), pp. 612–613, 622–623.

[69] "Vers le positivisme absolu," *ibid.,* Vol. 67 (1909), pp. 468–469, 476, 478. Alternatively he spoke of an "enlarged" or of a "realistic" positivism.

[70] *La philosophie moderne* (Paris, 1908), p. 6 n.

religious philosophy." [71] Comte was unsatisfactory, in short, both because in some respects he identified science and philosophy too closely and because in others he allowed philosophy to speculate too freely. By the turn of the century, by the time of Abel Rey, the ghost of Victor Cousin had been thoroughly laid (by Comte, very prominently, among others); French scientists and philosophers, no longer preoccupied with combating eclecticism, were ready to construct anew and to allow the mind freer rein than the Comte of the *Cours* seemed to do, but were unwilling to subscribe to the way in which, in the *Polity,* it developed that he had wanted all along to give it freer rein himself. In the dialectic of thought, Comte's Positivism was no longer acceptable as the final synthesis, although it could supply ingredients for an antithesis.

Comte himself had regarded his doctrine as an antithesis to that of Victor Cousin most particularly in the field of psychology, and his exclusion of psychology from the hierarchy of the sciences is not intelligible except in terms of the accepted current definition of "psychology" as that taught by Cousin, which relied heavily on introspection and was regarded with scorn by Comte as vague and "spiritualistic." Comte was determined to bring the study of the human mind, in the widest sense, within the range of determinism and to make it susceptible of being related to other studies and of contributing to the ultimate synthesis.[72] Therefore he made of psychology on the one hand a physiological discipline, in the course of which he came to subscribe in part to the phrenological doctrine of Franz Gall, and on the other hand a sociological discipline,

[71] *Les sciences philosophiques: Leur état actuel* (Paris, [1908?]), pp. 528, 550, 553–554; letters to Marcel Boll, cited by Boll in *R.P.I.,* [XXI] (1916), 75 n., [XXIII] (1917), 167–169. Rey was cited by Boll as the example *par excellence* of scholarly positivism.

[72] Indeed, one can go farther and say, with Gouhier, that the refusal to treat internal experiences, the results of introspection, as facts, and the consequent rejection not only of traditional psychology but of traditional logic, constituted the original point of departure for Comte's entire system (Introduction to Comte, *Oeuvres choisies* [Paris, n.d.], p. 7).

since the individual mind, we might say, was determined not only by its biological heredity but also, probably in fact more so, by its social environment. In fact Comte drew the logical conclusion from this situation by adding, in the *Polity,* a seventh science to the hierarchy, at its apex, which he christened ethics but which in fact, in many respects, was much closer to psychology.

Now it is not to be expected that we shall find many students of the human mind in the last hundred years who accepted the "cerebral table" which Comte adapted from Gall or, indeed, any of his specific psychological teachings. On the other hand, we certainly cannot ascribe to the influence of Comte every attempt made to construct a physiological psychology as a reaction against the "spiritualism" of Cousin. Particular caution, therefore, is called for in assessing Comte's influence in this field. The estimates, as usual, differ widely.[73]

The key figure is Théodule Ribot, "the real founder of experimental psychology in France," [74] and he was categorical:

The foundation of M. Comte's philosophy is in no way peculiar to him, but the general property of the age. . . . The philosophy called Positive is not a recent invention of M. Comte, but a simple adherence to the traditions of all the great scientific minds whose discoveries have made the human race what it is.

But Comte

has made the doctrine his own by his method of treating it. Positivism is, then, a form of the modern scientific spirit, but it is only a particular form of it, it is only a wave of the great current. . . . Between the positive mind and positivism we, for our part, discern as much differ-

---

[73] E.g., Gruber, *Positivismus,* p. 135; Lévy-Bruhl, *Philosophy of Comte,* p. 19; Cresson, *Courants,* II, 175–177; Benrubi, *Sources et courants,* I, 20, as against Parodi, *Philosophie contemporaine,* p. 78.

[74] Benrubi, *Sources et courants,* I, 43. Charlton, *Positivist Thought,* pp. 83–85, classifies Ribot with Claude Bernard as a "true positivist" according to his definition.

ence as between the philosophical mind and philosophy, [i.e.] between that which remains and that which passes away.

And he preferred Mill to Comte as an inspiration.[75] In defining the "old" and the "new" (physiological) psychology he allowed a place for introspection and made no mention of Comte or Positivism at all.[76] One of his students traced Ribot's intellectual debts back to Condillac and the Idéologues on the one hand and to his own medical studies on the other.[77] He and all other students or followers of Ribot preached a psychology free of metaphysics but with scarcely a reference or noticeable debt to Comte.[78] Even the promoter of Positivist educational principles talked of Comte's "fairy tale about the brain" and referred with approval to Victor Cousin.[79] It is with difficulty that we can scrape together even two psychologists who can be shown to have owed a significant debt to or even to have thought well of Comte or Positivism.[80]

[75] *English Psychology,* p. 80.

[76] *German Psychology of Today: The Empirical School* (tr. Baldwin, New York, 1886), pp. 1–3, 5–9, 11.

[77] Pierre Janet, "L'oeuvre psychologique de Th. Ribot," *Journal de psychologie normale et pathologique,* XII (1915), 269, 272–273. Cf. also the critique of Ribot by Wyrouboff in *P.P.,* XVI (1876), 468.

[78] See in the Bibliographical Appendix the works of Pierre Bovet, Georges Dumas, Théodore Flournoy, Pierre Janet, Frédéric Paulhan, Jules Payot, Charles Richet, and, the most eminent of them, Alfred Binet (still an eponymous hero of child testing), also his journal (with H. Beaunis), the *Année psychologique.*

[79] Alexis Bertrand, *La psychologie de l'effort et les doctrines contemporaines* (Paris, 1889), pp. 20, 181.

[80] See P. Froument, an "independent" contributor to the Positivist journals, *Recherches sur la mentalité humaine . . .* (Paris, [1902]), pp. vi–viii, x–xi, 2, *Les methodes de la raison précédées d'un exposé complet du travail cérébral* (Paris, 1908), p. viii; Ch. Blondel, "La psychologie selon Comte, Durkheim et Trade," *Journal de psychologie normale et pathologique,* XXIV (1927), 381–383, 387–399 (significance of Comte's system, fruitfulness of dependence of psychology on both biology and sociology, but falsity of his idea of "cerebral physiology" under the influence of "two fanatics, Gall

The reaction in Comte's favor against Cousin, therefore, occurred chiefly, not in the area in which Comte himself most consciously pitted himself against Cousin, but among philosophers and scientists. But although psychology, in the guise of ethics, came to crown Comte's second hierarchy of the sciences, it was with the regulation of man's social life that Comte had been from the very outset of his career supremely concerned, and this regulation depended on the science of which Comte called himself the founder, sociology.

---

and Broussais"). Aug. Georges, "Essai sur le système psychologique d'Auguste Comte," *Archives d'anthropologie criminelle, de médecine légale, et de psychologie normale et pathologique,* XXIII (1908), 749–809, called Comte's system in general worthless, though containing good individual points, original observations, and a new method.

Chapter V

FRANCE: HISTORY AND SOCIOLOGY

IN Comte's Classification of the Sciences, each science, though dependent on all the inferior ones and particularly on the one next preceding, was distinguished by following its own method, and the method that Comte assigned to sociology was "the method of filiation," i.e., the historical method. The study of history was important only insofar as it led to extrapolation and prediction, and hence to prescription, for the future. For this purpose, however, it was uniquely important. Comte in fact allowed no distinction between historians (that is, "good" historians) and sociologists, and certainly one test of his influence in this area will be the extent to which this distinction was in practice blurred, the extent to which history became the auxiliary, the handmaiden of sociology, and stressed social rather than individual causation in the historical process, for some such reasons as Comte gave. As Ernst Troeltsch points out, Comte's theory of historical development "benefited in the first place those areas of historical research which on account of a lack of literary remains in any event offer little of an individual nature," prehistory and the anthropological study of religion.[1] F. S. Marvin, on the contrary, held that intel-

[1] *Der Historismus und seine Probleme: Das logische Problem der Ge-*

lectual history was "the field in which Comte discovered the guiding line of common thought," the Law of the Three Stages, which was, of course, a law of intellectual development only (and sometimes objected to as such, although Comte did not omit to supply it with suitably symmetrical equivalents in political, military, and social development). "History, primarily regarded as the history of the development of the human mind, is the sole main road to intellectual synthesis. . . . That Comte stood practically alone, assuredly the most eminent, in pointing this way to attain the concentration and harmony of individual and national minds . . . is one of his most signal services." [2] That Comte pioneered in putting intellectual history to this use we would readily agree; that he pioneered in making history itself something besides "the account of the rise and government of states" is, after Voltaire, Condorcet, and even Saint-Simon, implausible. Apart from the mutual approach between history and sociology it was in an approach between history and science that Comte gave a lead, and that in two respects: in arousing an interest in the history of science and in trying to make history into a science. Of these two, he was far more original as well as influential in the former than in the latter. Paul Lacombe, the author of one of the early attempts to make a science of history, may be said to have adapted Comte's Classification of the Sciences, but he rejected the Law of the Three Stages and specifically allowed contingency as well as law in history and rebutted Comte's presumption of inevitable

---

schichtsphilosophie (Tübingen, 1922), pp. 414–417. In the documented areas of history, Troeltsch maintains, no significant work was written on the basis of Comte's method or results. See also Peter Stadler, Geschichtschreibung und historisches Denken in Frankreich 1789–1871 (Zurich, 1958), pp. 200–202, who ascribes very little influence to Comte, "the rigid limitations of whose preconceived view exclude all sense for living change, for the truly historical." By dint of a "fanatical effort of will power" Comte had "contrived to put together a structure of externally impressive dimensions out of his meager store of historical knowledge."

[2] *Comte,* pp. 204–205.

progress.[3] Other similar enterprises savored even less of Positivism.[4]

It was Taine who, like Renan in philosophy with whom he is often linked, was regarded as the most eminent representative of Comte's influence in historiography, and although there is no valid reason, in the one case as in the other, why the issue should stand or fall by this particular instance, certainly Taine is worth detailed examination as the author of "the most significant attempt yet made to constitute history as a science in the name of a philosophical conception." [5] Taine, it was recently written, "was not a genius: . . . he was not able . . . to construct new methods for investigating society. He relied on Comte." [6] What is usually singled out as the most important debt of Taine to Comte is his famous theory of the "milieu," his emphasis on the total condition of a society.[7] Alternatively it is suggested that it was not as a historian at all but as a psychologist that Taine, again by reaction

[3] *De l'histoire considérée comme science* (2nd ed., Paris, 1930), pp. vii–viii, xiii, 9, 11–13, 250, 289–291, 369. See Troeltsch, p. 398 n. 203; Henri Berr, *En marge de l'histoire universelle* (Paris, 1934–53), I, 36 n. 3; Paul Barth, *Die Philosophie der Geschichte als Soziologie* (3rd and 4th revised ed., Leipzig, 1922), I, 81–83, but cf. Benrubi, *Sources et courants,* I, 248–249.

[4] See, e.g., Paul Mougeolle, *Les problèmes de l'histoire* (Paris, 1886), pp. 75–77, 81, 94–95, 255; Henri Berr, *La montée de l'esprit: Bilan d'une vie et d'une oeuvre* (Paris, 1955), pp. 110, 123, 126–127, and his introduction to the journal that he founded, *Revue de synthèse historique,* I (1900), 4; and cf. Benrubi, *Sources et courants,* I, 252–258.

[5] Monod, *Renan, Taine, Michelet,* p. viii.

[6] *Times Literary Supplement,* 15 Nov. 1957, p. 692.

[7] Paul Barth, "Zum 100. Geburtstage Auguste Comte's," *Vierteljahrsschrift für wissenschaftliche Philosophie,* XXII (1898), 184–185; Victor Giraud, *Essai sur Taine* . . . (2nd ed., Paris, 1901), pp. 61–64. (See Taine's *History of English Literature* [tr. Van Laun, new ed., London, 1877], I, 17, 19.) Lamy, *L'Introduction,* pp. 28–29, ascribes this theory to the influence of Claude Bernard; cf. also Heinrich Ritter von Srbik, *Geist und Geschichte* . . . (Munich and Salzburg, 1950–51), II, 222.

against Victor Cousin, had affinities with Comte, though with Condillac, Mill, Bain, and Spencer as well.[8]

It is quite clear that any direct influence from Comte must have come fairly late in Taine's development, for he had not read him before 1864, when he was assigned to review the second edition of the *Cours;*[9] and it seems very doubtful if there was even any indirect influence.[10] Ernst Cassirer points out the very important fact that Taine, unlike Comte, was methodologically a monist, wishing to assimilate the social to the natural sciences,[11] and others deny to Taine the title of "positivist" or allow it to him only in a general way as an equally valid representative of it with Comte or Littré or Mill.[12] Even the orthodox disciples, usually eager to claim a supporter on the slightest provocation, rejected Taine as a Positivist historian.[13]

[8] Denroubi, *Sources et courants,* I, 26–27, 31–34; Harald Höffding, *Modern Philosophers* (tr. Mason, London, 1915), pp. 72–75; cf. Flint, *History of the Philosophy of History,* p. 630, and Cantecor, *Comte,* p. 168, who ascribe influence to Condillac principally and to Comte not at all (though Cantecor is mistaken in supposing that Taine may not even have read Comte, see below). Taine's *Les philosophes classiques du xixe siècle en France* (6th ed., Paris, 1888, first pub. 1857) dealt a decisive blow at Victor Cousin and his system.

[9] Taine in *Journal des débats,* 6 July 1864; cf. Giraud, *Essai sur Taine,* p. 63 n. 2.

[10] André Chevrillon, *Taine: Fondation de sa pensée* (Paris, 1932), p. 223 n. 2, states: "I have not come across the name of Comte a single time in the notes and writings of Taine's youth."

[11] *The Problem of Knowledge* . . . (tr. Woglom and Hendel, New Haven, 1950), pp. 244–247; cf. above, pp. 5–6.

[12] Monod, *Renan, Taine, Michelet,* pp. 137–140, 157; Edmond Scherer, "M. Taine ou la critique positiviste," in his *Mélanges de critique religieuse* (Paris, 1860), p. 487. Henri Bergson declared that Taine no more than Renan had any connection with Comte: "La philosophie française," p. 245. See also Charlton, *Positivist Thought,* chap. vii, who shows Taine to have been no positivist in either his sense or mine.

[13] Stupuy in *P.P.,* XXI (1878), 36, 55; Laffitte, *Grands types,* III, 651.

Taine himself used "positive" as meaning factual, unphilosophical, and as the opposite of "religious." Against Comte's Positivism he intended to restore the concept "cause" within the sphere of knowledge.[14] Of Comte himself, after criticizing his style, his egoism, his religion and politics, and other matters, Taine wrote:

His mind seems in all respects to be absolute, exclusive, narrow, vigorously and irrevocably immersed in its own evolution, confined to limited horizons and to a single conception. But this conception is worth universal attention, and in developing it he showed admirable vigor and persistence. On this score he is original and, if I am not mistaken, a part of his work will remain unshaken. For the first time a man has examined what *science* is . . . by looking at the existing and operating sciences . . . ; from which it follows that he said, not what science could or should be, but what it actually *is*.

Comte's lasting merit consisted in having been the first to sketch a theory of the sciences.[15] For the rest, Taine admired Charles Robin for having brought the light of his specialty to shine on philosophy and Littré for his philological writings and for restoring Comte's work to respectability.[16] None of this, especially in the light of his self-confessed ignorance of Comte's work until he was 37, gives warrant for attributing more than at most a minimal influence to Comte on Taine.

In the field of the history of science matters were different, for here Comte pioneered validly in practice as well as in theory; he can be said to have "constituted" this discipline, in a manner of speaking, as well as "instituting" it, inspired by the teleology of the Law of the Three Stages as well as by that of the Classifica-

[14] Taine, *Philosophes classiques,* pp. vii–ix, *Le positivisme anglais: Etude sur Stuart Mill* (Paris, etc., 1864), pp. 3–5, 60–61, 111, 145.

[15] Taine in *Journal des débats,* 6 July 1864.

[16] *Ibid.,* and letter to Sainte-Beuve, 14 Aug. 1865, in his *Life and Letters* (tr. Devonshire and Sparvel-Bayly, New York and London, 1902–8), II, 267–268, in which, significantly, the only other reference to Positivism or Positivists is to Frederic Harrison as a communist (III, 56).

tion of the Sciences, which in a sense made of the progress of science the vital part of all past history.[17] Paul Tannery, the rejected candidate for the succession to Laffitte at the Collège de France [18] and the most eminent historian of science of his generation in France, wrote for a large public that Comte's *Cours* "will always remain a valuable document of the general state of scientific ideas at the time that it was written," but more than that, although the Law of the Three Stages and the Classification of the Sciences could not suffice to rescue Comte's work from obsoleteness, the progress of science since his day had superseded that work

only in details. Its *positive* character, its insistence on reducing to their true value the *a priori* conceptions which it could not dispense with, have become, in fact, increasingly apparent. The small success that the *Positive Philosophy* enjoyed in France is due in great part to the sectarian character given it by its author.[19]

But a decade later Tannery declared that Positivism had become a part of history and Comte's influence was comparable to Descartes', since it was possible to be a Positivist without knowing it

[17] It is in this more specific way, and not in the general and negative way suggested by Marvin (above, pp. 126–127), that Comte made his mark in the field of historical study, as Marvin elsewhere acknowledges: "The type of research, directly inspired by him, is rather into the history of science than into that of social habits and institutions" (*Comte*, p. 63, see also pp. 180–181). See further H. B. Acton, "Comte's Positivism and the Science of Society," *Philosophy*, XXVI (1951), 298, and above all H. Guerlac, "Rapport," in IXᵉ Congrès International des Sciences Historiques, *Rapports* (Paris, 1950), pp. 186–187, 192, who cites as coming under Comte's influence, in addition to Tannery, Sarton, and Brunschvicg (discussed below), Boutroux, Meyerson, and Abel Rey (see above, pp. 103 n. 26, 106–107, and 120–122), Duhem, Mach, and Poincaré (see below, pp. 257–259 and 262), and Lalande and Milhaud (referred to in the Bibliographical Appendix).

[18] Cf. above, p. 87.

[19] *Mémoires scientifiques*, XVII, 375–376 (reprinted from Lavisse and Rambaud, *Histoire générale*, Vol. X [1893]).

merely by clinging to the concept of "positive knowledge." [20]

Tannery himself was quite early "pretty soaked in Comtian positivism," having no head for metaphysics.[21] In retrospect he recalled:

In my youth it so happened that I took part in the diffusion of positivist ideas . . . during the time when this movement, I believe, was at its most active. At that time positivism was in the truest sense a contemporary doctrine,

provoking many controversies which ceased as it gained ground among the younger generation.[22] In 1900, it is true, he admitted not having read Comte for a long time and therefore not knowing which parts of his work might be obsolete,[23] but nevertheless in the same year he wrote:

Only one attempt worth mentioning has hitherto been made at a historical synthesis of the sciences, that of Auguste Comte in the first volume of his *Leçons* [sic] *de philosophie positive*. But this one effort has at least yielded results of incontestable value which can serve as a point of departure for all work in the same direction and which are also of sufficient importance to deserve being emphasized in general histories.

The Classification of the Sciences and the Law of the Three Stages were both valid (with the exception that the latter did not really

[20] "Auguste Comte et l'histoire des sciences," *Revue générale des sciences pures et appliquées,* XVI (1905), 410.

[21] To Gustav Teichmüller, Sept. 1882, quoted by Sarton, "Paul, Jules, and Marie Tannery," p. 36 n. 5.

[22] "Comte et l'histoire des sciences," p. 410.

[23] To Gaston Milhaud, 10 Jan. 1900, in *Mémoires scientifiques,* XVI, 52, but cf. above, p. 131. The recipient of this letter wrote of Tannery in the same year: "I remember him . . . paying homage to the leader of positivism and to the services to philosophical thought formerly rendered by him, and then in a private conversation he told me that of all the influences exerted on him that of Comte had been the strongest, and that in particular his lively interest in the history of science derived from his reading of the *Cours*" (quoted *ibid.,* XVII, 30–31).

apply to pure mathematics).[24] Three years later, in his application for the chair at the Collège de France, he went out of his way to state that he had

never really adopted any philosophy besides Auguste Comte's, and that at age 22 [i.e., in 1865]; in fact it is his influence that gave rise to my work, whose object has been to verify and refine his ideas on the History of Science. Since then, however, Comtism itself has entered the domain of history.[25]

A little later still, having lost the appointment to the ex-Positivist Wyrouboff, he wrote to the press:

Clearly it is possible to do excellent specialized work in the history of science without bothering about positivist doctrine one way or the other. But when it is a question of *the general history of science* . . . one may have quite a different conception of it from Auguste Comte's, [but] seeing that this immortal thinker is the only one to have tried to reduce this history to laws, anyone who wishes to deal with it must be either for him or against him. Well, I am for him and with him, and against those who have attacked him as well as against those who have turned away from him, like Littré.[26]

His own conception of the history of science, Tannery wrote, was inspired by Comte's, which had guided him for thirty years, although he was the *only* historian of science who still credited the Law of the Three Stages.[27]

In a final article devoted specifically to Comte and published posthumously he said (having evidently reread Comte since 1900):

[24] "Revue générale: Histoire des mathématiques," *Revue de synthèse historique,* I (1900), 184–185.

[25] Letter of 29 April 1903, in *Mémoires scientifiques,* X, 134.

[26] Letter to *Le Radical,* 14 Feb. 1904, *ibid.,* X, 158; on the last rather surprising point see also his letter to Zeuthen, quoted by Sarton, "Paul, Jules, and Marie Tannery," p. 36.

[27] "De l'histoire générale des sciences," *Revue de synthèse historique,* VIII (1904), 15–16.

Comte was above all a simplifying and at the same time a powerfully systematizing mind. . . . [This] synthetic depiction of the mathematical, physical, and natural sciences . . . constitutes an invaluable document of the state of science and scientific ideas at the beginning of the 19th century.

But even by the standards of 1830 Comte had not been abreast of current work in mathematics and physics; it was in biology that he had continued to work after leaving the Ecole Polytechnique (1816) and made his greatest contribution. It was probable, Tannery thought, that there would never be another work so profound and so complete written by a single individual. The Classification, he now held, was of some provisional value, but it was *a priori* and not historical, it had the effect of limiting research, and it omitted medicine. The Law of the Three Stages was of some use as a formula, though, being among other things based on observation of only a single civilization, it did not fulfill the requirements of a law: it was not precise or universal and was inadequate for purposes of prediction. In the history of science it was necessary to consider political and economic as well as purely intellectual factors. Comte's basic fault, Tannery concluded, was that he was always trying to prove something [28] (or, we might say, that his contributions to the history of science were in Comte's mind chiefly contributions to his own system). It seems that in the last year of his life Tannery reviewed his own past dependence on Comte and decided that it had been too great.[29]

Less than ten years later, in 1913 in Belgium, George Sarton founded the journal *Isis,* which has been ever since the foremost international scholarly organ for the history of science. In his introduction Sarton wrote:

[28] "Auguste Comte et l'histoire des sciences," pp. 411–417.

[29] See also other almost entirely laudatory references to Comte in Tannery's *Mémoires scientifiques,* XI, 24–25, 76–77, 132, 166, XII, 177; and René Taton, "Paul Tannery (1843–1904)," *Revue d'histoire des sciences et de leurs applications,* VII (1954), 303–312.

One philosophical school in particular has contributed significantly to this resurgence [of the synthetic approach to science]: I mean the positivist school, represented in France by Auguste Comte and in England by Stuart Mill and Herbert Spencer [N.B.]. Our efforts are certainly a direct consequence of their activity.

But Positivism had been fruitful only since its narrow and dogmatic agnosticism had been mitigated by scientific progress, after the original school had died out. Nevertheless a reconciliation of the need for synthesis and the practical necessity of a division of labor was possible only in the manner suggested by Comte and practiced by him and his disciples, which was "to make of the study of scientific generalities one additional great specialty," namely, the history of science, of which Comte must be considered to have been the founder although (unlike Tannery) he had not really mastered the subject and had forced it into the rigid framework of the *Cours.* But he was one of the "great precursors of our discipline," and from the philosophical point of view, Sarton concluded, the task of *Isis* would be "to improve on [*refaire*] Comte's work on deeper and more solid scientific and historical foundations." [30] This was a considerable tribute.

After the war, Sarton recalled, he had been taken by Marvin to Chapel Street (this, of course, was after the reunification of English Positivism) where Marvin gave a "very moving" address on the Day of All the Dead (New Year's Eve), and Sarton himself also spoke. Thirty years later Sarton visited the rue Monsieur-le-Prince: "the place was dusty and dismal; yet, I bethought myself of the tragic heroism of the man who lived there and I communed with him. Every historian of science who happens to be in Paris should pay a visit to the Comtian shrine." [31] Yet despite what sounds almost like support for the doctrine of "subjective immor-

[30] "L'histoire de la science," *Isis,* I (1913), 4, 6–7, 9–10, 12, 42, 45. Cf. also below, p. 236, concerning Charles Singer.

[31] "Auguste Comte, Historian of Science: With a Short Digression on Clotilde de Vaux and Harriet Taylor," *Osiris,* X (1952), 357.

tality" Sarton wrote at the same time: "There is no doubt that Comte was crazy. . . . The prophet in him had killed the man of science. The less he knew the more he preached."[32] More important than these sentences, which refer to Comte's last years, was Sarton's view that, being neither a genuine historian nor a genuine scientist, Comte could not be a historian of science, although he had seen the need for such work. Sarton concluded: "Auguste Comte was a great man, one of the greatest of his time, even if he was crazy. He was a martyr to his own genius. We should respect him and be very grateful to him. He was one of the first men to popularize the history of science."[33]

Although, therefore, Sarton like Tannery became increasingly critical of Comte and ended by praising his qualities of character more than his intellectual achievement, Comte's influence on him at the outset of his own career, and through him on the whole organization of the history of science on an international professional scale, remains undiminished.[34] The latter can be seen, in France, in the work of a man like Léon Brunschvicg, who wrote that "the two great systems which raised the philosophical problems appropriate to the 19th century [were] Kantianism and positivism," and he saw Comte, indeed, as the heir of Kant in his view of the relations between the methods and results of science and his definition of mathematics as the model science.[35] On the

---

[32] *Ibid.,* pp. 345, 352; cf. his reference to "the religious aberrations of Comte's senility" ("Paul, Jules, and Marie Tannery," p. 40 n. 12). Most of the article, indeed, is devoted to a sarcastic discussion of Comte's Calendar (pp. 328–345, 351–354).

[33] "Auguste Comte, Historian of Science," pp. 352, 356, 357.

[34] See also the points of contact with Comte in Sarton's "The New Humanism," *Isis,* VI (1924), 2, 3, 9–11, 19, 21, but cf. p. 23 and Guerlac, "Rapport," p. 192.

[35] *Les étapes de la philosophie mathématique* (3rd ed., Paris, 1929), pp. 249, 283, see also p. 285, but these and other passages do not justify the extent to which Ducassé, "La pensée mathématique," p. 134 n. 3, and Mourélos, *Epistémologie,* pp. 201–202, use them to enroll Brunschvicg among the supporters of Positivism. Mourélos, pp. 193–194, 216 and *passim,* applies

other hand, Brunschvicg also saw Comte as a Romantic and as the creator of a "sectarian positivism" as distinct from "rational positivism" and criticized him on a number of scores,[36] but concluded that what was necessary was to proceed to the end of the path of positivism, which Comte had abandoned.[37] Recently an eminent French historian dedicated a book in the history of science to Comte on the hundredth anniversary of his death, paid tribute to his fruitfulness, and tried to explain away some of his shortcomings.[38]

Comte's influence on the historiography of science is not really dependent on such individual examples of direct debt; he had left his mark indelibly on the whole field by both precept and example, and through its earliest academic practitioners. The matter is rather less clear in the case of the discipline of sociology, both because the field mushroomed much more widely (so that there are many more people to consider) and because there were a number of possible sources of inspiration for the study of society conceived as a science. The eighteenth century was accustomed to the phrase "social physics," and in the more biologically minded nineteenth century the conception of society as an organism had considerable currency quite independent of Comte.[39] Nevertheless, at least in France, Comte was widely acknowledged as the

---

shoddy technique in attempting to do likewise for Gaston Bachelard; see, however, Bachelard's *Etude sur l'évolution d'un problème de physique* (Paris, 1928), pp. 56–57, 59, 67–68, 72, justifying Comte's interdicts against certain scientific research in terms of his correct understanding of scientific conditions at the time and particularly of the work of the mathematician Joseph Fourier.

[36] *Les âges de l'intelligence* (new ed., Paris, 1937), pp. 4–5, 7–8, and *Etapes*, pp. 306–307.

[37] *Ages de l'intelligence*, p. 9.

[38] Roland Mousnier, *Progrès scientifique et technique au xviiie siècle* (Paris, 1958), Dedication and pp. 19, 327–328, 386–388. Professor Mousnier did not respond to an invitation to discuss his view of Comte in greater detail.—See, further, the Bibliographical Appendix.

[39] Cf. my article "Herbert Spencer and the 'Social Organism,'" *Journal of the History of Ideas,* XXI (1960), 294–299.

"founder of sociology" even by many who owed nothing to him either in methods or in conclusions (and who often, in all probability, had not read him). But such a generalized obeisance is not enough for our purposes. In order to come within the orbit of genuine "influence" a sociologist would have to exhibit some specific marks: at least some agreement with Comte as to *why* sociology was to be regarded as a science (some version, however attenuated or modified, of the Classification of the Sciences) and as to its primarily predictive and reconstructive purposes. The latter should be in a form which gives, or which is accompanied by, some evidence that such views actually stem directly or indirectly from an acquaintance with Comte's doctrine. Adoption of Comte's own predictions and prescriptions is, of course, not required, although it constitutes strong supporting evidence.[40]

[40] For estimates of Comte's influence in sociology, see, on the affirmative side, Marvin, *Comte,* esp. pp. 178–180; Wyrouboff in *P.P.,* XXIV (1880), 318–319; Roberty, "Sociologie & psychologie . . . ," *Annales* de l'Institut International de Sociologie, X (1904), 100; Barth, *Philosophie der Geschichte,* I, 58–59, 166, 194 (whose analysis of divergent streams is somewhat similar to Roberty's); Charles Gide, *Principes d'économie politique* (Paris, 1884), p. 11 (qualified, and deleted altogether by the 10th ed., Paris, 1906); Millet, *La souveraineté d'après Auguste Comte,* pp. 219–220, 222 (qualified); Y. Fink, *Etude critique de la notion de la loi chez Comte et de son influence* (Paris, 1907), pp. 29, 30, 35, 68, 70 (qualified); Cresson, *Courants,* II, 177–181; Hans Freyer, *Soziologie als Wirklichkeitswissenschaft* . . . (Leipzig and Berlin, 1930), pp. 116–122 (Positivism as one of the philosophies of history from which sociology developed); R. H. Soltau, *French Political Thought in the 19th Century* (New York, 1959, first pub. 1931), pp. 214–215; Georges Davy, *Sociologues d'hier et d'aujourd'hui* (Paris, 1931), p. 2 (Saint-Simon and Comte as the sources of one of two streams); George A. Lundberg, "Contemporary Positivism in Sociology," *American Sociological Review,* IV (1939), 43–46 (very qualified and applying mainly to the U.S.); Berlin, *Historical Inevitability,* pp. 3–4. On economics specifically, see Roger Mauduit, *Auguste Comte et la science économique* (Paris, 1929), pp. 244–256. For negative estimates, see Waentig, *Auguste Comte,* pp. 180–211 (though with some concessions); Delvolvé, *Réflexions,* pp. 283–284; Raymond Aron, *German Sociology* (tr. Bottomore,

The first teaching position in sociology in France, like the first chair of the history of science, was inaugurated by a follower of Comte, though not as in the case of Laffitte an orthodox disciple. Emile Durkheim was appointed to lecture on sociology at Bordeaux in 1887 at the age of 29, and systematic cultivation of the discipline dates from then and grew rapidly. Of course study of the subject had preceded Durkheim (for that matter it had preceded Comte), but only scattered and for the most part vague examples of study of it in any manner that can be related to Comte can be found before the time of Durkheim's appointment.[41]

One school of sociologists, though not constituting in general an exception to this rule, nevertheless requires rather special attention and treatment: Comte's intellectual cousins the Saint-Simonians, the followers of the man with whom Comte had broken, to whom he denied any influence on himself, whom he later called, in his graceful fashion, "a depraved charlatan," [42] but in whose footsteps he in fact followed quite remarkably. If the Saint-Simonians, as Comte also said, proved to be merely "an ephemeral sect," [43] nobody turned this circumstance to better account than Comte, to whom it left a clear field in organizing "scientific religion." [44]

Melbourne, etc., 1957), pp. 121–122, *War and Industrial Society* (tr. Bottomore, London, 1958), p. 41, but cf. p. 16 (an Auguste Comte Memorial Lecture: "It seemed to me that there could be no worthier tribute to the memory of a great man than a consideration of one of his mistakes," p. 3).

[41] Cf. Parodi, *Philosophie contemporaine*, pp. 119–120, 122 *et seq*. Note that Alexis Bertrand, who a little later was so active on behalf of Positivist educational ideas, gave a "municipal" course in sociology as early as 1892; see his *Cours municipal de sociologie: Leçon d'ouverture* (Lyon, 1892), in which he said, among other tributes, that Comte had provided the "discourse on method" of the discipline (p. 26).

[42] *Polity*, III, xviii.

[43] *Ibid*.

[44] Cf. G. D. H. Cole, Preface to G. G. Iggers, ed. and tr., *The Doctrine of Saint-Simon: An Exposition. First Year, 1828–1829* (Boston, 1958), pp. vii–viii: "The Positivist and the Saint-Simonians were . . . rival schools despite their common origins; and the practical dissolution of the Saint-

The cleavage between Comte and Saint-Simon, insofar as it was not simply in Comte's mind, was fundamentally chronological in nature. In 1824–1825 Comte was not yet ready to design a religion, though in his essay on the "Spiritual Power" of 1825–1826 he gave clear notice of his intention of ultimately doing so. Nor was he yet in any position to form a school and to gather disciples. Saint-Simon, near the end of his life, sought to crown his career with a design for a "New Christianity" and had assembled the group of disciples and successors from which Comte himself seceded precisely for the reason that its purpose and nature were religious in the absence of the necessary scientific substructure. Nevertheless he did not allow his declaration of independence from Saint-Simon to deter him from contributing to the Saint-Simonian journal, the *Producteur,* over a year later.[45]

Not surprisingly the Saint-Simonians, though not themselves yet at the apogee of their mysticism, in turn tended to see Comte as an eighteenth-century skeptic and to reject the antagonism between religion and science that they saw in the Law of the Three Stages. Politically, also, Comte was for them too reluctant to jump to conclusions, the proper conclusion being the desirability of the technocratic state.[46] At any rate Comte's collaboration with the Saint-Simonians came to an abrupt end with his mental collapse [47] and never resumed. The Saint-Simonians for their part developed

Simonians after the 1840's left the road clear for Positivism and allowed Comte's debt [to Saint-Simon] to be largely forgotten." C. Bouglé and Elie Halévy in their Preface to the French edition (*Doctrine de Saint-Simon: Exposition, Première année, 1829* [Paris, 1924], p. 65) go even further in calling the Positivist movement "a dissident sect of the Saint-Simonian church" prospering on its ruins. I do not propose to ventilate here once more the vexed question of Saint-Simon's influence on Comte, having enough on my hands with the influence of Comte on others, and am content simply to register the two rival schools as similar. The classic treatments are Gouhier, *La jeunesse d'Auguste Comte,* methodologically a virtuoso performance, and Frank E. Manuel, *The New World of Henri Saint-Simon* (Cambridge, Mass., 1956).

[45] See Iggers, *Doctrine,* p. xxiv.   [46] *Ibid.,* pp. xxxii–xl.

[47] It is unnecessary to attribute this turn of events to a change of editor-

farther in a religious and mystical direction, and their intellectual spokesman, Bazard, inveighed against too rational, scientific, and "positive" an approach to human and social problems.[48] Henceforth the two schools moved along their separate lines, and very few disciples of Saint-Simon were converted to Positivism even when the Saint-Simonian leaders went completely off the rails.[49] Those who could not follow Enfantin to Ménilmontant were content to strike out for themselves, and in the case of such men as Buchez and Pierre Leroux made a considerable mark on the study of history and sociology without supplementing their Saint-Simonian upbringing with much or anything that could be attributed to Comte. It is, on the contrary, piquant to note that Leroux claimed to have influenced Comte through Clotilde de Vaux.[50]

ship of the *Producteur* (*ibid.*, p. 231 n.). Comte published nothing anywhere for over two years.

[48] *Ibid.*, pp. 41 n., 43, 49–50, 155, 222 n., 232–233, 235–237, 239–241, 266; see also n. 49 below.

[49] See the very telling testimony of Hippolyte Carnot, who in 1825 had been sent by Enfantin to attend Comte's lectures (Bouglé and Halévy, *Doctrine*, p. 8): Comte, "whatever judgment may be made of the ultimate value of his efforts, was one of the remarkable personalities of this century" whose work he, Carnot, had followed closely, but it did not occur to him to join the Positivists when he could no longer follow Père Enfantin (Carnot to Laffitte, 3 Aug. 1882, M-le-P). Gustave d'Eichthal, once a special intimate of Comte's, sent a copy of one of Comte's early works to Mill in 1828 and in the following year rejoined the Saint-Simonians (Comte to d'Eichthal, 1 May 1824, *Lettres à divers*, II, 40; Eugène d'Eichthal, ed. and tr., *John Stuart Mill: Correspondance inédite avec Gustave d'Eichthal* [*1828–1842—1864–1871*] [Paris, 1898], p. x, and G. d'Eichthal to Mill, 30 April 1830, *ibid.*, p. 141, on Comte *vs.* the Saint-Simonians).

[50] P. Félix Thomas, *Pierre Leroux* . . . (Paris, 1904), p. 177 n., and see further pp. 176–177, 186, 204–205; cf. also Deroisin, *Notes*, p. 122. On Buchez, see Flint, *Philosophy of History*, pp. 423–428; Barbara Patricia Petri, *The Historical Thought of P.-J.-B. Buchez* (Washington, 1958), pp. 37 n. 46, 46, 95; and Buchez's *Introduction à la science de l'histoire* (2nd ed., Paris, 1842), Vol. I *passim*.

Even at a later date, when the Saint-Simonians no longer existed as a school, their influence and that of their master may have been at work, by the side of Comte's, in the establishment of a scientific sociology.[51] This may well have been the case to a limited extent, for example, with Frédéric LePlay, who was subject more to Saint-Simonian than to Comtian indoctrination at the Ecole Polytechnique, but who, for the rest, was an orthodox Catholic and founded a rival school of sociology to Positivism, with emphasis on monographs, although he agreed with Comte on certain specific social measures.[52]

Very much in the category of a rival is also the famous social philosopher Proudhon, who, indeed, produced something resembling the Law of the Three Stages and may have owed to Comte some other conceptions on the relationship of society and the individual; but he also called Comte "the most pedantic of savants, the most shallow of all philosophers, the most insipid of Socialists, the most unbearable of all writers." [53] The scientific approach to

[51] In a sense the modern historiographical polemic in France about the relations between Saint-Simon and Comte may be regarded as in part a prolongation of the rivalry between the two schools. Thus I was told in Paris that both the historian of Saint-Simonism, Sébastien Charléty, and the sociologist Bouglé had at one time flirted with Positivism before reverting in a general way to being Saint-Simonians.

[52] LePlay, *La réforme sociale en France* . . . (3rd ed., Paris, 1867; first pub. 1864), I, 8, 11–13, 27, 57, 93, III, 505; cf. Leroy, *Histoire des idées sociales,* III, 280–281, and Madeleine Apchié, "Auguste Comte et le catholicisme social," *Archives de philosophie du droit et de sociologie juridique,* IV (1934), 223–224; also J. M. Robertson, *Buckle and His Critics* . . . (London, 1895), pp. 474–479, and Durkheim's criticism of LePlay referred to by Christian Chulliat, "LePlay et Durkheim: Essai de synthèse," in *Recueil d'études sociales publié à la mémoire de Frédéric LePlay* (Paris, 1956), pp. 15–16. Fink, *Etude critique,* pp. 90–91, finds Comtian influence on LePlay.

[53] The evidence concerning Proudhon is assembled by Henri de Lubac, *The Un-Marxian Socialist: A Study of Proudhon* (tr. Scantlebury, London, 1948), pp. 236–240.

society of the statistician Quetelet was parallel to rather than derived from Comte's.[54] I must demur to the categorical statement of the magisterial Emile Faguet that "there has never been a mind more soaked in Comtism than that of [Jean-Marie] Guyau. Guyau is the spiritual son of Auguste Comte," for although Guyau rejected traditional religion and ethics and tried to find new ones by social analysis, his conclusions and his specific method in no way resembled Comte's; a general negative influence there may have been.[55]

The first definite trace of Comte's influence (by the side of Spencer's) is to be found in Alfred Espinas, who was not deterred by his contempt for Comte's late religious construction from incorporating the notion of a socially induced altruism into an experimentally conducted sociology with the goal of prediction.[56] Then Comte's conception of social science, though not his practice of it, was praised in specific terms by an economist [57] (although Comte had slighted economics) and by a political scientist who related, interestingly, how as a youth he had asked himself why politicians never agreed, whereas scientists did, had concluded that it was because they did not use the scientific method, and had therefore determined to find out whether such a method could be applied to politics. In this quest he had turned to Comte's disciples and had been gratified to find that Comte stated very

[54] Ad. Quetelet, *Physique sociale* . . . (Brussels, etc., 1869), I, 97–98, 128–130, 149, II, 382, 384–385, 389–390; cf. F. A. Hayek, *The Counter-Revolution of Science* . . . (Glencoe, Ill., 1952), pp. 185–186.

[55] Faguet, "Comte et son siècle," *Revue bleue,* 4th series, VI (1896), 178; Guyau, *The Non-Religion of the Future* . . . (New York, 1897, first pub. 1887), esp. pp. 109–110, 365–366, *A Sketch of Morality Independent of Obligation or Sanction* (tr. Kapteyn, London, 1898; first pub. 1885), pp. 3–4 and *passim;* and cf. Benrubi, *Sources et courants,* II, 624–625.

[56] Espinas, *Des sociétés animales* (2nd ed., Paris, 1878), pp. 96–98, 108–109, 114–115, 149–153; cf. Benrubi, *Sources et courants,* I, 258–262.

[57] Paul Cauwès, *Cours d'économie politique* . . . (3rd ed., Paris, 1893; first pub. 1879), I, 19–20.

clearly that it could. But he had been put off by Comte's support of the *coup d'état* of 1851 and by the generally reactionary politics of his last years, which vitiated his doctrine, and had concluded that in the long run Comte, despite his brilliant beginnings, had ended by arousing more controversy than conviction. Comte had asked the right questions and shown how men should go about answering them; his mistake had been to try to answer them all himself.[58] Finally, a sociologist appeared who declared his ambition to be, as his title indicated, to reconcile Comte, Spinoza, and Descartes, Comte being the greatest philosopher of the nineteenth century by virtue of his combination of precision with generality.[59] Adolphe Coste produced something resembling the belief in "subjective immortality," consciously followed Comte and Littré, with reservations, on the spiritual power, in general praised Comte's and especially Littré's sociological method, defended Comte's Classification against Spencer's, and adapted the Law of the Three Stages. Despite some criticisms of detail, here is a clear case of Comtian influence in sociology, the only one to have for the most part preceded Durkheim's appointment.[60]

It was Durkheim who not only instituted sociology as a regular part of academic studies, but instituted it in a direct descent from Comte.[61] This is not to say that Comte's was the only or even necessarily the dominant influence on Durkheim: that of his own

[58] Léon Donnat, *La politique expérimentale* (2nd revised ed., Paris, 1891; first pub. 1885), pp. 2–4, 323–329.

[59] Adolphe Coste, *Dieu et l'âme: Essai d'idéalisme expérimental* (2nd ed., Paris, 1903; first pub. 1880), p. 106, but cf. p. 105; René Worms in the Preface, *ibid.*, pp. vii, xii–xiii; see also Wyrouboff's review of the first ed. in *P.P.*, XXIV (1880), 318–319.

[60] Coste, *Dieu et l'âme*, pp. 144–145, *Les conditions sociales du bonheur et de la force* (3rd ed., Paris, 1885; first pub. 1879), pp. 196–200, 204–205, 224–227, 249, *Les principes d'une sociologie objective* (Paris, 1889), pp. 2–4, 28, 37, 39–70, 77–95, 129–130, 191–192, 226.

[61] On Durkheim and Comte, see the Positivist Oscar d'Araujo in *R.O.*, n.s. XX (1899), 305–310; Fink, *Etude critique*, pp. 102, 114, 116; Barth, *Philosophie der Geschichte*, I, 289, 296; Roger Lacombe, *La méthode*

teacher, Emile Boutroux, and the neocriticist tradition from which he derived—which, however, in turn, had certain affinities with Positivism [62]—quite naturally weighed heavily in the balance; but Durkheim regarded Comte as both more and less than the founder

sociologique de Durkheim . . . (Paris, 1926), pp. 4, 9–12, 16–17, 51; G. L. Duprat, "Auguste Comte et Emile Durkheim." *Sozialwissenschaftliche Bausteine,* IV (1932), 109–140; Delvolvé, *Réflexions,* pp. 297–304; Ross, *Kritik,* pp. 258–259, 268, 273; George Simpson, Introduction to Durkheim's *On the Division of Labor in Society* (tr. Simpson, New York, 1933), pp. xxix, xxxi–xxxii; G. E. G. Catlin, Introduction to Durkheim's *The Rules of Sociological Method* (tr. Solovay and Mueller, Chicago, 1938), pp. xxix–xxx; René Hubert, "Essai sur l'histoire des origines et des progrès de la sociologie en France," *Revue de l'histoire de la philosophie et d'histoire générale de la civilisation,* n.s. VI (1938), 300–303; Talcott Parsons, *The Structure of Social Action* . . . (Glencoe, Ill., 1949), p. 307; C. Bouglé, Preface to Durkheim's *Sociology and Philosophy* (Glencoe, Ill., 1953), p. xxxv; Georges Davy, "L'explication sociologique et le recours à l'histoire d'après Comte, Mill et Durkheim," *Revue de métaphysique et de morale,* Vol. 54 (1949), pp. 330–331, 333, 353, and Introduction to Durkheim's *Professional Ethics and Civic Morals* (tr. Brookfield, London, 1957), pp. xxxi, xxxiv, xxxvi; Robert A. Nisbet, "Conservatism and Sociology," *American Journal of Sociology,* Vol. 58 (1952–53), pp. 172–175; Ranulf, "Methods of Sociology," pp. 109, 115; Henri Peyre, Foreword to Durkheim's *Montesquieu and Rousseau* . . . (Ann Arbor, Mich., 1960), pp. ix–x—all predominantly affirmative. See also Bréhier, *Histoire de la philosophie,* pp. 1128–1132; Simon Deploige, *Le conflit de la morale et de la sociologie* (Louvain, etc., 1911), pp. 127–139, 150–151; F. Pécaut, "Auguste Comte et Durkheim," *Revue de métaphysique et de morale,* XXVIII (1921), 639–655; Léon Brunschvicg, *Le progrès de la conscience dans la philosophie occidentale* (Paris, 1927), II, 563; Benrubi, *Sources et courants,* I, 153–160; Harry Alpert, *Emile Durkheim and His Sociology* (New York, 1939), pp. 15, 24–26; Alvin W. Gouldner, Introduction to Durkheim's *Socialism and Saint-Simon* (tr. Sattler, Yellow Springs, Ohio, 1958), pp. viii–xxv; John Rex, *Key Problems of Sociological Theory* (London, 1961), pp. 1, 8, 15–16, 99, 101—all giving a predominantly negative interpretation; and cf. Fouillée, *La science sociale contemporaine,* pp. ix–x, who wishes a plague on both houses. (Gouldner identifies Durkheim with Saint-Simon rather than with Comte.)

[62] See Bouglé, Preface to Durkheim's *Sociology and Philosophy,* p. xxxix; Alpert, *Emile Durkheim,* p. 24; and cf. above, pp. 101–103.

of the discipline which he himself was now officially inaugurating. More, because—though by no means uncritical of him from the start—Durkheim began by endorsing Comte on such questions as the subject matter of the discipline and its method (derived, of course, from the Classification of the Sciences), and on even more specific topics like the social as distinct from the economic nature of the division of labor and on the nature of society itself, where he defended Comte against Spencer; [63] less, because he attributed the fundamental ideas constituting the science of sociology to Saint-Simon.[64] But Durkheim's thought underwent a certain amount of change: he tended increasingly to distance himself from Comte.[65] He began to repudiate "positivistic metaphysics" and to call himself a "rationalist" rather than a positivist, and his fundamental work, *The Rules of Sociological Method* (first published in 1895), was almost consistently critical of Comte.[66] Never-

[63] See Durkheim, "Faculté de Bordeaux: Cours de science sociale, leçon d'ouverture," *Revue internationale de l'enseignement,* XV (1888), 30–31, and cf. criticisms, pp. 32–35; *Division of Labor,* esp. p. 62, also pp. 123, 251, 262 n., 278, 294, 356–359, 371–372, and cf. criticisms pp. 331, 363–364. Cf. for another "scientific" approach to the teaching of sociology Léon Duguit, "Un séminaire de sociologie," *Revue internationale de sociologie,* I (1893), 201–208.

[64] See the very similar statements in his two articles, "La sociologie en France au xixe siècle," *Revue bleue,* 4th series, XIII (1900), 611–612, and "La sociologie," in *La science française* (Paris, 1915), I, 41–42; see also his posthumous pieces, "Saint-Simon, fondateur du positivisme et de la sociologie," *Revue philosophique,* Vol. 99 (1925), pp. 321–341, and "Critique de Saint-Simon et du saint-simonisme . . . ," *Revue de métaphysique et de morale,* XXXIII (1926), 433–434.

[65] This view of Durkheim is suggested by H. Stuart Hughes, *Consciousness and Society* . . . (New York, 1958), pp. 73, 75, 278–279, 282–286 (although I think he places the beginning of Durkheim's turning away from Comte a little too early). This explanation may be a way of reconciling the conflicting estimates of Comte's influence on Durkheim.

[66] He accused Comte of such various errors as studying society too subjectively, confusing individual societies with mankind as a whole and

theless Durkheim continued to recommend the *Cours* as the best possible initiation into the study of sociology, declared that recent French sociological studies as they had developed under his own direction "derive directly from Comte," [67] and insisted, like Comte, on aiming at practical results in his academic studies.[68]

The upshot seems to be to place Durkheim in a category similar to Tannery's and Sarton's. All of them were assailed by a growing skepticism with respect to important, even fundamental parts of Comte's teaching, a skepticism which did not, however, prevent any of them from continuing to pass on to others, in their systematization and organization of their discipline, the influence that Comte had exercised on them in their initial dedication to that discipline.

The man who, after and even more than Durkheim, was the organizing and administrative genius of French sociology was René Worms,[69] who was at the same time the leader of one of the two contending schools which descended from conflicting tendencies within Comte's own analysis of sociology. For Comte had seen social events on the one hand as a continuation of (though not deducible from) biological events and on the other hand as intellectual events. The latter interpretation, though always im-

---

origins with functions, trying to explain sociological phenomena in terms of psychological laws, and making of progress a metaphysical concept; the Law of the Three Stages was at best only empirically true, and Comte's use of it was arbitrary. Above all, he rejected Comte's "particular conception of sociological laws" as revealing "not definite relations of causality but the direction which human evolution in general takes," and which in turn had led Comte into the error of applying the historical method to sociology (pp. xl, 18–20, 77, 89–91, 98, 109, 119, 125–126).

[67] "La sociologie," pp. 42, 45.

[68] *Education and Sociology* (tr. Fox, Glencoe, Ill., 1956, first pub. 1903–11), pp. 23, 152.

[69] In addition to his teaching and his numerous books, Worms very early in his career founded the *Revue internationale de sociologie,* the Institut International de Sociologie, and the Société Sociologique de Paris.

plicit in the Law of the Three Stages, increasingly gained the upper hand in Comte the more he came to see the social as well as the biological bases of psychology.[70] Accordingly, one school of sociologists followed Comte in this development, emphasizing the psychological and intellectual factors in sociology, while the other remained faithful to his earlier doctrine and continued to stress the biological and material elements.[71] It was with this latter, so-called "organicist" school (because they expounded the "biological analogy" which made of society an "organism") that Worms identified himself. Indeed, he went farther than and against Comte in insisting not only that sociology should model itself on the neighboring science of biology but that there was really one method, the method of observation, for all the sciences; and his introductory manifesto to a new journal contained only one reference to Comte and that a somewhat perverse one.[72] But he insisted, with Comte and Durkheim and against attack, that sociology was distinguished from the other social sciences by being concerned with the totality of social facts,[73] adopted Comte's Classification of the Sciences,[74] used one of Comte's aphorisms (though misquoting another), and accepted a version of the Law of the Three Stages.[75] In fact, in contrast to Durkheim, he seemed to draw somewhat closer to Comte with the passing years, his later

[70] See above, pp. 122–123.

[71] This useful and illuminating distinction, now generally accepted, was early suggested by both Barth, *Philosophie der Geschichte,* I, 58–59, and Roberty, "Sociologie & psychologie," p. 100.

[72] "La sociologie," *Revue internationale de sociologie,* I (1893), 9–10, 12, 15. He quoted Comte on behalf of the potential practical usefulness of all science, while himself stressing the normative character of sociology.

[73] "Sur la définition de la sociologie," *ibid.,* p. 177, and *Organisme et société* (Paris, 1896), p. 12, where his "organicism" is of course also clearly stated.

[74] *Ibid.,* p. 5; cf. also "Sociologie," p. 13.

[75] *Annales* de l'Institut International de Sociologie, IV (1898), 48, V (1899), 52, XIV (1913), 361–362.

works containing more frequent references praising or agreeing with Comte as a sociologist.[76] This evolution may be attributable to the necessity in which Worms found himself of taking a definite position on the correct interpretation of Comte as this became a controversial question among sociologists. From the point of view of the diffusion of the doctrine, at any rate, whereas in a pioneer like Durkheim it was important that he was influenced by Comte at the outset of his career, in a second-generation scholar like Worms it may well have been more advantageous that he became increasingly sympathetic to Positivism as he himself gained in authority.

Among his contemporaries and near-contemporaries there was considerable evidence of the impact of Positivism on the nascent discipline. A sociologically minded alumnus of the Ecole Polytechnique gave high praise to the *Cours* but advised caution with the *Polity,* although he not only adopted the Three Stages and admired the Classification but also agreed on the necessity of a spiritual power conceived along Comtian lines and produced a psychology closely following Comte's.[77] A more strictly academic sociologist criticized Comte on the score of not applying his criteria for truth to his own work, and for the rest adopted some of Comte's

[76] See his *Philosophie des sciences sociales* (Paris, 1907–13), I, 12–13, 17, 132–133, 171, 210, 217, III, 193, *Les principes biologiques de l'évolution sociale* (Paris, 1910), pp. 7, 11, 13–14 (cf. also P. Grimanelli's review in *R.P.I.,* IX [1910], 114 and *passim*), *La sociologie: Sa nature, son contenu, ses attaches* (Paris, 1921), pp. 2, 7, 16–17, 22–23, 57, 116–118, 137; of course all these books also contain much criticism of Comte's doctrine. See also Fink, *Etude critique,* p. 85.

[77] Léopold Bresson, *Les trois évolutions: Intellectuelle, sociale, morale* (Paris, 1888), pp. ii–iv, vi–x, 3–5, 49–58, 79, 343–346, 351, 375–388, 432–433. See also his earlier works: *Idées modernes: Cosmologie—sociologie* (Paris, 1880), pp. 44, 71, 175, 183–185, 200, 323, *Les connaissances nécessaires* (Paris, 1884), pp. 12, 54, and, much earlier still, his article "Considérations positives sur la science sociale" in the Fourierist journal *La Phalange,* esp. V (1847), 540–544, VII (1848), 287, 293. I owe this last reference to Mr. John Laffey.

language of historical analysis while regarding the Law of the Three Stages as a great obstacle to sociological studies.[78] The columns of Worms's journal offered a sociology of aesthetics that in many respects followed Littré.[79]

[78] Maurice Hauriou, *La science sociale traditionnelle* (Paris, 1896), pp. 26–27, 94–95, 197, 208–209, 214, 253–255; cf. Barth, *Philosophie der Geschichte*, I, 176–183.

[79] Edmond Galabert, "Les fondements de l'esthétique scientifique," "Le rôle social de l'art," "L'évolution esthétique," *Revue internationale de sociologie*, VI (1898), 13–15, 578, 590, 597–600, 603, 742, and see more generally his "Le pouvoir spirituel," *ibid.*, VII (1899), 321–331. For Littréist attempts at aesthetics (i.e., to make something definite of the general proposition that art was social in origin and therefore "relative") see H. Stupuy, "La liberté au théâtre," *P.P.*, I (1867), 51–66 (complaining, incidentally, of the absence of Positivism among writers), and "Question d'esthétique," *ibid.*, XXII (1879), esp. p. 295; Pierre Pétroz, "Etudes sur l'art moderne," *ibid.*, VIII (1872), esp. pp. 467–468, and *ibid.*, XX (1878), 82 —all fairly weak. The orthodox school did better in producing a respectable work in aesthetics: Christian Cherfils, *L'esthétique positiviste . . .* (Paris, 1909). The rue Monsieur-le-Prince even disposed of a tame poet; see Jean Canora, *Scène lyrique en l'honneur d'Auguste Comte* (Paris, 1902), and his attempt to introduce Positivist aesthetics to the general public in "L'évolution actuelle du roman," *Echo bibliographique du boulevard*, 15 June 1910, pp. 10–12. There was another prominent professional aesthetician besides Galabert who believed in the possibility of making an exact science of aesthetics, but he held Comte's sociology of art up to ridicule and contended that Comte had never understood anything about art, either when he treated it objectively or when he regarded it as related almost entirely to the feelings: Charles Lalo, *L'art et la vie sociale* (Paris, 1921), pp. 2, 194, *L'art et la morale* (Paris, 1922), pp. 35, 37–39, but cf. pp. 160–161, where he seems to accept the Classification of the Sciences, and also his Introduction to an edition of the first part of the *Cours* (Comte, *Cours de philosophie positive* [1re et 2^e leçons], ed. with an Introduction by Lalo [Paris, n.d.]), which though hostile to Comte personally was more sympathetic to the system and to the "esprit positif" generally, and to the problems that he had raised; cf. Benrubi, *Sources et courants*, I, 189–193. As for music, Georges Bizet once affirmed his disgust with fashionable philosophy and his desire to be a Positivist, and asked a friend what he should read of Littré and Comte (in that order) with this end in mind, but it is not known whether he did read them or, if he did,

Altogether more considerable were the writings of the Belgian Guillaume de Greef, a member of the rival "psychosociological" school to Worms's "organicist" one but equally and, like Worms, increasingly indebted to Positivism. In his first fundamental work he declared that Comte had abandoned the scientific method, and he ridiculed the Law of the Three Stages and in fact was uniformly critical of Comte on almost every detail while allowing that he was a genius.[80] But subsequently de Greef endorsed the Law of the Three Stages as well as the Classification within limits and spoke in broadly Positivist terms about sociological method and the relation of philosophy to the other disciplines, and about Humanity and Order and Progress.[81] Of course he still found much to object to in Comte's system; indeed, he believed in principle that any "system" sooner or later becomes an obstacle to further progress in the discipline, but he thought that Comte's had been beneficent and testified that his philosophical view of sociology and its method was widely followed in Brussels, while still objecting that Comte had crossed the border from a necessary "vue d'ensemble" to metaphysics.[82] This was the criticism made in much sharper form by perhaps the most respected French sociologist after Durkheim, Gabriel Tarde, who wanted a strictly empirical and philosophically uncommitted study of individual social phenomena while allowing that Comte "had traced once and for all the major role of the accumulation and connection of knowledge

---

what he thought of them (Bizet, *Lettres à un ami 1865–1872* [ed. Galabert, 2nd ed., Paris, n.d.], pp. 150–153).

[80] *Introduction à la sociologie* (Brussels and Paris, 1886–89), I, 3, 8–9, 16, 30, 38, 41, 45, 92, 159–161, 218, 225–228.

[81] *Les lois sociologiques* (Brussels, 1891), pp. 1–10, 14, 16–17, 20–26, 31–32, 56–57, 61 and *passim*.

[82] *Problèmes de philosophie positive* . . . (Paris, 1900), pp. i–ii, viii, x, 36–38, 45–46, 48–49, 60, 103, 167, cf. pp. 97–98, 130, 134. See also his Preface to Hector Denis, *Discours philosophiques* (Paris, 1919), pp. iv, ix–xii, xvi, on Comte's "two phases" and on the Classification. On de Greef cf. also Barth, *Philosophie der Geschichte,* I, 71–77; Waentig, *Auguste Comte,* pp. 197–198.

. . . in the ascending march of civilization." [83] Another sociologist indulged in almost a paean of praise to "the supreme thinker" Comte for the Classification and for his work in all the "inferior" sciences but denied Positivism much value for either its method or its content in the field of sociology beyond the idea of the desirability of such a discipline.[84]

Among sociologists particularly, the Classification of the Sciences (perhaps in part because it was flattering to their discipline) and the philosophical relatedness of knowledge implied by it appears to have been that part of Positivist doctrine that exercised the most attraction, although they were unwilling to follow Comte into the dogmatic parts of his philosophy or, still less, of his sociology. Like the sympathetic representatives of other disciplines, they saw both the pedagogical and the intrinsic advantages in being able to relate their chosen field of study to others in principle without being willing to adopt a substantive interdisciplinary system in practice; and insofar as they saw the latter as an indispensable ingredient of Positivist doctrine they repudiated it. Comte as much as, and probably more than, most original thinkers possessed and suffered from the defects of his virtues. He could be different things to different men, yet to all of them some of his conceptions were alien and they kept intruding.[85]

---

[83] *Etudes de psychologie sociale* (Paris, 1898), pp. 6–7, 9, 16, 20, 282, 285 n., 303 n.; cf. also his *The Laws of Imitation* (tr. Parsons, New York, 1903) for scattered references and the Introduction by F. H. Giddings, pp. iv–v, and Benrubi, *Sources et courants,* I, 344–345.

[84] Eugenio Rignano, "La sociologie dans le Cours de philosophie positive d'Auguste Comte," *Revue internationale de sociologie,* X (1902), 242–250, 337–338, 342, 347–349, 351–353, 355.

[85] Cf. Millet, *La souveraineté,* pp. 222–223, who approves of Comte's social and political conclusions while criticizing many of his premises and methods.—Before leaving the subject of sociology, I would like to note, merely as a curio, Comte's use of the phrase "la trahison de l'intelligence" (*Appel aux conservateurs* [Paris, 1855], p. 132); unfortunately I can find no evidence that this was where Julien Benda got it.

Chapter VI

FRANCE: FREETHINKERS, CATHOLICS, AND OTHERS

MORE, even than the allegiance of academic sociologists Comte would have valued that of men in a position to put sociological analysis to practical use: statesmen and politicians. Here again Positivism could both attract and repel by virtue of its susceptibility to mutually exclusive interpretations. Comte himself became ultraconservative in politics and had always, of course, had strong authoritarian tendencies, and some of the orthodox, especially the most orthodox, disciples followed him here;[1] the creator of the short-lived "liberal Empire," too, paid a sort of tribute to Comte;[2]

---

[1] Comte's own encounters, face to face or in writing, with highly placed public persons were almost uniformly catastrophic. See in particular the recollections of Guizot, whom Comte had importuned when he was minister of education in 1832, *Mémoires pour servir à l'histoire de mon temps* (Paris, 1858–67), III, 126–127, VI, 350 and n. (the first passage is completely garbled in the translation of J. W. Cole, *Memoirs . . .* [London, 1858–61]).

[2] Emile Ollivier to Léon Saléta, 2 Feb. 1873, in his "Lettres d'exil, II," *Revue des deux mondes,* 1 July 1919, p. 52: "As for me, I am at the point where I was left by Auguste Comte after his lectures at the Palais Royal, which I followed with care. I believe that positivism has rendered great service to the human mind by introducing, in every field, the method of

but both Littré and Laffitte, and almost all Positivists of the next generation, were republicans of various degrees of radicalism, and it was here that Positivist influence was most felt. Littré, in particular, was very prominent in radical and secularist republican circles during the 1860's and 1870's and must be taken to have insinuated Positivist doctrines into them.[3] Most important, of course, was the claim made by Positivism on two leading statesmen of the early years of the Third Republic, Léon Gambetta and Jules Ferry.[4] Gambetta, the strong man who molded democratic institutions to his liking, represented in fact, with Danton, the ideal of a statesman among the republican Positivists.[5] That Gambetta read Comte (at the very least the *Cours*) and was acquainted with the Littréists there is no room for doubt. He was a personal friend of two of them, Charles Robin and André Lavertujon, and had close connections with Littré himself. One of the intermediaries

---

experiment and observation." But he was actually concerned to point out the absurdity of a positivist political "faith."

[3] See Dansette, *Histoire religieuse,* I, 425, II, 59–60, and, despite some exaggerations and queer formulations, John Eros, "The Positivist Generation of French Republicanism," *Sociological Review,* n.s. III (1955), 255–256, 271–273. Cf. scattered tributes to Positivism even from socialists: Laffitte to Comte, 20 Oct. 1850, printed in *R.O.,* n.s. XXXVI (1907), 97; Eugène Fournière, Introduction to Alfred Dubuisson, *"Positivisme intégral . . ."* (Paris, 1910), pp. ii, v–vii.

[4] See in general Eros, "Positivist Generation," pp. 260, 271, and see also above, pp. 84–85.

[5] On Gambetta and Positivism, cf. *ibid.,* p. 261; his friend Eugène Spuller to Robinet, 1 April 1883, printed in *R.P.I.,* III (1907), 370–371; Frank Herbert Brabant, *The Beginning of the Third Republic in France* . . . (London, 1940), p. 366; and among Positivists and semi-Positivists André Lavertujon, *Gambetta inconnu* (Paris, n.d.), pp. 100–102, 106, 116; Wyrouboff in *P.P.,* XXVI (1881), 154; Robinet, "Gambetta positiviste," *R.O.,* X (1883), 207 and *passim;* Corra, *Gambetta,* pp. 3, 46, and *passim;* but cf. Deluns-Montaud, "La philosophie de Gambetta," *Revue politique et parlementaire,* XI (1897), 241, 247–248, 252, 265, whose argument seems to me to be weak.

was Eugène Spuller, a republican journalist with sympathies for Positivism, and all of them used to meet, in the last years of the Empire, at the salon of the writer Juliette Adam, wife of the radical politician Edmond Adam and herself a devotee of Littré. Gambetta also knew Laffitte.[6] He made three prominent references to Positivism in his speeches. In the first, at the height of his glory in 1871, he extolled the virtues of education and of science as the potential sources of France's regeneration and pointed to Comte, "one of the great thinkers of this century," for the role which science played in his educational scheme[7] (Gambetta appointed scientists to leading educational posts).[8] The second was at a banquet in honor of Littré in which, making all due allowances for flattery appropriate to the occasion, he made a pretty firm commitment:

My initiation to this rigorous and dependable method [i.e., the Positivist method] is not of recent date; . . . [it is] destined to render many services to the cause of science in general and of French civilization in particular. . . . We are honored to be the free and devoted servants of that doctrine which it is your [i.e., Littré's] mission to spread. . . . The day will certainly come when politics, restored to its true role, . . . will once again be what it should be, a moral science. . . . On that day your philosophy—and ours—will have triumphed.[9]

By 1880 Comte was no longer merely among the great thinkers of the century but the most powerful, and one whose ideas were penetrating everywhere.[10]

[6] C. de Freycinet, *Souvenirs 1848–1878* (Paris, 1912), p. 143; Corra, *Gambetta,* p. 45; Deluns-Montaud, "Philosophie de Gambetta," pp. 251–252; Eros, "Positivist Generation," pp. 267–269; Juliette Adam, *My Literary Life* (tr., New York, 1904), p. 127; cf. Aquarone, *Littré,* p. 168.

[7] Speech of 26 June 1871, in Bordeaux, in his *Discours et plaidoyers politiques* (ed. Reinach, Paris, 1881–1906), II, 20–26.

[8] Eros, "Positivist Generation," p. 272.

[9] Speech of 1873, printed in *P.P.,* X (1873), 304–305.

[10] Speech to the Association Polytechnique, 12 Dec. 1880, quoted by Wyrouboff in *P.P.,* XXVI (1881), 151–152. See further his statement, "We

Jules Ferry, Gambetta's younger associate and in some respects his successor, was also drawn by a mutual friend into Littré's circle, very early made admiring references to Positivism, and announced, in a famous dictum that echoed Comte: "My aim is to organize mankind without God and without kings." [11] He declared that from the day in which he read Comte's *General View* he had known that there was "a social art, distinct both from the bloodless [*impassible*] observation of the economists, satisfied with mere description and committed to fatalism, and the irrational and harmful utopianism of most of the socialist schools." Comte had found the proper mean between these two extremes in historical and social analysis and had, in particular, arrived at a correct diagnosis of the relationship of capital and labor.[12] Once the Third Republic was securely established, no later republican politicians were so intimately concerned as Gambetta and Ferry with finding philosophical support and justification for radicalism, though words and deeds of sympathy for Positivism were still occasionally to be found.[13]

---

propose to apply positivism to the field of politics," quoted by Dansette, *Histoire religieuse,* II, 61.

[11] Eros, "Positivist Generation," pp. 262, 274 n. 9, taken from Maurice Reclus, *Jules Ferry, 1832–1893* (Paris, 1947), pp. 116–117; *R.P.I.,* [XVII] (1914), 175–177; quoted by Jean Jaurès, *Discours parlementaires,* I (Paris, 1904), 29.

[12] Ferry, "Marcel Roulleaux," *P.P.,* I (1867), 297–298. (Roulleaux had been one of Ferry's links with the Littréists.)

[13] See, concerning Léon Bourgeois, J. E. S. Hayward, "The Official Social Philosophy of the French Third Republic: Léon Bourgeois and Solidarism," *International Review of Social History,* VI (1961), 22, 26, 29; Ant. Ritti in *R.O.,* n.s. II (1890), 126–127; Hillemand, *ibid.,* IV (1891), 268–274; and above, p. 86. See, concerning General André (minister of war), Corra in *R.P.I.,* [XIV] (1913), 291; concerning Waldeck-Rousseau, his letter to Hillemand quoted in the latter's *Vie et oeuvre de Comte et de Laffitte,* p. 72; the speech of the under-secretary of state at the ministry of fine arts, Dujardin-Beaumetz, in *R.O.,* n.s. XXXII (1905), 221; material connected with the classification of Comte's house as a national monument in *R.P.I.,* 1928, p. 299, 1929, pp. 61, 129–131, 191–192. (The under-

Meanwhile it is to be noted that one thread connecting the early republicans, particularly Ferry, with Positivism ran through Freemasonry and Littré's membership in that society,[14] and some Positivist doctrines were endorsed in other secularist and free-thinking circles, though often only with considerable caution.[15]

---

secretary of state responsible for the classification, André François-Poncet, was a friend of the family of the Positivist Gaston Prunières.) Georges Clemenceau, though a medical student under Charles Robin, was notably silent and even hostile to Positivism: he translated Mill's *Auguste Comte and Positivism* without comment, and his doctoral thesis, with an introduction by Robin, contains no noticeable debt to the latter's Positivist doctrines (*De la génération des éléments anatomiques,* Paris, 1867); cf. H. M. Hyndman, *Clemenceau, the Man and His Time* (London, 1919), pp. 25–26. S. I. Applebaum, *Clemenceau: Thinker and Writer* (New York, 1948), pp. 15–17, illustrates the dangerousness of a little knowledge.

[14] On a Masonic occasion in honor of Littré, Ferry referred to "the official entry of Positivism, in the person of one of its most illustrious representatives, into the ranks of Masonry," adding that this event was long overdue since there was "an intimate and secret affinity between Masonry and Positivism" and "Masonry had long been Positivist without knowing it" (Loge Française et Ecossaise de la Clémente Amitié, *Fête anniversaire de la réception du F∴ Littré* [Paris, 1876], pp. 89–90, also p. 98). On Ferry's connections with both the Masons and the Positivists, see also Reclus, *Ferry,* pp. 118–119, and [J.] Caubet, "Chronique," *Monde maçonnique,* XVII (1876), 153. On Positivism and Freemasonry generally, see Gruber, *Positivismus,* pp. 32–41 (of course hostile); Mildred J. Headings, *French Freemasonry under the Third Republic* (Baltimore, 1949), pp. 41–45; Léon Emery, "De Comte à Marx," *Le contrat social,* I (1957), 147 (in Masonry, Positivism may have survived more than commonly thought "in an innocuous, adulterated, diffuse form; what has survived has . . . gone into the public domain, merged in the anonymity of everyday thought"). Wyrouboff and at least one other prominent Littréist were also Masons: see Wyrouboff's Preface to Caubet, *Souvenirs (1860–1889)* (Paris, 1893); Emile Rigolage, "L'enseignement social," *R.O.,* n.s. XIX (1899), 370–380 (a speech to a Masonic meeting), and his opening of a lodge named "La philosophie positive," *ibid.,* XX (1899), 117–119. The Masonic dignitary Caubet, in turn, wrote occasional reviews for *P.P.*

[15] On Positivism and rationalist religion generally, see Raymond Aron, *The Opium of the Intellectuals* (tr. Kilmartin, New York, 1957), p. 279,

As late as 1935 a prominent freethinker proposed a reconciliation between rationalism and Positivism. He approved Comte's opposition to intellectual anarchy, his separation of religion from theology and his attempt to replace theology with scientific principles, and his emphasis on the importance of sentiment and of a ritual. Rationalism could in principle accept the spirit of the *Cours* and a religion of humanity based on science, love, and poetry. But on the other hand, Comte's particular religious construction was too much a *pastiche* of Roman Catholicism and too much directed against Protestantism, deism, and skepticism. Moreover, Comte had abandoned science in his "second phase." [16] These sentiments found a welcome among Positivists [17] but very little acceptance among a number of freethinking educators who answered a questionnaire on the subject,[18] and the Positivist movement was unable

and Caro, *Littré,* pp. 165–168. See, in particular, the freethinking journal *Morale indépendante,* published from 1865 to 1870 by two Masons, Massol and Caubet (with frequent friendly references to Littré and his journal, reprints from it, and original articles by Littréists, but frankly critical of Littréist views on ethics, liberty, and psychology though always preferring them to clerical views); G. Hubbard in *P.P.,* VIII (1872), 331; G. Persigout, "Le devoir des jeunesses laïques," *Annales de la jeunesse laïque,* IV (1905–6), 263, 296–298, 300, "Théorie des deux pouvoirs," *ibid.,* VI (1907–8), 85, 87, "Des 'pouvoirs spirituels' de Georges Guy-Grand," *ibid.,* VIII (1909–10), 179–180; the activities of a freethinking society in Lyon called "Le Chêne" in *R.O.,* n.s. XXIII (1901), 73; François Vermale, "L'enseignement intégral à Lyon," *ibid.,* XXIV (1901), 393–399, *ibid.,* XXVII (1904), 192; membership and activity of a number of Positivists in the Alliance des Savants et des Philanthropes, *ibid.,* 193–194; activity of Corra in the Union des Libres-Penseurs et des Libres-Croyants pour la Culture Morale, in *R.P.I.,* IX (1910), 371–373, 1925[1], pp. 101–105, but cf. Gabriel Séailles' letter to the Congrès de la Libre Pensée at Geneva in 1902, quoted by Hillemand in *Vie et oeuvre de Comte et de Laffitte,* p. 67.

[16] Albert Bayet, "Religion positiviste et rationalisme," *R.P.I.,* 1935, pp. 97–107; cf. also his *Histoire de France* (Paris, 1938), p. 298. (Bayet was secretary-general of the Union Rationaliste.)

[17] See G. Grimanelli and Hyard in *R.P.I.,* 1935, pp. 182–185.

[18] *Ibid.,* pp. 148–181. It is to be noted that two of the respondents (Alexandre Champeau and André Cresson, both secondary-school profes-

to rejuvenate itself significantly by accessions from that quarter.[19]

Evidently no cooperation on the English scale could be obtained in France by the twentieth century between organized Positivism and organized rationalism. Here again, Comte's doctrine suffered as well as profited from its eclecticism and the ambiguity of its appeal: thoroughgoing rationalists found Positivism in general giving too many hostages to traditional religion. On the other hand, the doctrine achieved a marked though very limited success within a group of militant Catholics despite the hostages it gave to scientific secularism. This was the Action Française group already mentioned, so that "Auguste Comte experienced the strange fate of being the inspirer both of the republican and of the monarchist party,"[20] for of course just as secularism went hand in hand with republicanism under the Third Republic, Catholicism was often coupled with monarchism, and the left and right wings of Positivism tended to represent opposite political and religious as well as doctrinal alignments. Thus, just as Littré and even Laffitte in cultivating Gambetta and accepting the republicanism of the Opportunists tacitly suppressed Comte's teaching concerning republican *dictatorship,* so the group of Comte's executors who agitated for Positivism within the Action Française glossed over his advocacy of *republican* dictatorship.

But the symmetry of political and religious alignment was certainly not complete. Just as, within Positivism, political orthodoxy was sometimes accompanied by marked religious skepticism, so within the otherwise aggressively Catholic Action Française no less a person than its leader combined reactionary political and social views with mere lip service to Catholic orthodoxy, and it was in fact this strange circumstance that made Charles Maurras accessible to Positivism, for he found it not only easy but useful to enlist Positivist help in the monarchist-corporatist cause and had no

sors of philosophy) were more sympathetic to Comte's second than to his first "phase."

[19] See the second questionnaire and answers, *ibid.,* 1936, pp. 3–28, 73–74.
[20] Dansette, *Histoire religieuse,* II, 566.

doctrinal scruples about accepting Comte's idea of a Religious League between believers of any sort, whether Catholic or Positivist, against the forces of anarchy and barbarism. He even did his Comtist colleagues the service of calling public attention to the activities of the committee of Comte's executors, praising them by comparison with the Laffittists. In general he said he knew of no man to whom the world ought to be more grateful than to Comte, and termed Comte's ethics and his logic a source of strength at a time of uncertainty and confusion even for those of his generation who could not subscribe to his entire system. He himself, Maurras said, had serious reservations about many of Comte's doctrines—including the Law of the Three Stages, the division between egoistic and altruistic instincts, and the degree of advancement of the science of sociology—but such doubts did not diminish the value of the doctrine as a whole, which in its general outlines stood firm. Comte had solved "the problem of positive reorganization" as to its essentials, but the value of his teaching above all others consisted in its providing a discipline, one which (he assured his colleagues) was compatible with Roman Catholicism. One had, admittedly, to penetrate through Comte's sometimes unfortunate choice of words to appreciate the merit of his ideas.[21] In fact, Maurras cared nothing about the scientific substructure of Comte's system, borrowing only those of Comte's political, social, and religious ideas that suited his purposes.[22]

[21] "Auguste Comte 15 janvier 1798–5 septembre 1857," *Minerva: Revue des lettres et des arts,* II (1902), 174–204 (also reprinted in his *L'avenir de l'intelligence* [2nd ed., Paris, 1918]). See further his endorsement of various of Comte's political and social ideas in his *Enquête sur la monarchie* (Paris, n.d.), pp. ciii, 108, 180 n. 1, 354 and nn. 1 and 3, 481.

[22] Cf., on Maurras and Positivism, Delvolvé, *Réflexions,* pp. 293–294; Michael Curtis, *Three against the Third Republic* . . . (Princeton, 1959), pp. 62–63, 69, 264; and Dimier (his colleague in the Action Française), *Vingt ans,* p. 18. Maurras himself stated (*Les princes des nuées* [Paris, n.d.], p. 59) that his political opinions had been derived originally from Renan, who had got them from Comte.

Actually Maurras and the specifically Comtist members of the Action Française had great difficulty in persuading any of their more orthodox Catholic colleagues to grasp the nettle of Comte's Religious League, however much his political ideas might be capable of being invoked in their cause. Although the Positivist Montesquiou held the "Auguste Comte chair" in the educational branch of the Action Française from which he dispensed Comte's religion as well as his politics, Positivism in fact never played more than a small part in the organization's activities.[23] But somewhat unexpected support came from an independent and genuinely Catholic conservative, the eminent literary critic Ferdinand Brunetière, who sought to show that Positivism had inevitably developed in a religious direction and to invoke it in its religious capacity in the Catholic cause. The history of Positivism demonstrated that

ethics could not be constituted, justified, or maintained independently of a religion; in the second place, that this religion, whatever it might be, could not be "natural" or "individual" but could only be "social" and based on an affirmation of the supernatural; and in the third place, but only *by the way,* that only Catholicism has historically corresponded to these needs, which are established and defined by science.

Brunetière went on to a discriminating evaluation of Comte, finding elements in all the stages of his teaching worthy of praise.[24] Comte himself was a "great philosopher . . . , so superior to the university men who affected to disdain him." [25]

At one time some Positivists also had hopes of the support of the Catholic Modernist Alfred Loisy, but were eventually disap-

[23] Dimier, *Vingt ans,* p. 18; on Montesquiou and his chair, see *ibid.,* pp. 95–98: it "made of our institute the organ of a sect, and the last of the refuges where Comte's doctrine was taught integrally." On Dimier's own view of Positivism, see *ibid.,* pp. 25–26. Cf. also *R.P.I.,* V (1908), 330–333.

[24] *Sur les chemins de la croyance. Première étape: L'utilisation du positivisme* (Paris, 1905), pp. xi, xiv–xvi, xxi–xxii, 19, 22–55, 129–182.

[25] *Honoré de Balzac* (tr. Sanderson, Philadelphia and London, 1906), p. 164.

pointed.[26] Thus, since Brunetière spoke for none but himself and since Maurras' irreligion did not represent the thinking of the Action Française, "right-wing" Positivism found far less support in Catholic conservative circles than "left-wing" Positvism found in freethinking circles,[27] and this despite the hard-pressed position of conservative Catholicism in the France of Waldeck-Rousseau and Combes.[28]

Brunetière thought he could discern in the novelist Balzac a mind sympathetic to Comte's "scientific" analysis of life and a common reaction against Romanticism, and a more recent critic also suggests that some of Balzac's reforming ideas on society and religion derive from Comte's early essays, although many of them, at least, could equally well have come from Saint-Simon, and Balzac mentions Saint-Simon but never Comte.[29] Potentially, of

[26] See Marcel Boll in *R.P.I.*, 1921[1], p. 87, and, of Loisy's writings, in particular his *La crise morale du temps présent et l'éducation humaine* (Paris, 1937), pp. viii–ix, 170, 197; but cf. Lubac, *Drama*, p. 102. More recently affinities with Comte have been claimed for Teilhard de Chardin, e.g., Manuel, *Prophets of Paris*, p. 281.

[27] See, however, favorable references by the Catholic journalist Le Guerdec, cited by Momenheim in *R.O.*, n.s. XI (1895), 152–155, and his comment, p. 151, also *ibid.*, XVII (1898), 127–138. For general comment on Positivism and Catholicism, see Benrubi, *Sources et courants*, I, 275–285, and particularly Ducassé, *Méthode et intuition*, pp. 562–563, 567, who thinks that, appearances to the contrary notwithstanding, Positivism has played a part in the changes that traditional organized religion has undergone.

[28] Compare the support offered to the Positivist Malcolm Quin in England by the Catholic Modernist George Tyrrell (Quin, *Memoirs of a Positivist* [London, 1924], p. 200; M. D. Petre, *Autobiography and Life of George Tyrrell* [London, 1912], II, 410–412). Quin thought that he and Tyrrell were converging on the same point from opposite directions. Orthodox English Catholicism, of course, had no need of Positivism; moreover there was no occasion there for a "throne-and-altar" alliance. On the other hand, its specifically anti-Protestant bias barred Comte's religious construction from any appeal to English Protestantism.

[29] Brunetière, *Balzac*, pp. 164, 197–199; Philippe Bertault, *Balzac et la religion* (Paris, 1942), pp. 409, 410, 412–416, 419. (I cannot find in Comte

course, belles-lettres would have provided the most rewarding of all propaganda outlets for Positivism, and Juliette Adam indeed declared: "The ideas of Auguste Comte and of Littré were influencing art [in the 1860's] in the most curious way. Altruism, association, synthesis, humanity, were everybody's watchwords and stock in trade." [30] Although she was scarcely an objective observer, being herself devoted to Littré,[31] it is nevertheless true that a certain number of literary figures were in varying degrees receptive to Positivist ideas. Prominent among them in the beginning were a number of other female writers, all enrolled by Littré: the Comtesse d'Agoult, who wrote under the pseudonym of Daniel Stern; [32]

---

the passage indicated on p. 413 as being similar to a passage of Balzac's.) On Balzac's Saint-Simonian connections and his silence concerning Comte, see also Bernard Guyon, *La pensée politique et sociale de Balzac* (Paris, 1947), pp. 315–329, 753–754. An even earlier literary derivation from Comte, Vigny's *Chatterton*, is suggested by D. O. Evans, "Alfred de Vigny and Positivism," *Romanic Review*, XXXV (1944), 288–295, but this seems speculative at best. (That Comte in his turn used a motto from Vigny's *Cinq mars* is not in dispute, *ibid.*, p. 296.)

[30] *My Literary Life*, p. 365.

[31] Of the influence of Positivism on her own life, she wrote that her first husband, Lamessine, had been a Positivist. "I was scarcely married before he began to fall upon me with his doctrines. . . . I listened, for a time, to these imposing affirmations, but finally they exasperated me to such a degree that I plunged headlong into the reading of Auguste Comte's very ponderous and very numerous volumes." (This was in 1855.) She objected equally to Comte's style and to his politics, as well as to the dogmatism of his orthodox disciples. Although her husband spoke enthusiastically of Clotilde de Vaux, "I took Positivism in utter abhorrence at that time." Eventually her husband's Positivist orthodoxy contributed to breaking up her marriage (*ibid.*, pp. 4–11, 289).

[32] Jacques Vier, *La comtesse d'Agoult et son temps: Avec des documents inédits* (Paris, 1955–61), II, 206, 228, 238, 242, 300 n. 24, 301 nn. 57 and 63, III, 168–170, 182–184, IV, 53; Suzanne Gugenheim, *Madame d'Agoult et la pensée européenne de son époque* (Florence, 1937), pp. 47, 133, 146–147; Fleuriot de Langle, ed., "Deux lettres de Littré," p. 501. Her well-known *Histoire de la révolution de 1848* (Paris, 1850–51), however, yields negative results in this respect.

George Sand;[33] and at a somewhat later time and in a very loose sense Louise Ackermann, who drew on any philosophy, including Comte's, which would undermine Faith in the name of Science.[34]

In addition to Balzac, Brunetière also mentions a fellow literary critic, Sainte-Beuve, in connection with Positivism.[35] Sainte-Beuve was, to be sure, a friend and admirer of Littré, but despite rather than because of his allegiance to Positivism and especially in connection with Littré's painful quarrel with Bishop Dupanloup arising out of the latter's campaign against Littré's election to the Académie Française. Littré, Sainte-Beuve wrote to a friend, suffered from a "lack of subtlety" (*manque de nuances*) which manifested itself in "that intellectual faith, which strikes me sometimes as a sort of superstition and credulity, in a system which does not appear to me necessarily to be identified with that obscure,

---

[33] See her letter to Littré printed by Aquarone, *Littré,* p. 191.

[34] Of her works see above all her poem "Le positivisme," *Oeuvres* (Paris, n.d.), pp. 91–92, also "De la lumière," pp. 136–137; cf. E. Caro, "La poésie philosophique dans les nouvelles écoles: Un poète positiviste," *Revue des deux mondes,* 15 May 1874, pp. 248, 261; Comte d' Haussonville, "Mme. Ackermann d'après des lettres et des papiers inédits," *ibid.,* Vol. 108 (1891), p. 336; Marc Citoleux, *La poésie philosophique au xixe siècle: Mme. Ackermann, d'après de nombreux documents inédits* (Paris, 1906), pp. 13, 101–106, 110–112, 167, 172–174; and Charlton, *Positivist Thought,* chap. viii, into whose definition of positivism she fits very well, as does Sully Prudhomme (chap. ix), but the latter fits into mine even less than Louise Ackermann. See the categorical statement of Clyde William Eichel, Jr., "Sully Prudhomme . . ." (Ph.D. thesis, Cornell University, 1954), p. 290, and the negative testimony of Camille Hémon, *La philosophie de M. Sully Prudhomme* (Paris, 1907), p. 42 and *passim,* and Sully Prudhomme, *Oeuvres: Prose, Testament poétique, Trois études sociologiques* (new ed., Paris, 1904), and *Journal intime: Lettres—pensées* (Paris, 1922); but cf. his letter (4 March 1898) accompanying his subscription to the fund for the Comte monument (*R.O.,* n.s. XX [1899], 320): "I regard Auguste Comte as a thinker of the first order. If his doctrine does not entirely satisfy all my aspirations, I nevertheless admire his genius." See in general the lists of subscribers, *ibid.,* XVII (1898), 464–466, XIX (1899), 141, 218, 311, 444, XX, 159, 314, 487, 495–496.

[35] *Balzac,* p. 284.

obstructed, and too often sick mind, Auguste Comte." [36] Much later, after Littré's death, Sainte-Beuve wrote publicly that Comte seemed to him to be "one of those men who since Lessing, Turgot, Condorcet, Saint-Simon, conceive of the progress of society and of the human understanding along a certain line which one can allow very generally but without pressing it too hard in its details." Comte himself had "considered that he had discovered the precise formula of this human development," which in fact, however, contained strange details compromising the value of the whole; Littré, on the contrary, had thought that the value of the whole more than made up for the defects of detail and had attached himself to Comte as a disciple, being led as a result "to press too hard in the application of certain laws which in a general sense are true." Sainte-Beuve concluded by admitting that an excess of order was perhaps a lesser evil than a lack of it.[37] In connection with this last remark it may be worth noting that Sainte-Beuve was a former Saint-Simonian.[38] At any rate this friendly notice of Littré, despite its reservations, was apt to throw Sainte-Beuve's prestige indirectly behind Littréist Positivism.

Another literary critic, this time a contemporary of Brunetière's, who was concerned with Positivism was Emile Faguet, whose praise was much more lavish. In two articles at the end of the century in journals of the widest circulation, this eminent national figure wrote what were virtually eulogies of Comte, "the great thinker too often unrecognized," and of his

great system, one of the strongest, best organized, and also most securely built on correct observations that has appeared not merely in modern times but in all history. The crucial observation that is its

[36] Letter to Henri Harrisse, 3 March 1867, quoted by André Billy in *Sainte-Beuve: Sa vie et son temps* (Paris, 1952), II, 268. Cf. the similar attitude to Littré of Renan, above, p. 97.

[37] "M. Littré," in his *Nouveaux lundis,* V (2nd ed., Paris, 1884), 234–236.

[38] On Sainte-Beuve, Littré, and the Saint-Simonians, see also Harold Nicolson, *Sainte-Beuve* (London, 1957), pp. 44–45, 258. On the effect of "positivism" in a very general sense on Sainte-Beuve's literary criticism, cf. Flint, *Philosophy of History,* pp. 621–622.

basis consists in having clearly seen the genuinely new and at the same time persistent tendency of human nature to attach to science the faith that it used to attach to mystery.

Comte's philosophy of history "is marvellous in its order, its clarity, even in its plausibility, and overflowing with ideas of detail which provide a feast for the mind." The trouble, Faguet added, was that as a whole it was questionable. In ethics, too, Comte had seen the problem but had not solved it successfully, and Faguet had in fact nothing but contempt and ridicule for Comte's religious construction. Nevertheless Comte had deserved the enormous influence that Faguet attributed to him: "No one has better traced the respective limits of science, philosophy, and religion. . . . No one has better defined the three essential tendencies of the human mind," although (a crucial reservation!) it was a mistake to translate these tendencies into historical periods. Faguet praised Comte's penetration, his intelligence, his impartiality, marred intellectually by his excessive optimism as well as emotionally by his pride and intransigence. All told, "he is the most powerful sower of ideas and stimulator of the intellect of our century and the greatest French thinker, in my opinion, since Descartes." Only anti-intellectualists, Faguet admonished in conclusion, should be against him.[39] In the second article, though it was much shorter, Faguet was in some respects more specific, particularly on Comte's influence which he held to be rising while Littré's was falling; in other words "positivism is languishing while Comtism prospers," a dictum which seems sarcastic in tone. But in general the article, which was in fact a review of Fouillée's book on Positivism,[40] defended Comte, particularly his psychology and his ethics, against Fouillée and pointed out that in his last years Comte had taken many of the steps that Fouillée was urging (but which Faguet himself deplored).[41] Some years later, however,

[39] "Auguste Comte," *Revue des deux mondes,* Vol. 130 (1895), pp. 296, 298–301, 548, 552–553, 557–559.

[40] Cf. above, pp. 103–105.

[41] "Comte et son siècle," pp. 177–181.

Faguet was markedly cooler toward Comte: only the "negative part" of his philosophy had endured and was "the *credo* or rather the *non-credo* of a fairly large number of minds." The Classification of the Sciences, with the Law of the Three Stages the "affirmative part" of Comte's ideas, "is generally considered by the learned as interesting but arbitrary." [42] Altogether the evidence of Faguet's writings is markedly unsatisfactory; I cannot rid myself of the suspicion that his commendation of Comte in his articles, though formal enough, had some ironical meaning or purpose, or else that they were in some way *pièces d'occasion* (which would not be out of character) written hastily. If Faguet was favorable to Positivism at all, it was to Littré's kind,[43] and his remark on the relative influence of "positivism" and "Comtism" remains puzzling. His attitude as a whole appears uncoordinated.

Much more easily disposed of is the case of Emile Zola, whose scientific realism came from Taine rather than from the Positivists, although he knew Littré and Wyrouboff and had at least met Laffitte.[44] The literary figure at the turn of the century who came into closest personal contact with the Positivists of the rue Monsieur-le-Prince was Anatole France, via his friendship with Laffitte. He declared himself to be, however, a stranger to the doctrine, to the extent, he added significantly, that it was possible "for any thinking person to be truly a stranger to positivism. Are not all cultivated minds today penetrated by the great ideas that Auguste Comte renewed or created and arranged in an order that adds strength to them?" Comte, declared Anatole France, was responsible for the destruction of metaphysics, for confidence in the scientific method, for the growth of instruction in the history of science and in the epochs of the human race, and for the idea of ethics

[42] *Initiation into Philosophy* (tr. Gordon, London, 1912), pp. 189–190.

[43] Scott, *Republican Ideas,* p. 105, sees Faguet as "for a quarter of a century the single most important exponent of Littré's ideas and the continuator of his method," but cf. p. 191.

[44] Ernest Alfred Vizetelly, *Emile Zola . . .* (London and New York, 1904), pp. 502–503, cf. p. 395.

founded on human solidarity. "Positivism has entered profoundly into the universal conscience, and there is not a free mind anywhere in the world who is not a debtor in some respect to the founder of your philosophy and to his first disciples." [45] The fact that this speech was made, as the pronoun "your" indicates, to a Positivist assembly—at Laffitte's funeral, in fact—cannot be considered as seriously diminishing its value as testimony to the extent of the vague and untraceable influence and penetration of Comte's ideas. Before other Positivist audiences but on less solemn occasions Anatole France gave a more balanced evaluation. He began with praise:

In inspiring yourselves to a just extent by positivism you have borrowed from western philosophy in the 19th century its most useful and most needed contribution to the human mind and human aspirations, at least at the time when that doctrine was conceived; you have embraced the noblest and most impartial thought of a great period of hope and restlessness, the generous idea which, more forcefully . . . than any other, attempted to reconcile science and feeling, the heart and the mind, reason and love. You have, finally, been pervaded by the philosophy most apt to excite ideas and to fertilize the mind.

He proposed, however, having said this much, to investigate the weak points of this system, "the vastest intellectual and moral machine of modern times," in order to demonstrate "the dead weight that immobilizes it." He himself, Anatole France declared, was no Positivist and never had been, and though a friend of Laffitte's he had never been tempted to become one. Among his reasons for this stand, he said, was a bad one: "I have not sufficient virtue to believe in and to profess the religion of humanity." He wanted the freedom to make mistakes and to indulge in fantasies. But, more specifically, he thought that Comte's doctrine gave aid and comfort to authoritarianism, and that the support claimed by the Action Française monarchists was all too plausible. Comte had

[45] *R.O.,* n.s. XXVII (1903), 181–182.

placed restrictions on research and had allowed no freedom of conscience in politics or ethics. He had subjected science to religion, and his religion, France said, echoing Huxley, was a Catholicism without God. The acceptable part of it, the homage paid to the dead, was practiced by every intelligent man anyway. As for the idea of the Virgin-Mother, this was "the strange inspiration of an ideal love in an overheated [*brûlant*] mind" and was rightly considered "the most incomprehensible of the mysteries of the positivist faith." Yet, he conceded, parthenogenesis had been shown to be possible with molluscs, and you never knew. In conclusion, Positivism contained many truths but did not contain "rigorous, scientific, and total truth," and this was fortunate since otherwise there would be no more freedom of opinion. He agreed, however, that no man had ever loved mankind in a fashion both so manly and so tender as Comte had done, and just as his work would rank among the great philosophical doctrines so "the beauty of his soul will serve as an eternal example to men. Without either believing in or desiring the triumph of positive philosophy in its doctrinal form, we all join its founder in his dream of concord, peace, and harmony." [46] Insofar as all this does not come down to the pious hope expressed in the last phrase, it is a vaguely Littréist version of Comte—vague in that it does not actually endorse any of Comte's teachings, Littréist in that it separates those teachings into two distinct parts and actively objects to the results of the second part. Indeed, Anatole France expressed his belief that the rue Monsieur-le-Prince had failed to take full advantage of the Positivist sympathies of Gambetta and Ferry and of the Dreyfus affair and had therefore left a clear field for the Littréists. [47]

[46] "Auguste Comte" and "Pierre Laffitte," in his *Oeuvres complètes illustrées,* XVII, 270–272, 279, 285–290, 310, 323–325 (lectures in South America in 1909). Cf. the negative emphasis of his earlier article in *Le Temps* (7 Feb. 1892), quoted by Laffitte in *R.O.,* n.s. VI (1892), 225.

[47] "Auguste Comte," pp. 273–275. Cf. also A. Armaingaud, "Anatole France à la recherche d'un idéal moral," reprinted from *Le Temps* of 24

Finally, a miscellaneous couple: a Lutheran who saw in Comte the antidote to Calvinist individualism and legalism, though, of course, criticizing Positivism for ignoring the supernatural and aiming to "complete" it in this direction,[48] and the journalist who wrote a sympathetic book about Comte's relationship with Clotilde de Vaux (without, however, glossing over Comte's carnal desires), in which he called him "the greatest philosopher of his day." [49]

All told, and making due allowance for sports of this nature, the impression is strong that the traceable influence of Positivism in France outside as well as within the universities was of a predominantly Littréist nature and often of Littréist origins. It was exercised, that is to say, on those who either were not interested in Comte as a person and were willing to take ideas which struck them favorably from anywhere and anyone or else shared Littré's charitable interpretation that Comte's "second phase" was unconnected with the "scientific" Positivism of the *Cours* and could be ignored. Those who could not accept this view tended for the most part to fight shy of Positivism altogether. But there were also cases, within and outside the universities, and they were important cases, of men who accepted something, at least, of Comte's specific political and religious construction, men who in one way or another, for one reason or another, still felt the need for "reorganization" which Comte's own post-Revolutionary generation had felt so strongly, men who, as even Anatole France said, thought that "Order and Progress" was "a maxim of the highest wisdom" and

March 1925 in *R.P.I.,* 1929, pp. 26–29, in which he says that A. France had repeatedly flirted with Positivism and frequently discussed it with him, but had never retained any Positivist convictions for long.

[48] Charles Gillouin, *Journal d'un chrétien philosophe (1915–1921)* (Paris, 1922), pp. 281–282 and cf. the Introduction by René Gillouin, p. xxxvii. C. Gillouin also wrote: "I think of Auguste Comte teaching astronomy to Parisian workmen. A good subject for study: 'the evangelical urge in Auguste Comte'" (p. 263).

[49] Maurice Wolff, *Le roman de Clotilde de Vaux et de Auguste Comte suivi d'un choix de leurs lettres et du roman* Wilhelmine (Paris, 1929), p. 3.

that Comte had indicated a way of putting it into practice. As for the Positivist penetration into the anonymous "thinking world" generally, to which men like Faguet and Anatole France referred, its predominantly Littréist nature is also implied in their testimony. But I would not want to accept that testimony completely. It does not, it seems to me, allow sufficiently for the multiplicity of possible sources of an antimetaphysical and scientific outlook. If, following good scientific method, one extrapolates from the known to the unknown, from the traceable cases of alleged Positivist influence to the anonymous, such reservations certainly suggest themselves.[50]

[50] Littré himself supplied what might be taken as a negative example, that of Marc Régis, from whose pen he published an article because it expressed ideas for the most part in conformity with Positivism though written without knowledge of it (see the editorial note, *P.P.*, XIX [1877], 378; cf. also *ibid.*, XXII [1879], 262 [Law of the Three Stages]).

Chapter VII

ENGLAND: THE AMBIANCE
OF JOHN STUART MILL

IT has occasionally been observed that Positivism achieved a greater measure of general diffusion in England than in France, or, alternatively, that it achieved success in France only after an interval and as a reimportation into France from England (and also from Germany) and that the name to be coupled with Littré's in this respect is that of John Stuart Mill.[1] Although Littré himself declined to be put in the same category as Mill philosophically and agonized over his defense of Comte against Mill, and although Mill, partly no doubt for temperamental reasons ultimately imponderable, for his part declined to be a "disciple" of Comte's even at the height of their friendship and agreement, it is true that Mill, for a while at least, played a role similar to Littré's in introducing Comte's *Cours* to the English public.

But although Mill had read one of Comte's early essays even before the *Cours* began to be published,[2] as to the *Cours* itself he did not quite have chronological priority, for the first public mention was in a favorable review article in 1838 by Sir David

[1] See, e.g., J. Martineau, *Types of Ethical Theory,* I, 398; Marcuse, *Geschichtsphilosophie Comtes,* pp. 20, 30.

[2] This was Comte's (first) *Système de politique positive,* written in 1822.

Brewster, the physicist, of the first two volumes, his attention having been called to them by another scientist, Sir Charles Wheatstone.[3] Mill first heard of the *Cours* at about the same time, and it was a nonconformist friend and pupil of his, William Smith, who wrote the first English notice of the complete *Cours,* markedly less favorable than Brewster's.[4]

[3] *Edinburgh Review,* Vol. 67 (1838), pp. 271–308. Brewster praised not only Comte's mathematics, astronomy, and physics, but also the Classification of the Sciences, the Law of the Three Stages, and his use of hypotheses. Incidentally, by implication he denied Wheatstone's claim to have been the first to bring these volumes to England; see also Mill to Comte, 27 Jan. 1845, in Lévy-Bruhl, ed., *Lettres,* p. 402, where he says that Neil Arnott, the scientist, knew and approved of them before he did. The situation should be compared with that in France, where the *Cours* received no notice whatsoever in the press until Littré's articles in the *National* in 1844 (Gouhier, *Vie,* p. 217).

[4] "Comte," *Blackwood's Edinburgh Magazine,* Vol. 53 (1843), pp. 397–414. The *Cours* was described as an "extreme, uncompromising, eccentric work," a strange mixture of "manifold blunder and great intellectual power." The historical survey was its "most remarkable" part, though guilty of a "singular negligence of the historical picture" redeemed by "traces of a deep penetration into the nature of man." Later periodical articles were also on the whole hostile: two by Henry Robert Reynolds in the *British Quarterly Review,* "Auguste Comte—His Religion and Philosophy," XIX (1854), 297–376, and "Auguste Comte, Life and Works," Vol. 44 (1866), pp. 59–89 (Reynolds was a Congregational minister); Anon., "Philosophy and Positivism," *London Quarterly Review,* XXXI (1868–69), 328–348, uniformly hostile; "Positivism . . . ," *North British Review,* Vol. 49 (1868), pp. 113–138, by one Henderson (hostile but sound); cf. also "The Worship of Humanity," *Spectator,* Vol. 55 (1882), pp. 9–11, scornful; and below, Chap. VIII, n. 44. The article "The Religion of Positivism," *Westminster Review,* n.s. XIII (1858), 305–350, is in a special category in that it is in two rather disparate parts, the first, by W. M. W. Call, descriptive and on the whole admiring with the exception of the politics, the second, by the editor, John Chapman, very critical, with the grudging concession that "the light which he kindled, such as it was, can never be put out." Call, who had forsaken Holy Orders, had earlier started on a translation of the *Cours* but abandoned it when informed of the one being undertaken by Harriet Martineau

Meanwhile Mill had written to his friend the Scottish philosopher Alexander Bain: "Have you ever looked into Comte's *Cours de Philosophie Positive?* He makes some mistakes, but on the whole, I think it very nearly the grandest work of the age." Bain forthwith read the work and subsequently discussed it with Mill in detail, agreeing that it was in general sound though wrong in specialized details. They admired the Law of the Three Stages, the Classification, the distinction between social statics and dynamics, and especially Comte's interpretation of history, though with reservations particularly concerning English and Protestant history. To Comte, Mill described Bain as a recruit of the first importance "for our common philosophy." Indeed, Bain did some recruiting himself among his circle of friends in Aberdeen, with whom he studied Comte, and read a paper to the local Philosophical Society on the classification of the sciences in which he introduced psychology into Comte's hierarchy.[5] Nevertheless it

---

(see below, pp. 213–215). It is stated that Comte "had at one time an almost tyrannous influence over him," but he eventually settled for agnosticism: Walter Lloyd, "Theological Evolution: W. M. W. Call," *Westminster Review,* Vol. 136 (1891), pp. 37, 40–41, 44; Call, *Final Causes: A Refutation* (London, 1891), pp. viii–ix, xlv–xlvi, 160; and cf. Congreve's Circular for 1891, *Essays,* II, 899.—I owe the identification of the authors of anonymous articles to the kindness of Prof. Walter Houghton of the Wellesley Index to Victorian Periodicals.

[5] For this account, see Bain, *John Stuart Mill . . .* (London, 1882), pp. 70–72, *Autobiography* (London, etc., 1904), pp. 112, 145, 153, 157–158, 223–225, closely followed by Anna Theresa Kitchel, *George Lewes and George Eliot . . .* (New York, 1933). Bain's study group included John Duguid Milne, George Walker, John Christie, David Mackinnon, and Alexander and John Cruickshank, the first two of whom went on to investigate Comte thoroughly; Milne even corresponded with Comte and received his circulars. Bain said in the prefatory notice to his *Astronomy* (London, 1848) that in arranging his material he had followed Comte's suggestions in his own astronomical writings; see also Mill to Comte, 26 April 1845, Lévy-Bruhl, ed., *Lettres,* p. 416. In 1851 Bain met Comte in Paris but was repelled by his political utopianism and his humorlessness (while he found Littré interest-

was mainly through Mill directly that the *Cours* received currency in Britain for ten years after its completion. Among those whose attention was attracted to it by Mill was Sir John Herschel, who in his presidential address to the British Association for the Advancement of Science in 1845 attacked Laplace's nebular hypothesis and in particular Comte's argument in support of it, which he said was circular.[6]

Mill's own attraction to Comte's orbit goes back historically at least as far as his meeting with Saint-Simon in Paris in 1820, when the latter was "not yet the founder either of a philosophy or a religion," while he himself was still completely under the spell of Bentham; and the "chief fruit" of this and subsequent visits "was a strong and permanent interest in Continental Liberalism."[7] By 1828–1829, however, after his own *crise,* when he became acquainted, through Gustave d'Eichthal, with the writings of the Saint-Simonians, including the early essay of Comte, he was "greatly struck with the connected view which they for the first time presented to me, of the natural order of human progress; and especially with their division of all history into organic periods and critical periods." "Among their publications . . . there was

---

ing), and Bain's later works show no appreciable trace of Comte's influence, although he wrote that he preferred Comte's general logic of the sciences to Mill's logic of moral and political science only. It is possible that Bain was a case of a recruit lost by personal contact with Comte.

[6] B.A.A.S., *Report* . . . (London, 1846), pp. xxxviii–xxxix. Cf. J. Martineau, *Types of Ethical Theory,* I, 415–418. Robert Chambers, in the famous *Vestiges of the Natural History of Creation* (London, 1844), p. 17 and n., on the contrary commended Comte on the same subject (while misspelling both Comte's name and the title of his book). Two philosophy textbooks in brief treatments praised separate aspects of the *Cours* but condemned it as a whole as materialistic and subversive: J. D. Morell, *An Historical and Critical View of the Speculative Philosophy of Europe* . . . (2nd ed., London and Edinburgh, 1847), I, 583–591; Robert Blakey, *History of the Philosophy of Mind* . . . (London, 1848), IV, 307–322.

[7] The meeting, in fact, took place in the house of the liberal economist J.-B. Say.

one which seemed to me far superior to the rest: in which the general idea was matured into something much more definite and instructive." This was Comte's essay, in which he first put forward the Law of the Three Stages.

This doctrine harmonized with all my existing notions, to which it seemed to give a scientific shape. I already regarded the methods of physical science as the proper models for political. But the chief benefit which I derived at this time from the trains of thought suggested by the St. Simonians and by Comte, was, that I obtained a clearer conception than ever before of the peculiarities of an era of transition in opinion. . . . I looked forward to a future which shall unite the best qualities of the critical with the best qualities of the organic periods; unchecked liberty of thought, unbounded freedom of individual action in all modes not hurtful to others; but also convictions as to what is right and wrong . . . deeply engraven on the feelings by early education and general unanimity of sentiment, and . . . firmly grounded in reason and in the true exigencies of life.[8]

To Comte himself Mill wrote later that this essay had helped to "shake his ideas loose" from Benthamism.[9] At the time, however, he had written to d'Eichthal:

I was no longer surprised at the high opinion which I had heard you express of the book and the writer, and was even seduced by the plausibility of his manner into forming a higher opinion of the doctrines which he delivers, than on reflection they appear to me at all entitled to. . . . It is only the *partie critique* which appears to me sound, the *partie organique* appears to me liable to a hundred objections. It abounds indeed with many very acute remarks,

but these, Mill said, were common property among *avant-garde* thinkers, and it was

a great mistake . . . which *this sect seem to be* in great danger of falling into, to suppose that a few striking and original observations are

[8] *Autobiography* (3rd ed., London, 1874), pp. 61, 163, 165–166.
[9] Lévy-Bruhl, ed., *Lettres*, p. 2.

sufficient to form the foundation of a *science positive*. Mr. Comte is an exceedingly clear and methodical writer, most *agreeable in style,* and *concatenates* so well, that one is apt to mistake the perfect coherence and logical consistency of his system for truth.

All of Comte's historical views were "warped and distorted by the necessity of proving that civilisation has but one law, and that a law of progressive advancement. . . . There is positively no place for England in Mr. Comte's system." If the "many excellent and true remarks" were taken up and the rest discarded, they would be valuable, but this would not happen "if the proselytes of Saint-Simon insist upon forming a sect, which is a character above all to be avoided by independent thinkers." [10]

This letter serves to emphasize the unity not only of Mill's thought but also of Comte's. The same class of objections were made by Mill to this early essay that he later made to the *Polity,* which was essentially an elaboration of the essay and the goal of Comte's activity from the beginning. The *Cours,* in Comte's own estimation, was only a means to that end, and was not to be considered in isolation, which is what Mill was doing when he admired it. Likewise, Mill's later objections to Comtist sectarianism were foreshadowed here in his strictures on Saint-Simonian sectarianism.

[10] Eugène d'Eichthal, ed., "Letters of John Stuart Mill to Gustave d'Eichthal," *Cosmopolis,* VI (1897), 29–32 (8 Oct. 1829). Nevertheless it appears that Mill owed the term "social science" to this essay (J. H. Burns, "J. S. Mill and the Term 'Social Science,' " *Journal of the History of Ideas,* XX [1959], 432). As to Comte's style, it was indeed much clearer in these early essays than in his works *de très longue haleine.* Cf. also the complaints about Comte's and the Saint-Simonians' style and sectarianism by Mill's friend Eyton Tooke to G. d'Eichthal, 29 Oct. 1829, 19 Jan. 1830, in E. d'Eichthal, ed., *Mill . . . correspondance,* pp. 35–37, 92–98, while praising their general tendency. Cf. also, on this early phase of Mill's contact with Comte's thought, Emery Neff, *Carlyle and Mill: An Introduction to Victorian Thought* (2nd ed., New York, 1926), pp. 10–11, 251, 255, 263, 376, who is, however, not entirely reliable on the facts.

D'Eichthal, indeed, tried to make of him the leader of an English Saint-Simonian school, which Mill of course declined.[11] He did, however, continue to cultivate the Saint-Simonians (whereas he lost sight of Comte for a number of years), including not only d'Eichthal but Bazard and Enfantin as well, "and as long as their public teachings and proselytism continued, I read nearly everything they wrote. Their criticisms on the common doctrines of Liberalism seemed to me full of important truth." [12] Again it was the critical parts of the doctrine that Mill stressed; as he wrote to d'Eichthal, he approved of the idea of a spiritual power,

a state in which the body of the people, *i.e.* the uninstructed, shall entertain the same feeling of deference and submission to the authority of the instructed, in morals and politics, as they at present do in the physical sciences. . . . [But] I object altogether to the means which the St. Simonists propose for organising the *pouvoir spirituel*. It appears to me that you cannot organise it at all. What is the *pouvoir spirituel*, but the insensible influence of mind over mind?

He agreed with the Saint-Simonians on the importance of ascertaining "what is the state into which, in the natural order of the advancement of civilisation, the nation in question will next come, in order that it may be the grand object of our endeavours to facilitate the transition to this state," but this information was to be had only by an empirical investigation, not by the application of a predetermined scheme, for these developments were not everywhere identical or even congruent.[13] He did admit to d'Eichthal that

[11] See G. d'Eichthal to Mill, 23 Nov. 1829, 30 April 1830, in E. d'Eichthal, ed., *Mill . . . correspondance,* esp. pp. 55, 59–60, 63–68, 144; Mill to G. d'Eichthal, 9 and 10 Feb. 1830, 1 March 1831, *Cosmopolis,* VI, 351–354, 356; Michael St. John Packe, *The Life of John Stuart Mill* (London, 1954), pp. 93–95; Iris Wessel Mueller, *John Stuart Mill and French Thought* (Urbana, Ill., 1956), pp. 54–56.

[12] *Autobiography,* pp. 166–167; Packe, *Mill,* p. 100.

[13] To G. d'Eichthal, 7 Nov. 1829, *Cosmopolis,* VI, 34–38. See also "Michelet's History of France" in Mill's *Dissertations and Discussions,* II (1859— first published in the *Edinburgh Review* in Jan. 1844), 129, 133–134, on the

the daily reading of the *Globe* [the Saint-Simonian organ], combined with various other causes, has brought me much nearer to many of your opinions than I was before. . . . I am now inclined to think that your social organisation, under some modification or other . . . is likely to be the final and permanent condition of the human race,

but this would require a very long time. Meanwhile the schism within the Saint-Simonian sect was a bad sign, and in any event he would not identify himself with it publicly. The doctrine was for him "only one among a variety of interesting and important features in the time we live in," and the Saint-Simonians had much to learn from other schools, particularly the English economists and the German philosophers.[14]

Meanwhile, in a series of articles published in the *Examiner* in 1831,[15] Mill was propagating certain Saint-Simonian doctrines: the philosophy of history, the conception of an age of transition, the idea of a spiritual power. But he used these ideas to further his own and not a Saint-Simonian argument, namely, that "worldly power must pass from the hands of the stationary part of mankind into those of the progressive part," an innocuous enough desire. "There must be a moral and social revolution, which shall, indeed, take away no men's lives or property, but which shall leave to no man one fraction of unearned distinction or unearned importance." This was in contrast to Saint-Simonian socialism; and, in contrast to both the Saint-Simonians and Comte, Mill thought it was unfortunately necessary for the social revolution to take place before the moral.[16] Moreover, he appeared to believe that Saint-Simonian ideas were far less applicable in England than in

---

predictive purpose of history and on the historical method of proceeding from the *ensemble* to the details (citing Comte).

[14] To G. d'Eichthal, 30 Nov. 1831, 30 May 1832, *Cosmopolis*, VI, 356–357, 361–362.

[15] Collected and reprinted as *The Spirit of the Age* (Chicago, 1942), with an introduction by F. A. von Hayek.

[16] *Ibid.*, pp. xxvii–xxx, 6, 12, 16–17, 21, 27–28, 31–34; cf. Packe, *Mill*, p. 98; Mueller, *Mill*, pp. 67, 75–78, 81, 84–85.

France.[17] But "he clearly lost heart and enthusiasm for the sect" altogether once they embarked on the road to Ménilmontant and points east, and in his "mixed attitude of sympathy, respect, and contempt" the latter ingredient gained the upper hand.[18] Nevertheless as late as 1841, when he had already read and recommended Comte, he still referred to "my friends the Saint-Simonians." [19]

In nearly every respect Mill's attitude to the Saint-Simonians, and its development, foreshadowed his later reaction to Comte's mature writings. By comparison with the evangelism of Bazard and the ravings of the later Enfantin, the *Cours* was intended to be and struck Mill as being eminently rational, tempting him to forget the Saint-Simonian origins and quasi-Saint-Simonian purposes of its author.[20] Having lost touch with the Saint-Simonians after 1832, he resumed intellectual contact with Comte by way of the first two volumes of the *Cours* in 1837 and started a personal correspondence in 1841 announcing his impatience for the remaining volumes (which he subsequently read "with avidity" [21]). In this first letter Mill offered Comte (who was little older than he) implicit deference and explicit "sympathy and approbation,"

[17] Mill to Sterling, 20–22 Oct. 1831, in Hugh S. R. Elliot, ed., *The Letters of John Stuart Mill* (London, etc., 1910), I, 19.

[18] Mueller, *Mill,* pp. 86, 88–90, with quotation from the *Examiner* of 9 Sept. 1832.

[19] To R. B. Fox, 6 May 1841, in Caroline Fox, *Memories of Old Friends* . . . (3rd ed., London, 1882), II, 324. Cf. Mill as late as 1869 condemning the Saint-Simonians' *gouvernementalisme à outrance* but paying tribute to the services they have rendered to women (to Dr. Cazelles, 30 May 1869, Elliot, ed., *Letters,* II, 204).

[20] The *Cours,* Mill wrote to a friend, was "one of the most profound books ever written on the philosophy of the sciences; and that of the higher branches of mathematics it appears to me to have *created*. . . . I shall be much astonished if this book of Comte's does not strike you more than any logical speculations of our time" (Mill to J. P. Nichol, 21 Dec. 1837, in William Knight, ed., "Unpublished Letters from John Stuart Mill to Professor Nichol," *Fortnightly Review,* Vol. 67 [1897], p. 674). Cf. also Mueller, *Mill,* pp. 91, 93.

[21] *Autobiography,* p. 210.

apart from secondary disagreements on which he was open to argument. Mill regarded Comte "with more esteem and admiration than any other of the great men of our time." [22] Amplifying a little later, he sought to soften and minimize his disagreements and reiterated his willingness to learn from Comte,[23] instancing only the issue of psychology. Meanwhile he impatiently awaited the final volume and the promised treatise on politics, where he hoped to find enlightenment "on many questions stated in the fourth and fifth volumes, which so far have only aroused intellectual needs in me without completely satisfying them." [24] His enthusiasm, Mill was writing by early 1842, was still growing; he gave evidence of his open-mindedness even in the field of psychology by asking for readings in phrenology, and he thought the sympathy between Comte and himself extended even to secondary questions and might continue to grow.[25] However, having read Gall on phrenology, he admitted to great difficulties in accepting his conclusions, but again softened the disagreement later.[26] One gets the persistent impression that Mill was trying to spare Comte's only too well advertised susceptibilities in order not to put an end to a correspondence which he valued: his agreement with Comte, he said, was growing the better he knew his doctrines; if before he started his own book on logic he had known of Comte's work perhaps he might merely have translated it instead.[27]

Then, finally, the last volume of the *Cours* arrived, "nobly com-

---

[22] Mill to Comte, 12 Nov. 1841, Lévy-Bruhl, ed., *Lettres,* pp. 1–2, 4.

[23] On Mill's passive attitude at this time, cf. Samuel Saenger, *John Stuart Mill* . . . (Stuttgart, 1901), p. 49.

[24] Mill to Comte, 18 Dec. 1841, Lévy-Bruhl, ed., *Lettres,* pp. 12–15. Later he wrote: "The fourth volume disappointed me: it contained those of his opinions on social subjects with which I most disagree. But the fifth, containing the connected view of history, rekindled all my enthusiasm" (*Autobiography,* p. 210).

[25] Mill to Comte, 25 Feb. and 22 March 1842, Lévy-Bruhl, ed., *Lettres,* pp. 26–32, 40–41.

[26] Same, 9 June and 11 July 1842, *ibid.,* pp. 66–68, 79–80.

[27] Same, 12 Aug. and 11 July 1842, *ibid.,* pp. 92–93, 77.

pleting a work necessarily unique in the development of mankind" (Mill was even falling into Comte's style of language, at least in French). Comte was the founder of true sociological method and therefore the author of the definitive systematization of human knowledge. This last volume was the greatest of them all, and Mill entirely adopted its conclusions except for some secondary questions which required further clarification but which in any event did not detract from "the essentially satisfying nature of this immense systematization." [28] Mill said that in the light of this and the two preceding volumes he was making some changes in his own book which was ready for publication.[29] The book in question was the now famous *System of Logic*,[30] in which Mill confirmed in public the recommendations of Comte that he was giving in private. He subsequently saw the work through many editions, by the last of which his approval of and acknowledgments of indebtedness to Comte were markedly reduced.[31]

Mill commented later, in his *Autobiography:*

My theory of Induction was substantially completed before I knew of Comte's book. . . . Comte is always precise and profound on the method of investigation, but he does not even attempt any exact definition of the conditions of proof: and . . . he never attained a just conception of them. . . . Nevertheless I gained much from Comte, with which to enrich my chapters in the subsequent rewriting: and his book was of essential service to me in some of the parts which still remained to be thought out. . . . In a merely logical point of view, the only leading conception for which I am indebted to him is that of the Inverse

[28] Same, 23 Oct. and 15 Dec. 1842, *ibid.,* pp. 119–120, 137.

[29] Same, 28 Jan. 1843, *ibid.,* p. 153. Bain, *Autobiography,* p. 146, testified that Mill "made a point" of completing Vol. VI of the *Cours* before publishing his own work.

[30] *A System of Logic, Ratiocinative and Inductive* (London, 1843).

[31] Eighth ed., London, 1872. See the comparative table in the first Appendix, below. Oskar Alfred Kubitz, *Development of John Stuart Mill's System of Logic* (Illinois Studies in the Social Sciences, Vol. XVIII, 1932), adds little of value to this comparison.

Deductive Method. . . . This was an idea entirely unknown to me when I found it in Comte. . . . My obligations to Comte were only to [those of] his writings [which preceded the *Logic*] . . . : and . . . the amount of these obligations is far less than has sometimes been asserted. The first volume, which contains all the fundamental doctrines of the book, was substantially complete before I had seen Comte's treatise. I derived from him many valuable thoughts, conspicuously in the chapter on Hypotheses and in the view taken of the logic of Algebra: but it is only in the concluding Book, on the Logic of the Moral Sciences, that I owe to him any radical improvement in my conception of the application of logical method.[32]

Neither these passages, nor the changes he made in the *Logic,* nor his letters to Comte warrant the assertion that Mill later deliberately minimized his debt to Comte.[33] The passages from the *Autobiography* seem to me a fair statement of the case. The changes in the *Logic* are mostly explicable in terms either of the reduced relevance and interest of references to Comte by 1872 or of a change of mind on Mill's part in the interval, particularly on the predictive and constructive parts of Comte's sociology. Insofar as he ever agreed with those, that agreement had already been accorded to the Saint-Simonians, including Comte's own essay of 1822. Insofar as he came to disagree more emphatically, that disagreement is largely attributable to his growing comprehension of the implications of Comte's doctrine, as revealed by Comte himself. It is to be noted that the later edition of the *Logic* suppressed disagreement as well as agreement and retained a considerable measure of tribute. As for the letters, those that preceded the publication of the *Logic* were so fulsome in praise that some degree of understandable flattery is to be suspected: Mill was anxious not to irritate Comte (the Preface to Vol. VI of the *Cours* had just indicated again how irritable Comte was) and preferred to gloss over their disagreements. But this forbearance never ap-

[32] *Autobiography,* pp. 209–210, 245 n.
[33] Lévy-Bruhl, ed., *Lettres,* Introduction, p. xx.

proached the point where he was willing to enroll as a Comtist, just as he had never, despite a comparable measure of agreement, been willing to enroll as a Saint-Simonian.[34] Moreover, the *Autobiography* and the last edition of the *Logic* must be read in conjunction with the essay on Comte and Positivism (still to be discussed), which is quite explicit in both praise and blame.

In any event, the reservations on so-called "secondary" matters that Mill indicated in the early letters to Comte, that he recorded in the *Logic,* and that eventually he could not forbear to bring out into the open in later letters did not in fact concern "secondary" matters. It is all very well to say that the only important disagreements between Mill and Comte were over the place of psychology in the sciences and the place of women in society,[35] but the second of these was a matter of deeply felt personal convictions on the part of both of them, and the first undermines their apparent agreement on the proper method for social science. Even in the first edition of the *Logic* Mill had stated his belief in the propriety in this field of the direct as well as the inverse deductive method, that is to say, the possibility of deducing sociological conclusions from psychological data concerning human nature. Mill, the descendant of Locke, Hartley, and his father, believed that "to create the moral sciences, we must start from a scientific psychology." [36]

[34] I do not think it is correct to attribute to Mill in the *Logic* (Mueller, *Mill,* pp. 67, 69) a greater degree of "acceptance of the intellectual directorate" than he manifested either earlier or later. He had accepted it in principle in the *Examiner* articles, he accepted it in principle in the *Utilitarianism* in the famous passage about Socrates and the pig, and the principle is all that he accepted in the *Logic.* He never endorsed, in fact he explicitly queried, specific designs to produce a social consensus. Cf. also Packe, *Mill,* pp. 273, 275.

[35] *Ibid.,* p. 276; Lévy-Bruhl, ed., *Lettres,* Introduction, pp. xxvi–xxviii.

[36] Leslie Stephen, *The English Utilitarians* (London, 1900), III, 155–157. See further, for methodological differences between Mill in the *Logic* and Comte, Saenger, *Mill,* p. 59; Fanja Finkelstein, *Die allgemeinen Gesetze*

These were not in fact the only issues on which Mill dissented from Comte in 1843. While assuring Comte that his judgment of the *Logic* was the only one he valued, he said that there were disagreements between them "on questions of major importance" (no longer "secondary") in connection with Comte's social statics, and despite continued deference he feared that these differences were not due only to his own as yet incomplete emancipation, as Comte, characteristically, maintained.[37] He declined Comte's invitation to collaborate on the journal proposed by Littré partly on the ground that to do so would reveal the differences of opinion between them on questions of current importance, as distinct from their agreement which he now reduced to philosophical method, historical doctrines, and laws of social development. Positivism, he warned, as he had warned d'Eichthal about Saint-Simonianism, was not yet ready to become a school, which would require a common corps of doctrine whereas at present there were only a common method and agreement on some general principles.[38]

---

bei Comte und Mill (Heidelberg, 1911); and particularly Cassirer, *Problem of Knowledge,* pp. 6–10, who says that Mill always remained an empiricist, for whom, in contrast to Comte, experience was simply "an aggregate," "a sum of individual observations," and for whom " 'universals' must be reduced to the individual particularities and resolved into the simple data of sense-perception," in contrast to Comte's pursuit of laws by means of "relational thinking" and of " 'general facts' " and his belief in a "logical *structure*" of knowledge. Cassirer concludes, unassailably I think, that Comte was closer to Hegel than to Mill "in basic tendency. What is common to Comte and Mill is basically only the negative tendency," the rejection of theology and metaphysics. Note, however, with respect to deduction from "human nature," that Comte and particularly Laffitte (see above, p. 43 and n. 60) practiced this, only not on the basis of empirical data. So, of course, did Mill, and for that matter Bentham.

[37] Mill to Comte, 13 March, 15 June, 13 July 1843, Lévy-Bruhl, ed., *Lettres,* pp. 166, 207–208, 221–224, and the entire letter of 30 Oct. 1843, pp. 259–271. Packe, *Mill,* pp. 277–278, says that Mill was encouraged by Harriet Taylor to take a firmer line with Comte.

[38] Mill to Comte, 27 Jan. 1845, *ibid.,* pp. 400–402.

At this point Comte's personal exigence, added to his philosophical domineering, drove a further breach between them. Comte, having been deprived of one academic post after another (for reasons of personality rather than competence), had appealed to Mill for financial help, and Mill had secured and transmitted to Comte contributions from a few of his friends. Comte at once regarded this as a normal state of affairs and affected injured surprise when the subsidy was not renewed in 1845, which he said was his due as a spiritual leader. Mill had to point out to Comte that neither he nor those who had contributed regarded him in fact as a spiritual leader. While they all considered the *Cours* as a philosophical work of the first rank in which Comte had applied the philosophical method to social questions, that did not imply acceptance of his dogmatic sociology or of his system as a whole.[39] And he came back to the crux of their disagreement: "I persist in thinking that sociology as a science can make no important progress without relying on a maturer [*plus approfondie*] theory of human nature." [40] Mill wrote later, concerning the end of their correspondence: "I found, and he probably found likewise, that I could do no good to his mind, and that all the good he could do to mine, he did by his books." [41] This was a very polite way of saying that he found personal contact with Comte unrewarding.[42] This personal estrangement did not prevent Mill from continuing to do justice to Comte both in public and in private.

The friends from whom Mill had solicited funds for Comte included the famous historian George Grote and the latter's pro-

[39] Same, 12 Jan. 1846, *ibid.,* pp. 499–504.

[40] Same, 26 March 1846, *ibid.,* p. 524, cf. above, p. 184.

[41] *Autobiography,* p. 211.

[42] Cf. Ernest Seillière, *Auguste Comte* (Paris, 1924), p. 50: Mill soon became tired of theoretical controversies in which he was "continuously confronted by maniacal preconceptions," and Mueller, *Mill,* p. 130: "Comte could never discuss 'opinions' with Mill because Comte had none, in the sense Mill used the term." See also Lewes' comment quoted by Eisen, "Harrison," p. 156.

tégé Sir William Molesworth, the radical politician,[43] both of whom were already acquainted with the *Cours*, probably through Mill. Grote wrote as early as 1838, concerning Vol. III:

It seems a work full of profound and original thinking. . . . [But] I do not find in it the solution of . . . perplexities respecting the fundamental principles of geometry. . . . Nor can I at all tolerate the unqualified manner in which he strikes out morals and metaphysics from the list of positive sciences.[44]

By 1840 he was in correspondence with Comte and in 1844 met him in Paris,[45] although Comte

was scarcely known to anyone with whom we habitually consorted. . . . Mr. Grote found M. Comte's conversation original and instructive, and on returning to London he became active in promoting the circulation of M. Comte's works, as being calculated to expand the range of speculative investigation among English students.[46]

In the same year, also, Grote contributed to Comte's financial support and procured something from Molesworth, likewise an "enlightened admirer" of the *Cours*, but neither of them was described by Mill as "capable of assimilating the method completely or of furthering the doctrine." [47] Mill nevertheless did his tactful best to get the subsidy renewed. He admitted, writing to Grote, that in Comte's position he would have taken more energetic steps in his own behalf; but "it is to be said for him . . . that he had every reason to believe his income a permanent one, and . . . that

[43] They also included Raikes Currie, about whom I can find nothing.

[44] Grote to Molesworth, 2 Oct. 1838, in Mrs. Grote, *The Personal Life of George Grote* (2nd ed., London, 1873), p. 129.

[45] Eisen, "Harrison," p. 145, thinks that they first met in 1840, but this conjecture seems unlikely in the light of the next quotation in the text.

[46] *Life of Grote,* pp. 157–158.

[47] Mill to Comte, 20 April 1843, 8 July 1845, 5 Oct. 1844, Lévy-Bruhl, ed., *Lettres,* pp. 181, 449, 356–357. Only Bain seemed to Mill to answer to this description. See also the similar state of affairs depicted as late as 1854 by Mill to Barbot de Chément, 7 Aug. 1854, in Elliot, ed., *Letters,* I, 182–183.

it is harder to be advised to break up all his arrangements and to alter his confirmed habits from a cause [i.e., his academic unemployment] which he firmly believes to be . . . of very short duration. If, therefore, you think that it would be possible and advisable to raise another subscription for him I should be happy, in case of need, to contribute my part towards it." [48] Mill had to report to Comte that none of the original subscribers would wish to support him indefinitely, and he himself was willing to do so only in case of absolute necessity. [49] Comte's attempt to establish the institution of a publicly supported priesthood, which he elaborated later in great detail in the *Polity,* therefore failed. Grote subsequently broke with Comte altogether when his sociological conclusions became even more explicit in 1848 in the *General View.* [50] Mill, however, made another contribution to Comte's support in that same year, writing to Littré: "I have a very high regard for his works so far as the theory of the positive method is concerned, but I am very far from approving his manner of applying this method to social questions. Most of his sociological opinions are diametrically opposed to mine." [51]

Comte, for his part, took his revenge for Mill's "ingratitude" by pronouncing on him, together with Littré, his peculiar species of

[48] Mill to Grote, July 1845, *ibid.,* I, 139–140. The letter is dated 1848 in Elliot, but this is clearly wrong, and Professor Francis E. Mineka of Cornell University, who is compiling a new edition of Mill's letters, confirms that 1845 must be the date.

[49] Mill to Comte, 8 July and 22 Sept. 1845, Lévy-Bruhl, ed., *Lettres,* pp. 449–450, 475–476.

[50] Eisen, "Harrison," p. 57, quoting Grote to Comte, 13 Oct. 1848; cf. Bain, *Mill,* p. 75.

[51] Mill to Littré, 22 Dec. 1848, Elliot, ed., *Letters,* I, 139. It is interesting that in 1844, on the occasion of Littré's articles in the *National,* Mill had spoken of the latter's "adhesion" to Comte in the same terms as of his own (Mill to Comte, 31 Dec. 1844, Lévy-Bruhl, ed., *Lettres,* p. 386), but here he was mistaken. Cf. also Seillière, *Comte,* pp. 49–50. See, further, Mill's diary for 21 Jan. 1854, in Elliot, ed., *Letters,* II, 361, and his letter to the Positivist Barbot de Chément, 7 Aug. 1854, *ibid.,* I, 182–183.

public denigration which he may have thought was less injurious
for not using their names:

Ever powerless to construct, the literateurs [*sic*] had their place only in
destruction. . . . A celebrated logician was the first to proclaim the
intellectual superiority of the new philosophy especially from the point
of view of method. He was soon followed by the able writer who . . .
was more successful in mastering, in its entirety, the conception of a
mission which was as much social as intellectual, and which he relieved from a concerted silence.

But their affinities proved to be only partial, since they were

unable to shake off the influence of their Protestant origin and revolutionary habits. After nobly introducing Positivism to the knowledge
of the public, the first early invented the tactic by which, ignoring the
indivisibility of my synthesis, the attempt is made to establish a contradiction between my philosophical creation and my religious construction.[52]

Yet even Comte continued to acknowledge that Mill had "introduced Positivism to the public." Mill gave the eminent jurist John
Austin an introduction to Comte, and Austin, who "became fast
friends" with Comte, in turn attempted to intervene with Guizot
in his behalf in his professional plight.[53] Subsequently Mill defended Comte against Austin in the matter of the subsidy.[54] To

[52] *Polity*, IV, 469–470; see also Comte to Laffitte, 30 Aug. 1855, in *C.I.*, II,
183, where he speaks of a "conspiracy" between Mill, Lewes, and Carlyle (!)
to suffocate social positivism under intellectual. Cf. Delvolvé, *Réflexions*,
p. 248, on Comte's repugnance toward Utilitarianism.

[53] Mill to Comte, 17 Oct. 1843, Lévy-Bruhl, ed., *Lettres*, p. 256; Packe,
Mill, p. 282; Eisen, "Harrison," pp. 151–152, 154 n. 2, 157; and Austin to
Mill, 25 Dec. 1844 (unpublished letter kindly supplied by Professor Mineka),
in which he praises Comte's character with the important exception of his
excessive self-confidence and the heedless contempt for public opinion that
followed from it.

[54] Mill to Austin, 13 April 1847, Elliot, ed., *Letters*, I, 132. (The purport
of this part of the letter is not different in the emended version supplied to

the politician and novelist Sir Edward Lytton Bulwer he recommended Comte as "the first speculative thinker of the age." [55] As late as 1848 Mill was writing about Comte's *General View* that it was

the first book which has given a coherent picture of a supposed future of humanity with a look of possibility about it. . . . To me the chief worth of the book seems to consist in, first, the systematic and earnest inculcation of the purely *subordinate* rôle of the intellect, as the minister of the higher sentiments,

secondly, in making a religion of humanity seem plausible despite the ridiculous attempts at defining its practices. "In most of the other doctrines of the book I wholly dissent from him." [56] Later still the politician and judge Sir Erskine Perry, having had Mill praise Comte to him and knowing of his financially straitened circumstances, visited the philosopher in Paris in 1853. He came away from the interview with a

warm regard for his benevolence and purity of views, . . . admiration for his profundity of ideas and brilliant elocution, but above all . . . wonder at the calm and well-assured self-complacency with which he regarded his own social theory to be as firmly established as any of the exact sciences.[57]

The philsopher Henry Sidgwick, alone among his contemporaries at Cambridge, was led by his study of Mill to a first-hand acquaintance with Comte's works and temporarily subscribed to the views of both, but later refuted Positivism.[58] The famous liberal econo-

---

me by Professor Mineka.) Austin's *Lectures on Jurisprudence* . . . (4th ed., London, 1873) do not seem to owe any definable debt to Comte's doctrines.

[55] Letter of 27 March 1843, Elliot, ed., *Letters,* I, 124.

[56] Mill to J. P. Nichol, 30 Sept. 1848, Knight, "Unpublished Letters," p. 676.

[57] "A Morning with Auguste Comte," *Nineteenth Century,* II (1877), 625, 630.

[58] William C. Havard, *Henry Sidgwick* . . . (Gainesville, Fla., 1959),

mist F. Y. Edgeworth, on the other hand, seems not to have gone beyond second-hand acquaintance with Comte's work by way of Mill's.[59]

All told, it can be said that Mill did his best to make Positivism known, but the seed fell on almost entirely barren soil. Moreover, he continued to propagate Comte's name long after he had become estranged from his person, and past the time when Comte had on the one hand publicly rebuked him and on the other made the social and political implications of his system unambiguously clear. In the essay *On Liberty* Mill was notoriously concerned to prevent undue pressure of public opinion on the individual,[60] and it may be thought that in this respect he had moved away from his acceptance of the idea of a "spiritual power," but in fact he defined his position in these years in almost precisely the same terms as he had done to d'Eichthal thirty years earlier: the spiritual power could not be organized; agreement if it was to come about at all must come about spontaneously. In Positivism, despite Comte's disclaimer of a desire to coerce, "public opinion, with a powerful moral authority as its focus, will always be in a position to exercise a tyrannical pressure on thought." [61]

---

pp. 7, 82–83; Sidgwick, *Philosophy: Its Scope and Relations* . . . (London and New York, 1902), pp. 4–17, 170, 195, 218–219, 227–230. Sidgwick saw some merit in the idea of consensus and in the Law of the Three Stages, but thought Comte's conception of metaphysics inadequate and constructed quite a different view of the relationship between science and philosophy.

[59] Edgeworth, *Mathematical Psychics* . . . (London, 1881), pp. 85, 91 n. 1.

[60] See also his specific reference to Comte, who "aims at establishing . . . a despotism of society over the individual surpassing anything contemplated in the political ideal of the most rigid disciplinarian among the ancient philosophers" (Everyman's ed., London and New York, 1947, p. 76).

[61] Mill to Blignières, 22 Jan. 1862, Elliot, ed., *Letters*, I, 252–254. Cf. also this passage from Mill's *Utilitarianism* (1863): "I entertain the strongest objections to the system of politics and morals set forth in . . . [the *Polity*]: but I think it has superabundantly shown the possibility of giving to the service of humanity, even without the aid of a belief in Provi-

This was written to the Littréist Blignières, approving of the latter's book, which had sent Comte into convulsions. Of Littré himself Mill also spoke well in the essay "Auguste Comte and Positivism," which he published in the *Westminster Review* in 1865,[62] a finely balanced piece of writing in which if anything he sought to do Comte's work in *all* its parts more rather than less justice than it deserved, going in some respects even farther than Littré himself. For he not only, as was to be expected, praised the *Cours* in general and in particular—the Law of the Three Stages, the classification and philosophy of the sciences, Comte's views on education and on history[63]—but also the *Polity* and even the *Synthèse subjective:* on religion, on ethics, on society, and on mathematics.[64] Conversely, he was emphatic about seeing anticipations of the objectionable parts of the *Polity* in the *Cours:* Comte's closed mind, his subjectivism, and his erroneous views on psychology, on history, on politics.[65] He concluded by comparing Comte to Descartes and Leibniz and thought him as great as either of them, "and hardly more extravagant."

Were we to speak our whole mind, we should call him superior to them: though not intrinsically, yet by the exertion of equal intellectual power in a more advanced state of human preparation; but also in an

dence, both the psychological power and the social efficacy of a religion" (Everyman's ed., as above, p. 31).

[62] Cited here after the second (revised) edition in book form, London, 1866. On Littré, see pp. 3, 82 n.

[63] Pp. 2, 3, 9, 12–13, 33, 40, 53–55, 76, 86, 106, 108, 113, 124, 199–200.

[64] Pp. 132, 133, 135–137, 147–148, 160–161, 165–166, 194; cf. his praise of the *Synthèse subjective* in his *Examination of Sir William Hamilton's Philosophy* . . . (London, 1865), p. 524 n., also his praise of Comte to Max Kyllman, 30 May 1865, in Elliot, ed., *Letters*, II, 40.

[65] *Auguste Comte and Positivism*, pp. 14–15, 62, 63–67, 70, 95–96, 98–99, 111–112, 118–121; see also pp. 10, 29, 51, 55–56, 59, 73, 80, 88–89, 91–92. For criticisms of the later writings, see pp. 4–5, 128–129, 138–142, 144–145, 149, 153, 158, 168–169, 171–173, 184–187, 190–192, 195, 196, 199, and of Comte's personality, pp. 127, 130, 153–154.

age less tolerant of palpable absurdities, and to which those he has committed, if not in themselves greater, at least appear more ridiculous.[66]

How very charitable this summing up was is indicated best, perhaps, by the grudging admission of Richard Congreve that Mill's article was "on the whole useful . . . to our cause. . . . Such is Mr. Mill's powerful position in England that it is really useful to have his voice or at any rate his neutrality." [67] Mill himself wrote to Congreve:

It is precisely because I consider M. Comte to have been a great thinker that I regard it as a duty to balance the strong and deeply felt admiration which I express for what I deem the fundamental parts of his philosophy by an equally emphatic expression of the opposite feelings I entertain towards other parts. It is M. Comte himself who, in my judgment, has thrown ridicule on his own philosophy by the extravagances of his later writings.[68]

And Mill went out of his way to assert his debt to Comte vis-à-vis Spencer and to defend Comte against Huxley's attack.[69]

His own account of his attitude toward Comte cannot be improved upon:

I had fully agreed with him when he maintained that the mass of mankind, including even their rulers in all the practical departments of life, must, from the necessity of the case, accept most of their opinions on political and social matters, as they do on physical, from the authority of those who have bestowed more study on those subjects than they generally have it in their power to do. . . . I agreed with him that the moral and intellectual ascendancy, once exercised by priests, must in time pass into the hands of philosophers, and will naturally do so when

[66] P. 200.

[67] Congreve to Edger, 5 May 1865, BM Add. MS 45232 f. 124.

[68] Mill to Congreve, 8 Aug. 1865, Elliot, ed., *Letters*, II, 42.

[69] Mill to Spencer, 3 April 1864, in David Duncan, *Life and Letters of Herbert Spencer* (New York, 1908), I, 149–150, to Dr. Cazelles, 23 Oct. 1869, Elliot, ed., *Letters*, II, 222.

they become sufficiently unanimous, and in other respects worthy to possess it. But when he exaggerated this line of thought into a practical system, in which philosophers were to be organised into a kind of corporate hierarchy . . . ; when I found him relying on this spiritual authority as the only security for good government, the sole bulwark against practical oppression, and expecting that by it a system of despotism in the state and despotism in the family would be rendered innocuous and beneficial; it is not surprising, that while as logicians we were nearly at one, as sociologists we could travel together no further. M. Comte lived to carry out these doctrines to their extremest consequences, by planning . . . the completest system of spiritual and temporal despotism which ever yet emanated from a human brain, unless possibly that of Ignatius Loyola. . . . [The *Polity*] stands a monumental warning to thinkers on society and politics, of what happens when once men lose sight in their speculations of the value of Liberty and of Individuality. . . . I had contributed more than anyone else to make . . . [Comte's] speculations known in England, and, in consequence chiefly of what I had said of him in my Logic, he had readers and admirers among the thoughtful men on this side of the Channel at a time when his name had not yet in France emerged from obscurity.

In the 1840's it had been more important to publicize Comte's "important contributions" to philosophical thought than to criticize his weaknesses; but this was no longer the case by the 1860's, when he was well known and when his worse aspects were riding on the coattails of his better; so Mill had undertaken "the task of sifting what is good from what is bad in M. Comte's speculations." [70]

This seems to me an entirely just description of the personal and intellectual relationship between Comte and Mill, and nothing in the latter's writings, private or public, negates it. All that can properly be objected is that Mill entertained too optimistic a view of the possibility of a voluntary social consensus and therefore grasped too readily at the ideas first of the Saint-Simonians, including Comte's essay of 1822, and then of the *Cours,* when he

[70] *Autobiography,* pp. 211–213, 277–278.

thought, or hoped, that this was all they were aiming at. When he suspected that they aimed at more, he rejected it at every turn. And his position was far more defensible than Littré's. Littré attempted to rescue Comte from himself, remaining in a posture of personal discipleship; Mill, instead, detached some of the doctrine from the man, and from the use to which he aimed to put it. Comte of course was also consistent: given that science could prescribe the course society should take, he undertook to prescribe it; given that a "spiritual power" could see to its enforcement, he undertook to install one. But Mill would not be driven to abandoning the empirical humanism which had first made him sympathetic to the thinking of Comte and the Saint-Simonians.[71]

In this respect he resembled the most important of the men whom he introduced to Positivism, G. H. Lewes. Not only did Lewes become almost as active as Mill in propagating the doctrine, but he never moved so far from it as Mill did. In commenting on Mill's articles on Comte in 1866, Lewes took the latter's side on the specific issue of the place of psychology among the sciences, acknowledging his own earlier mistake in this respect.

[71] Cf. Thomas Whittaker, "Comte and Mill," in his *Reason: A Philosophical Essay* . . . (Cambridge, 1934), p. 31, and see further pp. 50, 65–69, 73–76, 79–80. For other comparisons of the two, see on psychology, Ribot, *English Psychology,* pp. 78–85; Giacomo Barzellotti, *The Ethics of Positivism* . . . (tr., New York, 1878), pp. 48–49, 63–66, 124–135, 317–320; Caro, *Littré,* pp. 176–177; on ethics, Stephen, *English Utilitarians,* III, 300; on economics, Mauduit, *Comte et la science économique,* pp. 226–230; Mueller, *Mill,* pp. 115–123; on the individual and society, *ibid.,* pp. 106–114, 126–127; in general, Ferraz, *Socialisme, naturalisme et positivisme,* p. 403; Troeltsch, *Historismus,* pp. 417–419; Willey, *Nineteenth Century Studies,* pp. 150, 154–155; Mueller, *Mill,* pp. 94–105, 129–133. Cantecor, *Comte,* p. 166, seems to me to go much too far in maintaining that Mill accepted none of Comte's ideas. Gertrude Himmelfarb in her introduction to Mill, *Essays on Politics and Culture* (Garden City, N.Y., 1962), makes some interesting new suggestions about the various phases of Mill's life and casts doubt on the reliability of his *Autobiography,* but my analysis of his relations with Comte is not affected.

He also defended Comte against Mill on the score of his logic and the rules of proof. While emphatically dissociating himself from the "subjective method" of Comte's "second career," he asserted against Mill that it was precisely a change of method and not a change of purpose that marked the division between the two careers.[72]

It was in the period of Mill's honeymoon with Comte that Lewes got to know Mill and Comte's work through him,[73] and it was in the year of Mill's *Logic* that Lewes published the article in which he added his own first praise of the *Cours*. Comte's method, which made of philosophy a science instead of a literature, was of "the highest benefit to philosophy."

That the positive method is the only true one is readily to be proved: on it alone can *prevision* of phenomena depend. The characteristic of science is prevision. . . . The positive method is . . . the only one capable of furnishing to man the instrument whereby he may "interrogate nature" with success.

Lewes stressed the importance of the Law of the Three Stages and of Comte's diagnosis of the prevailing state of anarchy. As a remedy Comte offered the Classification of the Sciences, showing social science, "on the same method as the other sciences," to be possible, including a philosophy of history to unlock the mysteries of the past. Comte's "voluminous and systematic" work, with its "rigorous enchainment of views," contained "much of novelty" but also "necessarily many errors, and some points open to discussion." Yet Lewes concluded that Comte was the new "universal man," and one of incomparable philosophical power. "To a high and rare power of generalization, he adds a fulness of scientific knowledge seldom witnessed." [74] Two years later Lewes pub-

[72] "Comte and Mill," *Fortnightly Review,* VI (1866), 389–391, 394–396, 399.

[73] Packe, *Mill,* p. 291; Kitchel, *George Lewes and George Eliot,* p. 42.

[74] Lewes in *British and Foreign Review,* XV (1843), 395–396, 400–402, 405–406. See also his stress on ideas as the central forces in history, p. 354.

lished a history of philosophy which both began and ended with Positivism. In the preface he repeated that Positivism had made philosophy scientific by employing the scientific Method of Verification. At the same time Comte represented the culmination of a long line of philosophical development. His doctrine "is *positive,* because elaborated from the sciences and yet possessing all the desired *generality* of metaphysical doctrines, without possessing their vagueness, instability, and inapplicability." All told, the *Cours* was a work of unequaled eminence.[75]

In the following year Lewes went to see Comte in Paris and subsequently kept up a correspondence with him, which thus took up exactly where Mill left off, and by 1848, indeed, "Lewes had taken Mill's place in Comte's eyes as the hope of Positivism in England." Lewes accepted Comte's criticism of his recent *Biographical History* and was delighted "beyond measure" by the *General View,* especially its sections on society and the place of women in it; there was no word of criticism in his letters. Lewes thus went very much farther than Mill had done in submitting himself to Comte's domination: "he gave the impression of being the complete disciple." However, in 1852, in a series of articles in his journal *The Leader,* Lewes treated Comte in a manner not uniformly favorable. This show of independence, together with Lewes' alleged dilatoriness in collecting money on his behalf, was enough to make Comte dissatisfied with him, and Lewes, following Mill's example closely, allowed the correspondence to peter out.[76]

The *Leader* articles were expanded in Lewes' full-scale book on Comte, published in 1853, in which, despite the contrary indica-

[75] *The Biographical History of Philosophy from Its Origin in Greece down to the Present Day* (new ed., New York, 1879; first pub. 1845–46), pp. xiii–xv, xxx, 777–785, 788.

[76] Eisen, "Harrison," pp. 159–163, using Lewes' correspondence with Comte, 1846–1853, in M-le-P; cf. also Kitchel, *George Lewes and George Eliot,* pp. 42–43.

tion of the title, he did not confine himself to the *Cours*.[77] As a result of Comte's association with Clotilde de Vaux, Lewes said, he had "learned to appreciate the abiding and universal influence of the affections." Lewes agreed with Comte that "the intellectual aspect is *not* the noblest part of man" and that science was indeed only the basis for a social superstructure.

There never will be a Philosophy capable of satisfying the demands of Humanity, until the truth be recognised that man is moved by his emotions, not by his ideas: using his Intellect only as an eye to *see the way*. In other words, the Intellect is the servant, not the lord of the Heart; and Science is a futile, frivolous pursuit . . . unless it subserve some grand religious aim.

The Positive Philosophy, in fact, "is a doctrine capable of embracing all that can regulate Humanity."[78] Lewes had accompanied Comte a long part of the way from the *Cours* to the *Polity*, and it seems an understatement to say that agreement between them was still more prominent than differences.[79] The latter concerned mostly very specific technical scientific questions, apart from the issue of the place of psychology among the sciences, an allegation of confusion on Comte's part concerning the religious implications of astronomy, and the bare statements that "reverence is not incompatible with independence" and that Comte's "attempts to reorganise society" were premature.[80] The latter does not seem to me necessarily inconsistent with "proclaiming his general adherence even in matters concerning religion and politics."[81]

Comte, however, seized on the items of dissent and, with unconscious irony, wrote to one of his French disciples that Lewes was

[77] Cited here from the London edition of 1887: *Comte's Philosophy of the Sciences: Being an Exposition of the Principles of the Cours de Philosophie Positive of Auguste Comte.*

[78] *Ibid.*, pp. 5–6, 8–9.   [79] Eisen, "Harrison," p. 164.

[80] *Comte's Philosophy of the Sciences*, pp. 2, 87–92, 119 n., 122 n., 130, 181, 190, 210–232 (on psychology), 339.

[81] Cf. Eisen, "Harrison," p. 164.

interested in Positivism only in order to exploit it but that he might still be useful to the cause.[82] Publicly Comte ranked Lewes with Mill and Littré as "Protestant littérateurs": although "the least incomplete of the three," Lewes "offered a still more deplorable example than the others of the inherent inconsequence of literateurs [*sic*], by his definitive adhesion to the most despicable of all the systems of theological hypocrisy." [83] But Lewes, like Mill, did not repay Comte in kind. He continued to defend his relationship with Clotilde de Vaux and refused to take sides with Littré, the advocate of the interests of Mme. Comte. With Littré, however, Lewes asserted a "very wide divergence in Method" between Comte's two major works, giving ground for contradictory charges against him.

I accept with gratitude the Philosophy in all its cardinal views. . . . But in the *Politique Positive,* and the religious cultus, I can only see a magnificent utopia, and a prophetic vision of what the Religion of the future may become. As an utopia it commands a sentiment rather than an assent. As an attempt at social reorganisation, I not only resist many of the details, but altogether impugn the Method.

This was no longer the objective historical method, but an "unbridled employment of the deductive Method . . . on a topic which was destitute of the requisite inductions." But this approach, Lewes asserted, was inevitable, given "the tendencies towards despotic systematisation and arbitrary hypothesis" which were clearly evident in the *Cours*. Lewes therefore rejected Littré's attribution of the puerilities of the *Polity* to a mental deterioration in Comte. The *Polity,* Lewes wrote, exhibited "the same intellectual force, the same sustained power of conception and coordination, although with less successful result," as the *Cours*. It was a book which should be approached like that other utopia, Plato's *Republic:* students

---

[82] Comte to Deuillin, 17 Sept. 1853, *C.I.,* I, 269.
[83] *Polity,* IV, 470.

will find there an intellect greater than Plato's, a morality higher and purer, and an amount of available suggestion incomparably greater. . . . Hundreds of men have been as vain, as arrogant, as despotic in their ideas; but how many have been as severely ascetic, as profoundly moral, as devoted to high thoughts, and as magnificently endowed?

Positivism must not be judged by its "accessories": if it

is so far in harmony with demonstrated truths as to be a guide to us in our groping search for a solution of great problems, let us boldly declare as much and not reject so inestimable a benefit because Comte, or others, may have connected with the great central ideas certain ideas which seem false or ridiculous.

Lewes counted himself "a reverent heretic . . . : that is, I profoundly admire the greatness and sincerity of the thinker, although he seems to have attempted a task for which the materials were not ready." [84] It is difficult to imagine a more generous judgment, more generous even than Mill's both of the doctrine and, especially, of its author. Lewes was, in fact, more impressed by the *Polity* on a rereading than he had been at first, as well as "by what he is able to understand of the 'Synthèse.' " [85] Like Mill he disapproved of Huxley's attack on Comte,[86] and in reissuing the *History* of 1845 he deliberately drew a veil over Comte's attempts "to found a social doctrine, and to become the founder of a new religion." [87] Like Mill, if he can be accused of anything it is of an excess of charity to Comte, early and late, and he was not afraid to take up the cudgels for him even against Mill himself. If any-

[84] "Auguste Comte," *Fortnightly Review,* III (1866), 390, 400, 402–410.

[85] George Eliot to Mrs. Congreve, 22 Dec. 1866, 16 Jan. 1867, in Haight, ed., *George Eliot Letters,* IV, 324, 333; cf. Lewes' journal, 11 Jan. 1867, *ibid.,* 331; also his letter to Sara Hennell, 9 July 1860, *ibid.,* III, 320, and his diary for 18 July 1859, in Kitchel, *George Lewes and George Eliot,* p. 191 (conversation with Mrs. Congreve).

[86] George Eliot to Mrs. Congreve, 4 May 1869, Haight, ed., *George Eliot Letters,* V, 26.

[87] *Biographical History,* p. 787.

thing was likely to popularize Positivism, it was Lewes' two articles of 1866 in the *Fortnightly*.[88]

[88] Cf., on Lewes, Mathilde Blind, *George Eliot* (new ed., Boston, 1904), pp. 111-112; Edwin Mallard Everett, *The Party of Humanity: The* Fortnightly Review *and Its Contributors, 1865-1874* (Chapel Hill, N.C., 1939), p. 92; Thomas Nyland, "The English Positivists" (M.A. thesis, Universtiy of London, 1937), pp. 39-40; Cantecor, *Comte,* p. 167; and Eisen, "Harrison," pp. 159-163. Metz, *Hundred Years of British Philosophy,* p. 120, seems to me to exaggerate Lewes' divergence from Comte.

Chapter VIII

ENGLAND: SYMPATHIZERS

AND OTHERS

LEWES himself was in 1866 the editor of the *Fortnightly* (founded in the previous year). It was, however, not Lewes who subsequently opened its columns to Congreve, Bridges, and Harrison, but his successor, John Morley (the later famous writer and statesman). This succession was itself accomplished through the intervention of J. Cotter Morison, a Positivist disciple and one of the journal's original backers, who was a friend of Morley's from university days. Much like his predecessor, Morley had for a while been close to becoming a real disciple but had been held back by his "anti-sectarian instinct, confirmed by the influence of Mill" and by his association "with men like Spencer, Tyndall, Huxley, who bitterly condemned official Positivism as Catholicism minus Christianity." But he remained under Comte's influence in the sense, he said, "of Mill and Littré," was close to Lewes, was a lifelong friend of Harrison and admirer of Laffitte (whom he visited), and thought the Positivists "a remarkable group." [1]

[1] Morley, *Recollections* (New York, 1917), I, 68–72, 86; Morison to Laffitte, 14 July 1873, 28 Oct. 1875, M-le-P; Everett, *Party of Humanity,* pp. 17, 74–76; Basil Willey, *More Nineteenth Century Studies . . .* (London, 1956), pp. 253–258; F. W. Hirst, *Early Life & Letters of John Morley* (Lon-

Morley's adoption of some of Comte's ideas, particularly his interpretation of history, was nowhere so clear as in his book on Burke. He praised Burke for seeing "that in politics we are concerned not with barren rights, but with duties; not with abstract truth, but with practical morality."

It has been reserved for a great thinker of a later day [i.e., Comte] to explain the source and significance of absolute conceptions in social subjects, and to insist on the substitution of relative ideas in their place. This is the natural result of the substitution of the Positive for the Abstractional philosophy.

Morley went on to quote Comte on the absurdity of setting up absolute types of government, which Burke had seen but for which only Comte had provided a scientific basis. Morley alluded to Comte's formula of Order and Progress and condemned the French Revolutionary dogma of popular sovereignty in terms as similar to Comte's as to Burke's but maintained with Mill that political liberty was "the only possible guarantee that the principles, and methods, and purposes of a national government shall not sink below . . . [the] moral level of the nation itself." He made a special point, citing Comte, of the confusion of the spiritual and temporal powers during the Revolution.[2] In the following year, writing in the *Fortnightly,* Morley referred to Comte as "the thinker who has done more than any other towards laying the foundation of scientific history" and to the Law of the Three Stages specifically.[3]

Indeed, the *Fortnightly* was considered by some to be a Positivist organ,[4] and even Congreve could write of Morley:

---

don, 1927), I, 21; Morley to Harrison, 5 Jan. and 13 Nov. 1872, *ibid.,* I, 206–207, 223.

[2] Morley, *Edmund Burke: A Historical Study* (New York, 1924; first pub. 1866), pp. 18–20, 40–41, 232, 249, 251.

[3] Morley, "Mr. Froude on the Science of History," *Fortnightly Review,* VIII (1867), 229, 231.

[4] Everett, *Party of Humanity,* pp. 84, 91.

Outside of us he is one of the most useful men to our cause . . . , and though he does not share our convictions in all points . . . he is . . . a very great sympathiser with much. He is at present more useful to us in fact than if he were more fully with us. He has an acknowledged position . . . and he uses his pen and lets us use his periodical for the vulgarisation of Positivist doctrine.[5]

Morley in fact was driven to denying that the *Fortnightly* was a "consistent organ" of Positivism, citing the articles hostile to it that had been printed.[6] Privately he asserted that Harrison was "far from unanswerable," [7] and to Harrison himself he wrote:

You are all of you (when acting collectively) worshippers of abstractions; . . . you follow an absolute method; and you are penetrated with the vices of French political thinking. I don't believe there is a single leading principle of Comte's philosophy which has not been egregiously violated by the Church of Mecklenburgh Square since the outbreak of the German war with France.

Beesly and Congreve, particularly, Morley considered to be "not politicians, but clergymen," and he protested:

I see growing up among you—among us, if you like—tendencies to iterate the formulas of the master, instead of constantly applying, translating, and vivifying them: to pour malediction on men for not

[5] Congreve to Lobb, 4 Feb. 1870, BM Add. MS 45233 ff. 207–208.

[6] Morley, "The *Fortnightly Review* and Positivism; A Note," *Fortnightly Review,* n.s. VIII (1870), 118–120. The historian of the journal comments justly that it could be regarded as Positivist only in the broadest sense of the word: "If Positivism meant no more than faith in science and empiricism and the hope of eventually reducing all social concepts and institutions within the bounds of pure reason, then the review was Positivist, just as Aristotle was Positivist, or Voltaire, or Huxley" (Everett, *Party of Humanity,* p. 323). It is, of course, the contention of the present study that Positivism did mean more than this.

[7] Morley to Lady Amberley, 20 Dec. 1870, in Bertrand and Patricia Russell, ed., *The Amberley Papers* . . . (London, 1937), II, 387.

embracing Positivism, instead of explaining to them what Positivism is: to become more and more esoteric and special.[8]

"Why," he asked Harrison, "do you talk of Supreme Power with capital letters? It is the thin end of the wedge of a new theology"; he made fun of "Humanity, the Grand Etre, the Supreme Mother, and all the other capital letters of your faith," and contrasted "positive" with "positivist." [9]

Nevertheless that "among us, if you like" had not been a slip of the pen:

That my whole idea of history is . . . [Comte's] is certain: that my particular ideas in nearly all the subordinate points are his, is no less certain. . . . I agree with you and Bridges and Beesly and Crompton five million times more than I differ from you. . . . I am not Comtist but Positivist. I accept your statement . . . of the Positivist Problem.[10] I do not accept your solution—certainly not Comte's organisation, which I entirely dislike. . . . I don't know Comtism well enough to be competent either to accept or to repudiate it. I want three or four more years of reading him and of social observation. I believe I shall become more and more Millite, less and less Comtist.[11]

This prognostication proved correct; Morley, like Mill and Lewes, became progressively less enthusiastic about Comte. By 1874, in comparing Mill and Comte, Morley wrote that both had "wanted

[8] Morley to Harrison, 25 April 1871, Hirst, *Morley,* I, 187.

[9] Morley to Harrison, 7 May, 16 Oct., and 17 Nov. 1871, *ibid.,* I, 191–193, 222, 224; cf. also, on Congreve, to Harrison, 3 Oct. 1873, *ibid.,* I, 290, and on the Franco-Prussian war, to Congreve, 8 Jan. 1874, BM Add. MS 45241 ff. 61–62.

[10] Harrison's article under that title in the *Fortnightly,* XXXV (1869), 469–493.

[11] Morley to Harrison, 9 Dec. 1871, Hirst, *Morley,* I, 199–200. See also his letter to Mrs. Harrison, 29 Dec. 1873, *ibid.,* I, 301–302: "I am a Positivist— and a staunch repudiator of theology. . . . Only I am not, you know, of the straitest sect, and I disclaim all labels." But cf. his *Recollections,* II, 297 (written in 1909): "If I were to have a label, I should be called a Positivist."

to bring people to extend positive modes of thinking to the master subjects of morals, politics, and religion."

Mr. Mill, however, with a wisdom which Comte unfortunately did not share, refrained from any rash and premature attempt to decide what would be the results of this much-needed extension. . . . Comte . . . presumed at once to draw up a minute plan of social reconstruction, which contains some ideas of great beauty and power, some of extreme absurdity, and some which would be very mischievous if there were the smallest chance of their ever being realised.[12]

Two years later, in the article on Comte in the *Encyclopaedia Britannica,* he was still more severe. He chastised Comte's churlishness vis-à-vis Saint-Simon, his style, his "exaggerated egoism" and "absence of all feeling for reality," his "dogmatic and peremptory language," "his reactionary politics, and his perversity in clothing a philosophical doctrine, so intrinsically conciliatory . . . , in a shape that excites so little sympathy and gives so much provocation." Morley had no use for the Religion of Humanity in any aspect. But he called attention to the "magnitude and importance" of Comte's enterprise, his "sheer strength of thought" and "vigorous perspicacity." The strongest part of his work, Morley still thought, was the historical part of the *Cours,* "one of the great achievements of human intellect," and "his firm grasp of the cardinal truth that the improvement of the social organism can only be effected by a moral development." In general, Morley classified Comte as "the most eminent and important of that interesting group of thinkers whom the overthrow of old institutions in France turned towards social speculation."[13] This was a fair

[12] Morley, "Mr. Mill's Autobiography," *Fortnightly Review,* XXI (1874), 11–12. See also his reference to Comte in his *Voltaire* (1872), p. 37 n., quoted by Everett, *Party of Humanity,* p. 88 n.

[13] Cited after Morley's *Critical Miscellanies* (London, 1886), III, 337, 340–342, 355–356, 374–378, 380–384. Note, finally, his editorial admonition to Malcolm Quin, 18 Nov. 1884, quoted by Quin, *Memoirs,* p. 136: "Positivist views—yes, if you like; but not Positivist *dialect;* it is hated by men and

description, and for all its reservations the article as a whole was apt to stir interest in Positivism.

In the course of their correspondence Morley once chaffed Harrison: "Tush, my dear Harrison. There is not a Positivist among you. There are only two in England—Mill and George Eliot." [14] George Eliot "became familiar with Positivism in 1851 when she moved to London to assist John Chapman in the editing of the *Westminster Review,* and thereby came into close contact with the staff of the *Leader,*" [15] including, of course, Lewes. She had already abandoned traditional religion, translated Feuerbach, acquired an admiration of the certainty afforded by mathematics, and referred to "positive truths." [16] Nevertheless Lewes seems not to have influenced her much with respect to Positivism, for few references to it are to be found in her writings before 1859, when she and Lewes became neighbors of the Congreves in Wandsworth.[17] "She was deeply impressed by Comte's *Catéchisme posi-*

---

editors," and Harrison's irritable denunciation of him to Marvin, 28 Aug. 1908, FSM. Morley seems to have been partly instrumental, together with Harrison, Morison, and Beesly, in acquainting the novelist Meredith with Positivism (Mona E. Mackay, *Meredith et la France* [Paris, 1937], pp. 44-48; Lionel Stevenson, *The Ordeal of George Meredith: A Biography* [New York, 1953], p. 187; Jack Lindsay, *George Meredith: His Life and Work* [London, 1956], p. 196).

[14] Morley to Harrison, 22 Feb. 1871, Hirst, *Morley,* I, 178.

[15] Eisen, "Harrison," p. 171. Mrs. Chapman was also a great admirer of Comte (Harriet Martineau, *Autobiography* [London, 1887], III, 308-309).

[16] George Eliot to Mr. and Mrs. Charles Bray, 24 Oct. 1849, Haight, ed., *Letters,* I, 316; Nyland, "The English Positivists," pp. 43, 46-47; Willey, *Nineteenth Century Studies,* p. 207; and the rather special formulation of Gruber, *Positivismus,* pp. 77-78.

[17] Haight, ed., *Letters,* I, xlvi, lxi; Cross, *George Eliot,* II, 112, 118, 123-124; and P. Bourl'honne, *George Eliot . . .* (Paris, 1933), pp. 146-147, 151-154. She had, just previously, read and admired the article "The Religion of Positivism" in the *Westminster Reveiw,* an article taking a very reserved position (G. Eliot to Sara Hennell, 10-13 May 1858, Haight, ed., *Letters,* II, 456). Lewes had been recommended to Congreve by an Oxford friend

tiviste, translated by Congreve in 1858, and discussed it earnestly with her new friends." [18] It was in fact the religious side of Positivism that appealed to her, as distinct from Lewes, most strongly:

On many points where I used to delight in expressing intellectual difference, I now delight in feeling an emotional agreement. On that question of our future existence . . . my rooted conviction is, that the immediate object and the proper sphere of all our highest emotions are our struggling fellow-men and this earthly existence.[19]

From the *Catechism* George Eliot graduated to the *Cours* and thought Comte's survey of the Middle Ages full of "luminous ideas. I am thankful to learn from it." She admitted that Positivism was one-sided, "but Comte was a great thinker, nevertheless." [20] Congreve she diagnosed perceptively as "not at all a man to be free and easy with: he internally resents everything like a freedom, looking very benignant all the while," [21] and she felt more in sympathy with Harrison, whom she soon met at the Congreves'.[22] By the middle sixties she and Lewes were reading Comte systematically, and she was deeply moved at seeing Comte's house during a visit to Paris.[23] She defended the unity of Comte's thought; she and Lewes attended Congreve's first lectures to the Positivist Society and she contributed annually to the Society's funds thereafter; and she proposed to defray some of the expenses of publish-

---

of the latter as early as 1845 (Blackett to Congreve, 20 Aug. and 3 Sept. 1845, Wadham MS c. 185 f. 141).

[18] Haight, ed., *Letters,* I, lxii; cf. her journal for 9–10 Nov. 1859, *ibid.,* III, 197.

[19] G. Eliot to F. d'Albert-Durade, 6 Dec. 1859, *ibid.,* III, 231. The references are to Humanity and to "subjective immortality." See also her letter to S. Hennell, 13 July 1864, *ibid.,* IV, 158.

[20] G. Eliot to S. Hennell, 12 July 1861, *ibid.,* III, 438–439.

[21] Same, 21 May 1859, *ibid.,* III, 70.   [22] *Ibid.,* I, lxvii.

[23] G. Eliot to Mrs. Congreve, Oct. 1863, 27 Jan. 1865, 28 Jan. and 22 Dec. 1866, 16 Jan. 1867, *ibid.,* IV, 111, 176, 227, 324, 333.

ing the translation of the *Polity*.[24] She, like Lewes, approved of Congreve's reply to Huxley and went so far as to express fear that Harrison's disavowal of the religious aspects of Positivism would be misunderstood.[25]

Harrison, in his turn, also had occasion to be disappointed in George Eliot. He had suggested to her that "the grand features of Comte's world might be sketched in fiction in their normal relations though under the forms of our familiar life." He had outlined some of his ideas in this respect and concluded:

All that would be necessary to invent would be the condition which would give an organic unity to the good elements. . . . What the world yet wants to be shown is the possibility in real life of healthy moral control over societies—and the infinite scope and power of wealth used morally. . . . And nothing . . . but a miracle or a great work of art can flash it into their souls.[26]

The novelist replied that this idea would be tremendously difficult to execute. "On the other hand, my whole soul goes with your desire that it should be done, and I shall at least keep the possibility (or impossibility) perpetually in my mind, as something towards which I must strive." Then she mentioned, without any connection with what had gone before, that she was about to take up again an unfinished work, namely, *The Spanish Gypsy*.[27] The implica-

[24] *Ibid.,* I, lxii, to S. Hennell, 28 Oct. 1865, to Mrs. Congreve, 17 April 1868, *ibid.,* IV, 206–207, 430; see also her praise of the *Polity,* to Harrison, 19 Feb. 1875, *ibid.,* VI, 126. One of Congreve's lectures she found "chilling" (journal, 19 May 1867, *ibid.,* IV, 363 n. 8); see further, for criticism of Congreve, to S. Hennell, 13 May 1867, *ibid.,* IV, 363; Willey, *More Nineteenth Century Studies,* p. 254.

[25] G. Eliot to Mrs. Congreve, 4 May 1869, to Harrison, 15 Jan. 1870, Haight, ed., *Letters,* V, 26, 75.

[26] Harrison to G. Eliot, 19 July 1866, *ibid.,* IV, 286–289.

[27] G. Eliot to Harrison, 15 Aug. 1866, *ibid.,* IV, 301. A prefatory note to *The Spanish Gypsy* states that it was partly rewritten in the light of an intervening visit to Spain.

tion is that she had no notion of using this work to put Harrison's suggestion into practice, but she may have decided to do so as she went along. At any rate, when Congreve described *The Spanish Gypsy* on its appearance as "a mass of Positivism" she did not demur, allowing that it spread the doctrine.[28] Harrison also was polite enough to write that the work "truly idealized" "the profound truths and sacred principles" of Positivism: "I see in it the first fruits of the movement to the development of which we hope everything," [29] but actually he was dissatisfied with it as a Positivist poem.[30] Later Harrison asked George Eliot to write a Positivist liturgy, but she said this was beyond her powers, although she approved of prayers which kept "within the due limit of aspiration and do not pass into beseeching." [31]

As to whether *The Spanish Gypsy* or others of George Eliot's works were "Positivist" or not, in the sense of expressing Positivist ideas in some form or other, opinions may differ. Few are likely to go so far as to share Congreve's opinion of *The Spanish Gypsy;* on the other hand, given the biographical information available, it is certainly possible to discern Positivist ideas in that poem and elsewhere in her writings.[32] Perhaps the question is not very

[28] G. Eliot to Mrs. Congreve, 16 Dec. 1868, Haight, ed., *Letters,* IV, 496. Cf. Leslie Stephen, *George Eliot* (New York and London, 1902), p. 165.

[29] Harrison to G. Eliot, 11 Nov. 1868, Haight, ed., *Letters,* IV, 484.

[30] *Ibid.,* I, lxvii; Harrison, "George Eliot," *P.R.,* X (1902), 160, explicitly takes issue with Congreve in the matter and denies the Positivist content of *The Spanish Gypsy.*

[31] G. Eliot to Harrison, 14 June and 26 Dec. 1877, Haight, ed., *Letters,* VI, 387–388, 439; cf. I, lxviii. This episode is interesting, incidentally, as showing Harrison interested in a liturgy just before the break with Congreve. In the schism George Eliot sided with Harrison (*ibid.,* I, lxii, VII, 260 n. 6).

[32] With respect to George Eliot's literary works, with the best will in the world I cannot find more than a half-dozen brief passages each in *The Spanish Gypsy* and the 800 pages of *Daniel Deronda* which bear any sort of Positivist interpretation, and the principal message of both works is a paean to nationalism. Apart from her poem "O May I Join the Choir Invisible"

important, since even at best her allusions were not of a nature to exercise a "profound influence on the philosophy of her day," [33] and concerning her own attitude the evidence of the literary works is not necessary.

There is, however, as a matter of fact some evidence to suggest that George Eliot cooled somewhat in her enthusiasm toward Positivism. No doubt her husband, who was also her biographer, might be thought to have known best, and he declared that her adherence, though selective and limited, was profound: "For all Comte's writing she had a feeling of high admiration, intense interest, and very deep sympathy. I do not think I ever heard her speak of any writer with a more grateful sense of obligation for enlightenment." [34] Herbert Spencer, however, wrote that "during our last interview, which was on the very day she was taken ill, conversation brought out evidence that she was veering a good

(1867), which with its celebration of "subjective immortality" became a part of Positivist liturgy, I find Positivism, if anywhere, in her "College Breakfast-Party" (1878) (in her *Poems* [New York, 1886], pp. 201–202, 147–171 respectively). I confess to a suspicion that, the notion of Positivism in George Eliot's works once having got started (perhaps by Congreve's remark), it perpetuated itself, without much further thought, through the comments in the anonymous "George Eliot and Comtism," *London Quarterly Review*, Vol. 47 (1876–77), pp. 450–452, 464–465, 468–470; Blind, *George Eliot*, p. 10; Pond, *Idées morales*, pp. 79–80; Richard Stang, *The Theory of the Novel in England, 1850–1870* (New York and London, 1959), p. 42; Bourl'honne, *George Eliot*, p. 149 n. 4; Nyland, "English Positivists," pp. 49–51; and the Positivist Alfred Haggard, in *P.R.*, IX (1901), 27–28.

[33] Cf. Nyland, "English Positivists," pp. 51–52. There is tangible evidence of two cases of interest aroused in Positivism by George Eliot: Lord Houghton, who went with her to at least one of Congreve's lectures (G. Eliot to S. Hennell, Haight, ed., *Letters*, IV, 363; cf. T. Wemyss Reid, *Life, Letters, and Friendships of . . . Lord Houghton* [New York, 1891], II, 376), and one Samuel Pearson of Halifax, who read of Congreve in Cross's biography of her (Pearson to Congreve, 21 Dec. 1886, BM Add. MS 45240 ff. 228–229). It may be that she also interested her second husband in Positivism (Bridges to Laffitte, 10 Feb. 1881, M-le-P).

[34] Cross, *George Eliot*, III, 310–311.

deal away from Comte, and recognized the fundamental divergence from the Comtist conception of society, of views of mine which she accepted." [35] The magisterial Benjamin Jowett likewise testified that George Eliot "told me that she was never a Comtist, but as they were a poor and unfortunate sect, she would never finally renounce them." [36] Congreve also noted a decline in Positivist sympathy on George Eliot's part.[37]

But such a development occurred, if at all, only at the very end of her life, and of her earlier sympathy for the Religion of Humanity, over a period of twenty years, there can be no doubt.[38]

[35] Spencer to "my American friend" (Youmans?), 1880 or 1881, in his *Autobiography* (New York, 1904), II, 430.

[36] Jowett to Morier, 15 Jan. 1881, in Evelyn Abbott and Lewis Campbell, *Life and Letters of Benjamin Jowett* (New York and London, 1899), II, 182. Jowett himself had studied Comte about 1850 and had valued his historical method, remarking: "The world will not be again deceived by a metaphysical system.—Comte has such great knowledge of the world in one way, so little in another." But he became steadily less favorably inclined. He disapproved of Lewes' *Biographical History* and "looked with interest but with imperfect sympathy upon the rise of the Positivist sect in Oxford." To Harrison he wrote (30 April 1861): "I was glad to hear that you were not a Positivist. Not that I do not respect Comte. . . . But he seems to me to have got a false and absorbing hold on some minds" and to be a metaphysician in Positivist clothing. Rereading Comte in 1882, Jowett made disparaging observations while appreciating his genius. The science of sociology, in particular, was "a monstrous fiction" (*ibid.*, I, 130–131, 261, II, 187; Abbott and Campbell, ed., *Letters of Benjamin Jowett* [2 vols., London, 1897], p. 16). See, further, the views of another great Oxford figure of the time, Mark Pattison, who took issue with Harrison in the *Contemporary Review* ("The Religion of Positivism," XXVII [1875–76], 593–614), distinguishing between the "positive spirit" to which the future belonged and Positivism as a false system and a ridiculous religion, in which Pattison doubted whether Harrison really believed.

[37] Congreve to Sophia Edger, 10 May 1880, Haight, ed., *Letters,* I, lxii.

[38] See the conclusions of G. W. Cooke, *George Eliot: A Critical Study* (London, 1883), pp. 193–194; Marie Dronsart, *Portraits d'Outre-Manche* (Paris, 1889), p. 236; Blind, *George Eliot,* pp. 281–283 (placing her closer

In this respect her closest spiritual affinity was probably with Harrison. Like him she was of a profoundly religious temperament: having lost her old faith she "clung for years to the hope of finding a substitute for it in the Religion of Humanity." [39] The difference between them, though of great importance, was fine: where Harrison became persuaded that the Religion of Humanity was compatible with his "philosophy of common sense" and that by adopting it he did not give up his intellectual independence, George Eliot could not take that last step: "I cannot submit my intellect or my soul to the guidance of Comte." [40] She differed very much more from Lewes and all the other partial adherents to Positivism, who were least attracted by its religious aspects.

This description serves also for that other Victorian bluestocking, Harriet Martineau, who performed a task more fundamental to the understanding of Comte in England than did any of the others: she translated the *Cours* and, more important still, in doing so she abridged it. In her preface she explained that she had undertaken the work in the hope of aiding "scientific progress" by diffusing Comte's ideas and of providing "a rallying-point of . . . scattered speculations" in an age of transition; "it gives us the basis that we demand, the principle of action that we want." It was true that sociology was "as yet too crude and confused" to be established by Comte, like the other sciences,

by a review of what had before been achieved: but . . . by the hand of our master, discriminated, arranged, and consolidated, so as to be ready to fulfil the conditions of true science as future generations bring their contributions of knowledge and experience to build upon the foundation here laid.

---

to Lewes' position than I think is warranted); Pond, *Idées morales,* pp. 80, 82, 178; also Stephen, *George Eliot,* pp. 199–200, and, with more discernment for the negative as well as the affirmative side of the case, Bourl'honne, *George Eliot, passim.*

[39] Haight, ed., *Letters,* I, xlvi.

[40] Quoted by Blind, *George Eliot,* p. 283.

The study of Comte, she concluded, was the best remedy for the prevailing anarchy of opinion; his philosophy was morally edifying, "a train of noble truths." She had, she said, deliberately refrained from criticism.[41] She also deliberately refrained from translating, in her abridgment, the last few programmatic pages of the *Cours* which pointed most clearly in the direction of the *Polity,* in process of publication while the translation of the *Cours* was under way. Harrison, indeed, introducing a reissue of the Martineau translation, pronounced himself dissatisfied with it on this ground among others, and a beginning was made later on a new and complete translation.[42] Comte himself, on the contrary, was delighted with the Martineau translation and preferred it to the original, and it was subsequently retranslated and published in France.

Harriet Martineau later touched briefly on her relationship to Comte and his system:

After hearing Comte's name for many years, and having a vague notion of the relation of his philosophy to the intellectual and social needs of the time, I obtained something like a clear preparatory view, at second-hand, from a friend . . . in 1850. What I learned then and there impelled me to study the great book for myself.

She then read Lewes' and Littré's summaries of Comte and conceived the scheme of translating the *Cours,* an activity which she greatly enjoyed: "The vast range of knowledge, . . . the clear enunciation, and incessant application of principles. The weak part of the book,—the sacrifices made to system and order" were

[41] Comte, *The Positive Philosophy* (tr. and condensed by Harriet Martineau, Intro. by Frederic Harrison, London, 1896; first pub. 1853), I, xxiii–xxx.

[42] Comte, *The Fundamental Principles of the Positive Philosophy* (tr. Paul Descours and H. Gordon Jones, with a Biographical Preface by Edward Spencer Beesly, London, 1905). On Harrison's estimate, see also R. K. Webb, *Harriet Martineau: A Radical Victorian* (London, etc., 1960), pp. 304–305.

counterbalanced by Comte's "philosophical sensibility and honest earnestness," and she defended him against various critics.[43]

Recent scholarship has done something to eke out these tantalizing references. Harriet Martineau in the 1840's had already been intellectually and theologically radical, with a phenomenalistic epistemology and a sociologically and deterministically oriented interpretation of history. In short, and despite disagreement with Comte on a number of specific issues (e.g., feminism, Protestantism), she was attracted to his work "because he offered an entire system which at one point after another struck familiar notes" and which had the advantage, precisely, of being a system. Although she did not accept the ritual of Comte's religion, she welcomed a solution to the problem of religion in terms which included "a belief in progress and a passion for serving humanity." [44]

This analysis is not only informative about Harriet Martineau but suggestive about Comte and illustrative of the reasons for his

[43] Harriet Martineau, *Autobiography*, II, 371, 390–391, 393–396. The "friend" was apparently H. G. Atkinson, a writer with whom she had collaborated for many years and who had in turn learned of Positivism from reading Lewes and Littré (Webb, *Harriet Martineau*, p. 303).

[44] *Ibid.*, pp. 253, 281, 294, 303–308, 364. Cf. also Nyland, "English Positivists," pp. 29–34. Harriet Martineau's brother James, the famous Unitarian minister and theologian, was severer on Positivism than was Harriet. After an early essay ("Comte's Life and Philosophy," in his *Essays, Reviews, and Addresses* [London and New York, 1890–91], I, 331–380; first pub. in the *National Review* in July 1858) mixing sarcasm about "the puerilities of his later writings" with recognition of Comte as "the most powerful and constructive thinker of the modern scientific school" whose assumptions, however, are exposed as untenable, Martineau returned to the subject again in his maturer *Types of Ethical Theory*, where he approved of the Classification of the Sciences as a heuristic device, called Comte's historical survey "brilliant," saw wisdom and nobility in his ethical and religious ideas but also still much that was grotesque, and severely criticized his dogmatism in general and his dogmatic exclusion of certain branches of inquiry specifically (I, 398–399, 419–420, 423, 427–428, 430, 455, 461, 468–469, 475, 477–480, 482, 497–502, 505, 507).

adoption. Comte's ideas came if not precisely "out of the common-places of his time" [45] yet out of the climate of opinion of "advanced" thinkers of his time, including above all an admiration for science and a belief that a "scientific" analysis of history could show the way to a cure for the ills of society deriving from the political and economic revolutions of the past half-century. Mill, Lewes, Harriet Martineau, and their associates in England, more than most of the first generation of academic sympathizers with Positivism in France, appreciated the virtue of Comte's system as a system just because they were not closely wedded to some one academic discipline and even though they found both the extent and many of the contents of the system ultimately unacceptable. Comte himself had always conceived of his system in at least the etymological sense of the word "religion," as a bond among men, and in this sense Comte's English friends or admirers welcomed it in principle too, Lewes the most unequivocally of them all and including the necessity of the appeal to the emotions. They differed from the Wadham nucleus of disciples in that they did not follow Comte (not even George Eliot, finally) into the institutionalization of religion in the conventional sense of the word, or into the organization of society that it implied in the light of the doctrine of the "spiritual power." They differed from Littré, who rejected these elements too, in that they detected the germs of them in the *Cours* and were thus deterred, as well as by their revulsion from Comte personally and their different temperament generally, from accepting the Comte of the *Cours* as a source of unalterable truth. But they differed equally from men like Grote, who was so put off by the as yet relatively mild mania for *concrete* systematization in the *General View* that he abandoned Positivism altogether. Harriet Martineau with her single isolated contribution to the diffusion of Positivism, Mill and Lewes with their sustained,

[45] Webb, *Harriet Martineau*, p. 308. Cf. Gouhier, *La jeunesse d'Auguste Comte*, II, 348, on the climate of "pre-positivism" that nourished both Saint-Simon and Comte.

lifelong efforts in its behalf, Morley during the period of his flirtation with Positivism, agreed not only with Comte's method but with his purpose, which he shared with the Saint-Simonians, of reorganizing society. They disagreed with his specific conclusions, and even more with the proposed method of putting them into operation, but they did not disagree that conclusions could and should be arrived at, that Comte was asking the right questions. In this position they differed only from the most intransigent of Comte's disciples, who also admitted that the *Polity* still left sociology "instituted" but not yet "constituted." Only the disciples believed that it must be "constituted" along the lines prescribed by Comte, whereas the sympathizers held that scientific sociology might well lead to quite different conclusions from those to which its founder had forced it. In so doing they, like Littré, made Positivism accessible and palatable for persons of their own generation and of the next who often found Comte's systematization excessive even in principle but who came in this way to appreciate some of his ideas independent of their "rigorous enchainment" which had so attracted Lewes. George Eliot played rather a lone hand in this company.[46]

In his remarks concerning his last interview with George Eliot, Herbert Spencer indicated a feeling of rivalry rather than of cooperation between himself and Comte.[47] Spencer indeed found it necessary specifically to repudiate the suggestion of his indebtedness to Comte, asserting that he resembled the latter only with respect to ideas not original with Comte, ideas which both of them took from the general "atmosphere of scientific thought"— the idea of sociology as a science and of society as an "organism." Spencer's claim to independence seems justified both historically and doctrinally. He first learned about Comte in 1852 (that is, after the publication of his *Social Statics*) from Lewes and George

[46] Compare these reflections with Eisen, "Harrison," p. 358.
[47] On George Eliot and Spencer, see also Bourl'honne, *George Eliot*, pp. 145–146.

Eliot; subsequently he read in Lewes' *Biographical History* and in Mill's *Logic* passages concerning Comte and started to read Harriet Martineau's translation of the *Cours* but did not get very far with it because, as he said, he could never read books with which he disagreed (in this, at least, he resembled Comte).[48] Moreover, Spencer's doctrinal differences from Comte (whom he called "a very undignified little old man" and whom he accused of exhibiting a "lack of mental balance"[49]) were important and specific and outweigh the very generalized similarity. Spencer emphatically rejected the Law of the Three Stages, the Classification of the Sciences, and Comte's whole emphasis on the importance of ideas in history and indeed on the importance of history at all; and he accused Comte of not understanding biological evolution and of ignoring the "indefinite modifiability of species" and the "universal redistribution of matter and motion."[50] Spencer not merely ridiculed the Religion of Humanity but (in a famous controversy with Harrison) denied the necessity of a religious basis for ethics and defended agnosticism in the form of a *"deliberate assertion* of an unknown cause of phenomena," the so-called Unknowable, denounced by all Positivists as a metaphysical notion.[51] In politics, Spencer's extreme advocacy of a free society

[48] Spencer's essay "The Filiation of Ideas," to Lewes, 21 March 1864, and to Leslie Stephen, 2 July 1899, in Duncan, *Life of Spencer,* II, 317, 320–321, 568, 146–147.

[49] Spencer to his mother, 20 Oct. 1856, *ibid.,* I, 107; "Retrogressive Religion," *Nineteenth Century,* XVI (1884), 12.

[50] Spencer, *Essays: Scientific, Political & Speculative* (London and Edinburgh, 1891), II, 125–132, *The Study of Sociology* (New York, 1906), pp. 299–300, letter to Edward Lott, 23 April 1852, in Duncan, *Life,* I, 80–81.

[51] *Essays,* II, 125–132; "Religion: A Retrospect and Prospect," "Retrogressive Religion," and "Last Words about Agnosticism and the Religion of Humanity," *Nineteenth Century,* XV (1884), 1–12, XVI (1884), 3–26, 826–839; letters to the *New Englander,* Nov. 1863, and to E. L. Youmans, 4 Dec. 1869, in Duncan, *Life,* I, 147, 206. Cf. Harrison's "The Ghost of Religion," *Nineteenth Century,* XV (1884), 494–506, "Agnostic Metaphysics,"

contrasts obviously with Comte's authoritarian conception. Even in the field of scientific education Spencer heavily qualified his agreement with Comte.[52] In short, Spencer's disclaimer of Comtian influence, though violent, was nonetheless warranted; and recent scholarship has for the most part not repeated with Spencer the mistake made, for example, in the case of Taine of inferring historical derivation from a few very general resemblances.[53]

Resembling Taine more than Spencer in his historical interests, that archetype of English amateur scholarship, Henry Thomas Buckle, has also on the whole escaped being classified as a Positivist, and rightly so.[54] Nevertheless Buckle himself was not so eager as

---

ibid., XVI (1884), 353–378, and his well-balanced, nonpolemical *Herbert Spencer Lecture* (Oxford and London, 1905), esp. pp. 11–12, 16–17, 22, 24, 27. Spencer had been really annoyed by Harrison (Spencer to Congreve, 10 July 1884, BM Add. MS 45240 ff. 260–261).

[52] Spencer, *Education: Intellectual, Moral, and Physical* (New York and London, 1912), p. 117.

[53] On Spencer and Comte, see Whittaker, "Comte and Mill," pp. 77–78; Gruber, *Positivismus*, p. 113; Barth, *Philosophie der Geschichte*, I, 91–93, and "Herbert Spencer und Albert Schäffle: Zu ihrem Gedächtnis," *Vierteljahrsschrift für wissenschaftliche Philosophie und Soziologie*, XXVIII (1904), 231–235; Metz, *Hundred Years*, pp. 100–101; Cantecor, *Comte*, p. 166; Ribot, *English Psychology*, pp. 192–193; and the Positivist P. Pichard in his review of Spencer's *Study of Sociology* in *P.P.*, XIV (1875), 22–23, all distinguishing between them. See also Troeltsch, *Historismus*, pp. 420–429, somewhat more *nuancé* but in the end reducing the similarity to a desire for a scheme of human development; John C. Greene, "Biology and Social Theory in the Nineteenth Century: Auguste Comte and Herbert Spencer," in Marshall Clagett, ed., *Critical Problems in the History of Science* (Madison, Wis., 1959), pp. 419–446, an acute analysis in which differences outweigh similarities and no derivation is alleged. Waentig, *Comte*, pp. 231–236, and J. M. Robertson, *Modern Humanists Reconsidered* (London, 1927), p. 195, claim that Spencer protested too much in denying his debt to Comte. The subtlest analysis of all is perhaps that of Delvolvé, *Réflexions*, pp. 279–281: in Darwinian evolution Spencer supplied the final universal principle after which Comte had thirsted, and did so under Comte's influence via Mill.

[54] See, however, Louis Etienne, "Le positivisme dans l'histoire," *Revue*

Spencer to repudiate all connection with Comte or to denigrate him and, publishing as he did immediately after Comte's death, in a sense invited comparison with him. He quoted Comte, in the beginning of his famous *History,* on the deficiencies of traditional historiography and said that he had done more than any living writer to raise the standard. "There is much in the method and in the conclusions of this great work [the *Cours*] with which I cannot agree; but it would be unjust to deny its extraordinary merits." [55] Buckle had evidently read Comte with care and commented approvingly, in passing, on his treatment of one or two specific points.[56] But beyond these incidental references Buckle's *History,* neither in its programmatic statements nor in the actual execution, contains anything that strikes a Positivist chord apart from his hope "to accomplish for the history of man something equivalent, or at all events analogous, to what has been effected by other inquiries for the different branches of natural science," [57] which is in all conscience generalized enough and may, if one wishes, be

---

des deux mondes, Vol. 74 (1868), esp. pp. 403–407, and Carl Brinkmann, "Ernst Friedrich Apelt und Henry Thomas Buckle . . . ," *Archiv für Kulturgeschichte,* XI (1914), 316–318. His own compatriots have been more discerning with Buckle, beginning with Mill, who said that Buckle was not Comte's adherent "except in the opinion common to both, that history may be made a subject of science" (*Auguste Comte and Positivism,* p. 46 n.); see particularly Robertson, *Buckle,* esp. p. 377. The Positivists themselves repudiated Buckle. See above all Littré, "De l'histoire de la civilisation en Angleterre par Buckle," *P.P.,* II (1868), 54–84 *passim.* See also Charles de Rémusat, "De la civilisation moderne," *Revue des deux mondes,* XVIII (1858), 5–44, paying tribute to both Buckle and Comte but minimizing the link between them.

[55] Buckle, *History of Civilization in England* (New York, 1879, first pub. 1857–61), I, 4 and n. On the "conclusions" with which he disagreed, cf. his remark, in his essay on "Mill on Liberty," *Fraser's Magazine,* Vol. 59 (1859), p. 48: "Comte, the most comprehensive thinker France has produced since Descartes, did in his last work deliberately advocate, and wish to organise, a scheme of polity . . . monstrously and obviously impracticable."

[56] Buckle, *History,* I, 137 n. 24, 269 n.

[57] *Ibid.,* I, 5, and cf. Mill, quoted in n. 54 above.

attributed in part to Buckle's known acquaintance with Comte's work. On some specific matters Buckle explicitly differed from Comte: on determinism, for example, on the limitations of historical knowledge, on psychology, on economics, on the relationship between intellect and morality.[58] Another famous amateur historian, Lecky, contemporary with Buckle but living longer and accomplishing more, admired Buckle but repudiated Positivism.[59]

Leslie Stephen, the progenitor of Bloomsbury and prodigious man of letters, read the *Cours* while at Cambridge in 1859 (and long afterwards said that if he had been at Oxford instead he might have become a Positivist). Even as it was, he was sympathetic to the movement, believed it had "leavened the thoughts of the rising generation," and continued, in contact with Lewes, to occupy himself with Comte. As late as 1882 he wrote: "I consider myself to have learnt very much from Comte, and I take a higher estimate of him than most people do. . . . Much of my morality is contained in his."[60] By contrast, Walter Bagehot thought that Comte was "dead" as early as 1854[61] and in his famous *Physics and Politics* satirized the political views of the

[58] *Ibid.,* I, 6, 13–15, 94, 113–120, 151, 161. He agreed, however, that "a discovery of the laws of European history is resolved, in the first instance, into a discovery of the laws of the human mind" (*ibid.,* I, 112–113).

[59] Letters of 12 Sept. 1861 and March 1869, in H. Montgomery Hyde, ed., *A Victorian Historian: Private Letters of W. E. H. Lecky, 1859–1878* (London, 1947), pp. 40–41, 75. Lecky's own works contain no relevant material. Simply as a curio, before abandoning amateur historians, I note that Hilaire Belloc, with the encouragement of Harrison, wrote to the French Positivist Robinet concerning Danton (17 Sept. 1898, A.N., AS 2).

[60] Frederic William Maitland, *The Life and Letters of Leslie Stephen* (New York and London, 1908), pp. 73, 165, 172, 185, 352; cf. also Noel Gilroy Annan, *Leslie Stephen* . . . (London, 1951), pp. 43, 52, 143, 148 n., 184, 278, who on p. 212, no doubt following Stephen's last-quoted remark, calls his *Science of Ethics* (London, 1882) "a by-product of Comte," but that seems to me to be going very much too far; and Troeltsch, *Historismus,* p. 415.

[61] Alastair Buchan, *The Spare Chancellor: The Life of Walter Bagehot* (London, 1959), p. 77.

English Positivists.[62] The allusion of Jacques Barzun to "the Positivism of Comte and Huxley"[63] must be taken loosely, since Huxley, far more vociferously than Spencer (Huxley did nothing by half-measures), was the sworn opponent of the Positivists and the coiner of the description of it as "Catholicism *minus* Christianity." He found in Positivism "little or nothing of any scientific value, and a great deal, which is as thoroughly antagonistic to the very essence of science as anything in ultramontane Catholicism."[64] Comte, he continued in a second installment, "had but the most superficial and merely second-hand knowledge of most branches of what is usually understood by science." Huxley alluded to Comte's "want of apprehension of the great features of science; his strange mistakes as to the merits of his contemporaries; and his ludicrously erroneous notions about the part which some of the scientific doctrines current in his time were destined to play in the future." The Law of the Three Stages was "a series of more or less contradictory statements of an imperfectly apprehended truth," and the Classification "is, in my judgment, absolutely worthless." Comte had exhibited the "papal spirit" not merely at the end, but throughout.[65] This blast might be partially offset by a scholar, no doubt of lesser rank than Huxley but still a pioneering sociologist and president of the Royal Statistical Society, Charles Booth, who was related to Beesly and also knew Congreve. He was "fairly captivated" by their talk in the 1860's, "and his formal adhesion to the ranks of Positivism was held to be only a matter of time." In 1870 he wrote: "I feel assured that the principles of Positivism will lead us on till we find the true solution of the problem of government," though he was not prepared to accept Comte's "exact scheme of a Utopia" and began to cast about for an alternative to Positivism. Booth's nature,

[62] Cited after the New York ed. of 1948, pp. 61–62 (first pub. 1869).

[63] *Darwin, Marx, Wagner,* p. 123.

[64] Huxley, "On the Physical Basis of Life," *Fortnightly Review,* n.s. V (1869), 141.

[65] "The Scientific Aspects of Positivism," *ibid.,* 654, 659, 668–669.

though enthusiastic, had many needs, many aspirations difficult to satisfy, within the limits of any formal body of doctrine; and although the
writings of Comte affected him powerfully, and ever kept an influence
over his mind, he never took the step of joining the Positivist body, and
as time went on became less occupied with the movement.[66]

The failure of Positivism (intended to be *par excellence* the comprehensive system appealing to and satisfying all the many sides
of human nature) to hold the loyalty of this man of "many needs
and many aspirations" is perhaps as eloquent a commentary as any
on the movement's vicissitudes.

A few men in English public life (fewer than in France) came
in contact with Positivism and recorded their impressions. Lord
and Lady Amberley (the parents of Bertrand Russell) went to
Congreve's early lectures and they and their cousin Arthur Russell
knew Beesly and Harrison, but they were unfavorably impressed
by them in general and on such specific subjects as the Franco-
Prussian War and the role of workers in society.[67] John Bright
wrote to Congreve: "I hold that what is good in modern nations
is the outcome of Christianity and intimately allied to it. . . . I
am glad that you are willing to promote Christian morals if you
refuse the Christian faith." [68] W. S. Robson, later Lord Robson
and Solicitor-General, knew Congreve and once sent five pounds
after attending a Positivist service, saying that he had admired
the address and that his belief in God had not prevented him from
benefiting greatly from Positivism. He thought that "the noble

[66] T. S. and M. B. Simey, *Charles Booth: Social Scientist* (London, 1960),
pp. 44, 48; anon., *Charles Booth: A Memoir* (London, 1918), pp. 8–9; cf.
F. W. O[gilvie], "Charles Booth," *Dictionary of National Biography, 1912–
1921*, pp. 48–50. Another famous scientist wrote: "I never made a study of
Comte: his awful verbosity and great self-sufficiency frightened me" (A. de
Morgan to Sir W. R. Hamilton, 26 March 1854, in Robert Perceval Graves,
Life of Sir William Rowan Hamilton [Dublin and London, 1882–89], III,
476).

[67] Letters and diaries, 1867–72, in Russell, ed., *Amberley Papers*, II, 33,
40, 254–255, 376, 417, 462–468, 473–477, 479–481.

[68] Bright to Congreve, 25 Sept. 1876, BM Add. MS 45241 f. 27.

conception of Humanity" would be a permanent one. "Hence the importance of your work to those who share only part of your creed." [69]

Matthew Arnold considered Harrison "a very clever writer" who had "developed, in the systematic and stringent manner of his school," "that body of truth with which the earlier Liberals merely fumbled," but he regarded Harrison and Congreve—"an old friend of mine, and I am glad to have an opportunity of publicly expressing my respect for his talents and character"— as Jacobins and therefore hostile to "culture." [70] The only professional writer after George Eliot, in fact, to take much notice of Positivism was George Gissing, introduced to the Newton Hall group in 1882 by Harrison, whose sons he was tutoring; but his interest in the doctrine in fact antedated this event—and did not long survive it. Gissing had studied Comte at Jena in 1877 and "was obsessed with systems and science," and Positivism "seemed to offer a non-theological system that accounted for the great achievements of humanity as well as for the presence of the almost sub-human." Gissing called the *Cours* "a most wonderful résumé of human knowledge"; Positivism was both a "Religion of Humanity" and a "science of social life" which attracted members precisely "because it tried to do the impossible."

I always refer, in speaking of Positivism, to its *intellectual* side, its inculcation, for instance, of a system of politics based upon a study of the laws of human development. . . . Of course, with myself, its emotional side, the so-termed Religion of Humanity has also vast influence.

In his first novel he wrote: "Comte came to me with his lucid unfolding of the mystery of the world, and taught me the use to which my sympathy should be directed." Nevertheless, although he continued for some years to date some of his letters according

[69] Quin, *Memoirs*, pp. 113–114.

[70] *Culture and Anarchy* (ed. Knickerbocker, New York, 1925; first pub. 1869), pp. 35, 45, 62–63.

to the Positivist calendar, he began by the end of 1882 to veer away from Positivism and toward the less insistently optimistic agnosticism of a Stephen or a Lecky. He later said that his "temporary Positivist pose" had been "entirely due to his gratitude" to Harrison. Harrison, in his turn, was much disappointed in Gissing and even in his very generous introduction to Gissing's posthumous novel *Veranilda* did not mention his Positivism.[71]

It is, nevertheless, clear that Positivism came to the notice of many (with whatever effect) through the personal and political prominence of Harrison, as well as of Beesly, Congreve, and other Positivists, and if some (like John Morley or the Amberleys) were repelled by their politics, others were attracted. This was particularly true of the nascent Labour Movement.[72] The Socialist historian E. B. Bax later recalled how at the time of the Paris Commune

I became convinced that the highest and indeed only true religion for human beings was that which had for its object the devotion to the future social life of Humanity. . . . The idea of human progress as the proper object of religion led me some time after this to attach myself somewhat, although I never formally joined it, to the Positivist

[71] T. S(eccombe), "George Gissing," *DNB,* 2nd suppl., II, 114; *Letters of George Gissing to Members of His Family* (London, 1927), pp. 42, 92, 120; Mabel Collins Donnelly, *George Gissing: Grave Comedian* (Cambridge, Mass., 1954), pp. 10–11, 41–45, 50–51, 53, 80; Morley Roberts, *The Private Life of Henry Maitland: A Portrait of George Gissing* (ed. Bishop, London, 1958), pp. 44, 96; Gissing's *Workers in the Dawn* (pub. 1880), quoted by Frank Swinnerton, *George Gissing: A Critical Study* (new ed., London, 1924), p. 27; cf. Austin Harrison (one of Gissing's former pupils), "George Gissing," *Nineteenth Century and After,* Vol. 60 (1906), pp. 453–463, and in his biography of his father: "I think my father was disappointed in Gissing's sociology, which was purely fictional. . . . He had little sense of religion. . . . My father tried to stimulate some moral enthusiasm in him, but Gissing could not respond" (pp. 82–83).

[72] Cf. also above, pp. 80–81, for the Fabian Society as a medium of Positivist diffusion.

body. . . . I was the more attracted to the Positivists from the fact that they were the only organised body

except the Marxists who had espoused the cause of the Commune.[73] Sidney Ball, an Oxford friend of Marvin's, wrote in a Fabian Tract, quoting Comte, that the requisite "moral dynamics of Socialism" could be supplied by the Religion of Humanity.[74]

It was Beatrice Webb, however, who represented the greatest potential catch for Positivism in the Labour Movement. From Harrison she learned some of the fundamental principles of socialism, but despite favorable predisposition she was less apt a pupil in the doctrines of Positivism which he also tried to inculcate. She was originally attracted by the attempt to combine the intellectual appeal with an emotional one. She had earlier read Lewes, Mill, and George Eliot, but was persuaded by Harrison to read "all the works" of Comte himself and copied some passages in her diary, but "it certainly never occurred to me to join the Church of Humanity." She recorded how she had once been taken by Harrison to Newton Hall: "His address seemed to me forced— a valiant effort to make a religion out of nothing; a pitiful attempt by poor humanity to turn its head round and worship its tail." [75]

---

[73] Ernest Belfort Bax, *Reminiscences and Reflections of a Mid and Late Victorian* (London, 1918), pp. 29–30. But cf. his distinction between Socialism and Positivism (which performed a "travesty of Christian rites") in his *The Religion of Socialism* . . . (London, n.d.), pp. 52–53.

[74] Ball, *The Moral Aspects of Socialism* (London, 1908; Fabian Tract No. 72, first pub. 1896 in the *International Journal of Ethics*), p. 23. Cf. his rather lukewarm references to Positivism in his letters to Marvin, 29 Jan. 1890, 7 March 1895, and n.d. (1895), FSM. According to Margaret Cole, *The Story of Fabian Socialism* (London, etc., 1961), p. 6, the author of the first Fabian Tract, W. L. Phillips, was a house painter "who had embraced the Positivist philosophy of Auguste Comte"; the tract itself, "Why Are the Many Poor" (1884), in any event bears no traces of Positivist doctrine.

[75] Beatrice Webb, *My Apprenticeship* (London, etc., 1950), pp. 123–129. It may be worth noting that the library of another prominent Socialist, George Howell, included the following books: Bridges' *Unity of Comte's*

This comment seems to me to epitomize the reactions of many (including George Eliot) who came to Positivism because they shared the desire of Comte and his disciples for a comprehensive, nontheological guide for life, who were indeed attracted, as Gissing wrote, because Positivism promised the impossible, but who could not in the end say: "Credo quia impossibile." In fact, as soon as the problem presented itself as a religious one, people tended to shy away; and the problem presented itself far more readily as a religious one in England than in France because of the absence of a Littréist *via media,* of a way of "belonging" without committing oneself to a form of "believing"—because of the implied claim of the disciples, whether of Chapel Street or of Newton Hall, to some sort of orthodoxy.[76]

Life and Doctrine, Comte's *Polity,* Congreve's *Essays,* H. Crompton's *Religion of Humanity,* Lewes' *Comte's Philosophy of the Sciences,* and Mill's *Auguste Comte and Positivism;* see also allusions to Harrison in Howell's own *Conflicts of Capital and Labour* . . . (2nd ed., London and New York, 1890; first pub. 1878).

[76] For the sake of completeness I give here some references to a few miscellaneous persons, not of particular prominence, who came in contact with Positivism: Sir Thomas Allbutt went to medical school as a result of reading the *Cours* in 1858 (Sir Humphry Davy Rolleston, *The Rt. Hon. Sir Thomas Clifford Allbutt* . . . [London, 1929], p. 12). Auberon Herbert and Grant Duff requested introductions to Laffitte from Harrison (Harrison to Laffitte, 13 March 1876, 12 March 1879, M-le-P). The alienist Henry Maudsley, in his *The Physiology of Mind* (3rd ed., New York, 1883) cited Comte approvingly on various matters of specific method and content in psychology (though not including phrenology) and on altruism, the family, and society and made use of the Law of the Three Stages (pp. 1-11, 17-18, 48-49, 53, 69 n. 2, 132, 262, 330 n., 358, 376, 390, 399, 406, 505). Congreve wrote of him: "He allows his obligation to Comte and is not unprepared to admit that there is no other force than our own against Roman Catholicism. . . . My difficulty he continued is that I can get no sort of warm feeling for Humanity" (to Geddes, 2 July 1879, BM Add. MS 45231 f. 278). P. G. Hamerton, the artist and essayist, read the *Cours* in 1853 and accepted the Law of the Three Stages and Comte's division of the fine arts, but did not "admire the human race sufficiently to worship it," and he thought that

Comte had thought that men were becoming more and not less religious, and that nothing was destroyed until it was replaced ("On ne détruit que ce qu'on remplace"); hence he had striven to construct a new religion, more in tune with the modern world than the old one that he sought to replace. But not everyone who had struggled free from traditional religion would, like Congreve or Harrison, accept one which they recognized as contrived. The *locus classicus* of this problem is to be found in the relations between Positivism and the various forms of organized Humanism and Rationalism. The Positivists regarded the latter as incomplete, negative, destructive, and certainly felt a sense of deprivation when, at the end, they could find nothing better to do than join the Ethical societies.[77] On the other hand, it tended to raise the hackles of a Rationalist or Humanist to be asked to believe any-

Harrison's "advocacy of Positivism has put a weapon into the hands of his enemies who can . . . accuse him (a perfectly sane man) of sharing all the mental aberrations of Auguste Comte" ("The Chief Influences on My Career," *Forum*, XVIII [1894-95], 423-424). One James Hamilton, a pupil of Comte's in Paris in 1836, recalled Comte as "one of the greatest intellects of his generation" whose system's "pure morality and true conceptions" were his own while its "childishness and pedantry" were characteristically French (*Personal Recollections of Auguste Comte* [London, 1897], pp. 3-4, 12). Harrison declared his friend Matilda Betham-Edwards to have been in sympathy with Positivism but "by temperament and training . . . averse to any type of religious organisation" (*P.R.*, XXVII [1919], 41), but her only reference in her *Memories* is sarcastic (p. 23).

[77] Cf. above, p. 62; also information from Mr. H. J. Blackham. The tone was set by Comte himself in one of his brief but involuted demolitions: concerning the Secularist George Jacob Holyoake, to Winstanley, 16 July 1857, *C.I.*, III, 328. Holyoake did, however, manifest unquestionable affinities with Positivism (see his *English Secularism: A Confession of Belief* [Chicago, 1896], p. 73) and in transmitting to Congreve some letters of Comte's wrote: "If they bring honour to Comte it is his due and if they serve or interest any promoting his views that is his right" (9 April 1890, BM Add. MS 45240 f. 157). But he thought that the Secularist convert F. J. Gould made too many concessions to Christianity (Introduction to Gould's *Stepping-Stones to Agnosticism* [London, n.d.], p. 1).

thing. Not only, therefore, were the cases of two of the later Positivist leaders, F. J. Gould and Philip Thomas, who actually crossed the line, exceptions: even to sympathize cost a considerable effort. As another disciple once remarked of the Rationalist Press Association, "they are very suspicious of us (the suspicion of friends who are rivals in business)." [78]

Still, some cautious and perhaps rather condescending collaboration had gone on for some time. Dr. Moncure Conway, the American who became the leader of the South Place Ethical Society, recalled that the Church of Humanity "touched my sentiment of reverence." Congreve was "a phenomenal man, a refined scholar, . . . but his statements impressed me as curiously academic. He had such unquestioning faith in his creed and church." But to Conway, Positivist worship was merely "pathetically picturesque, . . . because this positivist deity was to me another 'Incomprehensible' like the triune." Several Positivists lectured for him at South Place, but none defined Humanity. "I gradually reached a belief that positivist religion is a refined variety of the general democratisation of Christianity. . . . But how precious were, and are, these high-principled men and women, with their unique philosophical faith, amid the sea of doubts and polemics mostly aimless!" [79] Conway's successor, Stanton Coit, striking an unwonted patriotic note, considered that, in order to find a program for ethical democracy "when applied to the existing conditions of Great Britain and Ireland," it was necessary to go neither "to Germany and to Karl Marx . . . , nor to France and Auguste Comte, as the English Positivists have done." Ethical culture was not "another name for positivism," but he admitted that "the two have much in common." Indeed, it is thought probable that,

[78] S. H. Swinny to Marvin, 25 April 1914, FSM.

[79] Conway, *Autobiography* . . . (London, etc., 1904), II, 345–349; see also his "What Is the Religion of Humanity?" *Free Religious Index*, n.s. I (1880–81), 278, and Mary Elizabeth Burtis, *Moncure Conway, 1832–1907* (New Brunswick, N.J., 1952), p. 194; cf. Harrison in *P.R.*, XV (1907), 285.

in breaking away from South Place and forming what became the Ethical Church, Bayswater, he was influenced by the Positivist church organization.[80] A follower of his, and a correspondent of Marvin's, perhaps put the matter more clearly than Coit himself. Having read an article of Marvin's on the Ethical societies in the *Positivist Review* he wrote that he himself, like Marvin, objected to "the want of backbone" in the Ethical movement,

but I would rather have too much sentiment to start with, than too much system and detail. . . . Of course . . . there must be some definite doctrine sooner or later, and also it must be laid down on Positivist lines. . . . It is a pity people always want to start something absolutely new in the way of religion. . . . Comte certainly was rather original, but I believe his weak point was a tendency to begin at the wrong end.[81]

Another member of the Ethical movement wrote to Marvin of his "pleasant surprise" that a pamphlet of his had been well received among the Positivists: "So, after all, ethicists and positivists are both of the modernist type—and could travel together." [82]

[80] Coit in *Ethical Democracy: Essays in Social Dynamics,* edited by himself (London, 1900), p. 346, *Ethical Culture as a Religion for the People* (London, n.d.), pp. 162–163; Mr. J. Hutton Hynd, secretary of the South Place Ethical Society, to the author, 13 Jan. 1958. This society commemorated the centenary of Comte's death with two lectures. S. K. Ratcliffe, in his *Story of South Place* (London, 1955), reports nothing of consequence in the present connection and is reported to have been little interested in the history of Positivism (Mrs. Ratcliffe to the author, 24 Jan. 1958). Coit's Ethical Church later became the West London Ethical Society, now under the leadership of Mr. H. J. Blackham, who considers Comte more important for his political and social than for his religious views and regards "secular religion" as a contradiction in terms and the "Religion of Humanity" as never viable (interview with the author, 30 Jan. 1958).

[81] L. Hale Pickle to Marvin, 26 April 1899, FSM. He had evidently not read Comte with much care. Cf. Marvin, "The Ethical Movement," *P.R.,* VI (1898), 187–191.

[82] Gustav Spiller to Marvin, 22 Dec. 1913, FSM. See also Spiller's *Outlines of a New World Religion in Fullest Harmony with Modern Scientific*

Marvin's most illustrious friend in this quarter was certainly Gilbert Murray, whom he introduced to Comte's writings when they were at school together in the 1870's. Murray subsequently went to Chapel Street sometimes and although he never joined the movement he "seemed to find under these guides an escape from cruel superstition and at the same time a fairly clear explanation and justification of the moral law and the ultimate duty of man." [83] Later, at Oxford, he considered the *Positivist Review* "a most interesting and able paper," and though he still did not think there was "much chance of my becoming a professed Positivist, . . . I feel clearly and strongly the value of having such subjects religiously and frankly treated by thinkers who are free of superstition." He wondered about the possibility of inviting Laffitte to give the Gifford Lectures (probably not knowing about his poor health or his bad English).[84] He himself wrote about the Positivist elements in his own lectures and appeared to be interested in spreading Positivist ideas at Oxford.[85] Many years later he reminisced to Marvin: "You and I have worked very much for the same causes and I expect we have the same mixed feeling as to their success and failure. Liberalism and Positivism can be represented as almost dead, and yet so much of their spirit has got abroad and permeated other bodies." [86]

------

and *Religious Demands* (London, 1918), p. 10, in which he finds Positivism close to his ideal, and his *New System of Scientific Procedure* . . . (London, 1921), pp. 20, 34 n. 1, 98, 104, 185, 191, 197, 396, mixing approval with disapproval of Comte.

[83] Gilbert Murray, *An Unfinished Autobiography* (London, 1960), p. 83.

[84] Murray to Marvin, 22 March 1896, FSM. See his own solitary contribution to the *Positivist Review* (without Positivist content): "What the Imperialists Mean by 'Imperialism,'" VIII (1900), 195–199.

[85] Murray to Marvin, 3 Jan. 1907, 21 April 1908, 4 Feb. 1909, 30 May 1914, FSM.

[86] Murray to Marvin, 24 Jan. 1936, FSM. Later still, Murray summed up Comte and Positivism as follows: "Comte was a very great figure in the history of thought, and Positivism remains a great coherent statement, im-

Certainly the greatest admirer of Positivism, or perhaps only of Comte, in Secularist circles was the famous Annie Besant, who wrote a little book on "the greatest thinker of the century."

Auguste Comte may have been either right or wrong in his opinions. . . . His mighty brain, his tender heart, his earnest and disinterested labour, his laborious and self-sacrificing life, his pure and noble character—these are the titles of Auguste Comte to the admiration and the homage of the Humanity he loved so well.

While maintaining the unity of his life, she thought that the *Cours* was his best work and that he later became a prophet and forbade criticism. She even went so far as to say: "Positivism is the death of all individualism, and therefore of all liberty and of all life." The polity was "noble in its scope, but childish in its details." [87] Others were more consistent, both in praise and in criticism.[88] As recently as 1958 the *Humanist,* the organ of the

---

perfect indeed and showing signs of its period, of certain permanent and all-important truths." But "he attempted too much; he tried to build a great structure almost complete in detail when he had materials only for a foundation and some outside walls, and even those subject to reformation." Yet "his system forms a wonderful achievement of sincere and constructive thinking, and secondly, . . . the thing he is trying to say, if only he could succeed in saying it, is not only sublime but true" ("What Is Permanent in Positivism," in his *Stoic, Christian, Humanist* [Boston, 1950], pp. 154, 188–189).

[87] Annie Besant, *Auguste Comte* . . . (London, n.d.), pp. 3, 19, 26–27, 30, 39. She had first written about Comte in the *National Reformer* (a radical journal) in 1875, having read the *Cours* the previous year (Arthur H. Nethercot, *The First Five Lives of Annie Besant* [Chicago, 1960], pp. 59, 82).

[88] See G. W. Foote, *Secularism the True Philosophy of Life* . . . (London, 1879), p. 29 (Comte had demonstrated the possibility of religion without theology, but his followers had served him ill by making a god of him); J. M. Robertson, "The Past and Future of Women: Two Lectures," *National Reformer,* n.s. Vol. 55 (1890), pp. 395–396 (Comte not positivist but metaphysical), *Buckle,* p. 20 (Comte's plans unworkable), *Modern Humanists* . . . (4th ed., London and New York, 1908), pp. 222, 227, 229, 238 (against

Rationalist Press Association, commissioned an article on Comte partly in defense of him against the "rough handling" he had received by Sir Isaiah Berlin in his Auguste Comte Lecture. The article made no mention of the Religion of Humanity, speaking of Positivism as "a remarkable effort to impose order on a chaotic universe," though the system contained "many debatable points." Comte's "establishment of sociology as a science was a step of immense value." [89]

It was certainly a step which gained him more recognition in the academic world in England than in any other, although English sociologists were less sympathetic than their French colleagues. The nearest equivalent to Durkheim was L. T. Hobhouse, the first professor of sociology in England (at the London School of Economics), who was related by marriage to J. H. Bridges, edited the latter's *Essays and Addresses,* and who, Marvin thought, was "perhaps the nearest to Comte of all post-Comtian sociologists in following what we hold to be the most important truth in Comte's system, viz., that the evolution of mind . . . should be the guiding principle in sociology." [90] Certainly he appears to have been first directed to sociology as a discipline, and to a generally humani-

Positivist religion), but he admitted that, though still metaphysical, Comte's method had been an improvement over previous ones (in *Sociological Papers* [I, London, 1905], p. 215); Charles E. Hooper, *Common Sense and the Rudiments of Philosophy* (2nd ed., London, 1920), pp. 58–59, 65, 122 (praise of Comte, especially for his concept of Humanity).

[89] Merle Tolfree, "Comte's Religion of Humanity," *Humanist,* Vol. 73 (1958), pp. 9–12; Mr. Hector Hawton, managing director of the R.P.A., to the author, 15 Dec. 1958. Mr. Hawton nevertheless regards the Religion of Humanity as a "cold-blooded invention" (to the author, 10 Feb. 1958). Rev. C. Maurice Davies, *Unorthodox London: or, Phases of Religious Life in the Metropolis* (2nd ed., London, 1876), pp. 435–436, found Chapel Street by far the most agreeable and instructive of the places he had to visit: "I must confess I should vastly like to see the full ritual as organised by Comte himself carried out."

[90] Marvin, *Comte,* pp. 184–185.

tarian motive in the study of it, by Comte, and in his historical and synoptic treatment of it he was closer to Comte than to Spencer. The same was true of his political sympathies, which were collectivist rather than liberal. On the other hand, he repudiated the antimetaphysical posture of Positivism and was strongly affected by his study of Plato and philosophical idealism at Oxford.[91] This was a rather more remote affinity with Positivism than Durkheim's; in any case Hobhouse did not guide the development of English academic sociology to the extent that Durkheim and Worms did French. To be sure, Hobhouse's successor and biographer, Morris Ginsberg, paid considerable tribute, in the second Auguste Comte Memorial Lecture, to Positivism for its psychological and historical approach to ethics, although even here Ginsberg was more impressed with Comte's effort than with his achievement, while elsewhere he concluded more firmly that "Comte attempted too much. Sociology cannot provide a complete philosophy. . . . Nor had he adequate materials for the sociological inductions that he claims to have established." [92]

In fact the most persistent sympathizers with Positivist sociology

[91] See Ernest Barker, "Leonard Trelawny Hobhouse, 1864–1929," *Proceedings* of the British Academy, 1929, pp. 543, 548, 553–554; Metz, *Hundred Years,* pp. 152–155, 169–170; J. A. Hobson and Morris Ginsberg, *L. T. Hobhouse: His Life and Work* (London, 1931), Hobson, *passim,* Ginsberg, pp. 100–105; Ginsberg, *Reason and Unreason in Society* . . . (Cambridge, Mass., 1948), pp. 44–48, 50; Hobhouse, *Development and Purpose* . . . (London, 1913), pp. xviii–xix (Idealism and Positivism), 371 (on Humanity), and particularly "The Law of the Three Stages," *Sociological Review,* I (1908), 262, 264–266, 268–269, 277, 279: its "general notions . . . have passed into ordinary thought and common language," but it cannot be taken over integrally although "it at least expresses certain aspects of the movement of thought" and any criticism leaves unchanged the fact that "we are creatures of a development which has been unconscious and stand at the point at which it begins to understand itself and so to become self-directing," which is "the central conception of Comte's sociology."

[92] Ginsberg, *Reason and Experience in Ethics* (Oxford and London, 1956), pp. 3–6, 22, 24, "Comte: A Revaluation," in *Sociologica, Frankfurter Beiträge zur Soziologie,* I (Frankfurt, 1955), 318 and *passim.*

were two students and followers of LePlay, Victor Branford and Patrick Geddes. Branford insisted on the "architectonic value" of Comte's sociology. More important because more specific was his declaration that "a controlling science of sociology is, as Comte showed, a necessary postulate of science itself." [93] In a joint work Branford and Geddes, placing Comte below LePlay but above Spencer, praised his pioneer attempt to enlist history in an optimistic prevision of the future.[94] Geddes, by profession actually a biologist, whose attention had first been drawn to Comte by Huxley's attack, attended some of Congreve's Chapel Street functions in the 1870's, became intimate with Bridges, and attempted without much success to bring Positivism to the notice of the Sociological Society.[95] He thought of himself as an empirical scientist with an interest "in the synthetic presentment of the sciences, and of sociology above all," and therefore in Positivism, but he always felt among the Positivists "a real dislike of scientific research, a disdain for it," and what he appreciated most in Comte himself was the introduction of the human, creative, and historical element into science.[96]

Even Marvin conceded that Comte's "master-thought" of the

[93] Branford, "Note on the History of Sociology . . . ," *Sociological Papers* [I] (London, 1905), 33–36, "On the Relation of Sociology to the Social Sciences and to Philosophy," *ibid.*, 202; cf. H. Gordon Jones in *P.R.*, XV (1907), 281–282 (also on Hobhouse).

[94] *The Coming Polity* (new ed., London, 1919), pp. viii, 18, 22, 25–26, 28–29, 41, 52–54, 62.

[95] Geddes, Introduction to Liveing, *Bridges*, pp. 1–2, and cf. Philip Boardman, *Patrick Geddes: Maker of the Future* (Chapel Hill, N.C., 1944), pp. 32–33, 240–241; Philip Mairet, *Pioneer of Sociology: The Life and Letters of Patrick Geddes* (London, 1957), pp. 19–20, 23, 122; Desch in *R.P.I.*, 1938, pp. 98, 102; Geddes to Laffitte, 6 Dec. 1881, M-le-P, and to Robinet, 29 Dec. 1883, A.N., AS 2; cf. Quin, *Memoirs,* pp. 100–101, and the disappointment with Geddes of Beesly, to Marvin, 11 June 1895, FSM.

[96] Geddes, in Liveing, *Bridges,* pp. 13–14, in *P.R.*, XXIX (1921), 146–147, and to Marvin, 12 Aug. 1926, FSM; cf. Sir J. Arthur Thomson and Patrick Geddes, *Life: Outlines of General Biology* (London, 1931), I, xi, II, 1119, 1122, 1126–1127, 1371.

steady evolution of mankind in terms of the increasing ascendancy of humanity over animality "is certainly not in accord with the mass of later work in sociology itself," which under the influence of Spencer had rather been more strictly empirical. The type of research "directly inspired" by Comte had been more "into the history of science than into that of social habits and institutions." [97] In England, however, the history of science as an academic discipline began to be cultivated even later than sociology and seems to have been inspired by Positivism at most indirectly, through Sarton, except perhaps in the case of Charles Singer, whom Marvin persuaded to lecture to the Positivist Society once or twice in the early 1920's and who had attended two or three meetings in the Newton Hall days. [98] Among "ordinary" historians Positivism made scarcely any headway. Goldwin Smith (by this time, of course, in America) wrote that Congreve, who had begun life "with high promise," was ending it "as the farcical anti-Pope of a moribund conventicle." He thought, however, that he would like "to be a member of the circle of Positivist Cooks. I could overlook their self-respect for the sake of their Poulet à la Clotilde de Vaux." Nevertheless he felt himself to be "not very far from certain Positivists who are essentially theological" and hoped that the Positivists could "put a new foundation under the national character." He admired Harrison, broke with him, and then was reconciled with him again on account of their agreement on the Boer War, but never "learned to find much comfort in Comte." [99] The only English historian who can be said to have had any appreciable contact with Positivism was A. J. Grant, and even he was really

[97] Marvin, *Comte,* pp. 61–63.

[98] Dr. Charles Singer to the author, 16 Jan. 1958.

[99] G. Smith to Mrs. Hertz, 17 Sept. 1879, 8 Aug. 1880, 30 Jan. 1882, 28 Dec. 1884, to Briton Riviere, 18 April 1889, to Harrison, 2 March 1900, 20 Feb. 1908, in Arnold Haultain, ed., *A Selection from Goldwin Smith's Correspondence* (Toronto, n.d.), pp. 84, 91, 103, 162, 222, 346, 494; Harrison in *P.R.,* XVIII (1910), 147.

more a personal friend of Marvin than a follower of the doctrine.[100] The position in economics was scarcely better.[101] That in philosophy was more hopeful, but since English "logical positivism" derived from the Vienna Circle a detour via Positivism in Germany and Austria is indicated.

[100] See his antiscientistic introduction to his edition of *English Historians* (London, etc., 1906), pp. lxxxii, lxxxiv–lxxxv, his recommendation of Bridges' *France under Richelieu and Colbert* (new ed., London, 1912), pp. vi–vii, for its abstention from propaganda, and his criticism of Marvin's *Century of Hope* for its tendentiousness, though he praises the chapters on the history of science (*History*, n.s. IV [1919–20], 228–229); Swinny to Marvin, 6 Oct. 1918, FSM. Grant's own writings were strictly in the tradition of political history, and his correspondence with Marvin did not touch on Positivist subjects. Quin was hopeful about him at one time (to Congreve, 8 June 1898?, BM Add. MS 45229 f. 229); in fact, he attended the Chapel Street Commemoration Service after Congreve's death (Grant to Mrs. Congreve, 13 Aug. 1899, Wadham MS c. 186 ff. 162–163), and he did possess an unusually large number of books by Positivists (according to list of books presented by Grant to the Leeds University Library in 1928, kindly supplied to me by Mr. G. Woledge, librarian of the British Library of Political and Economic Science).—Marvin also corresponded with A. J. Carlyle and H. A. L. Fisher, but this did not amount to anything in terms of Positivism, although Fisher did praise the *Calendar* (Beesly in *P.R.*, XVII [1910], 45). J. B. Crozier had been struck by Comte's historical treatment of science and religion but rejected "the assumption that there is nothing more requiring explanation" (*Civilization & Progress* [new ed., London, 1888], pp. 192–194). For Sir Isaiah Berlin see above, p. 92, and below, p. 270 n. 16.

[101] See, however, T. E. C. Leslie, "On the Philosophical Method of Political Economy," *Hermathena*, No. IV (1876), pp. 294–296; David Syme, *Outlines of an Industrial Science* (London, 1876), pp. 160, 162–163; Alfred Marshall, *Principles of Economics* (London and New York, 1890), pp. 72–74; cf. Fink, *Etude critique*, p. 19, and Jean Cuisenier, "Auguste Comte et la sociologie économique," *Cahiers internationaux de sociologie*, n.s. V (1958), 135, 136.

Chapter IX

POSITIVISM IN GERMANY

IF France by the 1860's was ready to react against the eclecticism of Victor Cousin, it might be thought that Germany would be infinitely more surfeited with the metaphysics of Fichte, Schelling, and Hegel, and that this revulsion would redound even more noticeably to the benefit of Positivism. But in fact the historical position was different in Germany.[1] On the one hand, a reaction against Hegel had occurred earlier, taking the form both of the materialistic philosophy of his own followers of the Left, particularly Feuerbach,[2] and of the empirical abstention from philosophy

---

[1] This term includes German-speaking Austrians. However, some of the general statements made in the first and last paragraphs of the chapter do not apply to Austria, where Kant never gained much support. On the changing reasons for this rejection of Kant in Austria in the course of the nineteenth century, see Otto Neurath, *Le développement du cercle de Vienne et l'avenir de l'empirisme logique* (Paris, 1935), pp. 32–33, 39–40, who reports that at first Kant was regarded as too radical, later as not radical enough. The scientific antimetaphysics of Mach (see below, p. 258) was not only non-Comtian but also non-Kantian.—I owe this distinction of Austria from the rest of Germany to the cautioning of Professor Carl Schorske.

[2] Although it appears that Feuerbach knew of the existence of Positivism, and although certain parallels can be drawn between Feuerbach's and Comte's teachings, no one suggests that the former drew on the latter; see Laffitte to Comte, 29 Sept. 1850, *R.O.*, n.s. XXXVI (1907), 87; David Koigen, *Zur Vorgeschichte des modernen philosophischen Socialismus in*

adopted by many natural scientists and, perhaps most prominently, by historians. On the other hand, a counterreaction had also already begun, but it was not predominantly a return to Hegel but rather a movement "back to Kant." The "critical philosophy" of Kant, which was important in France too, took a good deal of the wind out of the sails of any more dogmatically antimetaphysical philosophy in Germany. In addition, Hegel was of course throughout far from being forgotten. The area available for exploitation by other, especially by foreign, systems was thus rather small.

Deutschland . . . (Berne, 1901), pp. 114–116; Albert Lévy, *La philosophie de Feuerbach* . . . (Paris, 1904), pp. 31, 33, 42; S. Rawidowicz, *Ludwig Feuerbachs Philosophie* . . . (Berlin, 1931), pp. 141, 251, 310–311, 340–344. Even more obvious and very interesting comparisons can be made between Comte and Marx (see Th. G. Masaryk, *Die philosophischen und sociologischen Grundlagen des Marxismus* . . . [Vienna, 1899], pp. 35–36, 65–72, 76, 81–82, 86, 116–118, 125, 157–158, 196, 203, 210–211, 482, 488, 510–511, 555; Henri Wallon, Introduction, in *A la lumière du marxisme: Essais,* Vol. II: *Karl Marx et la pensée moderne,* Part I [Paris, 1937], pp. 9–11; Prenant, "Karl Marx et Auguste Comte," *ibid.,* pp. 17–76; R. Harrison, "Beesly and Marx," pp. 217, 234–235; and Marx's letters quoted by Bernhard J. Stern in "A Note on Comte," *Science and Society,* I [1936–37], 114 n. 2, 118 n. 14) or for that matter between Comte and Hegel (see Hayek, *Counter-Revolution of Science,* pp. 192–203; also Flint, *Philosophy of History,* p. 582; Bréhier, *Histoire de la philosophie,* pp. 756, 762, 767, 774, 784; Friedrich Dittmann, "Die Geschichtsphilosophie Comtes und Hegels . . . ," *Vierteljahrsschrift für wissenschaftliche Philosophie und Soziologie,* XXXVIII [1914], 281–312, XXXIX [1915], 38–81; G. Salomon-Delatour, "Comte ou Hegel?" *R.P.I.,* 1935, pp. 220–227; 1936, pp. 110–118). On Comte and Lorenz von Stein, see Gottfried Salomon's Preface to the latter's *Geschichte der sozialen Bewegung in Frankreich* . . . (Munich, 1921), I, xxv–xxvii; Heinz Nitzschke, "Die Geschichtsphilosophie Lorenz von Steins . . . ," Beiheft 26 der *Historischen Zeitschrift* (Munich and Berlin, 1932), pp. 8–9, 18, 97, 125–130, and *passim;* Herbert Marcuse, *Reason and Revolution: Hegel and the Rise of Social Theory* (London, New York, and Toronto, 1941), pp. 378–388. See in general, on Positivism in Germany, Gruber, *Positivismus,* pp. 139–140.

Indeed, the first substantial discussion of Comte and Positivism in Germany was written by a man who had learned of Comte's writings during a visit to Paris. Karl Twesten, soon to gain fame in the political arena, had become disgusted with the abuses practiced by metaphysical philosophy and had embarked on a quest for a new philosophy of history, based on the fundamental conceptions of Comte, which would analyze "all spheres of human life, and especially the state and politics, in the manner of the exact sciences in the factual terms of intellectual, moral, and material needs, without admitting any theological or metaphysical theory." The "undeniable decline of metaphysical philosophy" as well as "the positive progress of the natural sciences and the more or less conscious directions of recent historiography" seemed to Twesten to point to the eventual victory of such a method. Twesten insisted that his position was not to be identified with "mere empiricism": "I claim the same truth for the laws of positive science, that is for the general conditions which underlie individual phenomena, ascertained by observation, calculation, or experiment, as for the facts of experience themselves." [3]

As a by-product of his work Twesten published a short essay on Comte's life and work in which he again insisted, in the spirit of Comte himself, that philosophy must have an encyclopedic and universal character, "not in the sense of an external compilation, but in the higher sense of an internal objective connection. . . . Any philosophy that renounces this quality is no longer a true philosophy." Nevertheless Twesten paid far more attention, proportionately, than Comte to epistemology and to the problem of proof, and he went out of his way to emphasize that sufficient observations had not yet been made to permit the construction of social laws. In this situation recourse must be had to hypotheses.

[3] Twesten to Haym, 8 April and 28 June 1859, in Julius Heyderhoff, "Rudolf Haym und Karl Twesten . . . ," *Preussische Jahrbücher*, Vol. 161 (1915), pp. 237, 247–248. For an early German admirer of Comte (of whom nothing more was heard), see Comte to Buchholz, 18 Nov. 1825, *C.I.*, I, 5–6.

"Nevertheless we may regard a series of fundamental propositions in moral and social science as positively ascertained." Comte's own detailed propositions in the *Polity,* however, were arbitrary and in part idiosyncratic (*abenteuerlich*).

Some perceptive, imaginative, and interesting investigations and combinations are offered, but the whole is evidently a premature and hasty conception which contradicts Comte's own . . . principles as to the prior necessity of elaborating and propagating the theory. . . . His generalizations are not infrequently more glittering than true. His historical knowledge is not very thorough.

But despite his increasing sentimentality and arrogance Comte deserved "very serious study" for his reduction of the moral and political sciences to their first and most general principles.[4]

This was a friendly introduction, comparable perhaps to some of the early articles on Comte in England but certainly without any commitment on Twesten's part to much more than the possibility of a "positive" social science. Twesten returned to the subject in a lengthy introduction to a work of cultural anthropology. He premised that he was seeking historical laws empirically, defending this quest on the basis of the Law of the Three Stages and Comte's Classification of the Sciences. Positive philosophy was nothing but "the systematic coordination of the several sciences." Beyond this there was no science and no philosophy. He echoed Comte on the abstention from seeking absolute principles, on the substitution of laws for causes; he praised Comte as the author of the first coherent, encyclopedic theory based purely on the positive method and as the creator of sociology as the preeminently philosophical discipline. As before, Twesten rejected the *Polity* and the other later works but, like Mill and unlike Littré, pointed out that even in the *Cours* Comte had made impossible claims and demands. Comte's fame, nevertheless, was secure:

[4] "Leben und Schriften August Comte's," *Preussische Jahrbücher,* IV (1859), 280, 283–284, 300–301.

Inspired by the most ardent devotion to truth, he developed the outlines of positive philosophy for all realms of knowledge and of life in
a manner both acute and imaginative, and he equipped his encyclopedic
work, emphatically oriented though it was toward synthesis, with a
profusion of profound insights and brilliant ideas the like of which is
not easily to be found in the writings of a single man.[5]

This generous introduction was followed after a further interval
by a number of translations that began to make Comte's works
more readily available to the German reader,[6] and indeed there
had been only isolated discussion of them before about 1880 even
in academic circles. While criticizing Comte severely for defects of
method, the great economic historian Gustav Schmoller paid tribute to him for having founded both sociology and the philosophy
of history and may have resembled him more than he thought
in his hankering after general laws, though his antimetaphysical
orientation came from Spencer as well as from Comte.[7] Much

[5] *Die religiösen, politischen und socialen Ideen der asiatischen Culturvölker* . . . (ed. Lazarus, Berlin, 1872), I, 1–5, 7–8, 64–65, 83–85; cf. also
9–13, 23, 66–67, 72–74, 137.

[6] The following translations appeared: *Einleitung in die positive Philosophie* (tr. Schneider, Leipzig, 1880), the first two lessons of the *Cours; Die
positive Philosophie* (tr. Kirchmann, Heidelberg, 1883–84), translation of
the abridgment by Jules Rig, *La philosophie positive par Auguste Comte*
(Paris, 1881), with an appreciative though not uncritical translator's Introduction; *Katechismus der positiven Religion* (tr. Roschlau, Leipzig, 1891);
Der Positivismus in seinem Wesen und seiner Bedeutung (tr. *id.*, Leipzig,
1894), the *General View.* See also the article "Comte" by Ludwig Noack in
Philosophie-geschichtliches Lexikon . . . (Leipzig, 1879), pp. 206–208, ap-
preciative of the *Cours,* mildly sarcastic on the *Polity.* Cf. further Rudolf
Eucken, "Zur Würdigung Comte's und des Positivismus," in *Philosophische
Aufsätze* dedicated to Eduard Zeller (Leipzig, 1887), pp. 53–82, an ana-
lytical summary; Erich Rothacker, *Einleitung in die Geisteswissenschaften*
(Tübingen, 1920), pp. 137, 199–201.

[7] Heinrich Herkner, "Gustav Schmoller als Soziologe," *Jahrbücher für
Nationalökonomie und Statistik,* Vol. 118 (1922), pp. 1–2, 6; Otto Hintze,
article "Schmoller" in *Deutsches biographisches Jahrbuch,* Überleitungsband

more definitely favorable to Comte's historical method, as well as very influential, was Ernst Bernheim, the guide for generations of students of historical method. While cautioning against Comte's excessive emphasis on laws, and on society to the detriment of the individual, Bernheim called attention to his "extraordinarily keen sense of historical reality" and to his influence on historiography and historical philosophy, which, however, unfortunately did not yet extend to Germany. History was not a natural science and was not identical with sociology, but Comte, with Buckle, had rightly compelled recognition of the physical factors in historical evolution while on the other hand he had contributed to the development of the history of ideas. Volume IV of the *Cours* contained the basis of scientific sociology and the outlines of a philosophy of history and provided "a first grandiose attempt at a methodologically justified and genuinely socio-psychological interpretation." If Comte's alleged laws, including the Three Stages, were regarded instead as descriptive formulas and analogies, they could be extremely fruitful. Bernheim rejected the Comte of the "second phase" as semipathological, but acknowledged the importance of his effort to harmonize reason and emotion.[8]

II: 1917–1920 (Berlin and Liepzig, 1928), p. 131; and Schmoller's "Zur Methodologie der Staats- und Sozialwissenschaften," *Schmollers Jahrbuch,* VII (1883), 993, *Grundriss der allgemeinen Volkswirtschaftslehre* (Leipzig, 1900–4), I, 71–72, 138, II, 661. Schmoller's predecessor of an earlier generation, Karl Knies, stated explicitly that Comte had been unknown to him and probably to all his colleagues in the 1840's and 1850's at the time of the founding of the so-called "Historical School" in economics (*Die politische Oekonomie vom geschichtlichen Standpunkte* [2nd ed., Braunschweig, 1883], pp. 516–518; see also pp. 494, 515–516, 519). Cf. Mauduit, *Comte et la science économique,* pp. 232–235; Fink, *Etude critique,* pp. 31–33; Cuisenier, "Comte et la sociologie économique," pp. 135–136.

[8] Bernheim, *Geschichtsforschung und Geschichtsphilosophie* (Göttingen, 1880), pp. 51, 57–58, *Lehrbuch der historischen Methode und der Geschichtsphilosophie* (3rd and 4th ed., Leipzig, 1903; first pub. 1889), pp. 86–87, 91, 100–101, 569, 592, 624, 651–652, 656–665.

Bernheim also indicated in some detail the debt that he thought was owed to Comte by the contemporary cultural historian Karl Lamprecht.[9] The latter, however, "obstinately refused," as he himself put it, to acknowledge any such debt. His own conceptions, he said, had been formed before he knew of Comte and derived from the total climate of thought created in common by Condorcet, Saint-Simon, Comte, Herder, Kant, and Hegel. History, he affirmed, was "a socio-psychological science," applied psychology, and as such dependent on the progress made in that discipline. This pronouncement indicates Lamprecht's debt to the eminent psychologist Wilhelm Wundt, and even if the latter's influence affected Lamprecht only relatively late in his career, there seems no sufficient warrant for quarreling with his repudiation of Comtian influence even for his earlier development, except insofar as it may have been exercised through Bernheim during his student days in Göttingen. Lamprecht began by rejecting Ranke's "historische Ideenlehre" as metaphysical, but neither his postulation, in its place, of "cultural epochs" nor his treatment of these in an empirical manner exhibits more than the most general kind of affinity with Comte's *a priori* historical constructions. Lamprecht's principal disciple, Kurt Breysig, likewise repudiated any direct influence of Comte on himself and criticized the latter severely as to both method and results, though conceding that Comte had con-

---

[9] *Ibid.*, pp. 660–665. For Lamprecht see his *Die kulturhistorische Methode* (Berlin, 1900), pp. 33–34, "La science moderne de l'histoire . . . ," *Revue de synthèse historique*, X (1905), 257–258, and *What Is History?* . . . (tr. Andrews, New York and London, 1905), pp. 3, 29–31; Rothacker, *Einleitung,* pp. 249–253; Troeltsch, *Historismus,* pp. 459–461; Srbik, *Geist und Geschichte,* II, 228–229; Cassirer, *Problem of Knowledge,* pp. 284–285; Emil Jakob Spiess, *Die Geschichtsphilosophie von Karl Lamprecht* (Erlangen, 1921), pp. 30, 35–39, 66 ff.; Heinrich Borchert, *Der Begriff des Kulturzeitalters bei Comte* . . . (Halle, 1927), p. 216; and above all Georg Jahn, "Karl Lamprecht als Wirtschafts- und Kulturhistoriker . . . ," *Schmollers Jahrbuch,* Vol. 76 (1956), pp. 129–142.

tributed many original and central ideas to sociology, especially the division into statics and dynamics.[10]

The most interesting relationship to Positivism in German historiography was certainly that of Wilhelm Dilthey. Trained to be skeptical of Hegel and of idealism, he was not content to go uncritically to the opposite extreme of naturalism but entertained the ambition "of reconciling the traditional idealism of German historians [e.g., J. G. Droysen] with the scientific requirements of a positive age," and it was in pursuit of this aim that (possibly through Twesten) he became interested in Comte in the 1860's as one manifestation of "positivism." [11] It was not until 1875, however, that he published the results of his examination.[12] There was only one interpretation, he wrote, which "while acknowledging the validity of the positive sciences uproots philosophy [*in ihrer Wurzel auflöst*], the interpretation of Comte, which repudiates psychology and logic" and allots to philosophy the task of forming a new discipline out of the generalizations of science. But such a task could now be performed only by dilettantes; nobody could master the foundations of both the natural and the moral sciences, as demonstrated by Hegel's mistakes in the former and Comte's ignorance of the latter. It was necessary to distinguish between

[10] Breysig, *Aufgaben und Massstäbe einer allgemeinen Geschichtsschreibung* (Berlin, 1900), pp. 213–215, and especially *Gestaltungen des Entwicklungsgedankens* (Berlin, 1940), pp. 158–200; cf. Srbik, *Geist und Geschichte,* II, 240–243.

[11] See Jean-François Suter, *Philosophie et histoire chez Wilhelm Dilthey* (Basel, 1960), pp. 30–31 and 1–48 *passim;* Dilthey's letters to his father, 1853–54, to Hermann Usener, July 1864, in Clara Misch, ed., *Der junge Dilthey* . . . (Leipzig and Berlin, 1933), pp. 10, 23, 185. He had already criticized Buckle for confining intellectual history to the history of scientific ideas (diary, 1860, *ibid.,* p. 124).

[12] "Über das Studium der Geschichte der Wissenschaften vom Menschen, der Gesellschaft, und dem Staat," in his *Gesammelte Schriften,* V (Leipzig and Berlin, 1924), 49–56.

Comte's valid point of departure for the historiography of science (i.e., the Classification of the Sciences) and his vague and unverifiable historical generalizations (e.g., the Law of the Three Stages) and undemonstrable assumption of the assimilability of the human, social, and historical sciences to the natural sciences.

Even this treatment seemed to Dilthey, in retrospect, too generous. At the time of its writing, he reflected, he had still felt an affinity with Positivism in reaction against Hegel in the name of the natural sciences:

The tremendous strength of the Positivists lay in their refusal to have anything put over on them [*sich nichts vormachen lassen*]; but their corresponding weakness was their misrepresentation of the world of the mind in order to fit it into the framework of an external world [as part of the order of nature].[13]

Nevertheless, even in his fundamental "Introduction to the Moral Sciences," written eight years after the first essay, Dilthey still acknowledged that Comte had created "the basis for a true philosophy of the sciences" by examining the relation between the logical and the historical connections among propositions. On the other hand, he was possessed of an excessive *esprit de système* at the expense of an "intimate feeling for historical reality." The Positivists had constructed a system no more tenable than "the bold speculations of Schelling and Oken on nature." Comte's sociology was founded on a "crude naturalistic metaphysics." [14] Despite this

[13] "Vorrede" (1911), *ibid.,* pp. 3–5.

[14] "Einleitung in die Geisteswissenschaften . . . ," *ibid.,* I (1923), xvi–xvii, 23–24, 107, see also 96, 101, 108, 134–136, 140–141. On Dilthey cf., besides Suter, H. A. Hodges, *Wilhelm Dilthey: An Introduction* (London, 1944), pp. 4, 82, and *The Philosophy of Wilhelm Dilthey* (London, 1952), pp. xx, 18, 23, 161, 164, 215, 339; Gerhard Masur, "Wilhelm Dilthey und die europäische Geistesgeschichte," *Deutsche Vierteljahrsschrift für Literaturwissenschaft und Geistesgeschichte,* XII (1934), 492–493; and Carlo Antoni, *From History to Sociology* . . . (tr. White, Detroit, 1959), pp. 8, 18, who writes: "One should not exaggerate . . . the importance of his

severity it seems clear that a consideration of Comte had forced Dilthey to refine his own ideas and to decide just what a rejection of metaphysics implied for the study of history. Comte's influence on Dilthey, negative in character, may nevertheless be regarded as formative.[15]

If German historiography was not on the whole hospitable to Positivism, the climate in the new discipline of sociology, contrary to what one might expect, was scarcely more favorable. There was no German equivalent of Durkheim,[16] and there were only half a dozen or so German sociologists who even paid much attention to one of the founders of their discipline. Perhaps the most interesting case was that of Theodor Gomperz, who, led to Mill's *Logic* in 1853 by James Mill's psychological studies and to Comte, presumably, by the *Logic,* came to prefer Comte's total achievement to Mill's. Despite appearances, he wrote, Comte turned out to have a surer instinct for the desirable and attainable. His social ideals were being realized, and his insistence on the modification of opinion, culminating in his doctrine of the spiritual power, was justified.[17] This approval, however, was of social aims rather than of sociological achievement, and practicing sociologists

---

revolt against Comte and Mill. . . . Dilthey's originality lay in the fact that he turned the criteria of the positivists against themselves and thus undermined their intrusion into the historical sciences. More positivistic than the positivists, he refused to subordinate empirical facts to laws and methods not growing out of the facts themselves." It may be doubted whether this was so original. Antoni even claims that a positivistic residue filtered through from Dilthey to Troeltsch (p. 60); cf. Troeltsch, *Historismus,* pp. 417, 462–463. See in general Waentig, *Comte,* pp. 252–255.

[15] In some such way as in the case of Meyerson, cf. above, pp. 106–107.

[16] See, in general, Aron, *German Sociology,* p. 108; Waentig, *Comte,* pp. 247–252, 261–265, 279–282; Theodore Abel, *Systematic Sociology in Germany* . . . (New York and London, 1929), pp. 5–8 (stressing the empirical character of more recent work in Germany).

[17] Gomperz, *Essays und Erinnerungen* (Stuttgart and Leipzig, 1905), pp. 33–38.

were generally hostile to Positivism or at best grudging in their praise.[18] The only real exception to this rule was Ludwig Stein, who about the turn of the century endorsed Comte's definition of philosophy and of the relation between the individual and society, his conceptions of altruism and of Humanity, his predictive purpose, and the optimism of the Law of the Three Stages, while rejecting the division into statics and dynamics and criticizing Positivism on a number of other grounds.[19] Even the creator of

[18] See Paul von Lilienfeld, *Gedanken über die Socialwissenschaft der Zukunft* (Mitau, 1873–81), I, *passim* (rejection of metaphysics), II, 224 (Praise of Classification, but not original with Comte), 330, 428, III, xiv, V, vi (statements of his differences with Positivism), and cf. Barth, *Philosophie der Geschichte,* I, 128–138; A. Schäffle, *Bau und Leben des socialen Körpers* (2nd ed., Tübingen, 1896; first pub. 1875–78), I, 1, 8–24, 563 (sociology as a "philosophy of the special social sciences," the biological analogy, the political function of sociology, rejection of a "metaphysics of evolution"), and cf. Barth, *op. cit.,* I, 138–139, 145, and "Spencer und Schäffle," pp. 236–237 (Schäffle's debt to Spencer rather than to Comte); Dr. Kohn, "Beiträge zur Kenntniss und Würdigung der Sociologie," *Jahrbücher für Nationalökonomie und Statistik,* XXXV (1880), 407–433 (calls attention to Comte as too little known, but critical of him on almost every count); Ludwig Gumplowicz, *The Outlines of Sociology* (tr. Moore, Philadelphia, 1899; first pub. 1885), pp. 23–25, *Die sociologische Staatsidee* (Graz, 1892), pp. 75–77 (Comte had been the first to recognize the nature of sociology and to promote sociological analysis of the state, but had done nothing substantial himself); Ferdinand Tönnies, *Gemeinschaft und Gesellschaft* . . . (Leipzig, 1887), p. xxvi (tribute to general significance of Comte and Spencer); F. Müller-Lyer, *Der Sinn des Lebens und die Wissenschaft* . . . (2nd ed., Munich, 1923; first pub. 1910), pp. 5, 29–37, 139, 153, "Die phaseologische Methode in der Soziologie," *Vierteljahrsschrift für wissenschaftliche Philosophie und Soziologie,* XXXVI (1912), 241–242, 255 (adaptation of Three Stages and Classification, restriction to phenomenal world, suggestions for making sociology a predictive science as defined by Comte); see also Franz Oppenheimer, *System der Soziologie* (Jena, 1922) in connection with Aron, *German Sociology,* p. 38.

[19] Stein, *Die soziale Frage im Lichte der Philosophie* . . . (3rd and 4th ed., Stuttgart, 1923; first pub. 1897), pp. 9, 112, 303, 314, 323, 336, 362, 452, *Der soziale Optimismus* (Jena, 1905), pp. 69, 100, 161, 218, 225, 259–260.

248

a "positive monism" was at particular pains to repudiate allegations of discipleship of Comte, declaring that the latter had violated his own principles by departing from a strictly factual basis for his philosophy.[20] Others who specifically repudiated Positivism included the eminent Max Weber.[21]

In the neighboring field of psychology there is really only one candidate for Positivist influence, but an important one, Wilhelm Wundt, who in his turn gave Lamprecht his psychological orientation in his historical work.[22] An opponent of extreme naturalism and of purely physiological psychology in quest of some compromise with traditional idealism, Wundt moved within the orbit of

[20] Gustav Ratzenhofer, *Der positive Monismus* . . . (Leipzig, 1899), p. 15 n., *Die Kritik des Intellects* . . . (Leipzig, 1902), pp. v–vi. Comte had given sociology its name but had not treated it consistently (*Die sociologische Erkenntnis* . . . [Leipzig 1898], p. 1; see also pp. 11, 13, 17, 19), and his ethics, also, was worthless (*Positive Ethik* . . . [Leipzig, 1901], pp. 10–11, 28–29). Cf. Otto Gramzow, *Gustav Ratzenhofer und seine Philosophie* (Berlin, 1904), pp. 56–57.

[21] M. Weber, *Gesammelte Aufsätze zur Wissenschaftslehre* (2nd ed., ed. Winckelmann, Tübingen, 1951), pp. 149, 411–413, 424, and cf. the Introduction by H. H. Gerth and C. Wright Mills to their edition of *From Max Weber: Essays in Sociology* (New York, 1946), pp. 44, 57. See also Wilhelm Metzger, "Geschichtsphilosophie und Soziologie," *Vierteljahrsschrift für wissenschaftliche Philosophie und Soziologie*, XL (1916), 279–281 and *passim* (rejection of Comte's sociology as mere philosophy of history). The "positivism" that Alfred Vierkandt saw a necessity to "overcome" ("Die Überwindung des Positivismus in der deutschen Soziologie der Gegenwart," *Jahrbuch für Soziologie*, II [1926], 66–90) was no offspring of Comte's: he had in mind merely the overvaluation of society at the expense of the individual and the crude confrontation of "experience" with "metaphysics." See also his *Naturvölker und Kulturvölker* . . . (Leipzig, 1896), pp. 42–43, and cf. Abel, *Systematic Sociology*, pp. 73–76, 78–79.

[22] On German psychology in general, see Barth, "Spencer und Schäffle," p. 482, and cf. H. Reybekiel-Schapiro, "Die introspektive Methode in der modernen Psychologie," *Vierteljahrsschrift für wissenschaftliche Philosophie und Soziologie*, XXX (1906), 84. On Wundt see above all Troeltsch, *Historismus*, pp. 434–458; also Gruber, *Positivismus*, p. 152.

Kant rather than of Comte in trying to extend causality from the natural to the human sciences and at the same time to retain some notion of purpose and progress in history. In this respect he struggled, like Comte and many others, with the old problem of freedom and determinism, of the role of the individual in society, which Comte had met with his formula of *fatalité modifiable*. But Wundt called Comte's definition of philosophy a "play on words," rejected the Classification, and called Comte a dogmatist who had produced neither a tenable psychology nor a tenable epistemology. His only important achievement had been to turn the philosophy of history in the direction of sociology.[23]

Likewise, the so-called "positivist" movement in German aesthetics and philology had nothing to do with Comte; it was merely a quest for objective laws in reaction against metaphysical teleology.[24] Among professional philosophers there was some genuine discussion of the Positivism of Auguste Comte,[25] and two of the first to engage in it were prominent and interesting men. One, surprisingly enough, was the Catholic philosopher Franz Brentano, who in an article in 1869 called attention to Comte as one of the outstanding thinkers of the century whose influence in France and England was growing, and from whose insights as well as

[23] See above all Wundt's *Einleitung in die Philosophie* (Leipzig, 1901), pp. 2, 56, 58–59, 268–269, also his "Ueber die Definition der Psychologie," *Philosophische Studien*, XII (1896), 1–66, *Logik* . . . (3rd ed., Stuttgart, 1906–8; first pub. 1880–83), II, 87–88, III, 144, 164, 424, 471, *System der Philosophie* (4th ed., Leipzig, 1919; first pub. 1889), p. 9.

[24] Cf. Rothacker, *Einleitung*, pp. 196–197, 200–201, 205–206, 244–248; Karl Vossler, *Positivismus und Idealismus in der Sprachwissenschaft* . . . (Heidelberg, 1904), pp. 2–4, 6–10.

[25] See in general Srbik, *Geist und Geschichte*, II, 221, 227; Bréhier, *Histoire de la philosophie*, pp. 944–945; but particularly T. K. Oesterreich, ed., *Die deutsche Philosophie des XIX. Jahrhunderts und der Gegenwart* ("Ueberweg," Vol. IV) (Basel, 1951), pp. 378 *et seq.* (Comte's influence on German "positivism" was small).

errors much could be learned. Comte had seen clearly what was wrong with the philosophy and with the general conditions of his time, and even his errors, for example his religious development, were "evidence of important truths." He had been misled by his own confused terminology to deduce a denial of God from the correct denial of the possibility of knowledge of causes. Again, given Comte's definitions, the Law of the Three Stages contained much truth.[26] A few years later Brentano returned to the subject. Although criticizing Comte's denial of introspection and rejecting a purely physiological psychology, Brentano declared himself, as to method in the social sciences, to be a follower of Comte and of nobody else, adding, significantly enough, that few of his readers probably knew anything of the latter's views. He therefore provided a brief summary and concluded by defending Comte in this respect against Mill.[27]

In the same year as Brentano's first essay considerable attention was devoted to Positivism by Eugen Dühring, the object of Engels' famous diatribe. In his history of philosophy Dühring called Comte the only great French philosopher of the century, who should be considered on a par with Descartes, Spinoza, Locke, and Hume. It was in his method, especially in his reflections on the relationship between the general and the particular, that Comte's philosophy was of particular value; his encyclopedia of knowledge was worthless, though not without brilliant individual ideas like the Law of the Three Stages and his insistence on a constructive outlook in politics. But he lacked all capacity for self-criticism and

[26] Brentano, "Auguste Comte und die positive Philosophie," in his *Vier Phasen der Philosophie* . . . (ed. Kraus, Leipzig, 1926), pp. 99–133.

[27] *Id., Psychologie vom empirischen Standpunkt* (ed. Kraus, Leipzig, 1924–25; first pub. 1874), I, 9–10, 28–30, 44–46, 66–67, 93, II, 310–317. Cf. Kraus in Oskar Kraus, Carl Stumpf, and Edmund Husserl, *Franz Brentano* . . . (Munich 1919), p. 7, who is of course right in saying that Brentano cannot be called a Positivist.

251

hence lapsed into mysticism; even so he was superior to the two critics of his "second phase," Littré and Mill.[28] The opposite view was taken ten years later by Ernst Laas, who regarded the Three Stages and the Classification as ingenious and partially true notions but "so vitiated by accesses of arbitrary fabrication as to border on the enterprises of Hegel." For the rest, the "positivism" that Laas was defending against idealism was that of Hume and Mill.[29] Another decade, in fact, elapsed before Comte got another genuine admirer. Hermann Lietz, while considering Comte the greatest social philosopher of the century, at least in France, approved above all of his method and of his historical analysis and not even by any means of all of the latter; in his later years Comte's idealism gained the upper hand over scientific empiricism. Yet, on the other hand, his devotion to his social ideals, as well as the ideals themselves, was admirable and he had contributed to the possibility of their realization.[30] More significant, however, because incorporated in a general work by a respected philosopher, were the tributes to various parts of Comte's work by Friedrich Jodl: to his linking of functions with organs and his treatment of egoism and altruism (irrespective of the merits of Gall), his views on marriage and the family, his mastery of the history of science, his insistence on studying the mind in a social and historical context, and above all the combination of historical and critical analysis that had gone into the construction of the Religion of Humanity. The theocratic

[28] Dühring, *Kritische Geschichte der Philosophie* . . . (3rd ed., Leipzig, 1878; first pub. 1869), pp. 495–512; and see also his *Natürliche Dialektik* . . . (Berlin, 1865), p. xii, and his *Kritische Geschichte der allgemeinen Principien der Mechanik* (3rd ed., Leipzig, 1887; first pub. 1873), pp. 478–480 (balanced judgment of Comte as a mathematician). Cf. Gruber, *Positivismus,* pp. 140–142.

[29] Laas, *Idealismus und Positivismus* . . . (Berlin, 1879), I, 183 n. 2 (and *passim*), cf. also his *Literarischer Nachlass* (ed. Kerry, Vienna, 1887).

[30] Hermann Lietz, *Die Probleme im Begriff der Gesellschaft bei Auguste Comte* . . . (Jena, 1891), esp. pp. 8, 62–66, 68–73, 75–78, 84–87, 90–92, 96–98.

despotism rightly criticized by Mill was not a necessary consequence of Comte's basic premises.[31]

By the last decade of the century two distinct trends became discernible in German philosophy which, while far from following Comte, yet concerned themselves specifically with problems raised by Positivism: the school which called itself empirio-critical, seeking to improve further the "critical" philosophy of Kant by reference to the methods of natural science, and the school of materialistic monism, seeking its basic support, rather, in the *results* of natural science.[32] One of the two principal representatives of the latter school, which was closest to Positivism in its social aspects, was Wilhelm Ostwald, who, though by profession a chemist, in 1902 established a journal which was to act, under the auspices of Kant and Helmholtz, as a link between the natural sciences and philosophy.[33] Ostwald became increasingly interested in Positivism. In 1908–1909 he adopted a heavily modified version of the Classification of the Sciences;[34] in 1912 he changed the

[31] Jodl, *Geschichte der Ethik* . . . (2nd ed., Stuttgart and Berlin, 1906–12; first pub. 1882–89), II, 331, 334, 341, 348, 371, 378–380, 684 n. 26, 687 n. 50; cf. also 326–330, 332–333, 335–338. Contrast the criticism of Theodor Ziehen, *Erkenntnistheorie* . . . (Jena, 1913), pp. 548–549 and *Zum gegenwärtigen Stand der Erkenntnistheorie* . . . (Wiesbaden, 1914), p. 21, from an "empirical" point of view.

[32] On monism and Positivism in general, see Lily Herzberg, "Die philosophischen Hauptströmungen im Monistenbund," *Annalen der Philosophie und philosophischen Kritik,* VII (1928), 113–135, 177–199. (The other leader of German monism was of course Ernst Haeckel.) See also the precursor F. A. Lange, *History of Materialism* . . . (tr. Thomas, London, 1892), III, 176.

[33] Ostwald, "Zur Einführung," *Annalen der Naturphilosophie,* I (1902), 1–4.

[34] *Natural Philosophy* (tr. Seltzer, New York, 1910; first pub. 1908), pp. 54–55, "Das System der Wissenschaften," *Annalen der Naturphilosophie,* VIII (1909), 266–272; cf. also his *Monistische Sonntagspredigten* (Leipzig, 1911–12), I, 332–335, and *Monism as the Goal of Civilization* (Hamburg, 1913), pp. 33–35.

name of the journal to indicate its broad scope;[35] and in 1914 he published both a translation of Comte's *Système* of 1822 and a full-length biography of him. He referred to Comte as a "creative mind of the first rank," a "pioneering scholar," and an "eminent man" and described the problem of social reorganization posed by him as still relevant and his proposals as still applicable. Comte's notion of the "spiritual power" corresponded closely, he said, with the social aims of organized Monism. He endorsed the Law of the Three Stages, Comte's idea of cultural progress, and his view of the relationship between biology and sociology.[36]

It was organized Monism (the so-called Monistenbund), indeed, that ultimately reaped whatever benefit there was in the only attempt made in Germany to establish a Positivist movement. The initiator, and Comte's only active disciple in Germany, was Heinrich Molenaar, who, having abandoned Anabaptism, became interested in Positivism through his Paris contacts as a teacher of Romance languages, by the campaign for funds for the Sorbonne monument, and by Lévy-Bruhl's book. He forthwith translated the latter, calling Comte a "great thinker" whose ideas were "powerful and still relevant."[37] He became active on the international Positivist committee and founded successively three short-lived journals in which he attempted, partly by his own original contributions, partly by translating various French and English Positivist writings, to propagate the faith.[38] His own emphasis

[35] Ostwald and Rudolf Goldscheid, "Nachricht," *Annalen der Naturphilosophie,* XI (1912), 305–306. It was henceforth to be called *Annalen der Natur- und Kulturphilosophie.*

[36] Comte, *Entwurf der wissenschaftlichen Arbeiten* . . . (tr. and ed. Ostwald, Leipzig, 1914), pp. vii–ix, 200 n. 8, 202 n. 12, 204 n. 18, 211 n. 36; Ostwald, *Auguste Comte: Der Mann und sein Werk* (Leipzig, 1914), p. v. See also his late *Die Pyramide der Wissenschaften* . . . (Stuttgart and Berlin, 1929), taking in general a similar and if anything more friendly position toward Positivism (esp. pp. 48, 52–53, 61, 64, 135, 148).

[37] Lévy-Bruhl, *Die Philosophie August Comte's* (Leipzig, 1902), Preface.

[38] These journals were *Religion der Menschheit: Monatsschrift zur Ver-*

was on Positivism as a bridge between freethought and the religious instinct, and particularly on the idea of sociocracy as a political rallying point for freethinkers.[39] He followed the orthodox Positivist line that freethought itself, while useful for destroying theology, was "negative" and unsatisfying. Nevertheless he published a good deal of freethinking, secularist, and Monist material in his journals, joined the Monistenbund, and urged his readers to do so too. After nine years of not only writing but also financing these journals almost singlehandedly, with almost no apparent impact, Molenaar turned away from Positivism in order to devote himself to two other causes: a campaign against vaccination and advocacy of an international language which he claimed to be superior to Esperanto.[40] Comte's lone German disciple, therefore, deserted the cause even before the First World War disrupted communications between Munich and the Paris headquarters of international Positivism. There had never been any prospect of creating an organized Positivist movement in Germany.

The Positivist disciples elsewhere, for their part, were suspicious of Monism as a violation of the Master's prohibition of attempts at an "objective synthesis" and in the light of his denunciation of materialism as metaphysical. Likewise the other movement characteristic of German philosophy about the turn of the century,

---

breitung der positiven Weltanschauung (1901–3), Positive Weltanschauung (1904–6), and Menschheitsziele (1907–9). They differed little from one another.

[39] See the journals, passim, especially Positive Weltanschauung, I, 132, II, 107; letter to Corra, 5 Feb. 1907, A.N., AS 6; undated MS of a speech delivered as a Monist delegate to a Positivist celebration, given to the author by Dr. Molenaar in 1958. I also incorporate some information gleaned from conversation with him.

[40] Molenaar to Corra, 29 May 1914, A.N., AS 10; oral information. The single rather pathetic sign of success in propagating Positivism came from one reader who declared that he contemplated "a cult of Comte's teaching" and considered himself "a not unworthy disciple of Auguste Comte" (Menschheitsziele, II, 372).

empirio-criticism, in its attempt at an epistemology more sophisticated than Kant's had little in common with the epistemological poverty of Positivism, even if the end result of naïve realism was similar in the two cases. Nor did the pragmatic test of knowledge— the so-called economy of thought—proposed by the founder of empirio-criticism, Richard Avenarius, have any historical or substantive connections with Comte's relativism or his notion of a "subjective synthesis." [41] Even Avenarius' definition of philosophy and of its relationship with the several sciences, though strongly reminiscent of Comte, does not seem to have been derived from him.[42] After Avenarius' death his journal did, to be sure, receive a more sociological orientation on the ground that sociology and scientific philosophy were inseparable,[43] but in substance it exhibited few if any signs of a closer approach to Positivism. Even

[41] Avenarius' main work was *Kritik der reinen Erfahrung* (2nd ed., Leipzig, 1907–8; first pub. 1888–90).

[42] Avenarius, "Zur Einführung," *Vierteljahrsschrift für wissenschaftliche Philosophie,* I (1877), 7–8, 11–14; see also the importance attached to psychology in his "Ueber die Stellung der Psychologie zur Philosophie . . . ," *ibid.,* 473–476, 481–487. Cf. the castigation administered by Wyrouboff, "Remarques sur la philosophie critique en Allemagne," *P.P.,* XXII (1879), 375–392: empirio-criticism was metaphysics, slightly corrected in the light of science, but still imposing logic on science instead of finding logic in science. I should like to call attention here, although they are only tangential to my concerns, to the reflections on the relations among Schopenhauer, Hegel, Avenarius, Comte, and Croce in Patrick Romanell, "Romanticism and Croce's Conception of Science," *Review of Metaphysics,* IX (1956), 506–508, 513–514.

[43] This was the work of the new editor, Paul Barth; see his justification of the journal's new name, "Zur Einführung der neuen Folge dieser Zeitschrift," *Vierteljahrsschrift für wissenschaftliche Philosophie und Soziologie,* XXVI (1902), 1–2. In a rare personal remark in his history of sociology Barth commended Comte's insistence on the necessity of a generally accepted view of life for a healthy society and criticized versions of the biological analogy more stringent than Comte's (*Philosophie der Geschichte,* I, 164–166).

when Avenarius' disciple Joseph Petzoldt founded another journal which had the word "positivist" in its title, it had nothing to do with the Positivism of Comte.[44] Still a third journal was founded by a dissenting disciple of Avenarius, Hans Vaihinger, dedicated to a combination of "realism, idealism, and positivism," but again, neither here nor in the pragmatism of Vaihinger's famous "philosophy of As-if" was there any appreciable trace of Comte.[45]

Both in Vaihinger and in Petzoldt there was, on the other hand, considerable trace of a philosophy parallel but unconnected with Avenarius', that of Ernst Mach. In this connection it is of some interest that Vaihinger referred to his own system not only as "critical positivism" but also as "logical positivism," for he and particularly Mach constituted probably the only links, such as they were, between Comte and the burgeoning "logical positivism" of the twentieth century.[46] Mach, by training a physicist, was in-

[44] See Petzoldt's fundamentally empirical inaugural article "Positivistische Philosophie," *Zeitschrift für positivistische Philosophie,* I (1913), 1-3, 15-16. Cf. his *Das Weltproblem vom Standpunkte des relativistischen Positivismus aus* (4th ed., Leipzig and Berlin, 1924; first pub. 1906), pp. 178-179, where he calls Comte's phenomenalism idealistic. Also interesting is his claim to attract the common man to science again by validating common-sense naïve realism (which cannot be said to have been successful); see *Einführung in die Philosophie der reinen Erfahrung* (Leipzig, 1900-4), II, 329-330. See the critique of Petzoldt as well as of Ostwald by the English Positivist C. H. Desch (Littréist and lacking any social outlook) in *P.R.,* XXVIII (1920), 242-243.

[45] Vaihinger and Raymund Schmidt, "Programm der Zeitschrift," *Annalen der Philosophie,* I (1919), iv-v; Vaihinger, *The Philosophy of As-if . . ."* (tr. Ogden, London and New York, 1924; first pub. 1911), pp. xxxvi-xlviii, on his own intellectual development (greatest debt to Hume and Mill, but on p. 153 Comte is associated with Hume as a desirable corrective to the errors of the Kantians).

[46] For Vaihinger see "Programm" cited in prec. note and *Philosophy of "As-if,"* p. 163; for Petzoldt see also Walter Dubislav, "Joseph Petzoldt in memoriam," *Annalen der Philosophie und philosophischen Kritik,* VIII (1929), 290-291.

creasingly drawn toward the philosophy of science and ended his teaching career as a professor of philosophy; but he never forgot his scientific orientation and remained a rigorous empiricist. Philosophy, he taught, was valid only insofar as it grew out of the special sciences and was not distinct from them, and he consistently rejected all "constructions" of the universe, even materialistic ones. He also rejected causes in favor of laws and held that the legitimate demand for prediction could be satisfied adequately by description and could in any case be satisfied in no other way. To this extent there are echoes of nineteenth-century Positivism in Mach, but this extent reduces itself ultimately to little more than a thoroughgoing rejection of metaphysics—more thoroughgoing, in fact, than Comte's, since Mach refused to classify the sciences in a hierarchy which implied value judgments among them: all sciences were of equal value and provided similar information. There was, indeed, only one way in which information was to be had, the reception of sensations, among which Mach included the psychical sensations of introspection, rejected by Comte. In fact Mach formally traced his own intellectual ancestry back to Hume and Kant, stated the similarity of his views to those of Avenarius, and mentioned Comte only in a negative connection. This did not prevent him on an appropriate occasion from paying tribute to Comte's work and to his influence, and insofar as all historical approaches to natural science originate with Comte, Mach's interest in this subject may be taken as an instance of that influence, including even a friendly reference to the Law of the Three Stages.[47]

[47] Mach, *Popular Scientific Lectures* (tr. McCormack, Chicago, 1895), pp. 207–208, 210, 211, 253–254, 257–258, "Sur le rapport de la physique avec la psychologie," *Année psychologique,* XII (1906), 303–304, 318, *The Analysis of Sensations* . . . (tr. Williams, Chicago and London, 1914), pp. viii–ix, xiii, 30 n., 46–47, 49–50, 55–56, letter to Hillemand of 1901 *re* the Sorbonne monument, quoted by Hillemand, *Vie et oeuvre de Comte,* p. 51, *The Science of Mechanics* . . . (tr. McCormack, 2nd ed., Chicago, 1902), *re* history of science, *Erkenntnis und Irrtum* . . . (3rd ed., Leipzig, 1917), p. 99; cf.

Mach at the turn of the century held a chair of philosophy in Vienna, and it was very largely owing to his precepts and example that the so-called "Vienna Circle" of "logical positivists" was formed. The members of this circle, as well as outside observers, are agreed that Comte, whether directly or through Mach, was at best a minor influence on the group. Obviously they did not need Comte to teach them an aversion to metaphysics, and insofar as their essential achievement was to evolve "a logical method of antimetaphysical thought" and to show that metaphysical assertions "are not simply useless or indemonstrable" but meaningless and nonsensical, they ran counter to and exceeded Comte's principal concerns. Likewise they had little use for the historical cast of mind which was so strong in Comte. It was only in these last two matters—the historical outlook and the literal meaninglessness of metaphysical propositions—that Mach constituted some sort of a connecting link.[48] Indeed, so conscious were some members of the differences between themselves and "traditional" Positivism that they preferred to call themselves "logical empiricists"

Robert Bouvier, *La pensée d'Ernst Mach* . . . (Paris, 1923), pp. 299, 301–305; Desch in *P.R.*, XVII (1909), 131; Joergen Joergensen, "The Development of Logical Empiricism," *International Encyclopedia of Unified Science,* II, No. 9 (Chicago, 1951), p. 10.

[48] *Ibid.,* pp. 6–7, 11; Bertrand Russell, "Logical Positivism," *Revue internationale de philosophie,* IV (1950), 3–5; Åke Petzäll, "Logistischer Positivismus . . . ," *Göteborgs Högskolas Årsskrift,* XXXVII (1931), 6–7; Albert E. Blumberg and Herbert Feigl, "Logical Positivism . . . ," *Journal of Philosophy,* XXVIII (1931), 281–282; Julius Rudolph Weinberg, *An Examination of Logical Positivism* (New York and London, 1936), pp. 1–9; Philipp Frank, *Modern Science and Its Philosophy* (Cambridge, Mass., and London, 1950), pp. 1–16; I. M. Bocheński, *Contemporary European Philosophy* (tr. Nicholl and Aschenbrenner, Berkeley and Los Angeles, 1956), pp. 52–55; Richard von Mises, *Positivism* . . . (Cambridge, Mass., 1951), pp. 359–361 (Comte's "great accomplishment . . . lies behind us as a relatively closed chapter"), and cf. also his rejection of classifications of science, pp. 215–16; Herbert Feigl, "Moritz Schlick," *Erkenntnis,* VII (1937–38), 399; Schlick, "Positivismus und Realismus," *ibid.,* III (1932–33), 2–3, 5.

rather than positivists.[49] On the other hand, one of these, Otto Neurath, attempted to reintroduce into the movement a social orientation and to produce a substantive synthesis (a "unified science"), which Comte would no doubt have denounced as "objective" and hence metaphysical but which may nevertheless go to show that twentieth-century antimetaphysics labored under some of the same pressures as nineteenth-century antimetaphysics.[50] This congruence does not of course imply any historical derivation, any more than the fact that the semantic preoccupations of orthodox contemporary logical empiricists have a precedent in the recurrent concern of Comte and his disciples for the clarification of words.[51] In sum: twentieth-century logical positivism (or empiricism) may share with its nineteenth-century predecessor "the image of an, in principle, unmysterious world" (Dilthey's "refusal to have anything put over on them") and a propensity for equipping "common sense" with capital letters, but it was entirely original in devising for itself what has been called the role of "the

[49] See, on Rudolf Carnap (the real synthesizer of the movement), Victor Kraft, *The Vienna Circle* . . . (tr. Pap, New York, 1953), pp. 24–25, cf. Frank, *Modern Science,* pp. 33–34; and Otto Neurath, "The Orchestration of the Sciences . . . ," *Philosophy and Phenomenological Research,* VI (1945–46), 500–501 ("We should solemnly cut the strings which connect us with the positivism of the past"). On a very large canvas, however, Neurath pointed out that, as distinct from England and France where a line was traceable from nominalism through positivism and materialism to logical empiricism, Germany had seen no contribution oriented toward empiricism to compare with Comte's (*Développement du cercle de Vienne,* pp. 28–29).

[50] See Neurath, "Unified Science . . . ," *International Encyclopedia of Unified Science,* I (1955), 8, but cf. his "Wege der wissenschaftlichen Weltauffassung," *Erkenntnis,* I (1930–31), 107–108; and see Frank, *Modern Science,* pp. 34–37, and Charles Morris, "The Significance of the Unity of Science Movement," *Philosophy and Phenomenological Research,* VI (1945–46), 511–514.

[51] But see Berlin, *Historical Inevitability,* p. 4, who thinks that there is a historical connection.

night-watchman philosophy," guarding language against misuse.[52]

This severe, self-denying-ordinance outlook was also that of a special brand of the general Vienna prototype of "positivism" in the early twentieth century known as "legal positivism" (*Rechtspositivismus*). The central proposition of this school was that "positive law," the actual body of laws enacted by a sovereign state, was *ipso facto* valid and could not be overruled by reference to "Natural Law." Clearly the point of contact with both Comte and the Vienna Circle is the view that "Natural Law" is a metaphysical concept, but of a historical connection with the Positivism of Comte there is little trace. On the contrary:

While Comte subordinated all law to ethics, the essence of modern positivist theory is the refusal to go outside the legal system for any criteria of the validity of law and the rejection as legally irrelevant of any ethical principles whether of the law of nature or of a rational morality or of revealed religion.[53]

It was not only the legal aspects of this neopositivism that were exported from Vienna, especially to the English-speaking world. In fact, as is well known, there was a certain amount of mutual influence, particularly between Vienna and Cambridge, first in such persons as G. E. Moore and Russell and later in the peregrinations of Wittgenstein and A. J. Ayer, who represented per-

[52] Ernest Gellner, "Reflections on Linguistic Philosophy, II," *Listener,* Vol. 58 (1957), pp. 237, 240–241; cf. also Hughes, *Consciousness and Society,* pp. 400–401.

[53] Ginsberg, *Reason and Unreason,* p. 232. The principal exponent of "legal positivism," Hans Kelsen, seems totally independent of Comte. In France the sociologist Léon Duguit, in constructing a theory of "objective law," realized that he could derive some support for it from the *Polity;* see *Le droit social, le droit individuel et la transformation de l'Etat* (Paris, 1908), pp. 12–13, also pp. 17, 24, 149, 151. Cf. the critique of Gaston Richard, "Le positivisme juridique et la loi des trois états," *Archives de philosophie du droit et de sociologie juridique,* I (1931), 311–340; also Julius Stone, *The Province and Function of Law* . . . (Sydney, 1946), pp. 343–344.

haps the climax of this whole development toward purely linguistic philosophy in what has been called "therapeutic positivism." [54] Professor Ayer, however, emphatically and justly disclaims any important connection between Comte and twentieth-century neopositivism and confines any historical link to the mediation of Mach. He considers Comte not so much a metaphysician as a bad scientist and his Positivism as an untenable form of humanism.[55]

Finally, it seems clear that, by contrast with the intimate relationship between mathematical logic and physics on the one hand and neopositivism on the other, recent and contemporary philosophy of science owes little if anything to the Positivism of Auguste Comte. The relativistic physics of Einstein, and the relativistic philosophy that has been built upon it, have nothing to do with Comte's pragmatic relativism or with his "subjective synthesis," and the critique of science of such men as Pierre Duhem and Henri Poincaré has nothing to do with Comte's dogmatic scientism, deriving, rather, through Boutroux from Kant and Renouvier.[56]

In summary, Germany made little use of Positivism either for domestic consumption or for reexport.[57] There was a brief period shortly after the middle of the century when Comte became a focus of the revulsion from Hegel (this was true above all in Dilthey), but in the long run German thought found a better

[54] Frank, *Modern Science,* p. 32; Bochénski, *Contemporary Philosophy,* pp. 46–47, 60; J. O. Urmson, *Philosophical Analysis* . . . (Oxford, 1956), pp. 4, 103, 106–107; Max Black, ed., *Philosophical Analysis* . . . (Ithaca, 1950), p. 13 n. 26.

[55] Interview with Professor Ayer, Feb. 1958.

[56] See Bréhier, *Histoire de la philosophie,* pp. 1064–67. Mourélos, *Epistémologie,* chap. x, tries to rehabilitate Comte's philosophy of science in the light of twentieth-century physics and of the "applied rationalism" based on it by Gaston Bachelard in his *Le rationalisme appliqué* (Paris, 1949).

[57] The reliance on the "three stages" of the Catholic philosopher Hans Urs von Balthasar, *Science, Religion and Christianity* (tr. Graef, London, 1958), pp. 12–13, can be treated as an isolated "sport."

reagent against Hegel in Kant and in variously radical emendations of Kant, or else (especially in Austria) turned to Britain rather than to France for the empirical tradition of Hume, Mill, and Spencer. Hegel had immunized scientifically minded Germans against the appeal of historicizing metaphysics.

CONCLUSION

THE relative success of Positivism both as an organized movement and in propagating itself in the world outside is, as I have said, a phenomenon by no means to be taken for granted. Still, once it had taken place, the subsequent decline in popularity, like all historical change, equally requires explanation.

The high-water mark of Positivism in both respects can almost certainly be placed in the last two decades of the century, even though some of its best-known exponents, such as Littré and Mill, were by then dead. What can account for its steady descent thereafter? Why did its appeal diminish?

As to organized Positivism, it suffered, apart from anything else, serious personal losses at the turn of the century. Almost all the leading original disciples disappeared within a few years of each other: Laffitte, Congreve, Beesly, Bridges, and Harrison. The second generation, though perhaps no less vigorous, were certainly less respected and therefore less influential. In addition, in France they were occupied for years with the second schism, its preparation, and its aftermath. Both of these factors undoubtedly also affected the esteem in which Positivist doctrines were held outside the circle of devotees.

But these factors, though important, are almost certainly not the whole story. For one thing, its decreasing novelty was in all likelihood a significant element in the decreasing popularity of Positivism. It was its novelty that, on the one hand, had appealed to the temperamental hedgehogs perpetually on the lookout for a new, preferably the latest, intellectual panacea and that, on the other hand, had obscured its shortcomings to those who were inclined to adopt some of its individual ideas or who admired attempts at comprehensiveness, i.e., the asking of the large questions, even if they were not disposed to accept the answers.

Moreover, not only did the appeal of the doctrine fade with its novelty, but familiarity with it tended to breed contempt. It became less and less possible for outsiders to ignore the unsympathetically bizarre details of Comte's social and religious utopia,[1] and those of the disciples who were concerned with and sensitive to the public reaction therefore became increasingly uncomfortable with them too. Unfortunately for them their more orthodox colleagues, especially the zealots among the Executors, tended increasingly to identify orthodoxy with reverence toward the personality of Comte, and it was in this spirit of piety that, for example, they undertook the publication of the volume of Comte's Testament and letters to Clotilde de Vaux, which paradoxically revealed all his human frailties. But it was, of course, Comte himself who, by his overt acts and attitude as well as by the very fact of writing a Testament intended for publication and preserving the letters, had committed the orthodox disciples to this commingling of his person with his doctrine.[2] Once again: the mere existence of "disciples" had the defects of its qualities so far as the diffusion of the doctrine was concerned; and disciples were necessarily involved in the construction of a religion as distinct from a conventionally philosophical system. The Littréist *via media* became less and less viable the more the orthodox disciples insisted on the religion and

[1] See the concluding paragraph of Chap. VI, above.

[2] Cf. above, p. 5 n. 3. It seems that some letters from Comte to Lewes have been suppressed as liable to misunderstanding (T. S. Lascelles to the author, 1 June 1958).

drew attention to the unpleasant aspects of Comte's personality.

John Stuart Mill, in defending Comte, was irrefutable when he said that for nine out of ten of Comte's readers

to have no God, and to talk of religion, is to their feelings at once an absurdity and an impiety. Of the remaining tenth, a great proportion, perhaps, will turn away from anything which calls itself by the name of religion at all. Between the two, it is difficult to find an audience who can be induced to listen to M. Comte without an insurmountable prejudice.[3]

This prejudice, I suggest, was in fact temporarily overcome (owing not least to Mill's own efforts) but soon emerged again, nourished by the disciples' activities which displayed the narrow dogmatism of the founder and of his doctrine too ostentatiously to be passed over.[4]

Moreover, especially in France, the political climate had changed by the beginning of the new century. The militant first republican generation, which had seen an ally particularly in Littréist Positivism, was passing away, while on the other hand the activities of some of the disciples gave increased color to the charge that Positivism was in fact a doctrine of political and social reaction.[5] In England, likewise, the political and social appeal of the radical aspects of Positivism became less and less relevant.[6] Anyway, for the new "progressive" generation in both countries a new social

[3] *Auguste Comte and Positivism,* pp. 132–133, and cf. M. T. Hindson in a lecture of 1947 entitled "A. Comte: Philosopher and Moral Reformer," p. 13 (MS, Papers of Otto and Clair Baier, in the latter's possession).

[4] Cf. D. Parodi, *Du positivisme à l'idéalisme: Philosophies d'hier. Etudes critiques* (Paris, 1930), p. 7; Delvolvé, *Réflexions,* pp. vi–viii, 9–11; also Laffitte, Annual Circular for 1887; Quin, *Memoirs,* pp. 99, 112, 145, 175–176; F. J. Gould quoted by F. H. Hayward and E. M. White, eds., in *The Last Years of a Great Educationist* . . . (Bungay, Suffolk, n.d.), p. 271; further confirmed by Mr. F. O. Ellis in conversation with the author.

[5] See Paul Hyacinthe Loyson in *Bulletin Auguste Comte,* I (1921), 39.

[6] Cf. Cochrane in *DNB, 1922–1930,* p. 406, and Geddes in Liveing, *Bridges,* pp. 9–10.

266

prophet was available of equal scientific pedigree and greater immediate applicability, Karl Marx.[7] At the same time the external events of World War I not only disrupted the organization of the Positivist *cénacles* but also diverted people's attention from idealistic demands not connected with the war, such as those made by Positivism.[8] Nor should the snowball effect of a falling off in enthusiasm be underestimated in a movement entirely dependent on voluntary effort and, equally important, voluntary financial contributions.

If from religious and political aspects conditions in various ways turned increasingly against the diffusion of Positivism, no compensating gain could be expected in its purely intellectual adoption, for Positivism if taken seriously and as a whole was a most difficult and unaccustomed system for laymen to absorb.[9] In fact Positivism could conceivably have become a mass movement only *qua* religion;[10] but as soon as the disciples attempted to augment their numbers by emphasizing religion, even larger numbers were correspondingly repelled. There, as many of the disciples themselves saw, was the crucial issue raised by the form in which Comte had cast his ideas and by the expectations which he had entertained and bequeathed.

M. Ducassé argues on these premises that Positivism gave too many hostages to popularity:

[7] Cf. Willey, *Nineteenth Century Studies*, p. 187. Those to whom Marx did not appeal for any of a variety of reasons might turn instead to Sigmund Freud, misconstrued in general as an oracle and in particular as the prophet of antiscientific disillusionment (see Hughes, *Consciousness and Society*, *passim* and esp. pp. 36–37). The day is not far off when an attempt must be made to write the history of the misunderstanding of Freud.

[8] See Corra in *R.P.I.*, 1933, p. 53, who also refers to the postwar economic crises, and Auzende to Corra, 29 Aug. 1922, A.N., AS 10. Mr. M. T. Hindson in conversation with the author argued similarly.

[9] See Jeannolle in *R.O.*, XIV (1885), 111–113; Quin, *Memoirs*, p. 105, on the illusion that Positivism could appeal to workmen.

[10] Cf. Congreve, above, p. 51.

Since the separation of "intellectual" from "religious" Positivism the militant history of the doctrine consists of a steady impoverishment. With most of the disciples as among those men of science who desired to attach themselves to Positivism the spirit of Comtism was increasingly replaced by modern substitutes held to be more satisfying. With each succeeding compromise even the word Positivism moved farther away from its original meaning: the name of Auguste Comte, once a watchword, tended more and more to turn into a label.[11]

Whether a more rather than a less rigorous insistence on orthodoxy would have succeeded in increasing or preserving the diffusion of Comte's ideas may be thought doubtful; but that his ideas, in the course of propagation, were in fact distorted is quite certain. This is a phenomenon apt to take place when any doctrine whatsoever is popularized, and because of it, among other things, intellectual history is different from the history of philosophy. But it is a phenomenon which is bound to take place as soon as a closed system so dependent as Comte's on its internal coherence is communicated to anyone else at all. Among the disciples, original thought about the system tended to lead to schism or at least to violent disagreements and disturbances; among the heathen, it led to dismemberment and the selection of more or less isolated parts of the system for emphasis, adaptation, and incorporation into other clusters of ideas. While painful for the original system, this disjoining of disparate elements initially joined only by will power was intellectually salutary. Some of Comte's most original ideas were in this way allowed to play a role for which they were genuinely suited, instead of being condemned to consort exclusively and fruitlessly with each other. Though products of the *esprit de système,* they could sail before the wind only when emancipated from it. This is not to say that this process did not also do an injustice to Comte by omitting his subtleties and quali-

[11] *Essai sur les origines,* pp. 7–9; see also his remarks as recently as 1950 in the discussion printed in the *Revue de synthèse,* n.s. XXVI, 174–175. Cf. with this Deroisin, *Notes,* pp. 185–186.

fications (which made him so long-winded) as well as by tearing his ideas out of their context; on the other hand, Comte certainly laid himself open to such operations by the latent tensions within his own system.[12] The tension within the history of Positivism is that for the disciples, especially the more orthodox, the influence of Comte's ideas was directly related to his personal reputation, whereas for sympathizers and potential sympathizers the two tended to be inversely related. This circumstance leads to the further tension, or even paradox, in the disciples' own estimate of the diffusion of the doctrine: for on the one hand they tended to set their sights very high and to require the formation of a "school," while on the other hand they tended to grasp at straws and claim them as straws in the wind indicating Comte's influence. It is rather pathetic to be given long lists of books said to derive from Comte which contain nothing specifically from him and sometimes, indeed, contain explicit rejections of him and of his system.[13]

But the disciples' understandable overestimate should not cause us to go to the other extreme. The firm establishment of the history of science and of sociology as academic disciplines, and the encouragement given to the more general tendency to regard society as an object of "scientific" study, are no mean achievements. The eclipse of Cousin as the dominant figure in France was an event of general intellectual significance. The Positivist contribution to a secular outlook—especially in education—in France and to the trade-union movement in England is by no means negligible. The Classification of the Sciences, probably the most widely accepted of all of Comte's ideas,[14] has indeed been a fruitful device, even if sometimes abused in the service of scientism.

Yet the most interesting problem remains, not the acceptance of

[12] Cf. the analysis of Delvolvé, above, pp. 112–113.

[13] See the Bibliographical Appendix.

[14] See even Isaiah Berlin, "History and Theory: The Concept of Scientific History," *History and Theory,* I (1960), 16.

separate ideas of Comte's, but the struggle over his system as a whole in the minds of sympathizers and disciples alike. In France, the Littréist movement and the quarrels engendered by it; in England, the travail of Harrison, Mill, Lewes, George Eliot— these were the real crucibles of Positivism, and there can be little question that the persons involved emerged from the struggle stronger intellectually and, perhaps, morally than when they entered it. Nor was the dividing line between those who became disciples and those who could not make the necessary submission always the most significant. Surely the differences, not only of character but of cast of mind, between Harrison and Congreve or Laffitte and Audiffrent were greater than those between Harrison and Lewes or Laffitte and Alain. It is in fact surprising what widely different people the disciples really were. In all but one respect they represented, perhaps, a cross section of middle-class society. The exception, of course, was their abandonment of Christianity together with the strength of their need for a substitute religion, both as a framework for organized worship and as an explanation of the universe.[15] This hunger for systematic and comprehensive explanation was the distinctive hallmark of the Positivist.

Likewise it was his insistence on providing and on imposing such an explanation that was the distinctive hallmark of Comte himself, setting him apart from the exponents of mere scientism. It was this insistence that determined everything he wrote, and equally everything he did.[16] It determined the vicissitudes of his

[15] Organized Positivism cannot be understood except in the context of the general search for substitute religions in Europe since the Enlightenment whose history remains to be written. See D. G. Charlton, "New Creeds for Old in Nineteenth-Century France," *Canadian Journal of Theology,* VIII (1962), 258–269.

[16] Including all of the characteristics enumerated by Sir Isaiah Berlin: "His grotesque pedantry, the unreadable dullness of his writing, his vanity, his eccentricity, his solemnity, the pathos of his private life, his insane dogmatism, his authoritarianism, his philosophical fallacies, all that is bizarre and utopian in his character and writings. . . . This naïve craving for unity

teaching after his death and the violence with which people tended to disagree about it. It made sure that anyone who considered Positivism seriously at all was bound to confront ultimate questions not only of the intellect but also of temperament, and that even those who rejected it outright were bound to hold to their divergent opinions with a more enlightened awareness of their nature and implications.[17] And it is perhaps ultimately the function of attempts at comprehensive explanation to allow people, not to swallow them whole, but to sharpen their teeth on them. In this sense it is not altogether idle to award marks for effort rather than for success,[18] and of the heroism of Comte's effort there can be no question.

Explanation is the function of the historian too;[19] but perhaps the intellectual historian can learn from the history of Positivism, if he did not know it before, that he must beware of trying to explain everything. There is a difference between explaining something and explaining it away. If we attempt a complete explanation of the relative success of Positivism over more than half a century, we run the risk of explaining it away and turning it into an ideology.[20] There comes a point in the process of asking why people accepted it when we reach the residual and not further

---

and symmetry at the expense of experience," his "bureaucratic fantasies . . . , with his fanatically tidy world of human beings joyfully engaged in fulfilling their functions, each within his own rigorously defined province, in the rationally ordered, totally unalterable hierarchy of the perfect society" (*Historical Inevitability,* pp. 4–5, 22; cf. also *The Hedgehog and the Fox* . . . [Mentor Book ed., New York, 1957], p. 26).

[17] See the altogether remarkable article (although I do not entirely agree with it) of Paul Arbousse-Bastide, "Faut-il oublier Comte? . . . ," *Revue de synthèse,* Vol. 78 (1957), p. 450: "When a thinker has the curious privilege, in the eyes of posterity and particularly of his compatriots, of being held in both veneration and contempt we may be sure that, consciously or otherwise, he has put a fundamental question."

[18] See, e.g., Delvolvé, above, pp. 112–113.

[19] See William Dray, *Laws and Explanation in History* (London, 1957).

[20] I use the word in the technical sense of Karl Mannheim in *Ideology and Utopia.*

reducible answer: "Because they thought it was true." Likewise, in the case of those who after struggling with it in the end rejected it *qua* comprehensive explanation, the factors which tilted the delicate balance are not exhaustively explicable. In the decisions of Mill and of Harrison alike there are elements ultimately inaccessible to the historian, as they were inaccessible to Mill and Harrison themselves. The reconstruction of the "inside" of an event,[21] perhaps above all of a mental event, can never be either certain or complete; but it must be attempted if history is to be written.

[21] See R. G. Collingwood, *The Idea of History* (Oxford, 1948).

Appendices

APPENDIX TO CHAPTER VII

A COMPARISON of Mill's treatment of Comte in the first and eighth editions of his *System of Logic*. (See above, p. 182 and n. 31.)

First ed. (1843)	*Eighth ed. (1872)*
I, 421: The *Cours* "a work which I hold to be far the greatest yet produced on the Philosophy of the Sciences."	Omitted.
422: Agreement with Comte on the inaccessibility of ultimate causes and that "the 'constant relations of succession or of similarity' which exist among phenomena themselves, . . . are the only objects of rational investigation."	Omitted.
423: Defense of Comte against Whewell.	Omitted.
432: Reference to Comte.	Omitted.
537: "I am not quite prepared to agree with M. Comte, in deeming the science of society and government intrinsically a more difficult study than the science of organic and animal life."	Omitted.
538: Attribution to Comte of the view that pathology provides the nearest equivalent to experiment in the field of physiology.	Statement retained, attribution omitted.

I, 540 n.: Praise of Comte.	Omitted.
II, 8–9: Praise of Comte.	Very much toned down.
17: Agreement on hypotheses with Comte, "who of all philosophers seems to me to have approached the nearest to a sound view of this . . . subject."	Agreement retained, phrase quoted omitted.
19–20: Praise of Comte.	Toned down, and mention of his name omitted.
22: Agreement with Comte on the hypothesis of a "luminiferous ether."	Regarded as a possible hypothesis.
24–25: Agreement and two disagreements.	Omitted.
28: Comte's confirmation of Laplace cited.	Omitted.
105: Mention.	Name suppressed.
172: ". . . M. Comte, of whose admirable work one of the most admirable portions is that in which he may truly be said to have created the philosophy of the higher mathematics."	"The speculations of M. Comte on the philosophy of the higher branches of mathematics, are among the many valuable gifts for which philosophy is indebted to that eminent thinker."
178: Mention.	Preserved.
179: Praise.	Omitted.
200: Motto from Comte.	Preserved.
301: ". . . M. Comte, whose view of the philosophy of classification . . . is the most complete with which I am acquainted."	Paragraph omitted.
304: Mention.	Toned down.
321: Only Comte has systematically treated "the arrangement of the natural groups into a natural series."	Preserved. Substance of chapter (on Classification) also preserved.
327: Mention by name.	Converted to passive voice.
328: Mention.	Omitted.
Motto for Book VI from Comte.	Replaced by motto from Condorcet.
499: Disagreement on psychology.	Rephrased but meaning retained.
	Charge inserted against

Comte (II, 446) of devia-
tion from scientific spirit
in psychology.

II, 561: "The Social Science . . . (which I ". . . (which, by a con-
shall henceforth, with M. Comte, des- venient barbarism, has
ignate by the more compact term Soci- been termed Sociology)
ology) . . ." . . ."

564: "The . . . only philosopher who, with Substantially retained.
a competent knowledge of . . . [sci-
entific methods in general], has attempted to characterize the method of
Sociology, M. Comte, considers . . .
[the] inverse order as inseparably inherent in the nature of sociological
speculation. He looks upon the social
science as essentially consisting of generalizations from history, verified, not
originally suggested, by deduction from
the laws of human nature."

564: "Such an opinion [i.e., the above], "Though there is a truth
from such a thinker, deserves the most contained in this opinion,
serious consideration; but though I of which I shall presently
shall presently endeavour to show the endeavour to show the
eminent truth which it contains . . ." importance . . ."

564: "I cannot but think that this truth is Retained.
enunciated in too unlimited a manner,
and that there is considerable scope in
sociological inquiry for the direct, as
well as for the inverse, Deductive
Method."

573,
584,
589: Laudatory references to Comte. Omitted.
590–
591: Comte alone had seen the necessity of Substantially retained.
connecting historical generalizations
with the laws of human nature.

591: ". . . and he alone, therefore, has Omitted.
arrived at any results truly scien-
tific . . ."

II, 591,

592: Three laudatory references to Comte. Omitted.

594–

598: Comte's division into social statics and dynamics cited, followed by long quotation. Preserved.

598: "M. Comte proceeds to illustrate, with his usual sagacity and discrimination . . ." "These remarks are followed by illustrations of . . ."

610: "The investigation [into the historical method] which I have . . . endeavoured to characterise, has been systematically attempted, up to the present time, by M. Comte alone." Preserved.

610: "His works are the only source to which the reader can resort for practical exemplification of the study of social phenomena on the true principles of the Historical Method." Substantially retained.

610: "Of that method I do not hesitate to pronounce them a model." Omitted.

610: "What is the value of his conclusions is another question, . . . and one which this is not the place to decide." ". . . the worth of his conclusions, and especially of his predictions and recommendations with respect to the Future of society, which appear to me greatly inferior in value to his appreciation of the Past . . ."

610: Statement of the Law of the Three Stages, as having "that high degree of scientific evidence, which is derived from the concurrence of the indications of history with the probabilities derived from the constitution of the human mind." It lets in "a flood of light . . . upon the whole course of history." Preserved.

Addition of a long footnote (II, 528) defending Comte against Whewell and others, with respect to the Law of the Three Stages and to "the legitimacy of inquiry into all causes which are accessible to human investigation."

II, 612,
  620,
  621 n.: Laudatory references to Comte.   Omitted.

BIOGRAPHICAL APPENDIX

THIS appendix provides in brief form information relevant to Positivism on all Positivists mentioned by name in Chapter II.

AJAM, Maurice (1861–1939), lawyer and politician. Early emancipated from Catholicism, first heard of Positivism through Laffitte's public lectures ca. 1880. On recommendation of a friend read Littré and learned respect for Comte's philosophy; made the acquaintance of Corra, read some Positivist literature, corresponded with other Positivists, but still no more than a sympathizer until fully converted in 1900 by correspondence and lectures. His son also became a Positivist.

AUDIFFRENT, Dr. Georges (1823–1909), from Marseille. Attracted to Comte personally while a student at the Ecole Polytechnique, 1842, read first volumes of the *Cours;* finally converted ca. 1851.

BEESLY, Edward Spencer (1831–1914). Evangelical clergyman's son but agnostic by the time he went to Oxford. Political Radical. Indirectly introduced to Positivism by Congreve. Married into a Positivist family.

BLIGNIÈRES, Célestin de (1822–1905). A pupil of Comte at the Ecole Polytechnique, considered him the only one of his teachers who held an organized view of science, bought the *Cours* which confirmed this opinion. Resumed contact with Comte, 1849, while on leave from the army.

BRIDGES, Dr. John Henry (1832–1906). Evangelical clergyman's son. Indirectly introduced to Positivism by Congreve at Wadham; first read Comte 1853. As interne in London, 1855, lived in house of John Chapman, editor of *Westminster Review,* where Positivism was frequently discussed. Back in Oxford, 1857, made regular study of Comte. Fully converted by Congreve in Wandsworth ca. 1859.

CONGREVE, Dr. Richard (1818–1899). (Evangelical) Holy Orders, 1842, tutor at Wadham. Introduced to Positivism 1845–46, perhaps by his friend A. H. Clough, more probably by J. S. Mill's *Logic;* read Littré. In Paris, 1849, met Comte as a result of asking to buy the *General View;* was deeply impressed by the man and by the historical, political, and social parts of the doctrine. "My radicalism, or vehement dislike of the actual management of the world, was what I had to prepare me for taking with pleasure to the solution offered by Comte. —It was to me the offer of salvation" (letter to Mary Congreve, 25 Feb. 1893, Wadham MS c. 185 ff. 44–45). Spent the next few years studying the system. Corresponded with Comte and returned to see him, 1854; left Oxford, became disciple 1855–1856, returned his Holy Orders 1857; first public speech as Positivist 1859; began medical study as Positivist scientific training.

CORRA, Emile (1848–1933). First introduced to Positivism by Littré, ca. 1875, read the *Cours,* then followed up old scientific interest by going to Laffitte's public lectures beginning 1878, converted by them 1882; gave up radical journalism and politics and became civil servant in order better to devote himself to Positivism. His son and another relative also Positivists.

HARRISON, Frederic (1831–1923), writer and barrister. High Church upbringing. At Wadham in 1851 a friend brought him Littré's book on Positivism and showed him the passages on Comte in Mill's *Logic;* read the *Cours.* Indirectly influenced by Congreve. Accepted Comte's view of history and scheme for sociology, but no Positivist yet; still a Broad Churchman under influence of F. D. Maurice and a political Radical, though much impressed by interview with Comte in 1854. In London from 1855 in close association with Congreve, Beesly, and Bridges, and it was the latter rather than Congreve who by 1861–1862 converted Harrison. Married his cousin who was already a Positivist.

HILLEMAND, Dr. Constant (1859–1941). Initiated to Positivism by an abridgment of the *Cours* 1878. Later followed Laffitte's course in sociology, was converted, became Laffitte's secretary 1888.

JEANNOLLE, Charles (d. 1914), civil servant. Former student of mathematics with Laffitte and a friend of Laffitte's nephew. His son much interested in Positivism.

LAFFITTE, Pierre (1823–1903). In philosophic doubt since his break with Catholicism 1837. Was failed by Comte on his entrance examination to Ecole Polytechnique, 1839, prepared instead to teach mathematics. Became interested in this agent of his change in plans; read the *Cours,* 1842, which was a revelation to him; gave up reading all other philosophy. Met Comte, 1844, who persuaded him to study biology too; definitively adopted Positivism 1845.

LITTRÉ, Emile (1801–1881). Jacobin, nonreligious Protestant family. Intended for Ecole Polytechnique but instead studied medicine; turned to scientific journalism, interested in general implications of science. A friend lent him first four volumes of the *Cours,* 1840; Comte, hearing of this, sent him a copy of his own. He was enthralled by it, found in Positivism the solution to his problems, became Comte's first active disciple.

MARVIN, F. S. (1863–1943), historian, writer, educator. Read Comte at Oxford for historical and sociological content; always interested most in these aspects of Positivism; later also interested in science and history of science. Attended Newton Hall 1888 or earlier.

ROBIN, Dr. Charles (1821–1885), biologist. Introduced to Littré by a mutual friend; was taken by Littré to Comte's lectures 1847 (?).

ROBINET, Dr. J. F. E. (1825–1899). Born in Lorraine; in Paris for medical studies 1847; took part in February Revolution; attended Comte's lectures and converted by L. A. Segond (afterwards a Littréist), 1848; later met Comte and joined Positivist Society (1851). In turn actively recruited among his patients and colleagues and in his own family. His house at La Ferté-sous-Jouarre a Positivist center from 1859.

WYROUBOFF, G. (1843–1913), Russian-born geologist and philosopher. Introduced to Positivism at Russian lycée by French literature lectures of Edmond Pommier, long a friend of Littré, given a letter of introduction to Littré by Pommier; went to Paris and settled there, founding with Littré the journal *La philosophie positive*. After it ceased publication returned entirely to scientific pursuits.

BIBLIOGRAPHICAL APPENDIX

LISTED here are the works[1] of non-Positivists which were checked for evidence of the diffusion of Positivism. Brief comments indicate the nature of the evidence where any was found. Items listed without comment, therefore, are those where no such evidence was apparent to me, except writings which were mentioned in the text, indicated by an asterisk. Some works listed here contain useful general information; these, indicated by a dagger, appear here with a short title only but are given fully in the Bibliography.

The only comment that seems to be called for is that the results of the investigations represented by this Appendix are overwhelmingly negative. Most leads (many of them supplied by the disciples) proved abortive. The diffusion of Positivism was less wide than the disciples flattered themselves it was.

Abry, E., C. Audic, and P. Crouzet, *Histoire illustrée de la littérature française* (new ed., Paris, etc., 1930).
Ackermann, L., *Oeuvres* (Paris, n.d.).
——, *Pensées d'une solitaire précédées d'une autobiographie* (Paris, 1882).
Adam, Ch., *La philosophie en France (première moitié du xix⁰ siècle)* (Paris, 1894).
*Adam, Mme. Edmond (Juliette Lamber), *My Literary Life* (tr., New York, 1904).

[1] These do not include autobiographies, memoirs, letters, and the like. Such works are listed in the Bibliography.

——, *The Romance of My Childhood and Youth* (tr., New York, 1902). An additional reference.

[Adam, William], *An Inquiry into the Theories of History with Special Reference to the Principles of the Positive Philosophy* (London, 1862).

*Alain [Emile Chartier], *Humanités* (Paris, 1946).

*——, *Idées: Introduction à la philosophie. Platon, Descartes, Hegel, Comte* (7th ed., Paris, 1939).

*——, *Lettres au docteur Henri Mondor sur le sujet du coeur et de l'esprit* (Paris, 1924).

——, *Lettres sur la philosophie première* (Paris, 1955).

*——, *Propos sur l'éducation* (Paris, 1932).

——, Review, in *Revue de métaphysique et de morale, XII* (1904), 88–108.

Alex, P., *Du droit et du positivisme* (Paris, 1876). Science and the study of law and of society; Three Stages.

Anon., "Mr. Charles Gaskell Higginson," *Manchester Faces and Places,* VIII (1896–97), 108–110. Friendly.

*——, "Philosophy and Positivism," *London Quarterly Review,* XXXI (1868–69), 328–348.

*——, "The Worship of Humanity," *Spectator,* Vol. 55 (1882), pp. 9–11.

Apelt, E. F., *Die Epochen der Geschichte der Menschheit: Eine historisch-philosophische Skizze* (2nd ed., 2 vols., Jena, 1851).

Armstrong, Henry E., *The Teaching of Scientific Method and Other Papers on Education* (London and New York, 1903).

Auburtin, Fernand, ed., *Frédéric LePlay d'après lui-même: Vie— méthode—doctrine. Notices et morceaux choisis* (Paris, 1906).

*Austin, John, *Lectures on Jurisprudence or the Philosophy of Positive Law* (4th ed., Vol. I, London, 1873).

*Avenarius, Richard, *Kritik der reinen Erfahrung* (2nd ed., 2 vols., Leipzig, 1907–8).

——, *Der menschliche Weltbegriff* (Leipzig, 1891).

*——, "Ueber die Stellung der Psychologie zur Philosophie: Eine Antrittsvorlesung," *Vierteljahrsschrift für wissenschaftliche Philosophie,* I (1877), 471–488.

*——, "Zur Einführung," *ibid.,* 1–14.

Ayer, A. J., ed., *Logical Positivism* (Glencoe, Ill., 1959).

Bachelard, Gaston, *L'activité rationaliste de la physique contemporaine* (Paris, 1951).

*——, *Etude sur l'évolution d'un problème de physique: La propagation thermique dans les solides* (Paris, 1928).

——, *La formation de l'esprit scientifique: Contribution à une psychanalyse de la connaissance objective* (Paris, 1938).

——, *Les intuitions atomistiques (Essai de classification)* (Paris, 1933).

——, *Le matérialisme rationnel* (Paris, 1953).

——, *Le nouvel esprit scientifique* (Paris, 1937).

*——, *Le rationalisme appliqué* (Paris, 1949).

*Bagehot, Walter, *Physics and Politics: or, Thoughts on the Application of the Principles of "Natural Selection" and "Inheritance" to Political Society* (New York, 1948).

*Bain, Alexander, *Astronomy* (Edinburgh, 1848).

——, *Education as a Science* (New York, 1881).

——, *The Emotions and the Will* (3rd ed., London, 1880).

*†——, *John Stuart Mill.*

——, *Logic: Deductive and Inductive* (New York, 1889).

——, *Mental and Moral Science: A Compendium of Psychology and Ethics* (London, 1884).

——, *The Senses and the Intellect* (3rd ed., London, 1868).

*Ball, Sidney, *The Moral Aspects of Socialism* (London, 1908).

*Balthasar, Hans Urs von, *Science, Religion and Christianity* (tr. Graef, London, 1958).

*Barth, Paul, "August Comte als Soziologe," *Menschheitsziele,* I (1907), 193–194.

*——, "Zur Einführung der neuen Folge dieser Zeitschrift," *Vierteljahrsschrift für wissenschaftliche Philosophie und Soziologie,* XXVI (1902), 1–2.

Barthel, Napoléon, *Réforme sociale, religieuse, morale, politique et industrielle, suivant la philosophie normale ou le normalisme . . .* (Paris, etc., 1859).

Bastian, Adolf, *Der Mensch in der Geschichte: Zur Begründung einer psychologischen Weltanschauung* (3 vols. in 1, Leipzig, 1860).

Baudouin, C., *Suggestion et autosuggestion* (Neuchâtel and Paris, n.d.).

*Bax, Ernest Belfort, *The Religion of Socialism: Being Essays in Modern Socialist Criticism* (London, n.d.).

*Bayet, Albert, *Histoire de France* (Paris, 1938).

——, *La morale de la science* (Paris, 1947).

*——, "Religion positiviste et rationalisme," *R.P.I.,* 1935, pp. 97–107.

——, "Le sens de la vie," *Action laïque,* May 1958, pp. 2–3. Comte cited on behalf of altruism and of the superiority of love over thought.

Beaunis, H., "Introduction," *Année psychologique,* I (1895), iii–vii.

*Belot, Gustave, *Etudes de morale positive* (2nd ed., 2 vols., Paris, 1921).

*——, "L'idée et la méthode de la philosophie scientifique chez Aug. Comte," *Histoire de la philosophie,* Bibliothèque du Congrès International de Philosophie, IV (Paris, 1902), pp. 413–472.

*——, "Les principes de la morale positiviste et la conscience contemporaine," *Revue philosophique,* Vol. 56 (1903), pp. 561–591.

Bergmann, Gustav, "A Positivistic Metaphysics of Consciousness," *Mind,* Vol. 54 (1945), pp. 193–226.

*Bergson, Henri, "La philosophie française," *Revue de Paris,* 15 May 1915, pp. 236–256.

*†Berlin, Isaiah, *Historical Inevitability.*

*Bernard, Claude, *An Introduction to the Study of Experimental Medicine* (tr. Greene, [New York], 1949).

*——, *Pensées, notes détachées* (Paris, 1937).

*——, *Philosophie: Manuscrit inédit* (ed. Chevalier, Paris, n.d.).

——, *La science expérimentale* (3rd ed., Paris, 1890).

Bernard, Th[alès], *De l'esprit positif de notre temps* (Le Puy, 1861).

*Bernheim, Ernst, *Geschichtsforschung und Geschichtsphilosophie* (Göttingen, 1880).

*——, *Lehrbuch der historischen Methode und der Geschichtsphilosophie* (3rd and 4th ed., Leipzig, 1903).

——, " 'Naturwissenschaftliche' Geschichtsforschung?" *Deutsche Zeitschrift für Geschichtswissenschaft,* VI (1891), 356–357. Defense of determinism.

Berr, Henri, *L'avenir de la philosophie: Esquisse d'une synthèse des connaissances fondée sur l'histoire* (Paris, 1899).

*——, *En marge de l'histoire universelle* (2 vols., Paris, 1934–53).

*——, *La montée de l'esprit: Bilan d'une vie et d'une oeuvre* (Paris, 1955).

——, *La synthèse en histoire: Essai critique et théorique* (Paris, 1911).

Bert, Paul, *L'instruction civique à l'école* (*Notions fondamentales*) (29th ed., Paris, n.d.).

Bertauld, Pierre-Auguste, *Positivisme et philosophie scientifique* (Paris, 1899).

*Berthelot, [Marcelin], "Le rôle de la science dans les progrès des sociétés modernes," *Revue scientifique,* 4th series, VII (1897), 641–643.

*——, "La science idéale et la science positive: A M. Renan," in his *Science et philosophie* (Paris, 1886), pp. 1–40.

Berthonneau, M., and others, *La méthode positive dans l'enseignement primaire et secondaire* (Paris, 1913).

*Bertrand, Alexis, *Cours municipal de sociologie: Leçon d'ouverture* (Lyon, 1892).

*——, *L'égalité devant l'instruction: Crise de l'enseignement* (Paris, [1904]).

——, "L'enseignement secondaire," *Revue encyclopédique* (1899), pp. 75–78, 92–93.

*——, *Les études dans la démocratie* (Paris, 1900).

——, "Le lycée de demain," *Revue encyclopédique* (1899), pp. 310–313, 329–332. Further references to Positivist principles for education.

*——, *La psychologie de l'effort et les doctrines contemporaines* (Paris, 1889).

*——, "Un réformateur de l'éducation," *Nouvelle revue,* 15 Jan. 1898, pp. 286–304.

Bertrand, J., "Souvenirs académiques: Auguste Comte et l'Ecole Polytechnique," *Revue des deux mondes,* Vol. 138 (1896), pp. 528–548.

*Besant, Annie, *Auguste Comte: His Philosophy, His Religion, and His Sociology* (London, n.d.).

Biays, A., *Histoire sommaire de la littérature française des origines à nos jours* (2nd ed., Paris, n.d.).

Binet, Alfred, *L'âme et le corps* (Paris, 1905).

——, *L'étude expérimentale de l'intelligence* (Paris, 1903).

——, *Introduction à la psychologie expérimentale* (Paris, 1894).

——, "Pour la philosophie de la conscience," *Année psychologique,* XII (1906), 113–136.

Blackham, H. J., ed., *Stanton Coit 1857–1944: Selections from His Writings, with a Prefatory Memoir* (London, n.d.).

*Blainville, H. de, *Histoires des sciences de l'organisation et de leurs progrès, comme base de la philosophie* (ed. Maupied, 3 vols., Paris and Lyon, 1845).

*Blakey, Robert, *History of the Philosophy of Mind* . . . (4 vols., London, 1848).

[Blatin], "Discours de clôture de la session du Convent de 1883 du Grand Orient de France," *Bulletin* du Grand Orient de France, XXXIX (1883), 631–645.

Blondel, Charles, *La conscience morbide: Essai de psychopathologie générale* (Paris, 1914).

*†——, "La psychologie selon Comte, Durkheim et Tarde."

——, *La psycho-physiologie de Gall: Ses idées directrices* (Paris, 1914).

Blondel, Jules-Edouard, *La question sociale et sa solution scientifique* (Paris, 1887).

Booth, Charles, *Life and Labour of the People in London. Final Volume: Notes on Social Influences and Conclusion* (London and New York, 1902).

*Bouchard, Ch., and G.-H. Roger, eds., *Nouveau traité de pathologie générale* (2 vols., Paris, 1912–14).

Bouchereau, J., *Le positivisme et le droit* (Bordeaux, 1899).

*Bourdeau, Louis, *L'histoire et les historiens: Essai critique sur l'histoire considérée comme science positive* (Paris, 1888).

——, *Le problème de la mort: Ses solutions imaginaires et la science positive* (Paris, 1893).

*——, *Le problème de la vie: Essai de sociologie générale* (Paris, 1901).

*——, *Théorie des sciences: Plan de science intégrale* (2 vols., Paris, 1882).

*Bourdet, Edouard, *L'évolution de la médecine* (Paris, 1875).

Bourgeois, Léon, *Solidarité* (2nd ed., Paris, 1897).

Boutroux, Emile, "A. Comte et la métaphysique," *Revue des cours et conférences,* 2nd series, X (1902), 206–213, 547–554, 735–747.

——, "Comtisme et positivisme," *Revue bleue,* 4th series, XVII (1902), 161–165.

*——, *The Contingency of the Laws of Nature* (tr. Rothwell, Chicago and London, 1916).

——, *Historical Studies in Philosophy* (tr. Rothwell, London, 1912).

——, *Natural Law in Science and Philosophy* (tr. Rothwell, New York, 1914). Uses Comte's Classification.

——, *Nouvelles études d'histoire de la philosophie* (Paris, 1927).

——, *Science and Religion in Contemporary Philosophy* (tr. Nield, London, 1909).

Bouyx, Georges, *L'église de l'ordre,* Vol. I (Paris, 1929).

Bovet, Pierre, *L'instinct combatif: Psychologie—éducation* (Neuchâtel and Paris, 1917).

*Boysset, Charles, *Catéchisme du xixe siècle* (Paris, n.d.).

Branford, Victor, *Living Religions: A Plea for the Larger Modernism* (London, 1924).

*——, "Note on the History of Sociology in Reply to Professor Karl Pearson," *Sociological Papers,* [I] (London, 1905), 25–42.

——, "On the Origin and Use of the Word Sociology, and on the Relation of Sociological to Other Studies and to Practical Problems," *ibid.,* 3–24.

*——, "On the Relation of Sociology to the Social Sciences and to Philosophy, Abstract," *ibid.,* 200–203.

*—— and Patrick Geddes, *The Coming Polity* (new ed., London, 1919).

—— and Patrick Geddes, *Our Social Inheritance* (London, 1919).

Brentano, Franz, *Ueber die Gründe der Entmuthigung auf philosophischem Gebiete* (Vienna, 1874). An approximation to the Classification.

*——, *Psychologie vom empirischen Standpunkt* (ed. Kraus, 2 vols., Leipzig, 1924–25).

*——, *Die vier Phasen der Philosophie und ihr augenblicklicher Stand* (ed. Kraus, Leipzig, 1926).

Brentano, Lujo, *Die Arbeitergilden der Gegenwart* (2 vols., Leipzig, 1871–72). Praise of Comte's method.

*Bresson, Léopold, *Les connaissances nécessaires* (Paris, 1884).

*——, "Considérations positives sur la science sociale," *Phalange,* V (1847), 537–562, VI (1847), 48–71, 136–154, 275–296, 330–353, 441–464, 537–551, VII (1848), 54–72, 137–154, 285–316, 466–500, VIII (1848), 77–96, 161–174 (incomplete).

*——, *Idées modernes: Cosmologie—sociologie* (Paris, 1880).

*——, *Les trois évolutions: Intellectuelle, sociale, morale* (Paris, 1888).

*[Brewster, Sir David], Review article in *Edinburgh Review,* Vol. 67 (1838), pp. 271–308.

*Breysig, Kurt, *Aufgaben und Massstäbe einer allgemeinen Geschichtschreibung* (Berlin, 1900)

——, *Die Geschichte der Menschheit* (2nd ed., 5 vols., Berlin, 1955).

——, *Gesellschaftslehre, Geschichtslehre* (Berlin, 1958).

*——, *Gestaltungen des Entwicklungsgedankens* (Berlin, 1940).

——, *Der Stufen-Bau und die Gesetze der Weltgeschichte* (Berlin, 1905).

Briffault, Robert, *The Making of Humanity* (London, 1919). Humanity as an organism.

Brinkmann, Carl, *Versuch einer Gesellschaftswissenschaft* (Munich and Leipzig, 1919).

Brütt, Maximilian, "Der Positivismus nach seiner ursprünglichen Fassung dargestellt und beurteilt," in Realgymnasuim des Johanneums zu Hamburg, *Bericht über das 55. Schuljahr . . .* (Hamburg, 1889).

Brunetière, Ferdinand, "La formation de l'idée de progrès au xviiie siècle," in his *Etudes critiques sur l'historie de la littérature française,* 5th series (Paris, 1893).

*——, *Sur les chemins de la croyance. Première étape: L'utilisation du positivisme* (Paris, 1905).

*Brunschvicg, Léon, *Les âges de l'intelligence* (new ed., Paris, 1937).

*——, *Les étapes de la philosophie mathématique* (3rd ed., Paris, 1929).

——, *L'expérience humaine et la causalité physique* (3rd ed., Paris, 1949).

*——, *Le progrès de la conscience dans la philosophie occidentale* (2 vols., Paris, 1927).

*Buchez, P. J. B., *Introduction à la science de l'histoire* (2nd ed., 2 vols., Paris, 1842).

*Buckle, Henry Thomas, *History of Civilization in England* (2 vols., New York, 1879).

*——, "Mill on Liberty," *Fraser's Magazine,* Vol. 59 (1859), pp. 509–542.

Burns, C. Delisle, *A New Faith for a New Age* (London, n.d.).

——, *Old Creeds and the New Faith* (London, 1911).

*Burt, Thomas, "Working Men and War," *Fortnightly Review,* XXXVIII (1882), 718–727.

Busco, Pierre, *Les cosmogonies modernes et la théorie de la connaissance* (Paris, 1924).

Cairnes, J. E., *The Character and Logical Method of Political Economy* (2nd ed., New York, 1875).

*Calas, Alexandre, *Auguste Comte médecin* (Paris, 1889).

*Call, Wathen Mark Wilks, *Final Causes: A Refutation* (London, 1891).

*[―― and John Chapman], "The Religion of Positivism," *Westminster Review*, n.s. XIII (1858), 305–350.

Camus, Albert, *The Rebel* (tr. Bower, London, 1953). A tribute to Comte's influence, but critical.

*Canguilhem, Georges, *La connaissance de la vie* (Paris, 1952).

*――, "La philosophie biologique d'Auguste Comte et son influence en France au xixᵉ siècle," *Bulletin* de la Société Française de Philosophie, special no. (1958), pp. 13–26.

Carnap, Rudolf, "Die alte und die neue Logik," *Erkenntnis*, I (1930–31), 12–26.

――, *Der logische Aufbau der Welt* (Berlin, 1928).

*Cauwès, Paul, *Cours d'économie politique* (3rd ed., 4 vols., Paris, 1893).

Cavaillon, A., *Manuel pratique des lois sociales* (Paris, 1910).

Cazalas, Laurent, *Traitement systématique, préventif et curatif de la tuberculose pulmonaire par l'éducation ou l'hygiène et la morale pratique* (Paris, 1897). Led by reading of Comte, Laffitte, Audiffrent, to view that health is proper adaptation of organism to environment.

Cellérier, Lucien, *Esquisse d'une science pédagogique: Les faits et les lois de l'éducation* (Paris, 1910).

Chachoin, L., *Les religions: Histoire―dogme―critique* (Algiers, 1910).

Challaye, Félicien, *Philosophie scientifique et philosophie morale* (Paris, 1923). Considerable quotation of and agreement with Comte: consensus, Three Stages, sociology, method, Humanity; also disagreement.

*[Chambers, Robert], *Vestiges of the Natural History of Creation* (London, 1844).

Champeau, Alexandre, Articles in *R.P.I.*, 1935, pp. 68–75, 112–121, 1936, pp. 221–227, 1937, pp. 97–108, 1938, pp. 210–215, 1939, pp. 31–33, 101–106, 147–157, 180–184. All fairly orthodox articles by a professor.

C[harles], E[mile], Art. "Positivisme," in *Dictionnaire des sciences philosophiques,* ed. Franck (Paris, 1885), pp. 1370–1378.

*Clémenceau, G., *De la génération des éléments anatomiques* (Paris, 1867).

Clifford, William Kingdon, *Lectures and Essays* (ed. Stephen and Pollock, 2 vols., London and New York, 1901).

Coates, J. B., *A Challenge to Christianity* (London, 1958).

Cohen, Gustave, "Auguste Comte et sa conception du moyen âge," *Bulletin* de la Classe des Lettres et des Sciences Morales et Politiques, Académie Royale de Belgique, 5th series, XX (1934), 157–170.

Cohn, Gustav, "Die heutige Nationalökonomie in England und Amerika," *Schmollers Jahrbuch,* XIII (1889), 1–46, 947–982.

——, *A History of Political Economy* (tr. Hill, Philadelphia, 1894).

*Coit, Stanton, *Ethical Culture as a Religion for the People* (London, n.d.).

*——, ed., *Ethical Democracy: Essays in Social Dynamics* (London, 1900).

Compayré, Gabriel, *Eléments d'instruction morale et civique* (*degrés moyen et supérieur*) (new ed., Paris, n.d.).

——, *The History of Pedagogy* (tr. Payne, London, 1918).

——, *Lectures on Pedagogy Theoretical and Practical* (tr. Payne, Boston, 1893).

*Comte, Auguste, *Catéchisme positiviste ou sommaire exposition de la religion universelle* (ed. with an Introduction by P.-F. Pécaut, Paris, 1909).

*——, *Cours de philosophie positive* (1re et 2e leçons) (ed. with an Introduction by Charles Lalo, Paris, n.d.).

*——, *Entwurf der wissenschaftlichen Arbeiten welche für eine Reorganisation der Gesellschaft erforderlich sind* (*1822*) (tr., ed., and with an Introduction by Wilhelm Ostwald, Leipzig, 1914).

*——, *Die positive Philosophie* (abridged by Jules Rig, tr. Kirchmann, 2 vols., Heidelberg, 1883–84).

*——, *The Positive Philosophy* (tr. and condensed by Harriet Martineau, Introduction by Frederic Harrison, 3 vols., London, 1896).

——, *Der Positivismus in seinem Wesen und seiner Bedeutung* (tr. Roschlau, Leipzig, 1894).

——, *Sociologie* (ed. Laubier, Paris, 1957).

"Comte et la métaphysique," *Bulletin* de la Société Française de Philosophie, III (1903), 1–24.

Conway, Moncure D., *Addresses and Reprints 1850–1907* (Boston and New York, 1909).

*†——, *Autobiography*.

*——, "What Is the Religion of Humanity?" *Free Religious Index,* n.s. I (1880–81), 278–280.

Cordier, A., *Exposé et critique du positivisme prolongé ou doctrine de conciliation du Dr. Mougeot (de l'Aube)* (Paris, 1877).

Cornelius, Hans, *Psychologie als Erfahrungswissenschaft* (Leipzig, 1897).

*Coste, Adolphe, *Les conditions sociales du bonheur et de la force* (3rd ed., Paris, 1885).

*——, *Dieu et l'âme: Essai d'idéalisme expérimental* (2nd ed., Paris, 1903).

——, *L'expérience des peuples et les prévisions qu'elle autorise* (Paris, 1900).

*——, *Les principes d'une sociologie objective* (Paris, 1899).

——, *Les questions sociales contemporaines* (Paris, 1886). Some incidental references.

Cottin, cte. Paul, *Positivisme et anarchie: Auguste Comte—Littré—Taine* (Paris, 1908).

*Cournot, Antoine Augustin, *Considérations sur la marche des idées et des événements dans les temps modernes* (ed. Mentré, 2 vols., Paris, n.d.).

*——, *An Essay on the Foundations of Our Knowledge* (tr. Moore, New York, 1956).

——, *Recherches sur les principes mathématiques de la théorie des richesses* (Paris, 1838).

——, *Traité de l'enchaînement des idées fondamentales dans les sciences et dans l'histoire* (new ed., Paris, 1911).

Cresson, André, *Les courants de la pensée philosophique française* (2 vols., Paris, 1927). Critical of Comte's politics, but devotes half of his pages on the 19th century to Comte.

*——, "L'éducation positiviste," *R.P.I.,* 1938, pp. 1–13, 49–55.

*Crozier, John Beattie, *Civilization & Progress* (new ed., London, 1888).

*Davies, C. Maurice, *Unorthodox London: or, Phases of Religious Life in the Metropolis* (2nd revised ed., London, 1876).

Davy, Georges, "L'esprit ministre du coeur," *Bulletin* de la Société Française de Philosophie, special no. (1958), pp. 39–67. Plausibility of this idea of Comte's.

*†——, "L'explication sociologique."

*——, *Sociologues d'hier et d'aujourd'hui* (Paris, 1931).

Delbet, Pierre, *La science et la réalité* (Paris, 1913). Apostasy of a Positivist's son.

*†Deluns-Montaud, "La philosophie de Gambetta."

*Dilthey, Wilhelm, *Einleitung in die Geisteswissenschaften: Versuch einer Grundlegung für das Studium der Gesellschaft und der Geschichte* (Vol. I of his *Gesammelte Schriften*) (2nd ed., Leipzig and Berlin, 1923).

*——, *Die geistige Welt: Einleitung in die Philosophie des Lebens,* Part I (Vol. V of his *Gesammelte Schriften*) (Leipzig and Berlin, 1924).

Dimier, L., *Les maîtres de la contre-révolution au dix-neuvième siècle* (Paris, 1907).

*†——, *Vingt ans d'Action Française.*

*Donnat, Léon, *La politique expérimentale* (2nd revised ed., Paris, 1891).

Draper, Warwick H., "The Principles of State Interference," in *Pan-Anglican Papers: Capital and Labour* (London, 1908).

duBois-Reymond, Emil, *Culturgeschichte und Naturwissenschaft* (Leipzig, 1878).

——, *Über die Grenzen des Naturerkennens. Die sieben Welträtsel: Zwei Vorträge* (Leipzig, 1903).

Dühring, E., *Cursus der Philosophie als streng wissenschaftlicher Weltanschauung und Lebensgestaltung* (Leipzig, 1875).

*——, *Kritische Geschichte der allgemeinen Principien der Mechanik* (3rd ed., Leipzig, 1887).

*——, *Kritische Geschichte der Philosophie von ihren Anfängen bis zur Gegenwart* (3rd ed., Leipzig, 1878).

*——, *Natürliche Dialektik: Neue logische Grundlagen der Wissenschaft und Philosophie* (Berlin, 1865).

*†Dugas, [L.], "Auguste Comte."

——, *La mémoire et l'oubli* (Paris, 1917).

*——, *Le problème de l'éducation: Essai de solution par la critique des doctrines pédagogiques* (Paris, 1909).

*Duguit, Léon, *Le droit social, le droit individuel et la transformation de l'Etat* (Paris, 1908).

——, *L'état, le droit objectif et la loi positive* (Paris, 1901).

——, *Law in the Modern State* (tr. Laski, London, 1921).

*†——, "Un séminaire de sociologie."

Duhem, P., *Le mixte et la combinaison chimique: Essai sur l'évolution d'une idée* (Paris, 1902).

Dumas, Georges, and others, *Nouveau traité de psychologie,* Vol. I (Paris, 1930). Comte as a source of factual and social psychology.

*†Duprat, G. L., "Auguste Comte et Emile Durkheim." Attempt to redress the balance disturbed by the conspiracy of silence against Comte.

——, *Les causes sociales de la folie* (Paris, 1900).

——, *L'instabilité mentale: Essai sur les données de la psycho-pathologie* (Paris, 1899). Endorses Comte's definition of psychological normality.

——, *Morals: A Treatise on the Psycho-sociological Bases of Ethics* (tr. Greenstreet, London and Newcastle-on-Tyne, 1903). Statics and dynamics.

——, "La psycho-sociologie," *Revue internationale de sociologie,* XXII (1914), 656–677. Echo of the Classification.

——, *Science sociale et démocratie: Essai de philosophie sociale* (Paris, 1900).

*Durkheim, E., "Critique de Saint-Simon et du saint-simonisme: Derniers fragments d'un cours d'histoire du socialisme," *Revue de métaphysique et de morale,* XXXIII (1926), 433–454.

——, "Détermination du fait moral," *Bulletin* de la Société Française de Philosophie, VI (1906), 113–139.

*——, *Education and Sociology* (tr. and with an Introduction by Fox, Glencoe, Ill., 1956).

——, *L'éducation morale* (Paris, 1925).

——, *L'évolution pédagogique en France de la Renaissance à nos jours* (Paris, 1938).

*——, "Faculté de Bordeaux: Cours de science sociale, leçon d'ouverture," *Revue internationale de l'enseignement,* XV (1888), 23–48.

*——, *Montesquieu and Rousseau: Forerunners of Sociology* (tr. Manheim, Ann Arbor, 1960).

*——, *On the Division of Labor in Society* (tr. and ed. Simpson, New York, 1933).

*——, *Professional Ethics and Civic Morals* (tr. Brookfield, London, 1957).

*——, *The Rules of Sociological Method* (8th ed., tr. Solovay and Mueller, ed. Catlin, Chicago, 1938).

*——, "Saint-Simon, fondateur du positivisme et de la sociologie," *Revue philosophique,* Vol. 99 (1925), pp. 321–341.

*——, *Socialism and Saint-Simon* (*Le socialisme*) (tr. Sattler, ed. Gouldner, Yellow Springs, Ohio, 1958).

*——, "La sociologie," in *La science française* (Paris, 1915), I, 39–49.

*——, "La sociologie en France au xix⁰ siècle," *Revue bleue,* 4th series, XIII (1900), 609–613, 647–652.

*——, *Sociology and Philosophy* (tr. Pocock, Glencoe, Ill., 1953).

—— and P. Fauconnet, "Sociologie et sciences sociales," *Revue philosophique,* Vol. 55 (1903), pp. 465–497.

Earle, John Charles, "Leaders of Modern Thought," *Modern Thought,* I (1879), 63–66. Positivism remarkable; unity of Comte's thought, powerful even in its aberrations.

*Edgeworth, F. Y., *Mathematical Psychics: An Essay on the Application of Mathematics to the Moral Sciences* (London, 1881).

*Eliot, George, *Daniel Deronda* (International Novelists' Library, 2 vols., Boston, 1900).

*——, *Poems* (New York, 1886).

*——, *The Spanish Gypsy* (Standard Edition, Edinburgh and London, n.d.).

Enriques, F., "Philosophie scientifique," *Actes* du Congrès International de Philosophie Scientifique, Sorbonne, Paris 1935 (Paris, 1936), I, 23–27.

*Espinas, Alfred, *Des sociétés animales* (2nd ed., Paris, 1878).

*Etienne, Louis, "Le positivisme dans l'histoire," *Revue des deux mondes,* Vol. 74 (1868), pp. 375–408.

*Eucken, Rudolf, "Zur Würdigung Comte's und des Positivismus," in *Philosophische Aufsätze* dedicated to Eduard Zeller (Leipzig, 1887), pp. 53–82.

*Faguet, Emile, "Auguste Comte," *Revue des deux mondes,* Vol. 130 (1895), pp. 296–319, 534–559.

*——, "Comte et son siècle," *Revue bleue,* 4th series, VI (1896), 177–181.

*——, *Initiation into Philosophy* (tr. Gordon, London, 1912).

——, "La morale de Comte," *Annales politiques et littéraires,* Vol. 49 (1907), pp. 219–220. Tribute and criticism.

*†Ferraz, M., *Socialisme, naturalisme et positivisme.*

Ferré, Louise-Marie, *Féminisme et positivisme* (n.p., 1938).

*Ferry, Jules, "Marcel Roulleaux," *P.P.,* I (1867), 289–312.

Fiolle, Jean, *Scientisme et science* (Paris, 1936).

Flournoy, Th., *Métaphysique et psychologie* (Geneva, 1890).

*Foote, G. W., *Secularism the True Philosophy of Life: An Exposition and a Defence* (London, 1879).

*Fouillée, Alfred, *Histoire de la philosophie* (13th ed., Paris, n.d.).

——, *Le mouvement idéaliste et la réaction contre la science positive* (3rd ed., Paris, 1931)

*——, *Le mouvement positiviste et la conception sociologique du monde* (Paris, 1896).

——, *La propriété sociale et la démocratie* (2nd ed., Paris, 1895).

*——, *La science sociale contemporaine* (6th ed., Paris, 1922).

Fournière, Eugène, *Essai sur l'individualisme* (Paris, 1901).

——, *L'idéalisme social* (Paris, 1898).

——, *L'individu, l'association et l'état* (Paris, 1907).

——, *La sociocratie: Essai de politique positive* (Paris, 1910). Nothing, despite the title.

*France, Anatole, "Auguste Comte," in his *Oeuvres complètes illustrées,* XVII (Paris, 1928), 267–295.

*——, "Pierre Laffitte," *ibid.,* 297–325.

Franck, Ad., *Philosophie et religion* (Paris, 1867).

Freycinet, C. de, *Essais sur la philosophie des sciences* (Paris, 1896).

*Froument, P., *Les méthodes de la raison, précédées d'un exposé complet du travail cérébral* (Paris, 1908).

*——, *Recherches sur la mentalité humaine (ses éléments, sa formation, son état normal)* (Paris, n.d.).

Funck-Brentano, Th., "Positivisme et nihilisme," *Nouvelle revue,* Vol. 87 (1894), pp. 468–484.

Fyffe, C. A., *History of Modern Europe* (2 vols., London, etc., 1924).

*Galabert, Edmond, "L'évolution esthétique," *Revue internationale de sociologie,* VI (1898), 718–742.

*——, "Les fondements de l'esthétique scientifique," *ibid.,* 1–15.

*——, "Le pouvoir spirituel," *ibid.,* VII (1899), 321–331.

*——, "Le rôle social de l'art," *ibid.,* VI (1898), 577–603.

*Gambetta, Léon, "Discours," *P.P.,* XXVI (1881), 441–448.

*——, *Discours et plaidoyers politiques* (ed. Reinach, 11 vols., Paris, 1881–1906).

*——, Speech in *P.P.,* X (1873), 304–305.

Gaultier, Jules de, *La philosophie officielle et la philosophie* (Paris, 1922). Attempt to reconcile "idealist empiricism" with Positivism; school of L. Weber. Approval of Comte as a "philosopher of experience."

Geddes, Patrick, "Civics: As Applied Sociology," *Sociological Papers,* [I] (London, 1905), 101–118.

*——, A Current Evaluation of the Positivist School," *P.R.,* XXIX (1921), 145–147.

——, *John Ruskin, Economist* (Edinburgh, 1884).

—— and J. Arthur Thomson, *Evolution* (New York and London, 1911).

*Gensoul, L., *La république au-dessus du suffrage universel: Etude démonstrative de philosophie et de politique positives avec une lettre et des remarques de M. E. Littré* (Paris, 1871).

*Georges, Aug., "Essai sur le système psychologique d'Auguste Comte," *Archives d'anthropologie criminelle, de médecine légale, et de psychologie normale et pathologique,* XXIII (1908), 749–809.

*Gide, Charles, *Principes d'économie politique* (10th ed., Paris, 1906).

*Gillouin, Charles, *Journal d'un chrétien philosophe (1915–1921)* (Paris, 1922).

*Ginsberg, Morris, "Comte: A Revaluation," in *Sociologica: Frankfurter Beiträge zur Soziologie,* I (Frankfurt, 1955), 305–319.

*——, *Reason and Experience in Ethics* (Oxford and London, 1956).

*Goblot, Edmond, *Essai sur la classification des sciences* (Paris, 1898).

*——, *Traité de logique* (4th ed., Paris, 1925).

Goldscheid, Rudolf, *Entwicklungswerttheorie, Entwicklungsökonomie, Menschenökonomie: Eine Programmschrift* (Leipzig, 1908).

——, "Kulturperspektiven," *Annalen der Natur- und Kulturphiloso-*

phie, XII (1913), 3–27. Acknowledges Comte as the greatest sociologist.

Gomperz, Heinrich, *Philosophical Studies* (ed. Robinson, Boston, 1953).

*Gomperz, Theodor, *Essays und Erinnerungen* (Stuttgart and Leipzig, 1905).

Grant, A. J., *Outlines of European History* (London, etc., 1913).

*——, Review of F. S. Marvin, *The Century of Hope,* in *History,* n.s. IV (1919–20), 228–230.

*——, ed., *English Historians* (London, etc., 1906).

*Greef, Guillaume de, *Introduction à la sociologie* (2 vols., Brussels and Paris, 1886–89).

*——, *Les lois sociologiques* (Brussels, 1891).

*——, *Problèmes de philosophie positive: L'enseignement intégral— l'Inconnaissable* (Paris, 1900).

Gros, Johannès, "Auguste Comte et ses 'trois anges,'" *Revue hebdomadaire,* IX (1909), 350–366.

Guardia, J.-M., "Les sentiments intimes d'Auguste Comte," *Revue philosophique,* XXIV (1887), 59–74. Sympathy for Comte's person but not for his doctrine.

Guilleminot, H., *La matière et la vie* (Paris, 1919).

*Gumplowicz, Ludwig, *The Outlines of Sociology* (tr. Moore, Philadelphia, 1899).

——, *Sociologie und Politik* (Leipzig, 1892).

*——, *Die sociologische Staatsidee* (Graz, 1892).

*Guyau, M., *The Non-religion of the Future: A Sociological Study* (New York, 1897).

*——, *A Sketch of Morality Independent of Obligation or Sanction* (tr. Kapteyn, London, 1898).

Halbwachs, Maurice, "La loi en sociologie," in *Science et loi* (Paris, 1934), pp. 173–196. Comte the founder of sociology and correct as to its method.

Halleux, Jean, *Les principes du positivisme contemporain: Exposé et critique* (Paris, n.d.). Appreciation of the empiricism and relativism in Positivism.

*Hauriou, Maurice, *La science sociale traditionelle* (Paris, 1896).

Hayward, Frank H., *The Reform of Moral and Biblical Education on the Lines of Herbartianism, Critical Thought, and the Ethical Needs of the Present Day* (London, 1902). Interest in Gould as an agnostic.

—— and Arnold Freeman, *The Spiritual Foundations of Reconstruction: A Plea for New Educational Methods* (London, 1919).

Hellwald, Friedrich, *Culturgeschichte in ihrer natürlichen Entwicklung bis zur Gegenwart* (2nd ed., 2 vols., Augsburg, 1876–77).

*Helme, F., "L'opinion d'un médecin sur la Société Positiviste Internationale," *Revue moderne de médecine et de chirurgie,* July 1912, pp. 246–251.

*[Henderson], "Positivism: Its Nature and Influence as a Philosophy, a Polity, and a Religion," *North British Review,* Vol. 49 (1868), pp. 112–138.

Henne-am Rhyn, Otto, *Kulturgeschichte der jüngsten Zeit: Von der Errichtung des Deutschen Reiches bis auf die Gegenwart* (Leipzig, 1897).

——, *Kulturgeschichte der Urzeit und der morgenländischen Völker bis zum Verluste ihrer Selbständigkeit* (Leipzig, 1877).

Héron, A., *Le positivisme et la métaphysique* (Rouen, 1888).

Hesse, A., and A. Gleyze, *Notions de sociologie appliquée à la morale et à l'éducation* (3rd ed., Paris, 1927). Comte as forerunner of Durkheim.

*Hobhouse, L. T., *Development and Purpose: An Essay towards a Philosophy of Evolution* (London, 1913).

——, "Editorial," *Sociological Review,* I (1908), 1–11.

*——, "The Law of the Three Stages," *ibid.,* 262–279.

——, *Morals in Evolution: A Study in Comparative Ethics* (London, 1951).

Hobson, J. A., *Free-Thought in the Social Sciences* (New York, 1926).

——, *Rationalism and Humanism* (London, 1933).

*Holyoake, George Jacob, *English Secularism: A Confession of Belief* (Chicago, 1896).

Homberg, [Th.], *Le positivisme d'après un livre de M. Caro* (Rouen, 1884).

*Hooper, Charles E., *Common Sense and the Rudiments of Philosophy* (2nd ed., London, 1920).

*Howell, George, *The Conflicts of Capital and Labour Historically* *and Economically Considered* (2nd ed., London and New York, 1890).

*Hubbard, G., "Mémoire," *P.P.,* VIII (1872), 331–336.

Hubert, René, "Essai sur l'histoire de l'idée de progrès," *Revue d'histoire de la philosophie et d'histoire générale de la civilisation,* II (1934), 289–305, III (1935), 1–32. Positivism merely a philosophy of history and unscientific, but nevertheless powerful. Classification has become classical; Three Stages in general expresses intellectual progress.

*——, "Essai sur l'histoire des origines et des progrès de la sociologie en France," *ibid.,* VI (1938), 111–155, 281–310.

——, "Essai sur la systématisation du savoir scientifique," *Revue de métaphysique et de morale,* XXIX (1922), 311–358. Some favorable remarks.

——, *Histoire de la pédagogie* (Paris, 1949).

——, "La théorie de la connaissance chez Auguste Comte," *Revue philosophique,* Vol. 99 (1925), pp. 257–282. Attempt to supply Comte with an epistemology *malgré lui.*

——, *Traité de pédagogie générale* (Paris, 1946). Aproval of social relativism and of subjective religious synthesis.

——, ed., *Auguste Comte: Choix de textes et étude du système philosophique* (Paris, n.d.). A long and fairly sympathetic introduction; Comte as founder of sociology and history of science; approval of Humanity. Also criticism.

Huxley, Julian, *Essays of a Biologist* (London, 1923).

*Huxley, T. H., "On the Physical Basis of Life," *Fortnightly Review,* n.s. V (1869), 129–145.

*——, "The Scientific Aspects of Positivism," *ibid.,* 653–670.

Institut International de Sociologie, *Annales,* Vols. I–XIV (1895–1913). Organ of Worms's institute. Some references, by Positivists and others.

Izoulet, Jean, *La cité moderne: Métaphysique de la sociologie* (Paris, 1894).

Janet, Pierre, *L'automatisme psychologique: Essai de psychologie expérimentale sur les formes inférieures de l'activité humaine* (3rd ed., Paris, 1899).

Jankélévitch, S., *Nature et société: Essai d'une application du point de vue finaliste aux phénomènes sociaux* (Paris, 1906).

Jeanvrot, Victor, *La question du serment* (Paris, 1882).

Jevons, W. Stanley, *Political Economy* (London, 1878).

*Jodl, Friedrich, *Geschichte der Ethik als philosophischer Wissenschaft* (2nd ed., 2 vols., Stuttgart and Berlin, 1906–12).

——, *Lehrbuch der Psychologie* (4th ed., 2 vols., Stuttgart and Berlin, 1916).

Joint Committee of the Incorporated Association of Assistant Masters and the Science Masters' Association, *The Teaching of Science in Secondary Schools* (London, 1947).

Kelsen, Hans, *General Theory of Law and State* (tr. Wedberg, Cambridge, Mass., 1949).

——, *Die philosophischen Grundlagen der Naturrechtslehre und des Rechtspositivismus* (Charlottenburg, 1928).

Kern, Berthold von, *Die Willensfreiheit* (Berlin, 1914).

Kirchmann, J. H. von, *Katechismus der Philosophie* (Leipzig, 1877).

——, *Die Lehre vom Wissen als Einleitung in das Studium philosophischer Werke* (4th ed., Heidelberg, 1886).

Kleinpeter, Hans, "Die alte und die neue Logik," *Zeitschrift für positivistische Philosophie,* I (1913), 157–171.

*Knies, Hans, *Die politische Oekonomie vom geschichtlichen Standpunkte* (2nd ed., Braunschweig, 1883).

Kolb, G. Friedr., *Culturgeschichte der Menschheit . . .* (2nd ed., 2 vols., Leipzig, 1872–73).

*Kozlowski, W. M., "La réforme de l'enseignement philosophique à l'Université," *Revue philosophique,* Vol. 93 (1922), pp. 100–118.

*Krohn, Dr., "Beiträge zur Kenntniss und Würdigung der Sociologie," *Jahrbücher für Nationalökonomie und Statistik,* XXXV (1880), 407–433.

Krueger, Felix, *Über Entwicklungspsychologie: Ihre sachliche und geschichtliche Notwendigkeit* (Leipzig, 1915).

Kühnert, Herbert, *August Comtes Verhältnis zur Kunst* (Jena, 1910).

*Laas, Ernst, *Idealismus und Positivismus: Eine kritische Auseinandersetzung* (3 vols., Berlin, 1879).

*——, *Literarischer Nachlass* (ed. Kerry, Vienna, 1887).

*Lacombe, P., *De l'histoire considérée comme science* (2nd ed., Paris, 1930).

Lalande, André, *Les illusions évolutionnistes* (Paris, 1930).

——, *La raison et les normes* (Paris, n.d.).

——, *Vocabulaire technique et critique de la philosophie* (5th ed., Paris, 1947). Comtian definition of "positivism."

Lallemand, Jules, "La méthode et la définition de l'esthétique," *Esprit nouveau, revue internationale d'esthétique* [I] (1920), 257–267.

*Lalo, Charles, *L'art et la morale* (Paris, 1922).

*——, *L'art et la vie sociale* (Paris, 1921).

——, *L'esthétique expérimentale contemporaine* (Paris, 1908).

——, *Les sentiments esthétiques* (Paris, 1910).

Lamprecht, Karl, "Ueber den Begriff der Geschichte und über historische und psychologische Gesetze," *Annalen der Naturphilosophie,* II (1903), 255–278.

*——, *Die kulturhistorische Methode* (Berlin, 1900).

*——, "La science moderne de l'histoire: Quelques mots de réponse," *Revue de synthèse historique,* X (1905), 257–260.

*——, *What Is History? Five Lectures on the Modern Science of History* (tr. Andrews, New York and London, 1905).

*Lange, Friedrich Albert, *History of Materialism and Criticism of Its Present Importance* (tr. Thomas, 4th ed., 3 vols., London, 1892).

Lanson, Gustave, *Histoire de la littérature française* (7th ed., Paris, 1902). Praise of Comte as a thinker but not as a writer.

Lazarus, M., and H. Steinthal, "Einleitende Gedanken über Völkerpsychologie . . . ," *Zeitschrift für Völkerpsychologie und Sprachwissenschaft,* I (1860), 1–73.

Lecky, William Edward Hartpole, *Historical and Political Essays* (London, etc., 1908).

Le Dantec, Félix, *Le chaos et l'harmonie universelle* (Paris, 1911).

——, *De l'homme à la science: Philosophie du xxe siècle* (Paris, 1907).

——, *L'égoïsme seule base de toute société: Etude des déformations résultant de la vie en commun* (Paris, 1912).

——, *Lamarckiens et darwiniens: Discussion de quelques théories sur la formation des espèces* (Paris, 1899).

——, *Les limites du connaissable: La vie et les phénomènes naturels* (Paris, 1903).

——, *The Nature and Origin of Life in the Light of New Knowledge* (tr. Dewey, New York, n.d.).

Lefèvre, André, *L'histoire: Entretiens sur l'évolution historique* (Paris, 1897).

——, *L'homme à travers les âges: Essais de critique historique* (Paris, 1880).

——, *La philosophie* (2nd ed., Paris, 1884). Comte signaled return to objective and experimental method but achieved nothing valuable with it himself. Benefits of his influence on French medicine and on free thought.

Lemaitre, Jules, "Le style de Comte," *Annales politiques et littéraires,* Vol. 49 (1907), pp. 234–235. Virtues as well as vices.

Lenoir, Raymond, "Les astres et les nombres chez Auguste Comte," *Revue d'histoire de la philosophie,* IV (1930), 274–302. Comte right on the place of the intellect; mathematical discipline in sociology.

——, "Auguste Comte et Clotilde de Vaux vus par André Thérive," *Revue de synthèse,* Vol. 78 (1957), pp. 508–513. Very sympathetic.

——, "La sociologie moderne," *Revue de théologie et de philosophie,* n.s. XVI (1928), 125–152. Value of Comte's idea of fetishism.

Lenzen, Victor F., "Procedures of Empirical Science," *International Encyclopedia of Unified Science,* I (1955), 279–339. Acceptance of Three Stages.

LePlay, F., Preface to: *Programme de gouvernement et d'organisation sociale . . . par un groupe d'économistes* (Paris, 1881).

*——, *La réforme sociale en France déduite de l'observation comparée des peuples européens* (3rd ed., 3 vols., Paris, 1867).

——, *Textes choisis* (ed. Baudin, Paris, 1947).

*Le Roy, Edouard, "Un positivisme nouveau," *Revue de métaphysique et de morale,* IX (1901), 138–153.

*Leslie, T. E. Cliffe, "On the Philosophical Method of Political Economy," *Hermathena,* No. IV (1876), pp. 265–296.

——, "Political Economy and Sociology," *Fortnightly Review,* XXXI (1879), 25–46. Friendly.

Lestrade, Combes de, *Eléments de sociologie* (Paris, 1889).

Letourneau, Charles, *Sociology Based upon Ethnography* (tr. Trollope, new ed., London, 1893).

Levoix, E., "La fête de l'humanité chez les positivistes anglais," *Revue philosophique,* III (1877), 400–403. Rather sarcastic.

*Lewes, George Henry, "Auguste Comte," *Fortnightly Review,* III (1866), 385–410.

*——, *The Biographical History of Philosophy from Its Origin in Greece down to the Present Day* (new ed., 2 vols. in 1, New York, 1879).

*——, "Comte and Mill," *Fortnightly Review,* VI (1866), 385–406.

*——, *Comte's Philosophy of the Sciences: Being an Exposition of the Principles of the Cours de Philosophie Positive of Auguste Comte* (London, 1887).

*——, in *British and Foreign Review,* XV (1843), 353–406. (Unsigned.)

Lewis, George Cornewall, *A Treatise on the Methods of Observation and Reasoning in Politics* (2 vols., London, 1852). Induced to write by Comte, the author cites him with approval on a number of matters (particularly hypotheses) as well as sometimes with disapproval.

*Liard, Louis, *La science positive et la métaphysique* (3rd ed., Paris, 1893).

*Lietz, Hermann, *Die Probleme im Begriff der Gesellschaft bei Auguste Comte im Gesamtzusammenhange seines Systems* (Jena, 1891).

*Lilienfeld, Paul von, *Gedanken über die Socialwissenschaft der Zukunft* (5 vols., Mitau, 1873–81).

——, *La pathologie sociale* (Paris, 1896).

——, *Zur Vertheidigung der organischen Methode in der Sociologie* (Berlin, 1898).

Lippert, Julius, *Kulturgeschichte der Menschheit in ihrem organischen Aufbau* (2 vols., Stuttgart, 1886).

Lobley, J. Logan, "Positive Knowledge," *Journal* of the City of London College Science Society, X (1904–5), 16–21, 23–37.

Loge Française et Ecossaise de la Clémente Amitié, *Fête anniversaire de la réception du F.·. Littré* (Paris, 1876).

*Loisy, Alfred, *La crise morale du temps présent et l'éducation humaine* (Paris, 1937).

——, *La discipline intellectuelle* (Paris, 1919).

——, *La religion* (Paris, 1917).

——, *Religion et humanité* (Paris, 1926).

Lubbock, Sir John, *Fifty Years of Science* (London and New York, 1890).

——, *The Pleasures of Life* (New York, 1887).

——, *Scientific Lectures* (London and New York, 1890).

Lytton, Edward Lord, *Speeches* (2 vols., Edinburgh and London, 1874).

Maccall, William, *The Newest Materialism: Sundry Papers on the Books of Mill, Comte, Bain, Spencer, Atkinson and Feuerbach* (London, 1873).

*Mach, Ernst, *The Analysis of Sensations and the Relation of the Physical to the Psychical* (tr. Williams, revised Waterlow, Chicago and London, 1914).

*——, *Erkenntnis und Irrtum: Skizzen zur Psychologie der Forschung* (3rd ed., Leipzig, 1917).

*——, *Popular Scientific Lectures* (tr. McCormack, Chicago, 1895).

*——, *The Science of Mechanics: A Critical and Historical Account of Its Development* (tr. McCormack, 2nd ed., Chicago, 1902).

*——, "Sur le rapport de la physique avec la psychologie," *Année psychologique,* XII (1906), 303–318.

Malapert, P., *Leçons de philosophie* (2 vols., Paris, 1907-8).

Malet, Albert, *Nouvelle histoire de France* (Paris and London, 1922).

Mallock, William Hurrell, *Is Life Worth Living?* (New York, 1880).

Malon, Benoit, *Histoire du socialisme depuis les temps les plus reculés jusqu'à nos jours* (5 vols., Paris, n.d.).

Mannheim, Karl, *Systematic Sociology: An Introduction to the Study of Society* (ed. Eros and Stewart, London, 1957).

*Marshall, Alfred, *Principles of Economics,* Vol. I (London and New York, 1890).

*Martineau, James, "Comte's Life and Philosophy," in his *Essays, Reviews, and Addresses,* Vol. I (London, and New York, 1890), pp. 331–380.

*——, *Types of Ethical Theory* (3rd ed., 2 vols. in 1, Oxford and New York, 1891).

Masson-Oursel, Paul, *La philosophie comparée* (2nd ed., Paris, 1931).

Mathew, David, *Catholicism in England. The Portrait of a Minority: Its Culture and Tradition* (3rd ed., London, 1955).

*Maudsley, Henry, *The Physiology of Mind* (3rd ed., New York, 1883).

Maunier, René, "La sociologie chez les économistes," *Revue du mois,* XII (1911), 161–171.

*Maurras, Charles, "Auguste Comte 15 janvier 1798–5 septembre 1857," *Minerva: Revue des lettres et des arts,* II (1902), 174–204.

*——, *Enquête sur la monarchie* (Paris, n.d.).

*——, *Les princes des nuées* (Paris, n.d.).

Maxse, Captain [F. A.], R.N., *The Causes of Social Revolt* (London, 1872). Quotes the Positivists on social questions.

——, *Our Political Duty* (2nd ed., London, 1870).

——, *Reasons for Opposing Woman Suffrage* (new ed., London, 1884).

Menger, Carl, *Die Irrthümer des Historismus in der deutschen Nationalökonomie* (Vienna, 1884).

*Metzger, Wilhelm, "Geschichtsphilosophie und Soziologie," *Vierteljahrsschrift für wissenschaftliche Philosophie und Soziologie,* XL (1916), 279–292.

Meyerson, Emile, *Essais* (Paris, 1936)

*——, *De l'explication dans les sciences* (Paris, 1927).

*——, *Identity & Reality* (tr. Loewenberg, London and New York, 1930).

Miall, L. C., *History of Biology* (London, 1911).

——, *Thirty Years of Teaching* (London, 1897).

Milhaud, G., "L'idée d'ordre chez Aug. Comte," *Revue de métaphysique et de morale,* IX (1901), 385–406. Approves of Comte's quest and desire for order.

——, *Le positivisme et le progrès de l'esprit: Etudes critiques sur Auguste Comte* (Paris, 1902). Excellent analysis, but no particular sympathy.

*†Mill, John Stuart, *Auguste Comte and Positivism.*

*——, *An Examination of Sir William Hamilton's Philosophy and of the Principal Philosophical Questions Discussed in His Writings* (London, 1865).

*——, *On Liberty and Utilitarianism* (Everyman's ed., London and New York, 1947).

*——, "Michelet's History of France," in his *Dissertations and Discussions,* II (London, 1859), 120–180.

*——, *The Spirit of the Age* (ed. with an Introduction by Hayek, Chicago, 1942).

*——, *A System of Logic, Ratiocinative and Inductive* (2 vols., London, 1843, also 8th ed., 2 vols., London, 1872).

*Millet, André, *La souveraineté d'après Auguste Comte: Etude sociologique* (Poitiers, 1905).

Moore, G. E., *Philosophical Studies* (New York and London, 1922).

*Morell, J. D., *An Historical and Critical View of the Speculative Philosophy of Europe in the Nineteenth Century* (2nd ed., 2 vols., London and Edinburgh, 1847).

Morley, Henry, *Early Papers and Some Memories* (London, etc., 1891).

*Morley, John, "Auguste Comte," in his *Critical Miscellanies,* III (London, 1886), 337–384.

*——, *Edmund Burke: A Historical Study* (New York, 1924).

*——, "The *Fortnightly Review* and Positivism: A Note," *Fortnightly Review,* n.s. VIII (1870), 118–120.

*——, "Mr. Froude on the Science of History," *ibid.,* VIII (1867), 226–237.

*——, "Mr. Mill's Autobiography," *ibid.,* XXI (1874), 1–20.

*Mougeolle, Paul, *Les problèmes de l'histoire* (Paris, 1886).

Mourgue, Raoul, "La philosophie biologique d'Auguste Comte," *Archives d'anthropologie criminelle, de médecine légale, et de psychologie normale et pathologique,* XXIV (1909), 829–870, 911–945. A scholarly but sympathetic examination.

*Mousnier, Roland, *Progrès scientifique et technique au xviiie siècle* (Paris, 1958).

—— and Denis Huisman, *L'art de la dissertation historique* (Paris, 1960).

Müller-Lyer, F., *The History of Social Development* (tr. Lake, London, 1920).

*——, "Die phaseologische Methode in der Soziologie," *Vierteljahrsschrift für wissenschaftliche Philosophie und Soziologie,* XXXVI (1912), 241–255.

*——, *Der Sinn des Lebens und die Wissenschaft: Grundlinien einer Volksphilosophie* (2nd ed., Munich, 1923).

*Murray, Gilbert, "What Is Permanent in Positivism," in his *Stoic, Christian, Humanist* (Boston, 1950), pp. 153–189.

*——, "What the Imperialists Mean by Positivism," *P.R.,* VIII (1900), 195–199.

Neurath, Otto, "Foundations of the Social Sciences," *International Encyclopedia of Unified Science*, II, no. 1 (Chicago, 1944).

*——, "The Orchestration of the Sciences by the Encyclopedism of Logical Empiricism," *Philosophy and Phenomenological Research*, VI (1945–46), 496–508.

*——, "Unified Science as Encyclopedic Integration," *International Encyclopedia of Unified Science*, I (1955), 1–27.

*——, "Wege der wissenschaftlichen Weltauffassung," *Erkenntnis*, I (1930–31), 106–125.

*Noack, Ludwig, Art. "Comte," in his *Philosophie-geschichtliches Lexikon* . . . , (Leipzig, 1879), pp. 206–208.

Oliphant, James, *A Short History of Modern Europe 1450–1915 for the Young Student and the General Reader* (London and Toronto, 1915).

*Oppenheimer, Franz, *System der Soziologie*, Vol. I (Jena, 1922).

*Ostwald, Wilhelm, *Auguste Comte: Der Mann und sein Werk* (Leipzig, 1914).

*——, *Monism as the Goal of Civilization* (Hamburg, 1913).

*——, *Monistische Sonntagspredigten* (2 vols., Leipzig, 1911–12).

*——, *Natural Philosophy* (tr. Seltzer, New York, 1910).

*——, *Die Pyramide der Wissenschaften: Eine Einführung in wissenschaftliches Denken und Arbeiten* (Stuttgart and Berlin, 1929).

*——, "Das System der Wissenschaften," *Annalen der Naturphilosophie*, VIII (1909), 266–272.

*——, "Zur Einführung," *Annalen der Naturphilosophie*, I (1902), 1–4.

*—— and Rudolf Goldscheid, "Nachricht," *ibid.*, XI (1912), 305–306.

Pacheu, Jules, *Du positivisme au mysticisme: Etude sur l'inquiétude religieuse contemporaine* (Paris, 1906).

*Pagès, C., "Auguste Comte et la vétérinaire," *R.O.*, IX (1882), 365–372.

*Pasteur, Louis, "Discours de réception," *P.P.*, XXIX (1882), 128–139.

*Pattison, Mark, "The Religion of Positivism," *Contemporary Review*, XXVII (1876), 593–614.

Paul, C. Kegan, *Faith and Unfaith and Other Essays* (London, 1891).

Paul, Hermann, *Aufgabe und Methode der Geschichtswissenschaften* (Berlin and Leipzig, 1920).

Paulhan, Fr., *L'activité mentale et les éléments de l'esprit* (2nd ed., Paris, 1913).

——, "Le nouveau mysticisme," *Revue philosophique,* XXX (1890), 480–522. Propriety of Comte's desire for a human synthesis; failure of his attempt to provide one.

Paulsen, Friedrich, *A System of Ethics* (tr. Thilly, New York, etc., 1899).

——, "Ueber das Verhältniss der Philosophie zur Wissenschaft: Eine geschichtliche Betrachtung," *Vierteljahrsschift für wissenschaftliche Philosophie,* II (1877), 15–50.

Payot, Jules, *Cours de morale* (new ed., Paris, 1914).

——, *L'éducation et la démocratie* (Paris, 1895). Humanity the object of ethics; for an intellectual élite. Doubtful.

——, *The Education of the Will: The Theory and Practise of Self-Culture* (tr. Jelliffe, New York and London, 1919). Approval of Calendar only.

——, *La morale à l'école* (3rd ed., Paris, 1908).

*Pécaut, F., "Auguste Comte et Durkheim," *Revue de métaphysique et de morale,* XXVIII (1921), 639–655.

——, *Eléments de philosophie morale* (Paris, 1905).

——, *Eléments de philosophie scientifique* (Paris, 1905).

——, "La philosophie de la morale," in *Morale et science* (Paris, 1924), pp. 39–59.

*Pennetier, Georges, *Discours sur l'évolution des connaissances en histoire naturelle* (Actes du Muséum d'Histoire Naturelle de Rouen, XIV–XXX; Rouen, 1911–24).

——, *L'origine de la vie* (Paris, 1868).

Pensées choisies de nos maîtres (Paris, 1908). Published by Action Française, preface by Montesquiou; includes Comte.

Pérez, Bernard, *L'éducation morale dès le berceau* (3rd ed., Paris, 1896).

Perris, George Herbert, *The Industrial History of Modern England* (London, 1914).

*Petzoldt, Joseph, *Einführung in die Philosophie der reinen Erfahrung* (2 vols., Leipzig, 1900–1904).

*——, "Positivistische Philosophie," *Zeitschrift für positivistische Philosophie,* I (1913), 1–16.

*——, *Das Weltproblem vom Standpunkte des relativistischen Positivismus aus* (4th ed., Leipzig and Berlin, 1924).

[Phillips, W. L.], "Why Are the Many Poor?" No. 1 in *Fabian Tracts* (London, n.d.).

Picard, Emile, *Un coup d'oeil sur l'histoire des sciences et des théories physiques* (Paris, 1930). Importance of Comte for the history of science.

*——, *La science moderne et son état actuel* (Paris, 1914).

——, *Les sciences mathématiques en France depuis un demi-siècle* (Paris, 1917).

Picot, J.-J., *Projet de réorganisation de l'instruction publique en France* (Tours, 1871). Appears to draw on the Classification and favors encyclopedic instruction, but no explicit reference to Positivism.

*Pinet, G., *Auguste Comte: Notice biographique* (n.p., n.d.).

*——, *Ecrivains et penseurs polytechniciens* (2nd ed., Paris, 1902).

*——, "L'ensemble de la science mathématique: Résumé des idées d'Auguste Comte," *P.P.*, XXVII (1881), 165–186.

†——, *Histoire de l'Ecole Polytechnique.*

Poincaré, H., *The Foundations of Science: Science and Hypothesis, The Value of Science, Science and Method* (tr. Halsted, New York and Garrison, N.Y., 1921).

Pouchet, Georges, "Des études anthropologiques," *P.P.*, I (1867), 251–273.

——, "L'enseignement supérieur des sciences à Paris," *ibid.*, VIII (1872), 24–58.

——, *The Plurality of the Human Race* (tr. and ed. Beavan, London, 1864).

——, *Science et religion* (Paris, 1859).

Price, R. Arnold, *An Economic Basis for an Ethical Solution of the Social Problem* (London, 1920).

Proudhon, P.-J., *De la création de l'ordre dans l'humanité ou principes d'organisation politique* (new ed., Paris, 1873). A few piquant resemblances.

Pünjer, Bernhard, "Auguste Comte's 'Religion der Menschheit,'" *Jahrbücher für protestantische Theologie,* VIII (1882), 385–404, and "Der Positivismus in der neueren Philosophie," *ibid.*, IV (1878), 79–121, 241–272, 434–481. Grandeur of Comte's effort and tribute to his genius, but generally critical.

*Quetelet, Ad., *Physique sociale* . . . (2 vols., Brussels, etc., 1869).

Rabier, Elie, *Leçons de philosophie* (5th ed., 2 vols., Paris, 1896–1903). Approves of a few details but otherwise very critical.

Radcliffe-Brown, A. R., *A Natural Science of Society* (Glencoe, Ill., 1957).

*Ratzenhofer, Gustav, *Die Kritik des Intellects: Positive Erkenntnistheorie* (Leipzig, 1902).

*——, *Positive Ethik: Die Verwirklichung des Sittlich-Seinsollenden* (Leipzig, 1901).

*——, *Der positive Monismus und das einheitliche Princip aller Erscheinungen* (Leipzig, 1899).

*——, *Die sociologische Erkenntnis: Positive Philosophie des socialen Lebens* (Leipzig, 1898).

Rauh, F., *L'expérience morale* (Paris, 1903).

——, *De la méthode dans la psychologie des sentiments* (Paris, 1899).

*Rémusat, Charles de, "De la civilisation moderne," *Revue des deux mondes,* XVIII (1858), 5–44.

*Renan, Ernest, *L'avenir de la science: Pensées de 1848,* in his *Oeuvres complètes,* III (Paris, n.d.), 712–1151.

*——, "Réponse au discours de réception de M. Pasteur (27 avril 1882)," *ibid.,* I (Paris, n.d.), 759–777.

*Renouvier, Ch., *Essais de critique générale:* deuxième essai (2nd ed., 3 vols., Paris, 1875), troisième essai, quatrième essai (2 vols., Paris, 1864).

*Rey, Abel, "Ce que devient la logique," *Revue philosophique,* Vol. 57 (1904), pp. 612–625.

——, "Histoire de la notion de loi," in *Science et loi* (Paris, 1934), pp. 1–5.

——, *Leçons élémentaires de psychologie et de philosophie* (Paris, 1903). A few references.

——, *Logique et morale suivies de notions sommaires de philosophie générale* (4th ed., Paris, 1916). Some debts to Positivism.

——, "Une opposition de tendances dans la science des 'temps modernes,'" *Revue de synthèse,* II (1931), 111–125.

*——, *La philosophie moderne* (Paris, 1908).

——, "Physique et réel," in *L'évolution de la physique et la philosophie* (Paris, 1935).

*——, *Les sciences philosophiques: Leur état actuel* (Paris, n.d.).

——, *La théorie de la physique chez les physiciens contemporains* (Paris, 1907).

*——, "Vers le positivisme absolu," *Revue philosophique,* Vol. 67 (1909), pp. 461–479.

Reybaud, Louis, *Etudes sur les réformateurs ou socialistes modernes* (7th ed., 2 vols., Paris, 1864).

*[Reynolds, Henry Robert], "Auguste Comte—His Religion and Philosophy," *British Quarterly Review,* XIX (1854), 297–376.

*——, "Auguste Comte, Life and Works," *ibid.,* Vol. 44 (1866), pp. 59–89.

——, "Theism, Atheism, and the Popular Theology," *ibid.,* XXI (1855), 408–441.

*Ribot, Th., *English Psychology* (New York, 1874).

*†——, *German Psychology of Today.*

*†Robertson, John Mackinnon, *Buckle and His Critics.*

*——, "Discussion," *Sociological Papers* [I] (London, 1905), 214–215.

*——, *Modern Humanists Reconsidered* (London, 1927).

*——, *Modern Humanists: Sociological Studies of Carlyle, Mill, Emerson, Arnold, Ruskin, and Spencer* (4th ed., London and New York, 1908).

*——, "The Past and Future of Women: Two Lectures," *National Reformer,* n.s. Vol. 55 (1890), pp. 298–300, 309–311, 330–332, 342–343, 357–358, 380–381, 395–396, 411–413.

Rocholl, R., *Die Philosophie der Geschichte: Darstellung und Kritik der Versuche zu einem Aufbau derselben* (2 vols., Göttingen, 1878–93).

Rodrigues, Gustave, *L'idée de relation: Essai de critique positive* (Paris, 1903). Attempt at a new "rational positivism" to which Comte made valuable contributions: science, relativism, synthesis, Classification. But Comte not exempt from criticism.

Rosenstock, Eugen, *Soziologie, I: Die Kräfte der Gemeinschaft* (Berlin and Leipzig, 1925).

Rougier, Louis, *Les paralogismes du rationalisme: Essai sur la théorie de la connaissance* (Paris, 1920). Casual approving references to Classification, Three Stages, antimetaphysics.

Roulleaux, Marcel, *Fragments économiques publiés par ses amis* (Paris, 1867).

*Royer, Clémence, "Attraction et gravitation d'après Newton," *P.P.,* XXXI (1883), 206–226.

——, *Le bien et la loi morale: Ethique et téléologie* (Paris, 1881).

——, *Ce que doit être une église nationale dans une république, par un esprit religieux* (Lausanne, 1861). (Unsigned.)

*——, *Deux hypothéses sur l'hérédité* (Paris, 1877).

——, *Introduction à la philosophie des femmes* (Lausanne, 1859).

*——, "Lamarck: Sa vie, ses travaux et son système," *P.P.,* III (1868), 173–205, 333–372, IV (1869), 5–30.

——, *La matière* (n.p., 1895).

——, *La nation dans l'humanité et dans la série organique* (Paris, 1875).

——, *Origine de l'homme et des sociétés* (Paris, 1870).

——, *Les phases sociales des nations* (Paris, 1876).

——, *La question religieuse* (Paris, 1898).

*Sainte-Beuve, C.-A., "M. Littré," in his *Nouveaux lundis,* V (2nd ed., Paris, 1884), 200–256.

Saisset, Emile, "La philosophie positive," *Revue des deux mondes,* n.s. XV (1846), 185–220. Hostile.

*†Sarton, George, "Auguste Comte, Historian of Science."

*——, "L'histoire de la science," *Isis,* I (1913), 3–46.

*——, "The New Humanism," *ibid.,* VI (1924), 9–42.

*†——, "Paul, Jules, and Marie Tannery."

Schäfer, Dietrich, *Das eigentliche Arbeitsgebiet der Geschichte* (Jena, 1888).

*Schäffle, A., *Bau und Leben des socialen Körpers* (2nd ed., 2 vols., Tübingen, 1896).

——, *The Quintessence of Socialism* (3rd English ed., London, 1891).

Schilpp, Paul Arthur, ed., *The Philosophy of Bertrand Russell* (2nd ed., Evanston, Ill., 1946).

——, *The Philosophy of G. E. Moore* (2nd ed., New York, 1952).

Schinz, Albert, "Le positivisme est une méthode et non un système," *Revue philosophique,* Vol. 47 (1899), pp. 63–75. Endorses Positivism as a naturalistic scientific method; attacks it as a system.

Schlick, Moritz, *Allgemeine Erkenntnislehre* (Berlin, 1918).

——, *Gesetz, Kausalität und Wahrscheinlichkeit* (Vienna, 1948).

——, "Gibt es intuitive Erkenntnis?" *Vierteljahrsschrift für wissenschaftliche Philosophie und Soziologie,* XXXVII (1913), 472–488.

*——, "Positivismus und Realismus," *Erkenntnis,* III (1932–33), 1–31.

——, "Die Wende der Philosophie," *ibid.,* I (1930–31), 4–11.

*Schmoller, Gustav, *Grundriss der allgemeinen Volkswirtschaftslehre* (2 vols., Leipzig, 1900–1904).

*——, "Zur Methodologie der Staats- und Sozial-Wissenschaften," *Schmollers Jahrbuch,* VII (1883), 975–994.

Schuppe, Wilhelm, *Grundriss der Erkenntnistheorie und Logik* (Berlin, 1894).

Seal, Horace, *On the Nature of State Interference* (London and Edinburgh, n.d.).

†Sée, Henri, "Auguste Comte et la vie politique."

——, *Science et philosophie de l'histoire* (Paris, 1928).

Seliger, Paul, "Der Begriff der geschichtlichen Entwicklung bei Hegel und Comte," *Menschheitsziele,* I (1907), 201–206.

*Sidgwick, Henry, *Philosophy: Its Scope and Relations. An Introductory Course of Lectures* (London and New York, 1902).

Simiand, François, *La méthode positive en science économique* (Paris, 1912).

*[Smith, William Henry], "Comte," *Blackwood's Edinburgh Magazine,* Vol. 53 (1843), pp. 397–414.

Sommer, Hugo, "Die positive Philosophie August Comte's," *Sammlung gemeinverständlicher wissenschaftlicher Vorträge,* Series XX (Berlin, 1885), No. 480 (pp. 889–936).

Spann, Othmar, "Über die Einheit von Theorie und Geschichte," in *Aus Politik und Geschichte: Gedächtnisschrift für Georg von Below* (Berlin, 1928), pp. 303–337.

——, "Untersuchungen über den Gesellschaftsbegriff zur Einleitung in die Soziologie," Part I, *Zeitschrift für die gesamte Staatswissenschaft,* Vol. 59 (1903), pp. 573–596, Vol. 60 (1904), pp. 462–508, Vol. 61 (1905), pp. 302–344.

*Spencer, Herbert, *Education: Intellectual, Moral, and Physical* (New York and London, 1912).

*——, *Essays: Scientific, Political, & Speculative* (3 vols., London and Edinburgh, 1891).

——, *First Principles* (New York, 1958).

*——, "Last Words about Agnosticism and the Religion of Humanity," *Nineteenth Century,* XVI (1884), 826–839.

——, *The Man* versus *the State* (Caldwell, Idaho, 1940).

——, *The Principles of Sociology* (3 vols., New York, 1898).

*——, "Religion: A Retrospect and Prospect," *Nineteenth Century,* XV (1884), 1–12.

*——, "Retrogressive Religion," *ibid.,* XVI (1884), 3–26.

——, *Social Statics* (New York, 1954).

*——, *The Study of Sociology* (New York, 1906).

Spiller, G., *Darwinism and Sociology* (London, 1914).

†——, *The Ethical Movement.*

——, *Faith in Man: The Religion of the Twentieth Century* (London, 1908).

*——, *A New System of Scientific Procedure* . . . (London, 1921).

*——, *Outlines of a New World Religion in Fullest Harmony with Modern Scientific and Religious Demands* (London, 1918).

——, *The Possibility of a Universal Moral Code as a Basis for Educacation* (Rome, 1926).

Sprott, W. J. H., *Science and Social Action* (London, 1954).

Spuller, Eugène, *Au ministère de l'instruction publique* . . . (2 vols., Paris, 1888–95).

——, *Education de la démocratie* (Paris, 1892). A tribute to Laffitte, but not as a Positivist.

*——, *Figures disparues: Portraits contemporains politiques et littéraires* (3rd ed., Vol. I, Paris, 1894).

*Stein, Lorenz von, *Geschichte der sozialen Bewegung in Frankreich von 1789 bis auf unsere Tage* (3 vols., Munich, 1921).

*Stein, Ludwig, *Die soziale Frage im Lichte der Philosophie: Vorlesungen über Soziologie und ihre Geschichte* (3rd and 4th ed., Stuttgart, 1923).

*——, *Der soziale Optimismus* (Jena, 1905).

Steiner, Rudolf, *Cosmology, Religion and Philosophy* (London and New York, 1943).

——, *The Philosophy of Spiritual Activity: A Modern Philosophy of Life Developed by Scientific Methods* (tr. Hoernle, London and New York, 1922).

Steinthal, H., *Philologie, Geschichte und Psychologie in ihren gegenseitigen Beziehungen* (Berlin, 1864).

*Stephen, Leslie, *The Science of Ethics* (London, 1882).

*Stern, Daniel, *Histoire de la révolution de 1848* (2 vols., Paris, 1850–51).

Stocker, R. Dimsdale, *The God Which Is Man: The Message of Human Idealism* (London, 1912).

*Sully Prudhomme, *Journal intime: Lettres—pensées* (Paris, 1922).

*——, *Oeuvres,* Vol. IV: *Poésies 1878–1879* (Paris, 1925).

——, *Oeuvres: Prose. Testament poétique, Trois études sociologiques* (new ed., Paris, 1904).

——, *Que sais-je? Examen de conscience* (5th ed., Paris, 1896).

*Syme, David, *Outlines of an Industrial Science* (London, 1876).

Taine, H., *Essai sur Tite Live* (2nd ed., Paris, 1860).

*——, *History of English Literature* (tr. Van Laun, new ed., 4 vols., London, 1877).

——, *Notes on England* (tr. Hyams, Fair Lawn, N.J., 1958).

——, *On Intelligence* (tr. Haye, 2 vols., New York, 1884).

*——, *Les philosophes classiques du xixe siècle en France* (6th ed., Paris, 1888).

*——, Review of Comte's *Cours de philosophie positive,* 2nd ed., in *Journal des débats,* 6 July 1864.

*Tannery, Paul, "Auguste Comte et l'histoire des sciences," *Revue générale des sciences pures et appliquées,* XVI (1905), 410–417.

——, "De l'histoire générale des sciences," *Revue de synthèse historique,* VIII (1904), 1–16. A laudatory reference.

——, *Mémoires scientifiques* (ed. Heiberg and Zeuthen, 17 vols., Toulouse and Paris, 1912–50).

*——, "Revue générale: Histoire des mathématiques," *Revue de synthèse historique,* I (1900), 179–195.

Tarde, G., *Essais et mélanges sociologiques* (Lyon and Paris, 1900).

*——, *Etudes de psychologie sociale* (Paris, 1898).

*——, *The Laws of Imitation* (tr. Parsons, New York, 1903).

*Thamin, R., *Education et positivisme* (3rd ed., Paris, 1910).

*Thomas, P. Félix, ed., *De la méthode dans les sciences* (Paris, 1909).

*Thomson, Sir J. Arthur, and Patrick Geddes, *Life: Outlines of General Biology* (2 vols., London, 1931).

Thoré, T., "Salon de 1842," *Revue indépendante,* III (1842), 525–532.

*Tönnies, Ferdinand, *Gemeinschaft und Gesellschaft: Abhandlung des Communismus und des Socialismus als empirischer Culturformen* (Leipzig, 1887).

*Tolfree, Merle, "Comte's Religion of Humanity," *Humanist,* Vol. 73 (1958), pp. 9–12.

Torau-Bayle, X., *Introduction à l'étude de la philosophie* (Paris, 1919). Accepts Three Stages, Classification, statics and dynamics; generally admiring.

*†Troeltsch, Ernst, *Der Historismus und seine Probleme.*

*[Twesten, Carl], "Lehre und Schriften August Comte's," *Preussische Jahrbücher,* IV (1859), 279–307.

*——, *Die religiösen, politischen und socialen Ideen der asiatischen Culturvölker und der Aegypter in ihrer historischen Entwicklung* (ed. Lazarus, 2 vols., Berlin, 1872).

——, *Schiller in seinem Verhältniss zur Wissenschaft* (Berlin, 1863). Some traces of influence.

Tyndall, John, *Fragments of Science: A Series of Detached Essays, Addresses, and Reviews* (2 vols., New York, 1892).

Unold, Joh., *Der Monismus und seine Ideale* (Leipzig, 1908). Accepts Three Stages.

*Vaihinger, Hans, *The Philosophy of "As if": A System of the Theoretical, Practical and Religious Fictions of Mankind* (tr. Ogden, London and New York, 1924).

*—— and Raymund Schmidt, "Programm der Zeitschrift," *Annalen der Philosophie,* I (1919), iii–vi.

Véron, Eugène, *Aesthetics* (tr. Armstrong, London, 1879).

——, *La morale* (Paris, 1884).

——, *Supériorité des arts modernes sur les arts anciens* (Paris, 1862).

Viardot, Louis, *Reasons for Unbelief* (New York, n.d.).

*Vierkandt, Alfred, *Naturvölker und Kulturvölker: Ein Beitrag zur Socialpsychologie* (Leipzig, 1896).

*——, "Die Überwindung des Positivismus in der deutschen Soziologie der Gegenwart," *Jahrbuch für Soziologie,* II (1926), 66–90.

Volkelt, Johannes, *Erfahrung und Denken: Kritische Grundlegung der Erkenntnistheorie* (Hamburg and Leipzig, 1886).

Volkmar, Wilhelm Volkmann Ritter von, *Lehrbuch der Psychologie vom Standpunkte des Realismus und nach genetischer Methode* (4th ed., 2 vols., Cöthen, 1894–95). Rejects introspection but without reference to Positivism.

Wahl, Jean, *Vers le concret: Etudes d'histoire de la philosophie contemporaine* (Paris, 1932).

Waitz, Theodor, *Lehrbuch der Psychologie als Naturwissenschaft* (Braunschweig, 1849). Rejects introspection but without reference to Positivism.

Wallon, J., *Le positivisme ou la foi d'un athée* (Paris, 1858).

Webb, Sidney, "The Economics of a Positivist Community," *Practical Socialist,* I (1886), 37–39. Altruism a noble ideal, but practical proposals of Positivism unrealistic.

Weber, Louis, *Vers le positivisme absolu par l'idéalisme* (Paris, 1903).

*Weber, Max, *Gesammelte Aufsätze zur Wissenschaftslehre* (2nd ed., ed. Winckelmann, Tübingen, 1951).

——, *The Methodology of the Social Sciences* (tr. and ed. Shils and Finch, Glencoe, Ill., 1949).

Whewell, W., "Comte and Positivism," *Macmillan's Magazine,* XIII (1865–66), 353–362. Hostile.

Wicksteed, Philip H., *Our Prayers and Our Politics* (London, 1885).

——, "The Place of Sociology in the Circle of Theological Studies," in J. Estlin Carpenter and P. H. Wicksteed, *Studies in Theology* (London, 1907), pp. 283–300.

*Wilbois, Joseph, "L'esprit positif," *Revue de métaphysique et de morale,* IX (1901), 154–209, 579–645, X (1902), 69–105, 334–370, 565–612.

Wilson, J. M., "On Teaching Natural Science in Schools," in *Essays on a Liberal Education* (ed. Farrar, 2nd ed., London, 1868), pp. 241–291.

Winch, Peter, *The Idea of a Social Science and Its Relation to Philosophy* (London and New York, 1958).

Wolf, A., *Essentials of Scientific Method* (New York, n.d.).

*Wolff, Maurice, "Auguste Comte: Deux sanctuaires du positivisme," *Larousse mensuel illustré,* VIII (1929), 150–152.

——, "Le ménage d'Auguste Comte," *Mercure de France,* Vol. 226 (1931), pp. 557–605. Defense of Comte and Clotilde de Vaux against Littré and Mme. Comte.

*——, *Le roman de Clotilde de Vaux et de Auguste Comte suivi d'un choix de leurs lettres et du roman* Wilhelmine (Paris, 1929).

*Worms, René, *Organisme et société* (Paris, 1896).

*——, *Philosophie des sciences sociales* (3 vols., Paris, 1907–19).

*——, *Les principes biologiques de l'évolution sociale* (Paris, 1910).

*——, "La sociologie," *Revue internationale de sociologie,* I (1893), 3–16.

*——, *La sociologie: Sa nature, son contenu, ses attaches* (Paris, 1921).

*——, "Sur la définition de la sociologie," *Revue internationale de sociologie,* I (1893), 173–177.

Wright, Thomas, *Our New Masters* (London, 1873).

*Wundt, W., "Ueber die Definition der Psychologie," *Philosophische Studien,* XII (1896), 1–66.

*——, *Einleitung in die Philosophie* (Leipzig, 1901).

——, *Essays* (2nd ed., Leipzig, 1906).

*——, *Logik: Eine Untersuchung der Prinzipien der Erkenntnis und der Methoden wissenschaftlicher Forschung* (3rd ed., 3 vols., Stuttgart, 1906–8).

——, "Ueber naiven und kritischen Realismus," *Philosophische Studien,* XII (1896), 307–408, XIII (1898), 1–105, 323–433.

*——, *System der Philosophie* (4th ed., 2 vols., Leipzig, 1919).

Ziehen, Theodor, *Die Beziehungen der Lebenserscheinungen zum Bewusstsein* (Berlin, 1921).

*——, *Erkenntnistheorie auf psychophysiologischer und physikalischer Grundlage* (Jena, 1913).

——, *Die Grundlagen der Psychologie* (2 vols., Leipzig and Berlin, 1915).

*——, *Zum gegenwärtigen Stand der Erkenntnistheorie* (Wiesbaden, 1914).

Bibliography and Index

BIBLIOGRAPHY

THIS bibliography is divided into the following sections:

I. Manuscript collections.

II. Writings by Positivists. (Articles appearing in the various Positivist "house-organ" journals—*La philosophie positive, Revue occidentale, Revue positiviste internationale, Positivist Review,* and the journals edited by H. Molenaar [1]—are omitted for reasons of space.)

III. Writings about Positivists and Positivism.

IV. General works.

Categories II and III above aim at offering a complete bibliography. Works of some relevant interest, whether referred to in the text or not, are preceded by a double dagger. Some works in Category IV which were consulted but found altogether irrelevant are omitted.

Note that the Bibliographical Appendix (pp. 283–320) contains all the works by non-Positivists in which evidence on the influence of Positivism was sought.

[1] See above, Chap. IX, n. 38.

I. MANUSCRIPT COLLECTIONS

A. France

Letters and papers in the possession of La Maison d'Auguste Comte Association Internationale, 10 rue Monsieur-le-Prince, Paris VIᵉ (courtesy of M. Paul Carneiro). Abbrev.: M-le-P.

Papers of Emile Corra and of the Société Positiviste Internationale, in the Archives Nationales (Paris), Catalogue No. 17 AS 1–11 (deposited by and used with the permission of M. Calixte Corra and through the courtesy of Mme. Gille of the Archives Nationales). Abbrev.: A.N.

Papers of Maurice Ajam (in the possession and used through the courtesy of Prof. M. Bouvier-Ajam).

B. England

Papers of Clair and Otto Baier (in the possession and used through the courtesy of the former).

Papers of Richard Congreve in the British Museum, Add. MSS 45227–45264 (acquired in 1939 from Mrs. Congreve's niece, Emily Geddes). Abbrev.: BM Add. MS.

Papers of Richard Congreve at the Bodleian Library, Oxford (various catalogue numbers), formerly at Wadham College (the residue of the British Museum collection). Abbrev: Wadham.

Two MSS of C. H. Herford (in the possession and used through the courtesy of Mrs. Mary Braunholtz).

Papers of F. S. Marvin (in the possession and used through the courtesy of Mr. J. D. Marvin). Abbrev.: FSM.

Papers of Henry Tompkins and others (formerly in the possession and used through the courtesy of the late T. S. Lascelles, now mostly or entirely in the care of Mr. D. G. Fincham).

Minutes and Papers of the London Positivist Society (in the possession and used through the courtesy of Mr. D. G. Fincham).

Collections at the British Library of Political and Economic Science (London School of Economics): the Broadhurst, Courtney, Giffen, and Solly Collections.

Public Record Office, File No. B 17626, on Sir Godfrey Lushington.

Minutes of the Senate and of the Committees of the University of London.

Minutes of University College London.

II. WRITINGS BY POSITIVISTS
(EXCEPT ARTICLES IN POSITIVIST JOURNALS)

Ajam, Maurice, *Contre l'étatisme* (Paris, 1910).

‡——, "Les déformations du positivisme," *Grande revue,* Vol. 54 (1909), pp. 668–684.

‡——, "La faillite du socialisme," *ibid.,* Vol. 43 (1907), pp. 1–19.

‡——, *La morale laïque* (Saint-Dié, n.d.). Propaganda.

‡——, *Opinons d'un positiviste* (Paris, 1904). Reprints of newspaper articles; important as propaganda.

——, *La parole en public* (new ed., Paris, 1939).

‡——, *Transition: Roman positiviste* (Paris, 1905). Possibly influential as propaganda.

‡André-Nuytz, Louis, *Le positivisme pour tous: Exposé élémentaire des principes de la philosophie positive* (Paris, 1868).

‡Antoine, Emile, *Aperçu sommaire sur la vie et sur l'oeuvre de M. Pierre Laffitte, successeur d'Auguste Comte* (Havre, 1880).

Arréat, Lucien, *Les croyances de demain* (Paris, 1898).

‡——, *Dix années de philosophie: Etudes critiques sur les principaux travaux publiés de 1891 à 1900* (Paris, 1901). Lukewarm Positivism.

——, *Une éducation intellectuelle* (Paris, 1887).

——, *Journal d'un philosophe* (Paris, 1887).

——, "Le 'parlement des religions,'" *Revue philosophique,* XL (1895), 329–351.

‡——, *Le sentiment religieux en France* (Paris, 1903). Brief tribute to Positivism.

‡Audiffrent, G., *A M. Drumont, auteur de* La France juive *et de* La fin d'un monde (Paris, 1889).

‡——, *A Messieurs les membres du congrès ouvrier de Marseille* (Paris, 1879).

‡——, *A propos du centenaire de la naissance d'un maître vénéré* (Paris, 1898).

‡——, *Actualités politiques et sociales* (Paris, 1901).

‡——, *Une antique croyance* (Marseille, 1894). Fetishism.

‡——, *Appel aux médecins* (Paris, 1862). His basic scientific work.

‡——, *Appel aux positivistes* (Marseille, n.d.).

‡——, *Aux vrais catholiques: Lettre adressée à son eminence le Cardinal di Rende pendant sa nonciature auprès de la république française* (Marseille, 1892).

‡——, *Centenaire de la fondation de l'Ecole Polytechnique: Auguste Comte, sa plus puissante émanation. Notice sur sa vie et sa doctrine* (Paris, 1894).

‡——, *Circulaire exceptionnelle adressée aux vrais disciples d'Auguste Comte* (Paris, 1886).

——, *Contribution à l'étude du cerveau et de l'innervation* (Paris, 1909).

‡——, *Des épidémies: Leur théorie d'après Auguste Comte* (Paris and Marseille, 1866).

‡——, *Des maladies du cerveau et de l'innervation d'après Auguste Comte* (Paris, 1874).

‡——, *Des mouvements irrésistibles* (Paris, 1879). Positivist psychotherapy.

‡——, *Du cerveau et de l'innervation d'après Auguste Comte* (Paris, 1869).

‡——, *Etude sur la digestion* (Marseille, 1867).

‡——, *Exposé sommaire du positivisme ou Religion de l'Humanité d'après les derniers conceptions d'Auguste Comte: Lettre à M. le Colonel de Rochas* (Paris, 1896).

‡——, *La femme* (Paris, 1903). Virgin Mother.

‡——, *Fête de l'humanité* (Paris, 1881). Positivism in the rue Jacob.

‡——, *La loi des successions* (Paris, 1896).

‡——, *M. Laffitte et l'exécution testamentaire d'Auguste Comte* (Paris, 1903).

‡——, *Paris et la situation* (Paris, 1883).

——, *Parlementarisme, dictature* (Paris, 1888).

‡——, *Le positivisme des derniers temps* (Paris, 1880).

‡——, *Le positivisme et la science contemporaine* (Paris, 1896).

‡——, *Quelques mots pour servir à l'histoire du positivisme* (Marseille, 1895).

——, *Quelques mots sur la vie et l'oeuvre d'Auguste Comte: Réponse à M. Emile Ollivier, de l'Académie Française* (Paris, 1901).

——, *Réponse à M. de Boureuille au sujet de la question des quarantaines* (Marseille, 1866).

——, *Saint-Paul et l'Eucharistie* (Paris, 1882).

‡——, *Saint-Paul et son oeuvre* (Paris, 1899).

——, *Saint Paul, Saint Bernard, Auguste Comte: Sommaires considérations sur leur action respective* (Lyon, 1908).

‡——, *La seconde à M. Drumont* (Marseille, 1892).

‡——, *Le temple de l'humanité* (Paris, 1885).

‡——, *Théorie de la vision, suivie d'une lettre sur l'aphasie* (Paris, 1866). Based on Gall and Comte.

——, and E. Sémérie, *A Messieurs les députés membres de la commission relative aux associations syndicales* (Paris, 1881).

‡——, and E. Sémérie, *Après la légende, l'histoire: Réponse . . . à un écrit de MM. Monier & Boudeau ayant pour titre Une* question de fait (Paris, 1878).

‡Auzende, A. M., *Un pas en avant: Essai de philosophie populaire* (Marseille, 1935).

Avezac-Lavigne, C., *Diderot et la société du Baron d'Holbach: Etude sur le xviiie siècle 1713–1789* (Paris, 1875).

——, *Saint-Simonisme—positivisme: Etude comparative des deux doctrines* (Paris and Bordeaux, 1905).

‡Baenteli, Marcel, *Les différentes phases de l'évolution civilisatrice de l'humanité d'après le tableau des commémorations historiques établi par Auguste Comte* (Vol. I, Paris, 1913).

‡Baier, Otto, *An Address Delivered in the Temple of Humanity Liverpool on Sunday, 26 Homer 76 (23 February, 1930), in Memory of the Life and Work of Sydney Style Apostle of Humanity* (n.p., n.d.).

‡——, *An Address . . . in Memory of . . . Jane May Style* (Liverpool, 1938).

Barton, F. B., *An Outline of the Positive Religion of Humanity of A. Comte* (London, 1867).

——, *Positivism and Theism, an Answer to the Rev. C. Voysey's Criticism on the Positive Religion* (n.p., n.d.).

‡Baumann, Antoine, "Auguste Comte et la liberté de l'enseignement,"

Annales de philosophie chrétienne, 3rd series, I (1902–3), 399–413. Voluntary consensus under spiritual power.

——, *Le coeur humain et les lois de psychologie positive* (Paris, 1909).

‡——, *L'efficacité pratique de la sociologie d'Auguste Comte* (La Chapelle-Montligeon, 1902).

——, "Lettre d'un positiviste à M. le général André," *Action française,* VI (1902), 917–922.

‡——, "Le positivisme depuis Auguste Comte," *Annales de philosophie chrétienne,* n.s. Vol. 44 (1901), pp. 251–274.

‡——, *Le programme politique du positivisme* (Paris, 1904).

‡——, "La religion d'Auguste Comte," *Annales de philosophie chrétienne,* n.s. Vol. 44 (1901), pp. 383–404. Religious League.

‡——, *La religion positive* (Paris, 1903).

‡——, *L'union dans la famille, dans la patrie, dans l'humanité et au delà: Entretiens positivistes* (Paris, 1914).

‡——, *La vie sociale de notre temps: Notes, opinions et rêveries d'un positiviste* (Paris, 1900).

‡Beesly, Edward Spencer, *Comte as a Moral Type* (London, 1888).

‡——, "Mr. Kingsley on the Study of History," *Westminster Review,* n.s. XIX (1861), 305–336. (Unsigned.) History subordinated to sociology.

‡——, *Positivism before the Church Congress: A Reply to Mr. Balfour* (London, 1889).

——, *The Social Future of the Working Class* (London, 1881).

‡——, *Some Public Aspects of Positivism* (London, 1881).

Blake, W. F., *Some Neglected Passages on the "Culte historique," from Comte's Appeal to Conservatives* (London, 1890).

Blignières, C. de, *La doctrine positive: Projet de revue* (Paris, 1867).

——, *Du progrès des idées politiques: La liberté et la souveraineté nationale. Lettre à un positiviste (M. Ch. Mellinet fils, de Nantes)* (Paris, 1864).

‡——, *Exposition abrégée et populaire de la philosophie et de la religion positives* (Paris, 1857).

‡——, *Lettre sur la morale à M. l'évêque d'Orléans, l'un des quarante de l'Académie Française* (Paris, 1863).

——, *La vraie liberté: Conséquence nécessaire de la séparation des pouvoirs temporel et spirituel* (Paris, 1860).

Bockett, F. W., *The Workman's Life: What It Is, and What It Might Be* (London, n.d.).

‡Boell, Paul, *Document pour servir à l'histoire du positivisme* (Paris, 1906).

‡Boll, Marcel, "Ambiguïté de l'explication," *Les nouvelles littéraires, artistiques et scientifiques,* 31 March 1934. Defense of Comte against Meyerson.

‡——, "Les divers aspects de la connaissance scientifique," *ibid.,* 31 Aug. 1929. Likewise.

——, *L'éducation du jugement* (Paris, 1954).

——, *Manuel de logique scientifique* (Paris, 1948).

——, *Le mystère des nombres et des formes* (Paris, 1941).

——, *L'occultisme devant la science* (Paris, 1944).

——, "Pourquoi y-a-t'il encore des croyants?" *Raison militante,* Feb. 1949, p. 3.

‡——, *Le problème de la mort: Ses solutions actuelles* (Paris, 1912).

‡——, *La science et l'esprit positif chez les penseurs contemporains* (Paris, 1921).

‡——, *Trois conférences de philosophie scientifique* (Paris, 1913).

——, and Francis Baud, *La personnalité: Sa structure, son comportement* (Paris, 1958).

—— and André Boll, "L'art dans la société contemporaine," *Grande revue,* Vol. 126 (1928), pp. 401–420.

—— and André Boll, *L'élite de demain: Pour une culture objective au service des hommes* (Paris, 1946).

—— and Jean-Claude Pagès, *Les étapes de la connaissance* (Paris, 1953).

—— and Jacques Reinhart, *La conquête de la vérité* (Brussels and Paris, 1947).

—— and Jacques Reinhart, *Les étapes de la logique* (Paris, 1948).

Bombard, E., *La marche de l'humanité et les grands hommes d'après la doctrine positive* (Paris, 1900).

——, *Der Positivismus (die Religion der Menschheit) auf zehn Seiten* (tr., Munich, 1901).

Boudeau, E., and [C.] Monier, *Une question de fait* (Paris, 1878).

Bourdet, Eug., *De la morale dans la philosophie positive et de l'autonomie de l'homme* (Paris, 1866).

‡——, *Des maladies du caractère: Hygiène, morale et philosophie* (Paris, 1858). Accepts Comte's table of cerebral functions.

‡——, *Principes d'éducation positive* (2nd ed., Paris, 1877).

‡——, *Vocabulaire des principaux termes de la philosophie positive avec notices biographiques appartenant au calendrier positiviste* (Paris, 1875).

‡Bridges, J. H., "Comte's Definition of Life," *Fortnightly Review,* XXXV (1881), 675–688. Important as propaganda.

‡——, *Discourses on Positive Religion* (2nd ed., London, 1891).

‡——, "Discussion," in *Sociological Papers,* [I] (London, 1905), 206–209. Propaganda.

‡——, *Essays and Addresses* (London, 1907).

‡——, "Evolution and Positivism," *Fortnightly Review,* XXVII (1877), 853–874, XXVIII (1877), 89–114.

‡——, *Five Discourses on Positive Religion* (London, 1882).

‡——, *France under Richelieu and Colbert* (new ed., London, 1912).

‡——, *History an Instrument of Political Education* (London, 1882).

‡——, *Illustrations of Positivism* (new ed., ed. Jones, London, 1915).

‡——, *The Unity of Comte's Life and Doctrine: A Reply to Strictures on Comte's Later Writings Addressed to J. S. Mill* (London, 1866).

Cancalon, A.-A., *L'hygiène nouvelle dans la famille* (Paris, 1892).

‡Canora, Jean, "Le cinquantenaire d'Auguste Comte," *Annales politiques et littéraires,* Vol. 49 (1907), pp. 225–226. Propaganda.

‡——, "L'évolution actuelle du roman," *Echo bibliographique du boulevard,* 15 June 1910, pp. 10–12.

‡——, *Scène lyrique en l'honneur d'Auguste Comte* (Paris, 1902).

‡Carson, Thomas, *The Message of Humanity* (Liverpool, 1908).

Castelnau, Albert, *Aux riches* (Montpellier, 1851).

‡——, *La question religieuse* (Paris, 1861).

Celebration of the Golden Wedding of Sydney and Jane M. Style . . . (Liverpool, 1928).

Cherfils, Christian, *Auguste Comte au Panthéon* (Paris, 1910).

‡——, *L'esthétique positiviste: Exposé d'ensemble d'après les textes* (Paris, 1909).

‡Clavel, Dr. [Adolphe], *La morale positive* (Paris, 1873).

——, *Les principes au xix* siècle* (Paris, 1877).

Comte, Auguste, *Appeal to Conservatives* (tr. Donkin and Congreve, London, 1889).

‡——, *Appel aux conservateurs* (Paris, 1855).

‡——, *The Catechism of Positive Religion* (tr. Congreve, London, 1858).

‡——, *Correspondance inédite* (4 vols., Paris, 1903–4).

‡——, *Cours de philosophie positive* (6 vols., Paris, 1830–42).

——, *Cours de philosophie positive (première et deuxième leçons), Discours sur l'esprit positif* (ed. and with an Introduction by LeVerrier, 2 vols., Paris, [1949]).

‡——, *Discours sur l'ensemble du positivisme* (Paris, 1848).

——, *Discours sur l'esprit positif* (2nd ed., Paris, 1909).

‡——, *A Discourse on the Positive Spirit* (tr. and ed. Beesly, London, 1903).

‡——, *Eight Circulars* (tr. Lobb and others, London, 1882).

‡——, *The Fundamental Principles of the Positive Philosophy* (tr. Descours and Jones, Preface by Beesly, London, 1905).

‡——, *A General View of Positivism* (tr. Bridges, London, 1865).

‡——, *Lettres à des positivistes anglais* (London, 1889).

‡——, *Lettres à divers* (2 vols. in 3, Paris, 1902–5).

‡——, *Lettres à M. Valat 1815–1844* (Paris, 1870).

†——, *Lettres à Richard Congreve* (London, 1889).

‡——, *Lettres inédites à C. de Blignières* (ed. Arbousse-Bastide, Paris, 1932).

‡——, *Nouvelles lettres inédites* (ed. Carneiro, Paris, n.d.).

‡——, *Oeuvres choisies* (ed. and with an Introduction by Gouhier, Paris, n.d.).

‡——, *Pensées et préceptes* (ed. and with a Preface by Deherme, Paris, 1924).

——, *Die positive Philosophie im Auszug* (ed. Blaschke, Leipzig, 1933).

——, *Der Positivismus in seinem Wesen und seiner Bedeutung* (tr. Roschlau, Leipzig, 1894).

——, *Rede über den Geist des Positivismus* (ed., tr., and with an Introduction by Fetscher, Hamburg, 1956).

——, *Die Soziologie: Die positive Philosophie im Auszug* (ed. Blaschke, Leipzig, 1933).

‡——, *Synthèse subjective* . . . (2nd ed., Paris, 1900).

‡——, *System of Positive Polity* (tr. Bridges and others, 4 vols., London, 1875–77).

‡Congreve, Richard, *Essays: Political, Social, and Religious* (3 vols., London, 1874–1900).

‡——, *Religion of Humanity: The Annual Address Delivered at the Church of Humanity* . . . (*1 January 1899*) (London, 1899).

‡——, *The Sacraments of the Religion of Humanity as Administered at the Church of Humanity* . . . (London, 1893).

‡Corra, Emile, *L'amour de Comte pour Mme. de Vaux* (Paris, n.d.).

‡——, *Appréciation générale du positivisme précédée d'une notice sur la vie et l'oeuvre d'Auguste Comte par Ch. Jeannolle* (Paris, 1898). Poor.

‡——, *Centenaire de l'essor du génie d'Auguste Comte* (Paris, n.d.).

——, *Centenaire du dernier opuscule d'Auguste Comte. Examen du traité de Broussais: De l'irritation et de la folie* (n.p., n.d.).

‡——, *Cinquante-septième circulaire adressée à chaque coopérateur du libre subside institué par Auguste Comte pour l'organisation de la Religion de l'Humanité* (n.p., n.d.). (Not signed.)

‡——, *Compromissions de la science dans la démoralisation contemporaine: Nécessité d'une science morale distincte* (n.p., n.d.).

‡——, *Consécration positiviste de la retraite* (Paris, 1925).

‡——, *Le culte public de l'Humanité et les pèlerinages positivistes* (Paris, 1903).

——, *Le développement de la solidarité pendant la guerre* (Paris, 1916).

‡——, *Les devoirs naturels de l'homme* (Paris, 1905).

——, *La domesticité* (n.p., n.d.).

——, *Les enseignements philosophiques de la guerre* (Paris, 1915).

——, *L'ère de la sociabilité universelle* (Paris, 1920).

‡——, *L'évolution du culte et de la fête des morts* (Paris, 1919).

‡——, *La fête du feu* (Paris, 1912).

‡——, *Le fondateur du positivisme: Auguste Comte et son oeuvre* (Paris, 1923).

‡——, *La fraternité* (Paris, 1907).

‡——, *Gambetta* (Paris, 1917).

——, *Hommage aux héros de la défense nationale* (Paris, 1916).

——, *Hommage général aux morts de 1914–1918* (Paris, 1922).

‡——, *L'humanité* (Paris, 1914).

‡——, *La maladie occidentale* (Paris, 1917). Diagnoses absence of spiritual power.

‡——, *Le mariage* (Paris, 1909).

‡——, *La morale politique* (Paris, 1908).

——, *La morale primitive* (Paris, 1908).

‡——, *Nécessité et principaux caractères du positivisme* (Paris, 1924).

‡——, *La patrie* (Paris, 1913). Humanitarian nationalism.

——, *La philosophie positive* (n.p., 1904).

——, *Pierre Laffitte: Successeur d'Auguste Comte* (Paris, 1923).

‡——, *Portraits positivistes* (Paris, 1921).

‡——, *Le pouvoir spirituel* (Paris, 1918).

‡——, *La religion* (Paris, 1920).

‡——, *Rôle civilisateur des mères* (Paris, 1924). Astonishing version of Mother's Day.

‡——, *Rôle civilisateur du sentiment* (Paris, 1916).

——, *Le rôle social des animaux* (Paris, 1909).

‡——, *Le rôle social des morts* (Paris, 1907).

——, *Le rôle social des vieillards* (Paris, 1923).

——, *Le sentiment filial* (Paris, 1906).

——, *Sociologie positive: L'organisme social* (Paris, n.d.).

‡——, *La troisième république* (Paris, n.d.).

‡——, *L'unification du genre humain* (Paris, 1911).

——, *La vie éternelle: Ses conceptions mystiques, sa conception positive* (Paris, 1924).

‡——, ed., *Lettres d'Auguste Comte au docteur Robinet . . . : Précédées d'une notice sur la vie positiviste du dr. Robinet . . .* (Paris, 1926).

‡Cotard, Jules, *Etudes sur les maladies cérébrales et mentales* (Paris, 1891). Biographical notices.

‡Cotton, Sir Henry, *Indian & Home Memories* (London and Leipzig, 1911).

‡Crompton, Albert, *An Address . . . in Memory of the Life and Work of Thomas Carson, Apostle of Humanity* (n.p., n.d.).

‡——, ed., *Confessions and Testament of Auguste Comte and His Correspondence with Clotilde de Vaux* (Liverpool, 1910).

333

Crompton, Henry, *The Annual Address at the Church of Humanity . . . (1900)* (London, 1900).

‡——, *The Funeral Sermon Preached at the Church of Humanity . . . in Commemoration of Richard Congreve* (London, 1899).

‡——, *Letters on Social and Political Subjects* (London, 1870). Reprinted from the *Sheffield Independent;* propaganda.

‡——, *The Religion of Humanity* (London, n.d.).

‡——, *Special Circular . . . (30 September 1899)* (London, 1899).

‡——, *Thomas Sulman: A Memorial Sermon* (London, 1901).

‡——, *The Virgin-Mother: The Positivist Ideal of Humanity* (London, 1900).

‡Dally, Eugène, *De l'état présent des doctrines médicales dans leurs rapports avec la philosophie des sciences* (Paris, 1860).

‡——, *Remarques sur les aliénés et les criminels au point de vue de la responsabilité morale et légale* (Paris, 1864).

‡*La déchéance de M. Jeannolle* (Paris, 1906).

Deherme, Georges, *L'Afrique occidentale française: Action politique —action économique—action sociale* (Paris, 1908).

‡——, *Auguste Comte et son oeuvre: Le positivisme* (Paris, 1909).

‡——, *Aux jeunes gens. Un maître: Auguste Comte, une direction: le positivisme* (Paris, 1921).

‡——, *Les classes moyennes: Etude sur le parasitisme social* (Paris, 1912). Spiritual power will displace the bourgeoisie.

‡——, *La crise sociale* (Paris, 1910). The Religious League and social discipline.

——, *Croître ou disparaître* (Paris, 1910).

‡——, *Démocratie et sociocratie: L'immense question de l'ordre* (Paris, 1930). Sociocracy, Action Française, Mussolini.

‡——, *Les directions positives: Penser pour agir* (Paris, 1919).

‡——, *Les forces à régler: Le nombre et l'opinion publique* (Paris, 1919).

‡——, *Le positivisme dans l'action* (Paris, 1923).

——, "Rapport sur l'enseignement social en France," in *Congrès international de l'enseignement des sciences sociales, Paris, 30 juillet —3 août 1900* (Paris, 1900).

‡——, "La réforme et la critique positive," *Revue critique des idées et des livres,* X (1910), 193–198. Religious League propaganda.

334

Delbet, E., "Morale positive. Art et science: Vues d'ensemble," in *Morale sociale: Leçons professées au Collège libre des sciences sociales* (2nd ed., Paris, 1909), pp. 1–16.

——, "Rapports de la psychologie avec la sociologie," *Annales* de l'Institut International de Sociologie, X (1904), 275–279.

‡Delivet, Emile, *Les employés et leurs corporations: Etude sur leur fonction économique et sociale* (Paris, 1909). Only vaguely Positivist.

‡——, *Le positivisme et le mouvement social* (Paris, 1907).

‡Denis, Hector, *Discours philosophiques* (Paris, 1919). Belgian economist, Littréist. Moral approach to economics as part of sociology.

‡——, *Histoire des systèmes économiques et socialistes* (2 vols., Paris, 1904–7).

‡[Deroisin, Hippolyte Philémon], *Notes sur Auguste Comte par un de ses disciples* (Paris, 1909).

Desch, Cecil H., "Francis Sidney Marvin, 1863–1943," *Isis,* XXXVI (1945–46), 7–9.

‡——, *Science and the Social Order* (London, 1946).

Dessaint, J., *Avant tout, un pouvoir central! Les enseignements de la guerre* (Paris, 1916).

‡——, *Les conservateurs républicains et leur mission d'après Auguste Comte* (Paris, 1914).

‡Dubost, Antonin, *Danton et la politique contemporaine* (Paris, 1880). Some Positivist propaganda.

‡——, *Des conditions de gouvernement en France* (Paris, 1875).

‡Dubuisson, Alfred, *"Positivisme intégral": Foi—morale—politique, d'après les dernières conceptions d'Auguste Comte* (Paris, 1910). Right-wing Positivism of the Executors.

Dubuisson, Paul, *Comte et Saint-Simon: Comte n'est-il que le disciple de Saint-Simon?* (Paris, 1906).

——, *Le positivisme et la question sociale: Précédée d'une notice sur la société lyonnaise Le Chêne* (Paris, 1899).

‡—— and A. Vigoureux, *Responsabilité pénale et folie: Etude médico-légale* (Paris, 1911). Based on Positivist psychology and sociology.

Ducassé, Pierre, *Auguste Comte et Gaspard Monge* (Paris, 1937).

‡——, "Auguste Comte et le calcul des variations," *Thalès,* III (1936), 39–43.

‡——, *Essai sur les origines intuitives du positivisme* (Paris, 1939).

‡——, *Les grands philosophes* (Paris, 1941).

‡——, *Méthode et intuition chez Auguste Comte* (Paris, 1939).

‡——, *La méthode positive et l'intuition comtienne: Bibliographie* (Paris, 1940).

‡——, "Méthode positive et méthode cartésienne," *Revue de synthèse,* XIV (1937), 51–66.

‡——, "La pensée mathématique d'Auguste Comte," *Thalès,* I (1934), 133–143.

‡——, "Positivisme et spiritualité," *Revue de synthèse,* IV (1932), 173–192.

‡——, "La synthèse positiviste: Comte et Spencer," *ibid.,* n.s. XXVI (1950), 155–171.

——, *Les techniques et le philosophe* (Paris, 1958).

Dussauze, Walter, *Essai sur la religion d'après Auguste Comte* (Saint-Amand, 1901).

‡Ellis, Alexander J., *Auguste Comte's Religion of Humanity* (London, 1880). South Place lecture.

‡Ellis, Henry, "Can the Capitalist Be Moralized?" *To-Day,* n.s. IV (1885), 358–364, 367–375. Propaganda.

——, *What Positivism Means: A Brief Summary of Its Doctrine and Aims* (London, 1887).

‡Etex, Antoine, *Les souvenirs d'un artiste* (Paris, n.d.).

‡Favareille, René, *La dotation syndicale: Solution de la question sociale* (Nancy, etc., 1920). "Incorporation of the proletariat."

‡Finance, Isidore, *Des chambres syndicales ouvrières et des associations coopératives: Discours prononcé au congrès de Marseille* (Paris, n.d.). Propaganda among workers.

‡Foucart, J.-B., *La Toussaint* (Paris, 1864). Positivist poem.

Foucart, Paul, *De la fonction industrielle des femmes* (Paris, 1882).

Geddes, James, *The Month Gutenberg: or, Modern Industry* (London, n.d.).

Gould, F. J., *Auguste Comte* (London, 1920).

——, *Auguste Comte and Positivism: An Address Delivered at the Church of Humanity . . .* (London, 1916).

‡——, *A Catechism of Religion and the Social Life with Notes from the Writings of Auguste Comte* (London, 1908).

——, *The Enduring Life: An Address on the Positivist Conception of Immortality* (London, 1907).

‡——, *Humanism: The Religion of Humanity* (n.p., 1954).

——, *Is Religion Growing or Decaying?* (London, 1917).

‡——, *The Life-Story of a Humanist* (London, 1923).

——, *Moral Teaching as Life-Revelation* (London, 1915).

——, *The Religion of Humanity in Simple Outline* (London, 1924).

——, *The Religion that Fulfils: A Simple Account of Positivism, with Notes and Comments* (London, 1905).

‡——, *Stepping-Stones to Agnosticism* (London, n.d.).

‡Grimanelli, P., "Auguste Comte et la notion de solidarité," *Annales de l'Institut International de Sociologie*, XIII (1911), 159–184. Propaganda.

‡——, *La crise morale et le positivisme* (Paris, 1903).

——, *La femme et le positivisme* (n.p., 1905).

‡——, *L'idéologie démocratique et la politique positive* (Paris, 1922). Moderate Positivist politics.

——, *La morale positive et le bonheur: Etude de psychologie et de morale positives* (Paris, 1924).

‡——, "Quelques réflexions sur le progrès intellectuel," *Annales* de l'Institut International de Sociologie, XIV (1913), 265–299. Three Stages, etc.

‡Haggard, Alfred H., *The Annual Address . . . (1 January, 1901)* (London, 1901).

‡——, *The Principles of Positivism* (London, 1931).

‡Harrison, Frederic, "Agnostic Metaphysics," *Nineteenth Century,* XVI (1884), 353–378.

‡——, *Autobiographic Memoirs* (2 vols., London, 1911).

——, *The Centenary of the Revolution* (London, 1889).

‡——, *The Creed of a Layman: Apologia pro fide mea* (New York and London, 1907).

‡——, *De senectute: More Last Words* (London, 1923).

‡——, "The Ghost of Religion," *Nineteenth Century,* XV (1884), 494–506.

‡——, *The Herbert Spencer Lecture* (Oxford and London, 1905).

‡——, *Humanity* (n.p., 1957).

‡——, *In Memoriam James Cotter Morison* (London, 1888).

‡——, *The Meaning of History and Other Historical Pieces* (New York and London, 1894).

‡——, "Mr. Goldwin Smith on the Study of History," *Westminster Review*, n.s. XX (1861), 293–334. (Unsigned.) Early propaganda.

——, *National and Social Problems* (New York, 1908).

‡——, *New Year's Address, 1888* (London, 1888).

‡——, *On Society* (London, 1918).

‡——, *The Philosophy of Common Sense* (New York, 1907).

‡——, *Politics and a Human Religion* (London, n.d.). South Place lecture.

‡——, *The Positive Evolution of Religion: Its Moral and Social Reaction* (New York, 1913).

‡——, "The Positivist Problem," *Fortnightly Review*, XXXV (1869), 469–493.

——, *Realities and Ideals: Social, Political, Literary and Artistic* (New York, 1908).

‡——, "The Religious and Conservative Aspects of Positivism," *Contemporary Review*, XXVI (1875), 992–1012, XXVII (1875–76), 140–159. Propaganda.

‡——, *Science and Humanity: A Lay Sermon* (London, n.d.). (Unsigned.)

‡——, tr. and ed., *The Positivist Library of Auguste Comte* (London, 1886).

‡——, S. H. Swinny, and F. S. Marvin, eds., *The New Calendar of Great Men: Biographies of the 559 Worthies of All Ages & Nations in the Positivist Calendar of Auguste Comte* (new revised ed., London, 1920).

Higginson, Charles Gaskell, *Auguste Comte: An Address on His Life and Work* (London, n.d.).

‡Hillemand, Constant, *La vie et l'oeuvre de Auguste Comte et de Pierre Laffitte: Discours commémoratifs précédés d'un grand nombre d'aperçus sur le positivisme* (Paris, 1908).

‡Ingram, John Kells, *A History of Political Economy* (new ed., London, 1915). By an Irish Positivist; first published as an Encyclopaedia Britannica article and as such an important means of diffusion.

‡——, *The Present Position and Prospects of Political Economy* (Dublin, 1878). Speech to the B.A.A.S.

‡*International Policy: Essays on the Foreign Relations of England* (London, 1866).

Jabely, A., *Appel à la jeunesse des écoles et introduction au positivisme* (Paris, n.d.).

‡Kaines, J., "On the Anthropology of Auguste Comte," *Report* of the Forty-first Meeting of the British Association for the Advancement of Science [1871], p. 153. Abstract; propaganda.

——, *A Funeral Address Delivered at the Burial of Mrs. Edward Truelove* . . . (London, n.d.).

‡——, *Seven Lectures on the Doctrine of Positivism, Delivered at the Positivist School* . . . *in May, June, and July 1879* (London, 1880). Also published in the *Secular Review*—important for diffusion.

‡K[un], L[éon], ed., *Auguste Comte méconnu, Auguste Comte conservateur: Extraits de son oeuvre finale (1851 1857)* (Paris, 1898).

‡Lacassagne, A., *L'assassinat du président Carnot* (Lyon and Paris, 1894). Evils of anarchism as diagnosed by Comte.

——, *Peine de mort et criminalité: L'accroissement de la criminalité et l'application de la peine capitale* (Paris, 1908).

——, *Précis de médecine judiciaire* (Paris, 1878).

Lacombe, E. de, *La maladie contemporaine: Examen des principaux problèmes sociaux au point de vue positiviste* (Paris, 1906).

‡Laffitte, Pierre, *Cours de philosophie première* (Vol. I, 2nd ed., Paris, 1928; Vol. II, Paris, 1894).

‡——, *A General View of Chinese Civilization and of the Relations of the West with China* (tr. Hall, London, etc., 1887).

‡——, *Les grands types de l'Humanité: Appréciation systématique des principaux agents de l'évolution humaine* (Vols. I–II, 2nd ed., Paris, 1932; Vol. III, Paris, 1897).

‡——, "Philosophie seconde: Cosmologie . . . ," *Cours professé* . . . 1874–75, rédigé par M. Jeannolle, MS.

‡——, *The Positive Science of Morals* (tr. Hall, London, 1908).

‡——, *Le positivisme et l'économie politique* (2nd ed., Paris, 1867). Somewhat platitudinous assertion of Positivist economic doctrines vis-à-vis Littré.

——, *La révolution française* (*1789–1815*) (2nd ed., Paris, 1895).

‡Lascelles, T. S., "Comte's Positive Religion of Humanity: Can It Appeal Today?" MS.

——, *In Memoriam Cecil Henry Desch 1874–1958* . . . (n.p., n.d.).

‡Lavertujon, André, *La chronique de Sulpice Sévère: Texte critique, traduction et commentaire* (2 vols., Paris, 1896–99). Some Positivist allusions.

‡——, *Gambetta inconnu: Cinq mois de la vie intime de Gambetta* (Paris, n.d.).

‡——, ed., *Béllérophon: Vainqueur de la chimère* (Paris, 1900). An ephemeral periodical with many Positivist allusions and quotations.

‡Leblais, Alph[onse], *Matérialisme et spiritualisme: Etude de philosophie positive* (Paris, 1865). Preface by Littré.

‡Lefebvre de Rieux, C., *De la méthode comparative dans les sciences médicales* (Paris, 1926).

Lemoyne, Emmanuel, *Les conservateurs et l'instruction obligatoire* (Paris, 1872).

‡Lévy-Bruhl, L., *Die Philosophie August Comte's* (tr. and with a Preface by H. Molenaar, Leipzig, 1902).

‡Littré, Emile, *Analyse raisonnée du cours de philosophie positive de M. Auguste Comte* (Utrecht, 1845).

‡——, *Auguste Comte et la philosophie positive* (2nd ed., Paris, 1864).

‡——, *Auguste Comte et Stuart Mill* (Paris, etc., n.d.). First appeared in *Revue des deux mondes*.

‡——, "Circulaire positiviste," *Revue philosophique et religieuse,* VIII (1857), 156–159.

‡——, *Conservation, révolution et positivisme* (Paris, 1852; 2nd ed., Paris, 1879).

‡——, *De la philosophie positive* (Paris, 1845). Reprinted in *Fragments*.

‡——, "Du développement historique de la logique," *Revue des deux mondes,* n.s. II (1849), 79–101.

‡——, "Du progrès dans les sociétés et dans l'état," *Revue des deux mondes,* n.s. XX (1859), 796–823. Some propaganda.

——, *Etudes et glanures pour faire suite à l'*Histoire de la langue française (Paris, 1880).

‡——, *Etudes sur les barbares et le moyen âge* (2nd ed., Paris, 1869).

‡——, *Fragments de philosophie positive et de sociologie contemporaine* (Paris, 1876).

‡——, *Littérature et histoire* (2nd ed., Paris, 1877).

‡——, *Paroles de philosophie positive* (2nd ed., Paris, 1863).

‡——, "Préface d'un disciple," in Comte, *Cours de philosophie positive,* 4th ed., I (Paris, 1877), v–l.

‡——, *La science au point de vue philosophique* (4th ed., Paris, 1876).

‡—— and Ch. Robin, *Dictionnaire de médecine, de chirurgie, de pharmacie, de l'art vétérinaire et des sciences qui s'y rapportent* (13th ed., Paris, 1873).

‡Lombrail, A. M. de, *Aperçus généraux sur la doctrine positiviste* (Paris, 1858).

‡——, "Sommaire exposition du positivisme," *Revue philosophique et religieuse,* VII (1856), 357–384, VIII (1857), 57–80.

‡Lonchampt, Joseph, *Essai sur la prière* (3rd ed., Paris, 1878). Preface attributed to Robinet.

‡——, *Notice sur la vie et l'oeuvre d'Auguste Comte* (Paris, 1900).

‡——, *Positivist Prayer* (tr. Mills, Goshen, N.Y., 1877).

‡London Positivist Society, *Positivist Comments on Public Affairs: Occasional Papers* (London, n.d.).

‡Lushington, Vernon, *The Day of All the Dead* (London, 1883).

——, *Mozart: A Commemorative Address* (London, 1883).

‡——, *The Worship of Humanity: An Address* (London, 1886).

‡Magnin, Fabien, *Etudes sociales* (Paris, 1913).

‡Marvin, F. S., *The Century of Hope: A Sketch of Western Progress from 1815 to the Great War* (2nd ed., Oxford, 1921).

‡——, *Comte: The Founder of Sociology* (London, 1936).

‡——, "Frederic Harrison," *Isis,* VI (1924), 387–390.

——, *The Living Past: A Sketch of Western Progress* (5th ed., Oxford, 1931).

‡——, ed., *Progress and History* (London, etc., 1916).

‡——, ed., *Recent Developments in European Thought* (London, etc., 1920).

‡——, ed., *Science and Civilization* (London, etc., 1926).

——, ed., *The Unity of Western Civilization* (London, etc., 1915).

‡Mismer, Charles, *Mémoire sur le suffrage universel: Sa capacité or-*

ganique et sa compétence (Paris, 1880). Originally a lecture; some propaganda.

‡——, *Principes sociologiques* (2nd ed., Paris, 1898).

Mollin, Gabriel, *Rapport sur le congrès de Bâle* (Paris, 1870).

‡Monier, Camille, *Essai sur le langage: Résumé de cinq leçons au Collège de France* (Paris, 1903). Propaganda.

‡——, *Exposé populaire du positivisme* (new ed., Paris, 1911).

‡——, *Résumé de sociologie* (n.p., 1904).

‡Montesquiou, comte Léon de, *Les consécrations positivistes de la vie humaine* (Paris, n.d.).

‡——, *Le système politique d'Auguste Comte* (Paris, n.d.).

Montroui, M. de, *Pensées morales et religieuses* (Paris, 1875).

‡Morison, James Cotter, *The Service of Man: An Essay towards the Religion of the Future* (2nd ed., London, 1887).

‡Morlot, Emile, *Loi de l'histoire d'après Auguste Comte* (Belfort, 1864). Originally a lecture.

Naquet, Alfred, *L'anarchie et le collectivisme* (Paris, 1904).

——, *Collectivism and the Socialism of the Liberal School: A Criticism and an Exposition* (tr. Heaford, London, 1891).

‡——, *L'humanité et la patrie* (Paris, 1901). Quotes Littré.

——, *La loi du divorce* (Paris, 1903).

——, *Principes de chimie fondée sur les théories modernes* (3rd ed., 2 vols., Paris, 1875).

——, *Questions constitutionelles* (Paris, 1883).

——, *Religion, propriété, famille* (Paris, 1869).

——, *La république radicale* (Paris, 1873).

——, *Temps futurs: Socialisme—anarchie* (Paris, 1900).

Noël, Eugène, *Fin de vie (notes et souvenirs)* (Rouen, 1902).

‡——, *Mémoires d'un imbécile écrits par lui-même* (Paris, 1875).

‡Oliveira, José Feliciano de, *Mon action positiviste à Paris (à propos de la maison d'Auguste Comte)* (Paris, 1951).

‡——, *Le positivisme religieux: La religion de l'humanité* (Paris, 1957).

Papillon, Fernand, *Histoire de la philosophie moderne dans ses rapports avec le développement des sciences de la nature* (ed. Lévèque, 2 vols., Paris, 1876).

‡——, *Introduction à l'étude de la philosophie chimique: Ouvrage dans lequel les rapports de la chimie et de la biologie sont établis con-*

formément aux principes de la méthode positive (Paris, 1865).

——, *La nature et la vie: Faits et doctrines* (2nd ed., Paris, 1874).

Percival, P., *The Position of Positivism, with Some Remarks on the Position of Secularism* . . . (Manchester and London, 1891).

‡Persigout, G., "Des 'pouvoirs spirituels' de Georges Guy-Grand," *Annales de la jeunesse laïque*, VIII (1909-10), 178-183.

‡——, "Le devoir des jeunesses laïques," *ibid.*, IV (1905-6), 263-266, 296-300.

‡——, "Théorie des deux pouvoirs," *ibid.*, VI (1907-8), 83-88.

‡Pichard, Prosper, *Doctrine du réel: Catéchisme à l'usage des gens qui ne se paient pas de mots* (Paris, 1873).

‡Poëy, André, *M. Littré et Auguste Comte* (2nd ed., Paris, 1880).

Pompéry, Edouard de, *Despotisme ou socialisme* (Paris, 1849).

‡——, *Exposition de la science sociale, constituée par C. Fourier* (2nd ed., Paris, 1840). Of biographical interest.

——, *La femme dans l'humanité: Sa nature, son rôle et sa valeur sociale* (Paris, 1864).

‡——, *La morale naturelle et la religion de l'humanité* (Paris, 1891).

——, *Simple métaphysique* (Paris, 1891), and two *Suppléments* (1892).

‡*The Positivist Year Book 141 (1929). Annuaire Positiviste* (Paris, 1929).

‡Primot, Alphonse, *La psychologie d'une conversion du positivisme au spiritualisme* (Paris, 1914).

Quin, Malcolm, *The Angels of the Founder* (Newcastle-on-Tyne, 1902).

‡——, *An Apostolic Letter* (Newcastle, 1899).

‡——, *The Church of Humanity* (Newcastle, 1896).

‡——, *A Final Circular* (Newcastle, 1910).

‡——, *A First Annual Circular* (Newcastle, 1899).

‡——, *The Future of Positivism* (Newcastle, 1927).

——, *The Liberty of Humanity* (Newcastle, 1900).

‡——, *Memoirs of a Positivist* (London, 1924).

‡——, *On the Positive Idea of the Church* (Newcastle, 1903).

‡——, *The Politics of the Proletariat: A Contribution to the Science of Citizenship Based Chiefly on the Sociology of Auguste Comte* (London, n.d.).

——, *Positivism and Social Problems* (Newcastle, 1895).

‡——, *A Prefatory Note on Religious Positivism* (n.p., n.d.).

‡——, *Richard Congreve* (Newcastle, 1899).

——, *The Rule of Auguste Comte* (Newcastle, 1901).

——, *Science and Religious Unity: Letter Addressed to an Anglican Clergyman* (Penrith, 1935).

‡——, *Special Announcement* (Newcastle, 1901). Abandonment of his effort to lead Chapel St.

‡——, *A Special Circular* (Newcastle, 1901). Proposal to move to London.

——, *The Way of the Positivist Life* (n.p., n.d.).

——, *The Worship of Humanity* (Newcastle, 1897).

Rapport à la Société Positiviste, par la commission chargée d'examiner la question du travail (Paris, 1848).

‡*Religion of Humanity* (London, 1891).

Report of a Positivist Service Conducted in Liverpool by Dr. Richard Congreve . . . (Liverpool, 1880).

‡Rig, Jules, ed., *La philosophie positive par Auguste Comte* (2 vols., Paris, 1881).

‡Rigolage, Emile, ed., *La sociologie par Auguste Comte* (Paris, 1897).

‡Ritti, Ant., *Notice biographique sur H.-Ph. Deroisin ancien maire de Versailles* (Paris, 1911).

‡Ritti, J. M. Paul, *Une conversion: Roman social, avec préface du Dr. G. Audiffrent* (Paris, 1896). Propaganda for workers.

‡——, *De la méthode sentimentale* (Paris, 1904).

‡——, *De la notion de Dieu d'après la méthode sentimentale* (Paris, 1930).

‡——, "De la sentimentalité chrétienne selon la philosophie positive," *Annales de philosophie chrétienne,* 3rd series, IV (1904), 442–470. Propaganda for Religious League via ethics.

‡——, *De l'existence sociale d'après la méthode sentimentale* (Paris, n.d.).

‡——, *De l'intelligence d'après la méthode sentimentale* (Paris, n.d.). Heart over mind.

‡——, *Quelques vues théoriques sur la sympathie* (Paris, 1899). Sympathy as a method of knowledge. Unintelligible.

‡Roberty, E. de, *L'ancienne et la nouvelle philosophie: essai sur les lois générales du développement de la philosophie* (Paris, 1887).

344

——, "Les antinomies et les modes de l'Inconnaissable," *Revue philosophique*, XXX (1890), 569–581.

——, *Auguste Comte et Herbert Spencer: Contribution à l'histoire des idées philosophiques au xixe siècle* (Paris, 1894).

‡——, "Le concept sociologique de la solidarité," *Annales* de l'Institut International de Sociologie, XIII (1911), 185–197.

——, "Le concept sociologique de liberté," *Revue philosophique,* Vol. 56 (1903), pp. 488–494.

——, "Le concept sociologique du progrès," *Annales* de l'Institut International de Sociologie, XIV (1913), 397–413.

‡——, *Les concepts de la raison et les lois de l'univers* (Paris, 1912).

‡——, *Les fondements de l'éthique* (2nd ed., Paris, 1899).

‡——, "Morale et politique," in *Morale sociale: Leçons professées au Collège libre des sciences sociales* . . . (2nd ed., Paris, 1909), pp. 255–278.

‡——, *Nouveau programme de sociologie: Esquisse d'une introduction générale à l'étude des sciences du monde surorganique* (Paris, 1904).

‡——, *La philosophie du siècle: Criticisme—positivisme—évolutionnisme* (Paris, 1891).

‡——, *Pourquoi je ne suis pas positiviste* (Paris, 1900).

——, "Les préjugés de la sociologie contemporaine," *Annales* de l'Institut International de Sociologie, VII (1901), 239–259.

‡——, "Qu'est-ce que la philosophie?" *Revue philosophique,* Vol. 53 (1902), pp. 225–244.

‡——, *La sociologie: Essai de philosophie sociologique* (3rd ed., Paris, 1893).

‡——, "Sociologie & psychologie . . . ," *Annales* de l'Institut International de Sociologie, X (1904), 83–120.

‡Robin, Charles, "Analyse," *Journal de l'anatomie et de la physiologie normales et pathologiques de l'homme et des animaux,* I (1864), 308–326. On the second edition of the *Cours.*

‡——, *Anatomie et physiologie cellulaires* (Paris, 1873).

‡——, *L'instruction et l'éducation* (Paris, 1877).

‡[Robinet, J. F. E.?] *Auguste Comte et M. Aulard à propos de la révolution* (Paris, 1893).

‡Robinet, J. F. E., *Danton émigré: Recherches sur la diplomatie de la république (An Ier—1793)* (Paris, 1887). Some propaganda.

‡——, *Danton: Mémoire sur sa vie privée* (3rd ed., Paris, 1884). Likewise.

‡——, *Lettre à M. Emile de Girardin sur l'économie politique positiviste* (Paris, 1864). (Unsigned.) Against Littré among others.

‡——, *Lettres sur l'hippophagie* (Paris, 1864). Cites Laffitte as authority against eating horsemeat.

‡——, *M. Littré et le positivisme* (Paris, 1871).

‡——, *Notice sur l'oeuvre et la vie d'Auguste Comte* (3rd ed., Paris, 1891).

——, *La nouvelle politique de la France: Relations extérieures* (Paris, 1875).

——, *La philosophie positive: Auguste Comte & M. Pierre Laffitte* (Paris, n.d.).

Roussy, B., *Education domestique de la femme & rénovation sociale* (Paris, 1914).

‡——, *Les progrès de la science et leurs volontaires délaissés: Projet de réorganisation* (Paris, 1901). Propaganda.

‡——, *Science et démocratie* (Paris, 1902). Originally a lecture; some propaganda.

‡——, *Les universités populaires: Origines, destination & avenir* (Paris, 1901). Likewise.

‡——, in *Revue internationale de sociologie,* XV (1907), 203–207, 213–214.

Roux, Adrien, *La constitution prochaine* (Paris, 1922).

‡——, *La pensée d'Auguste Comte* . . . (Paris, 1920).

‡——, *Pour un gouvernement de salut public et la paix sociale* (Paris, n.d.).

‡Sabatier, Alfred, *Discours* (Paris, 1853).

‡——, *Programme d'éducation positive: Des écoles communales* (Paris, 1872).

‡Sanson, André, *Science sans préjugés* . . . (Paris, 1865).

‡——, *Semaines scientifiques (première année)* (Paris, 1866).

‡Sauria, Charles, *A MM. les élèves en médecine* (Paris, 1877). Comtist medicine.

‡——, "Riches et pauvres," *Bulletin* de la Société d'Agriculture, Sciences et Arts de Poligny (1874), pp. 47–49.

346

‡Segond, L. A., *Histoire et systématisation générale de la biologie* (Paris, 1851). Important for propaganda.

——, *Traité d'anatomie générale: Traité de la structure* (Paris, 1854).

‡Sémérie, Eugène, *La dernière incarnation d'Haussmann: Réponse d'un positiviste à MM. Asseline & Yves Guyot* (Paris, 1876).

‡——, *La grande crise (1789–1871)* (Neuchâtel, 1874).

‡——, *Lettre à M. Emile Laporte: Les éléments d'action de Pierre Laffitte* (Paris, 1880).

——, *La loi des trois états: Réponse à M. Renouvier, directeur de la Critique philosophique* (Paris, 1875).

‡——, *Positivistes et catholiques* (Paris, 1870).

‡——, *La république et le peuple souverain . . .* (Paris, 1871).

‡——, *Des sources biologiques de la notion d'humanité* (Vichy, 1883).

‡——, *Des symptômes intellectuels de la folie* (2nd ed., Paris, 1875).

——, *Théologie et science: Simple réponse à M. Dupanloup, évêque d'Orléans* (4th ed., Paris, 1875).

‡Société Positiviste Internationale, *Le jubilé de M. Emile Corra . . .* (Paris, 1928).

‡——, *Le positivisme et ses morts 1939–1945* (Paris, n.d.).

‡*Statuts de la maison d'Auguste Comte association internationale* (Paris, 1954).

Stawell, F. Melian, and F. S. Marvin, *The Making of the Western Mind: A Short Survey of European Culture* (London and New York, n.d.).

‡Stupuy, Hippolyte, *Discours à la distribution des prix du Collège Rollin le 31 juillet 1888* (Paris, 1888). Propaganda.

‡——, *Discours prononcé à la distribution des prix du collège Rollin le 28 juillet 1892* (Paris, 1892). Likewise.

‡Style, Jane M., *Auguste Comte, Thinker and Lover* (London, 1928).

‡——, *The Voice of the Nineteenth Century: A Woman's Echo* (London, 1920).

‡Style, Sydney, *An Address Delivered in the Church of Humanity . . . , Liverpool, . . . in Memory of the Life and Work of Albert Crompton* (Liverpool, 1908).

‡——, "In Memoriam Henry Crompton: Read at Falkland St. Liverpool 10 April 1904," MS. (Unsigned.)

347

——, *What Is Positivism?* (Liverpool, 1906).

‡Swinny, S. H., Art. "Positivism," *Encyclopedia of Religion and Ethics,* ed. Hastings (New York and Edinburgh, 1919).

‡——, "Sociology: Its Successes and Its Failures," *Sociological Review,* XI (1919), 1–10.

‡*Testament d'Auguste Comte avec les documents qui s'y rapportent: Pièces justificatives, prières quotidiennes, confessions annuelles, correspondance avec Mme. de Vaux, publié par ses exécuteurs testamentaires conformément à ses dernières volontés* (2nd ed., Paris, 1896). Contains the "secret codicil" about Mme. Comte which is omitted from the English translation ed. by A. Crompton.

‡Thomas, Philip, *Auguste Comte and Richard Congreve* (London, 1910).

——, *Auguste Comte on Marriage and Divorce* (London, 1910).

‡——, *Our Church and Faith of Humanity* (London, 1910).

‡——, *A Religion of This World: Being a Selection of Positivist Addresses* (London, 1913).

‡Tompkins, Henry, *The Human Universe* (n.p., 1952).

——, "Marvin Memorial Address Delivered at the Herts. Branch of the Historical Association November 10th, 1945," MS.

Urbain, Georges, and Marcel Boll, eds., *La science: Ses progrès, ses applications* (2 vols., Paris, 1933–34).

Williamson, Alexander W., *Address* [to the British Association] (n.p., n.d.).

‡——, *Development of Difference the Basis of Unity: Introductory Lecture to the Courses of the Faculty of Arts and Laws Delivered in University College, London, October 16, 1849* (London, 1849).

——, "Experimental Science the Basis of General Education," *London Student,* I (1868), 51–60, 67–76.

Wyrouboff, G., *Manuel pratique de la cristallographie* (Paris, 1889).

‡——, Memoirs [in Russian], *Vestnik Evropy,* Jan. 1910, pp. 26–56, Feb. 1910, pp. 1–26, Jan. 1911, pp. 3–44, Feb. 1911, pp. 92–125, Jan. 1913, pp. 53–98.

‡——, "Stuart Mill et la philosophie positive," in E. Littré, *Auguste Comte et Stuart Mill* (Paris, etc., n.d.), pp. 57–86.

III. WRITINGS ABOUT POSITIVISTS AND POSITIVISM

‡Acton, H. B., "Comte's Positivism and the Science of Society," *Philosophy*, XXVI (1951), 291–310.

‡Ageorges, Joseph, "Souvenirs inédits sur Auguste Comte," *La revue*, 6th series, Vol. 108 (1914), pp. 17–22.

Aimel, Henri, "Auguste Comte et Clotilde de Vaux," *Nouvelle revue*, Vol. 60 (1889), pp. 699–720.

‡Alengry, Franck, *Essai historique et critique sur la sociologie chez Auguste Comte* (Paris, 1900).

Ames, Percy W., "Positivism in Literature," *Transactions* of the Royal Society of Literature of the United Kingdom, 2nd series, XVII (1895), 79 121.

‡Annan, Noel, *The Curious Strength of Positivism in English Political Thought* (London, 1959).

‡Anon., "George Eliot and Comtism," *London Quarterly Review*, Vol. 47 (1876–77), pp. 446–471.

‡Apchié, Madeleine, "Auguste Comte et le catholicisme social," *Archives de philosophie du droit et de sociologie juridique*, IV (1934), 208–226.

‡Aquarone, Stanislas, *The Life and Works of Emile Littré 1801–1881* (Leyden, 1958).

‡Arbousse-Bastide, Paul, *La doctrine de l'éducation universelle dans la philosophie d'Auguste Comte: Principe d'unité systématique et fondement de l'organisation spirituelle du monde* (2 vols., Paris, 1957).

——, "Faut-il oublier Comte? A l'occasion du premier centenaire de la mort de Comte (1857–1957)," *Revue de synthèse*, Vol. 78 (1957), pp. 447–463.

Aubin, Victor, *Trahison positiviste* (Paris, 1881).

‡Audierne, R., "Note sur la classification des connaissances humaines dans Comte et dans Cournot," *Revue de métaphysique et de morale*, XIII (1905), 509–519.

Barth, Hans, "Auguste Comte und Joseph de Maistre," *Schweizer Beiträge zur allgemeinen Geschichte*, XIV (1956), 103–138.

‡Barth, Paul, "Zum 100. Geburtstage Auguste Comte's," *Vierteljahrsschrift für wissenschaftliche Philosophie,* XXII (1898), 169–189.

‡Barzellotti, Giacomo, *The Ethics of Positivism: A Critical Study* (New York, 1878).

‡Batault, Georges, "Le positivisme scientifique et son critique M. Emile Meyerson," *Mercure de France,* Vol. 94 (1911), pp. 449–464.

Bibliographie positiviste: Catalogue complet de tous les ouvrages existant sur Auguste Comte & le positivisme (Paris, n.d.).

‡Billington, James H., "The Intelligentsia and the Religion of Humanity," *American Historical Review,* Vol. 65 (1959–60), pp. 807–821.

‡Blondel, Ch., "La psychologie selon Comte, Durkheim et Tarde," *Journal de psychologie normale et pathologique,* XXIV (1927), 381–399, 493–519, 591–609.

Boivin, Pierre, "L'économie sociale d'Auguste Comte: La doctrine," *Revue d'histoire économique et sociale,* XXIII (1936–37), 193–227.

‡Borchert, Heinrich, *Der Begriff des Kulturzeitalters bei Comte: Nach dem "Cours de philosophie positive" unter Mitberücksichtigung der Jugendschriften* (Halle, 1927).

Boyer de Sainte-Suzanne, R. de, *Essai sur la pensée religieuse d'Auguste Comte* (Paris, 1923).

‡B[ridges], M. A., ed., *Recollections of John Henry Bridges, M.B.* (London, 1908).

Broglie, abbé de, *Le positivisme et la science expérimentale* (2 vols., Paris and Brussels, 1880–81).

‡Caird, Edward, *The Social Philosophy and Religion of Comte* (Glasgow, 1893).

‡Calas, Alexandre, *Auguste Comte médecin* (Paris, 1889).

‡Cantecor, G., *Comte* (Paris, n.d.).

——, "La science positive de la morale," *Revue philosophique,* Vol. 57 (1904), pp. 225–241, 368–392.

‡Caro, E., *M. Littré et le positivisme* (Paris, 1883).

‡Charlton, D. G., *Positivist Thought in France during the Second Empire, 1852–1870* (Oxford, 1959).

Chiappini, Toussaint, *Les idées politiques d'Auguste Comte* (Paris, 1913).

Claretie, Jules, "Les 'colles' de Comte," *Annales politiques et littéraires,* Vol. 49 (1907), p. 220.

‡Copaux, H., "Notice sur la vie et les travaux de Grégoire Wyrouboff (1843–1913)," *Bulletin* de la Société Chimique de France, 4th series, XV (1914), i–xxi.

Cristea, C., *La morale d'Auguste Comte* (Focchany, 1896).

‡Cuisenier, Jean, "Auguste Comte et la sociologie économique," *Cahiers internationaux de sociologie,* n.s. V (1958), 125–140.

D., E., "Alexander William Williamson, 1824–1904," *Proceedings* of the Royal Society of London, Vol. 78 (1907), pp. xxiv–xliv.

‡Defourny, Maurice, *La sociologie positiviste: Auguste Comte* (Louvain and Paris, 1902). Critical, Thomist.

‡Delvolvé, Jean, "Auguste Comte et la religion," *Revue d'histoire de la philosophie et d'histoire générale de la civilisation,* n.s. V (1937), 343–368.

‡——, "Examen critique des conditions d'efficacité d'une doctrine morale éducative," *Revue de métaphysique et de morale,* XVI (1908), 372–402, 515–545, XVII (1909), 136–159, 276–308, 448–459.

‡——, *Réflexions sur la pensée comtienne* (Paris, 1932).

‡Dittmann, Friedrich, "Die Geschichtsphilosophie Comtes und Hegels: Ein Vergleich," *Vierteljahrsschrift für wissenschaftliche Philosophie und Soziologie,* XXXVIII (1914), 281–312, XXXIX (1915), 38–81.

‡Dugas, [L.], "Auguste Comte: Etude critique et psychologique," *Revue philosophique,* XL (1895), 225–251, 360–398.

‡Dumas, Georges, *Psychologie de deux messies positivistes: Saint-Simon et Auguste Comte* (Paris, 1905).

‡Duprat, G. L., "Auguste Comte et Emile Durkheim," *Sozialwissenschaftliche Bausteine,* IV (1932), 109–140.

Dupuy, Paul, *Le positivisme d'Auguste Comte* (Paris, 1911).

‡Eisen, Sydney, "Frederic Harrison: The Life and Thought of an English Positivist" (Ph.D. thesis, The John Hopkins University, 1957).

‡Emery, Léon, "De Comte à Marx," *Contrat social,* I (1957), 142–148.

‡Eros, John, "The Positivist Generation of French Republicanism," *Sociological Review,* n.s. III (1955), 255–277.

‡Ferraz, M., *Socialisme, naturalisme et positivisme* (4th ed., Paris, n.d.).

‡Fink, Y., *Etude critique de la notion de la loi chez Comte et de son influence* (Paris, 1907).

‡Finkelstein, Fanja, *Die allgemeinen Gesetze bei Comte und Mill* (Heidelberg, 1911).

‡Fleuriot de Langle, P., ed., "Deux lettres de Littré à propos de la femme d'Auguste Comte," *Mercure de France,* Vol. 227 (1931), pp. 500–502.

Fleury, Maurice de, *Eloge de Littré prononcé à l'Académie de Médecine dans la séance annuelle du 16 décembre 1919* (Paris, 1920).

Gabriel, Leo, "Auguste Comte und der Positivismus: Zum hundertsten Todestag des Philosophen," *Wissenschaft und Weltbild,* X (1957), 161–169.

Gautier, Léon, "E. Littré," in his *Portraits du xixe siècle,* II (Paris, n.d.), 209–216.

‡Genty, Victor, *Un grand biologiste: Charles Robin (1821–1885). Sa vie, ses amitiés philosophiques et littéraires* (Lyon, 1931).

‡Gilson, E., "La specificité de la philosophie d'après Auguste Comte," in Congrès des Sociétés Philosophiques Américaines, Anglaises, Belge, Italienne et de la Société Française de Philosophie, Session extraordinaire tenue à la Sorbonne, du 27 au 31 décember 1921, *Communications et discussions* (Paris, n.d.), pp. 363–386.

‡Gouhier, Henri, "Auguste Comte: Esquisse d'un portrait," *Bulletin* de la Société Française de Philosophie, special no. (1958), pp. 3–12.

‡——, *La jeunesse d'Auguste Comte et la formation du positivisme* (3 vols., Paris, 1933–41).

‡——, "La philosophie 'positiviste' et 'chrétienne' de D. de Blainville," *Revue philosophique,* Vol. 131 (1941), pp. 38–69.

‡——, *La vie d'Auguste Comte* (Paris, 1931).

——, ed., "Lettres inédites de Saint-Simon à Blainville," *Revue philosophique,* Vol. 131 (1941), pp. 70–80.

‡Greene, John C., "Biology and Social Theory in the Nineteenth Century: Auguste Comte and Herbert Spencer," in Marshall Clagett, ed., *Critical Problems in the History of Science* (Madison, Wis., 1959), pp. 419–446.

‡Gruber, Hermann, *August Comte, der Begründer des Positivismus: Sein Leben und seine Lehre* (Freiburg im Breisgau, 1889).

‡——, *Der Positivismus vom Tode August Comte's bis auf unsere Tage (1857–1891)* (Freiburg im Breisgau, 1891).

Grunicke, Lucia, *Der Begriff der Tatsache in der positivistischen Philosophie des 19. Jahrhunderts* (Halle, 1930).

Guilmain, Léon Joseph, *La sociologie d'A. Comte: Ce qu'elle doit à la biologie du début du xixe siècle* (Algiers, 1922).

Guinet, L., "Emile Littré (1801–1881)," *Isis,* VIII (1926), 77–102.

Guthlin, A., *Les doctrines positivistes en France* (new ed., Paris, 1873).

Harris, Marjorie Silliman, *The Positive Philosophy of Auguste Comte* (n.p., 1923).

‡Harrison, Austin, *Frederic Harrison: Thoughts and Memories* (London, 1926).

‡Harrison, Royden, "E. S. Beesly and Karl Marx," *International Review of Social History,* IV (1959), 22–58, 208–238.

‡——, "Professor Beesly and the Working-Class Movement," in Asa Briggs and John Saville, eds., *Essays in Labour History* (London and New York, 1960), pp. 205–241.

‡Hayward, F. H., and E. M. White, eds., *The Last Years of a Great Educationist: A Record of the Work and Thought of F. J. Gould from 1923 to 1938* (Bungay, Suffolk, n.d.).

‡Knight, William, ed., "Unpublished Letters from John Stuart Mill to Professor Nichol," *Fortnightly Review,* Vol. 67 (1897), pp. 660–678.

Krynska, Salomea, *Entwicklung und Fortschritt nach Condorcet und A. Comte* (Berne, 1908).

Laberthonnière, L., *Positivisme et catholicisme: A propos de "L'Action Française"* (Paris, 1911).

Lacroix, Jean, *La sociologie d'Auguste Comte* (Paris, 1956).

‡Lévy-Bruhl, L., *The Philosophy of Auguste Comte* (tr. Beaumont-Klein, London, 1903).

‡——, ed., *Lettres inédites de John Stuart Mill à Auguste Comte publiées avec les réponses de Comte* (Paris, 1899).

‡Liveing, Susan, *A Nineteenth-Century Teacher: John Henry Bridges, M.B., F.R.C.P.* (London, 1926).

Lloyd, Walter, "J. S. Mill's Letters to A. Comte," *Westminster Review,* Vol. 153 (1900), pp. 421–426.

‡Lundberg, George A., "Contemporary Positivism in Sociology," *American Sociological Review,* IV (1939), 42–55.

‡McGee, John Edwin, *A Crusade for Humanity: The History of Organized Positivism in England* (London, 1931).

Mackintosh, Robert, *From Comte to Benjamin Kidd: The Appeal to*

Biology or Evolution for Human Guidance (New York and London, 1899).

‡Marcuse, Alexander, *Die Geschichtsphilosophie Auguste Comtes* (Stuttgart, 1932).

‡——, "La philosophie de l'"Aufklaerung' au temps du romantisme: Auguste Comte et Arthur Schopenhauer," *Revue de synthèse,* XIV (1937), 149–157.

Marjolin, Robert, "French Sociology—Comte and Durkheim," *American Journal of Sociology,* Vol. 42 (1936–37), pp. 693–704.

‡Mauduit, Roger, *Auguste Comte et la science économique* (Paris, 1929).

Mehlis, G., "Comte," in *Vom Messias: Kulturphilosophische Essays* (Leipzig, 1909), pp. 28–41.

‡Mill, John Stuart, *Auguste Comte and Positivism* (2nd ed., London, 1866).

Misch, Georg, "Zur Entstehungsgeschichte des französischen Positivismus," *Archiv für Geschichte der Philosophie,* XIV (1901), 1–39, 156–209.

‡Mises, Richard von, *Positivism: A Study in Human Understanding* (Cambridge, Mass., 1951).

‡Mourélos, Georges, *L'épistémologie positive et la critique meyersonienne* (Paris, 1962).

‡Nyland, Thomas, "The English Positivists" (M.A. thesis, University of London, 1937).

‡Pellarin, Charles, *Essai critique sur la philosophie positive: Lettre à M. E. Littré (de l'Institut)* (Paris, 1864). Littré to be respected despite his Positivism.

Peter, Johannes, *Auguste Comtes Bild vom Menschen (Der Philosoph und die Gemeinschaft im Positivismus)* (Stuttgart, 1936).

Pillon, F., "La brochure de M. Sémérie sur la loi des trois états," *Critique philosophique,* IV^1 (1875), 385–391. Critical.

——, "Positivisme et progrès," *ibid.,* 259–265.

——, "Un programme de morale positive," *ibid.,* IV^2 (1875), 1–5.

‡——, "Une question de priorité à propos de la loi des trois états," *ibid.,* IV^1 (1875), 116–118, 154–165, 372–375.

‡Pouchet, G., "Charles Robin (1821–1885), sa vie et son oeuvre," *Journal de l'anatomie et de la physiologie,* XXII (1886), i–clxxxiv.

‡Prenant, Lucy, "Karl Marx et Auguste Comte," in *A la lumière du marxisme: Essais,* Vol. II: *Karl Marx et la pensée moderne,* Part I (Paris, 1937), pp. 17–76.

Reiche, Kurt, *Auguste Comtes Geschichtsphilosophie* (Tübingen, 1927).

‡Richard, Gaston, "Le positivisme juridique et la loi des trois états," *Archives de philosophie du droit et de sociologie juridique,* I (1931), 311–340.

‡Rignano, Eugenio, "La sociologie dans le *Cours de philosophie positive* d'Auguste Comte," *Revue internationale de sociologie,* X (1902), 241–264, 337–355.

‡Robertson, J. G., *Charles Harold Herford 1853–1931* (London, n.d.).

‡Romanet, J. de, "La communauté terrestre et la marche vers l'unité selon Auguste Comte," *Cahiers du monde nouveau,* I (1945), 868–898, II (1946), 1036–1064. On Comte and "One World."

‡Rouvre, Charles de, *Auguste Comte et le catholicisme* (Paris, 1928). Influence of Clotilde de Vaux.

‡Sarton, George, "Auguste Comte, Historian of Science: With a Short Digression on Clotilde de Vaux and Harriet Taylor," *Osiris,* X (1952), 328–357.

‡——, "Paul, Jules and Marie Tannery (with a Note on Grégoire Wyrouboff)," *Isis,* XXXVIII (1947–48), 33–51.

Schaefer, Albert, *Die Moralphilosophie Auguste Comte's: Versuch einer Darstellung und Kritik* (Basel, 1906).

Scherer, Edmond, "Emile Littré," in his *Etudes sur la littérature contemporaine,* VII (Paris, 1882), 335–346.

Sée, Henri, "Auguste Comte et la vie politique et sociale de son temps," *Revue d'histoire moderne,* II (1927), 412–421.

‡Segond, J., "Le saint-simonisme d'Auguste Comte et le but pratique de la sociologie," *Revue de synthèse historique,* Vol. 41 (1926), pp. 63–80.

‡Seillière, Ernest, *Auguste Comte* (Paris, 1924).

Sellars, Roy Wood, "Positivism in Contemporary Philosophic Thought," *American Sociological Review,* IV (1939), 26–42.

Sokoloff, Boris, *The "Mad" Philosopher: Auguste Comte* (New York, etc., 1961).

Spielfogel, Rosa, *Comte's moralphilosophische Methode* (Zurich, 1909).

‡Stern, Bernhard J., "A Note on Comte," *Science and Society,* I (1936–37), 114–119.

‡ Sterzel, Georg Friedrich, *A. Comte als Pädagog: Ein Beitrag zur Kenntnis der positiven Philosophie* (Leipzig, 1886).

‡Thérive, André, *Clotilde de Vaux ou la déesse morte* (Paris, 1957).

Torlesse, Frances H., *Some Account of John Henry Bridges and His Family* (London, 1912).

‡"Trust Deed of the Auguste Comte Memorial Fund," MS.

‡Urbain, G., "La valeur des idées de A. Comte sur la chimie," *Revue de métaphysique et de morale,* XXVII (1920), 151–179.

Uta, Michel, *La loi des trois états dans la philosophie d'Auguste Comte* (Paris, 1928).

——, *La théorie du savoir dans la philosophie d'Auguste Comte* (Paris, 1928).

Veniamin, V., "La philosophie du droit d'Auguste Comte," *Archives de philosophie du droit,* n.s. I (1952), 181–196.

‡Verrier, René, *Roberty: Le positivisme russe et la fondation de la sociologie* (Paris, 1934).

‡Waentig, Heinrich, *Auguste Comte und seine Bedeutung für die Entwicklung der Socialwissenschaft* (Leipzig, 1894).

Watson, John, *Comte, Mill, and Spencer: An Outline of Philosophy* (Glasgow and New York, 1895).

‡Whittaker, Thomas, "Comte and Mill," in his *Reason: A Philosophical Essay with Historical Illustrations* (Cambridge, 1934), pp. 31–80.

IV. GENERAL WORKS

Abbott, A., *Education for Industry and Commerce in England* (Oxford and London, 1933).

‡ Abbott, Evelyn, and Lewis Campbell, *The Life and Letters of Benjamin Jowett* (2 vols., London, 1897).

‡—— and Lewis Campbell, eds., *Letters of Benjamin Jowett* (New York and London, 1899).

‡Abel, Theodore, *Systematic Sociology in Germany: A Critical Analysis of Some Attempts to Establish Sociology as an Independent Science* (New York and London, 1929).

Adamson, John William, *English Education 1789–1902* (Cambridge, 1930).

Addison, Christopher, *Four and a Half Years: A Personal Diary from June 1914 to January 1919* (2 vols., London, 1934).

Alain [Emile Chartier], *Correspondance avec Elie et Florence Halévy* (2nd ed., Paris, 1958).

Allier, Raoul, *La philosophie d'Ernest Renan* (Paris, 1895).

‡Alpert, Harry, *Emile Durkheim and His Sociology* (New York, 1939).

——, "France's First University Course in Sociology," *American Sociological Review*, II (1937), 311–317.

‡Annan, Noel Gilroy, *Leslie Stephen: His Thought and Character in Relation to His Time* (London, 1951).

‡Anon., *Charles Booth: A Memoir* (London, 1918).

——, *Gustave Spiller 1864–1940* (n.p., n.d.).

‡——, *Life and Letters of H. Taine* (tr. Devonshire and Sparvel-Bayly, 3 vols., New York and London, 1902–8).

‡Antoni, Carlo, *From History to Sociology: The Transition in German Historical Thinking* (tr. White, Detroit, 1959).

‡Applebaum, Samuel Isaac, *Clemenceau: Thinker and Writer* (New York, 1948).

Archer, C., *William Archer: Life, Work, and Friendships* (London, 1931).

Archer, R. L., *Secondary Education in the Nineteenth Century* (Cambridge, 1921).

Armytage, W. H. G., *Civic Universities: Aspects of a British Tradition* (London, 1955).

——, "J. F. D. Donnelly: Pioneer in Vocational Education," *Vocational Aspect of Secondary and Further Education*, II (1950), 6–21.

‡Arnold, Matthew, *Culture and Anarchy* (ed. Knickerbocker, New York, 1925).

Arnoux, Jules, *Collège et lycée de Digne: Etude historique* (Digne, 1888).

‡Aron, Raymond, *German Sociology* (tr. Bottomore, Melbourne, etc., 1957).

‡——, *The Opium of the Intellectuals* (tr. Kilmartin, New York, 1957).

‡——, *War and Industrial Society* (tr. Bottomore, London, 1958).

Bachelard, Suzanne, *La conscience de rationalité: Etude phénoménologique sur la physique mathématique* (Paris, 1958).

Bagenal, Philip H., "The International and Its Influence on English Politics," *National Review,* II (1883–84), 422–431.

Bagge, Dominique, *Les idées politiques en France sous la restauration* (Paris, 1952).

‡Bain, Alexander, *Autobiography* (London, etc., 1904).

‡——, *John Stuart Mill: A Criticism with Personal Recollections* (London, 1882).

Ball, Oona Howard, ed., *Sidney Ball: Memories & Impressions of "An Ideal Don"* (Oxford, 1923).

‡Barker, Ernest, "Leonard Trelawny Hobhouse, 1864–1929," *Proceedings* of the British Academy, 1929, pp. 536–554.

‡Barth, P., "Herbert Spencer und Albert Schäffle: Zu ihrem Gedächtnis," *Vierteljahrsschrift für wissenschaftliche Philosophie und Soziologie,* XXVIII (1904), 231–239.

‡——, *Die Philosophie der Geschichte als Soziologie* (3rd and 4th ed., Vol. I, Leipzig, 1922).

——, "Die Soziologie Albert Schäffles," *Vierteljahrsschrift für wissenschaftliche Philosophie und Soziologie,* XXXI (1907), 467–483.

Barzellotti, Giacomo, *La philosophie de H. Taine* (tr. Dietrich, Paris, 1900).

‡Barzun, Jacques, *Darwin, Marx, Wagner: Critique of a Heritage* (2nd ed., Garden City, N.Y., 1958).

‡Bax, Ernest Belfort, *Reminiscences and Reflexions of a Mid and Late Victorian* (London, 1918).

Bayer, Raymond, *Epistémologie et logique depuis Kant jusqu'à nos jours* (Paris, 1954).

Bellessort, André, *Les intellectuels et l'avènement de la troisième république (1871–1875)* (Paris, 1931).

‡Bellot, H. Hale, *University College London 1826–1926* (London, 1929).

‡Benrubi, J., *Les sources et les courants de la philosophie contemporaine en France* (2 vols., Paris, 1933).

‡Berlin, Isaiah, *The Hedgehog and the Fox: An Essay on Tolstoy's View of History* (New York, 1957).

‡——, *Historical Inevitability* (London, 1954).

‡——, "History and Theory: The Concept of Scientific History," *History and Theory,* I (1960), 1–31.

‡Bertault, Philippe, *Balzac et la religion* (Paris, 1942).

Besant, Annie, *An Autobiography* (Philadelphia, n.d.).

‡Betham-Edwards, Matilda, *Mid-Victorian Memories* (London, 1919).

——, *Reminiscences* (new ed., London, 1903).

‡Bibby, Cyril, *T. H. Huxley: Scientist, Humanist and Educator* (London, 1959).

‡Billy, André, *Sainte-Beuve et son temps* (2 vols., Paris, 1952).

‡Binet, A., "Une enquête sur l'évolution de l'enseignement de la philosophie," *Année psychologique,* XIV (1908), 152–231.

‡Bizet, Georges, *Lettres à un ami 1865–1872* (ed. Galabert, 2nd ed., Paris, n.d.).

‡Black, Max, ed., *Philosophical Analysis: A Collection of Essays* (Ithaca, N.Y., 1950).

‡Blind, Mathilde, *George Eliot* (new ed., Boston, 1904).

‡Blumberg, Albert E., and Herbert Feigl, "Logical Positivism: A New Movement in European Philosophy," *Journal of Philosophy,* XXVIII (1931), 281–296.

‡Boardman, Philip, *Patrick Geddes: Maker of the Future* (Chapel Hill, N.C., 1944).

Boas, George, *A Critical Analysis of the Philosophy of Emile Meyerson* (Baltimore, London, and Oxford, 1930).

‡Bochénski, I. M., *Contemporary European Philosophy* (tr. Nicholl and Aschenbrenner, Berkeley and Los Angeles, 1956).

Böckenförde, Ernst-Wolfgang, *Gesetz und gesetzgebende Gewalt: Von den Anfängen der deutschen Staatsrechtslehre bis zur Höhe des staatsrechtlichen Positivismus* (Berlin, 1958).

Boissonade, P., and J. Bernard, *Histoire du collège et du lycée d'Angoulême (1516–1895)* . . . (Angoulême, 1895).

Bonnard, E., *Le mouvement antipositiviste contemporain en France* (Paris, 1936).

‡Bouglé, C., and Elie Halévy, eds., *Doctrine de Saint-Simon: Exposition. Première année, 1829* (Paris, 1924).

‡Bourl'honne, P., *George Eliot: Essai de biographie intellectuelle et morale 1819–1854. Influences anglaises et étrangères* (Paris, 1933).

‡Boutroux, Emile, "La philosophie en France depuis 1867," *Revue de métaphysique et de morale,* XVI (1908), 683–716.

‡Bouvier, Robert, *La pensée d'Ernst Mach: Essai de biographie intellectuelle et de critique* (Paris, 1923).

Bower, F. O., *Sixty Years of Botany in Britain (1875–1935): Impressions of an Eye-Witness* (London, 1938).

‡Brabant, Frank Herbert, *The Beginnings of the Third Republic in France: A History of the National Assembly (February–September 1871)* (London, 1940).

‡Bréhier, Emile, *Histoire de la philosophie,* Vol. II: *La philosophie moderne* (Paris, n.d.).

‡Brinkmann, Carl, "Ernst Friedrich Apelt und Henry Thomas Buckle: Ein Beitrag zur Geschichte der historischen Methode im neunzehnten Jahrhundert," *Archiv für Kulturgeschichte,* XI (1914), 310–319.

‡British Association for the Advancement of Science, *Report of the Fifteenth Meeting Held at Cambridge in June 1845* (London, 1846).

‡Brodrick, George Charles, *Memories and Impressions 1831–1900* (London, 1900). On Wadham College.

‡Brunetière, Ferdinand, *Honoré de Balzac* (tr. Sanderson, Philadelphia and London, 1906).

‡Buchan, Alastair, *The Spare Chancellor: The Life of Walter Bagehot* (London, 1959).

‡Burns, J. H., "J. S. Mill and the Term 'Social Science,'" *Journal of the History of Ideas,* XX (1959), 431–432.

‡Burtis, Mary Elizabeth, *Moncure Conway 1832–1907* (New Brunswick, N.J., 1952).

Bush, Wendell T., *Avenarius and the Standpoint of Pure Experience* (Archives of Philosophy, Psychology and Scientific Methods, No. 2) (New York, 1905).

Cardwell, D. S. L., *The Organisation of Science in England: A Retrospect* (Melbourne, etc., 1957).

Carlisle, Robert Bruce, "The Saint-Simonians and the Foundation of the Paris-Lyon Railroad, 1832–52" (Ph.D. thesis, Cornell University, 1957).

Caro, E., *Etudes morales sur le temps présent* (Paris, 1855).

——, *L'idée de Dieu et ses nouveaux critiques* (Paris, 1864).

‡——, "La poésie philosophique dans les nouvelles écoles: Un poète positiviste," *Revue des deux mondes,* 15 May 1874, pp. 241–262. (L. Ackermann.)

Carter, Hugh, *The Social Theories of L. T. Hobhouse* (Chapel Hill, N.C., and London, 1927).

‡Cassirer, Ernst, *The Problem of Knowledge: Philosophy, Science, and History since Hegel* (tr. Woglom and Hendel, New Haven, 1950).

‡Caubet, "Chronique," *Monde maçonnique,* XVII (1876), 145–158.

‡——, *Souvenirs (1860–1889)* (Paris, 1893).

‡Caveribert, Raoul, *La vie et l'oeuvre de Rayer (1793–1867)* (Paris, 1931).

‡Chambers, R. W., *Man's Unconquerable Mind: Studies of English Writers from Bede to A. E. Housman and W. P. Ker* (London and Toronto, 1939). On Beesly as a professor.

Chambers, William, *Memoir of Robert Chambers with Autobiographic Reminiscences* (New York, 1872).

‡Charléty, Sébastien, *Histoire du saint-simonisme (1825–1864)* (n.p., 1931).

‡Charlton, D. G., "New Creeds for Old in Nineteenth-Century France," *Canadian Journal of Theology,* VIII (1962), 258–269.

Chastenet, Jacques, *Histoire de la troisième république* (6 vols., Paris, 1952–62).

‡Chevrillon, André, *Taine: Formation de sa pensée* (Paris, 1932).

‡Citoleux, Marc, *La poésie philosophique au xixe siècle: Mme. Ackermann d'après de nombreux documents inédits* (Paris, 1906).

Clarke, M. L., *George Grote: A Biography* (London, 1962).

Clément-Simon, G., *Histoire du collège de Tulle depuis son origine jusqu'à la création du lycée (1567–1887)* (Paris, 1892).

‡Cole, Margaret, *The Story of Fabian Socialism* (London, etc., 1961).

——, ed., *Beatrice Webb's Diaries 1912–1924* (London, etc., 1952).

Collinet, Michel, "Saint-Simon et la 'société industrielle,'" *Contrat social,* IV (1960), 340–347.

——, "Saint-Simon et l'évolution historique," *ibid.,* 287–294.

‡Conway, Moncure Daniel, *Autobiography: Memories and Experiences* (2 vols., London, etc., 1904).

——, *Centenary History of the South Place Society* (London, 1894).

‡Cooke, G. W., *George Eliot: A Critical Study* (London, 1883).

‡Cournot, A[ntoine Augustin], *Souvenirs (1760–1860)* (Paris, 1913).

‡Cresson, André, *Ernest Renan: Sa vie, son oeuvre avec un exposé de sa philosophie* (Paris, 1949).

——, *Hippolyte Taine . . .* (Paris, 1951).

‡Cross, J. W., *George Eliot's Life as Related in Her Letters and Journals* (3 vols., Boston and New York, 1909).

‡Crowley, D. W., "The Origins of the Revolt of the British Labour Movement from Liberalism, 1875–1906" (Ph.D. thesis, University of London, 1952).

‡Curtis, Michael, *Three against the Third Republic: Sorel, Barrès, and Maurras* (Princeton, 1959).

Curtis, S. J., and M. E. A. Boutwood, *A Short History of Educational Ideas* (London, 1953).

‡Dansette, Adrien, *Histoire religieuse de la France contemporaine* (2 vols., Paris, 1948–51).

‡Dauriac, Lionel, *Contingence et rationalisme: Pages d'histoire et de doctrine* (Paris, 1924).

‡——, *Croyance et réalité* (Paris, 1899).

‡——, "La philosophie au collège," *Critique philosophique,* n.s. I (1885), 17–24.

‡——, "Les sources néocriticistes de la dialectique synthétique," *Revue de métaphysique et de morale,* XVII (1909), 483–500.

‡Davy, Georges, "L'explication sociologique et le recours à l'histoire d'après Comte, Mill et Durkheim," *ibid.,* Vol. 54 (1949), pp. 330–362.

Defries, Amelia, *The Interpreter Geddes: The Man and His Gospel* (London, 1927).

Dejob, Charles, *L'instruction publique en France et en Italie au dix-neuvième siècle* (Paris, n.d.).

Delbos, Victor, *La philosophie française* (Paris, 1921).

Delfour, J., *Histoire du lycée de Pau* (Pau, 1890).

‡Deluns-Montaud, "La philosophie de Gambetta," *Revue politique et parlementaire,* XI (1897), 241–265.

‡Deploige, Simon, *Le conflit de la morale et de la sociologie* (Louvain, etc., 1911).

‡Dimier, Louis, *Vingt ans d'Action Française et autres souvenirs* (Paris, 1926).

Dingler, Hugo, *Die Grundgedanken der Machschen Philosophie* (Leipzig, 1924).

‡Donnelly, Mabel Collins, *George Gissing: Grave Comedian* (Cambridge, Mass., 1954).

‡Dronsart, Marie, *Portraits d'Outre-Manche* (Paris, 1889).

‡Dubislav, Walter, "Joseph Petzoldt in memoriam," *Annalen der Philosophie und philosophischen Kritik,* VIII (1929), 289–294.

Duboc, Julius, *Hundert Jahre Zeitgeist in Deutschland: Geschichte und Kritik* (Leipzig, 1889).

Dürr, Karl, *Der logische Positivismus* (Berne, 1948). Bibliographical.

‡Duguit, Léon, "Un séminaire de sociologie," *Revue internationale de sociologie,* I (1893), 201–208.

‡Duncan, David, *Life and Letters of Herbert Spencer* (2 vols., New York, 1908).

Dupréel, E., *Deux essais sur le progrès* (Brussels, 1928).

Duroselle, J.-B., "Michel Chevalier saint-simonien," *Revue historique,* Vol. 215 (1956), pp. 233–266.

Duruy, Victor, *Notes et souvenirs (1811–1894)* (2 vols., Paris, 1901).

Duveau, Georges, *Les instituteurs* (Bourges, 1957).

——, *La pensée ouvrière sur l'éducation pendant la Seconde République et le Second Empire* (Paris, n d).

Eaglesham, Eric, *From School Board to Local Authority* (London, 1956).

‡Eichel, William, "Sully Prudhomme: An Intellectual Biography. A Struggle for Idealistic Reconstruction in the Age of Positivism" (Ph.D. thesis, Cornell University, 1954).

‡Eichthal, Eugène d', ed., *John Stuart Mill: Correspondance inédite avec Gustave d'Eichthal (1828–1842—1864–1871)* (Paris, 1898).

‡——, "Letters of John Stuart Mill to Gustave d'Eichthal," *Cosmopolis,* VI (1897), 20–38, 348–366.

‡Elliot, Hugh S. R., ed., *The Letters of John Stuart Mill* (2 vols., London, etc., 1910).

Ensor, R. C. K., *England 1870–1914* (Oxford, 1936).

‡Evans, D. O., "Alfred de Vigny and Positivism," *Romanic Review,* XXXV (1944), 288–298.

‡Everett, Edwin Mallard, *The Party of Humanity: The Fortnightly Review and Its Contributors, 1865–1874* (Chapel Hill, N.C., 1939).

Eyre, J. Vargas, *Henry Edward Armstrong 1848–1937: The Doyen of British Chemists and Pioneer of Technical Education* (London, 1958).

Faber, Geoffrey, *Jowett: A Portrait with Background* (Cambridge, Mass., 1957).

Faure, Jean Louis, *Claude Bernard* (Paris, 1925).

Fawcett, Mrs., *Life of the Right Hon. Sir William Molesworth, Bart.* (London and New York, 1910).

‡Feigl, Herbert, "Moritz Schlick," *Erkenntnis,* VII (1937–38), 393–419.

‡Flint, Robert, *History of the Philosophy of History* (New York, 1894).

Foulquié, Paul, *Alain* (Paris, n.d.).

‡——, *Claude Bernard* (Paris, n.d.).

‡Fox, Caroline, *Memories of Old Friends: Being Extracts from the Journals and Letters* (ed. Pym, 3rd ed., 2 vols., London, 1882).

‡Frank, Philipp, *Modern Science and Its Philosophy* (Cambridge, Mass., and London, 1950).

‡Freycinet, C. de, *Souvenirs 1848–1878* (Paris, 1912).

‡Freyer, Hans, *Soziologie als Wirklichkeitswissenschaft: Logische Grundlegung des Systems der Soziologie* (Leipzig and Berlin, 1930).

‡Froude, James Anthony, *Thomas Carlyle: A History of His Life in London 1834–1881* (2 vols., New York, 1904).

Galabert, Edmond, *Georges Bizet: Souvenirs et correspondance* (Paris, 1877).

Gehlke, Charles Elmer, *Emile Durkheim's Contributions to Sociological Theory* (New York and London, 1915).

‡Gellner, Ernest, "Reflections on Linguistic Philosophy, II," *Listener,* Vol. 58 (1957), pp. 237–241.

‡Gerth, H. H., and C. Wright Mills, eds., *From Max Weber: Essays in Sociology* (New York, 1946).

Gheusi, P. B., *Gambetta: Life and Letters* (tr. Montagu, London and Leipzig, 1910).

‡Gilson, Etienne, *Choir of Muses* (tr. Ward, New York, 1953). On Clotilde de Vaux.

‡Ginsberg, Morris, *Reason and Unreason in Society: Essays in Sociology and Social Philosophy* (Cambridge, Mass., 1948).

‡Giraud, Victor, *Essai sur Taine: Son oeuvre et son influence d'après des documents inédits* (2nd ed., Paris, 1901).

Gissing, George, *Autobiographical Notes, with Comments upon Tennyson and Huxley* (Edinburgh, 1930).

——, *Letters to Edward Clodd* (London, 1914).

——, *Selections Autobiographical and Imaginative* (London, 1929).

‡Gley, E., *Essais de philosophie et d'histoire de la biologie* (Paris, 1900).

‡——, "Les sciences biologiques et la biologie générale," *Revue scientifique,* Vol. 47 (1909), pp. 1–11.

‡Gramzow, Otto, *Gustav Ratzenhofer und seine Philosophie* (Berlin, 1904).

‡Graves, Robert Perceval, *Life of Sir William Rowan Hamilton* (3 vols., Dublin and London, 1882–89).

Gresham University Commission, *The Report of the Commissioners* (London, 1894).

‡Grote, Mrs. [Harriet], *The Personal Life of George Grote* (2nd ed., London, 1873).

Guérard, Albert, *Fossils and Presences* (Stanford, Calif., 1957).

‡Guerlac, H., "Rapport," in IXᵉ Congrès International des Sciences Historiques: I, *Rapports* (Paris, 1950), pp. 182–211.

‡Gugenheim, Suzanne, *Madame d'Agoult et la pensée européenne de son époque* (Florence, 1937).

‡Guizot, [François], *Mémoires pour servir à l'histoire de mon temps* (8 vols., Paris, 1858–67).

‡——, *Memoirs to Illustrate the History of My Time* (tr. Cole, 4 vols., 1858–61).

‡Guyon, Bernard, *La pensée politique et sociale de Balzac* (Paris, 1947).

‡Haight, Gordon S., ed., *The George Eliot Letters* (7 vols., New Haven and London, 1954–55).

Haldane, Elizabeth S., *George Eliot and Her Times: A Victorian Study* (New York, 1927).

Hamburger, Maurice, *Léon Bourgeois 1851–1925* (Paris, 1932).

‡Hamerton, P. G., "The Chief Influences on My Career," *Forum,* XVIII (1894–95), 415–424.

‡Hamilton, James, *Personal Recollections of Auguste Comte* (London, 1897).

‡Harrison, Austin, "George Gissing," *Nineteenth Century and After,* Vol. 60 (1906), pp. 453–463.

‡Haultain, Arnold, ed., *A Selection from Goldwin Smith's Correspondence* (Toronto, n.d.).

‡Haussonville, [comte d'], "Mme. Ackermann d'après des lettres et

des papiers inédits," *Revue des deux mondes,* Vol. 108 (1891), pp. 318–352.

‡Havard, William C., *Henry Sidgwick & Later Utilitarian Philosophy* (Gainesville, Fla., 1959).

‡Hayek, F. A., *The Counter-Revolution of Science: Studies on the Abuse of Reason* (Glencoe, Ill., 1952).

‡Hayward, J. E. S., "The Official Social Philosophy of the French Third Republic: Léon Bourgeois and Solidarism," *International Review of Social History,* VI (1961), 19–48.

‡Headings, Mildred J., *French Freemasonry under the Third Republic* (Baltimore, 1949).

‡Hémon, Camille, *La philosophie de M. Sully Prudhomme* (Paris, 1907).

Henning, Hans, *Ernst Mach als Philosoph, Physiker und Psycholog* (Leipzig, 1915).

‡Herford, C. H., *Philip Henry Wicksteed: His Life and Work* (London and Toronto, 1931).

‡Herkner, Heinrich, "Gustav Schmoller als Soziologe," *Jahrbücher für Nationalökonomie und Statistik,* Vol. 118 (1922), pp. 1–8.

‡Herzberg, Lily, "Die philosophischen Strömungen im Monistenbund," *Annalen der Philosophie und philosophischen Kritik,* VII (1928), 113–135, 177–199.

‡Heyderhoff, Julius, "Rudolf Haym und Karl Twesten: Ein Briefwechsel über positive Philosophie und Fortschrittspolitik, 1859–1863," *Preussische Jahrbücher,* Vol. 161 (1915), pp. 232–256.

‡Hintze, Otto, Art. "Gustav v. Schmoller," in *Deutsches Biographisches Jahrbuch,* Überleitungsband II: 1917–1920 (Berlin and Leipzig, 1928).

‡Hirst, F. W., *Early Life & Letters of John Morley* (2 vols., London, 1927).

‡Hobson, J. A., and Morris Ginsberg, *L. T. Hobhouse: His Life and Work* (London, 1931).

‡Hodges, H. A., *The Philosophy of Wilhelm Dilthey* (London, 1952).

‡——, *Wilhelm Dilthey: An Introduction* (London, 1944).

‡Höffding, Harald, *Modern Philosophers* (tr. Mason, London, 1915).

‡*Hommage à Alain* (Paris, 1952).

Hommage à Gaston Bachelard: Etudes de philosophie et d'histoire des sciences (Paris, 1957).

366

‡Hughes, H. Stuart, *Consciousness and Society: The Reorientation of European Social Thought, 1890–1930* (New York, 1958).

‡Hyde, H. Montgomery, *A Victorian Historian: Private Letters of W. E. H. Lecky, 1859–1878* (London, 1947).

‡Hyndman, H. M., *Clemenceau: The Man and His Time* (London, 1919).

Iggers, Georg G., *The Cult of Authority: The Political Philosophy of the Saint-Simonians, a Chapter in the Intellectual History of Totalitarianism* (The Hague, 1958).

‡——, ed. and tr., *The Doctrine of Saint-Simon: An Exposition. First Year, 1828–1829* (Boston, 1958).

‡Jahn, Georg, "Karl Lamprecht als Wirtschafts- und Kulturhistoriker: Zur 100. Wiederkehr seines Geburtstages," *Schmollers Jahrbuch*, Vol. 76 (1956), pp. 129–142.

‡Janet, Paul, *La crise philosophique: MM. Taine, Renan, Littré, Vacherot* (Paris, 1865).

——, "La philosophie de Pierre Leroux," *Revue des deux mondes*, Vol. 152 (1899), 767–788, Vol. 153 (1899), pp. 379–406.

‡Janet, Pierre, "L'oeuvre psychologique de Th. Ribot," *Journal de psychologie normale et pathologique*, XII (1915), 268–282.

‡Jaurès, Jean, *Discours parlementaires*, Vol. I (Paris, 1904).

‡Joergensen, Joergen, "The Development of Logical Empiricism," *International Encyclopedia of Unified Science*, II, no. 9 (Chicago, 1951).

‡Jones, Thomas, *A Diary with Letters 1931–1950* (London, etc., 1954).

Judges, A. V., ed., *Education and the Philosophic Mind* (London, etc., 1957).

Kelly, Thomas R., *Explanation and Reality in the Philosophy of Emile Meyerson* (Princeton, London, and Oxford, 1937).

‡Kent, William, *London for Heretics* (London, 1932). Some notes on Positivist physical arrangements.

Keynes, John Maynard, *Essays in Biography* (new ed., London, 1951).

‡Kitchel, Anna Theresa, *George Lewes and George Eliot: A Review of Records* (New York, 1933).

‡Koigen, David, *Zur Vorgeschichte des modernen philosophischen Socialismus in Deutschland: Zur Geschichte der Philosophie und Socialphilosophie des Junghegelianismus* (Berne, 1901).

‡Kraft, Victor, *The Vienna Circle: The Origin of Neo-Positivism. A Chapter in the History of Recent Philosophy* (tr. Pap, New York, 1953).

‡Kraus, Oskar, Carl Stumpf, and Edmund Husserl, *Franz Brentano: Zur Kenntnis seines Lebens und seiner Lehre* (Munich, 1910).

‡Kubitz, Oskar Alfred, *Development of John Stuart Mill's* System of Logic (Illinois Studies in the Social Sciences, Vol. XVIII, 1932).

‡Lacombe, Roger, *La méthode sociologique de Durkheim: Etude critique* (Paris, 1926).

Lamy, Pierre, *Claude Bernard et le matérialisme* (Paris, 1939).

‡——, *L'introduction à l'étude de la médecine expérimentale: Claude Bernard, le naturalisme et le positivisme* (Paris, 1928).

Larguier des Bancels, J., "L'oeuvre d'Alfred Binet," *Année psychologique,* XVIII (1912), 15–32.

Lauzun, Philippe, *Notice sur le collège d'Agen depuis sa fondation jusqu'à nos jours (1581–1888)* (Agen, 1888).

Lavisse, Ernest, *Victor Duruy* (Paris, 1895).

‡Le Gendre, Paul, *Un médecin philosophe: Charles Bouchard, son oeuvre et son temps (1837–1915)* (Paris, 1924).

‡Leroy, Maxime, *Histoire des idées sociales en France* (3 vols., Paris, 1946–54).

‡*Letters of George Gissing to Members of His Family* (London, 1927).

‡Lévêque, Raphaël, *L'élément historique dans la connaissance humaine d'après Cournot* (Paris, 1938).

‡Levin, Rudolf, *Der Geschichtsbegriff des Positivismus unter besonderer Berücksichtigung Mills und der rechtsphilosophischen Anschauungen John Austins* (Leipzig, 1935).

‡Lévy, Albert, *La philosophie de Feuerbach et son influence sur la littérature allemande* (Paris, 1904).

‡Lévy-Bruhl, Lucien, *Carnets* (Paris, 1949).

Liard, Louis, *L'enseignement supérieur en France 1789–1893* (2 vols., Paris, 1888–94).

Lindley, Dwight Newton, "The Saint-Simonians, Carlyle, and Mill: A Study in the History of Ideas" (Ph.D. thesis, Columbia University, 1958).

‡Lindsay, Jack, *George Meredith: His Life and Work* (London, 1956).

‡Lloyd, Walter, "Theological Evolution: W. M. W. Call," *Westminster Review,* Vol. 136 (1891), pp. 36–45.

London, School Board, *Reports of Debates . . . , with Division Lists, etc., 1891–94* (2 vols., London, 1895).

‡Lubac, Henri de, *The Drama of Atheist Humanism* (tr. Riley, New York, 1950).

‡——, *The Un-Marxian Socialist: A Study of Proudhon* (tr. Scantlebury, London, 1948).

McCabe, Joseph, *Life and Letters of George Jacob Holyoake* (2 vols., London, 1908).

‡Mackay, Mona E., *Meredith et la France* (Paris, 1937).

‡Mairet, Philip, *Pioneer of Sociology: The Life and Letters of Patrick Geddes* (London, 1957).

‡Maitland, Frederic William, *The Life and Letters of Leslie Stephen* (New York and London, 1908).

‡Manuel, Frank E., *The New World of Henri Saint-Simon* (Cambridge, Mass., 1956).

‡——, *The Prophets of Paris* (Cambridge, Mass., 1962).

‡Marcuse, Herbert, *Reason and Revolution: Hegel and the Rise of Social Theory* (London, etc., 1941).

‡Martineau, Harriet, *Autobiography* (3 vols., London, 1877).

‡Masaryk, Th. G., *Die philosophischen und sociologischen Grundlagen des Marxismus: Studien zur socialen Frage* (Vienna, 1899).

Massip, Maurice, *Le collège de Tournon en Vivarais d'après les documents originaux inédits* (Paris, 1890).

‡Masur, Gerhard, "Wilhelm Dilthey und die europäische Geistesgeschichte," *Deutsche Vierteljahrsschrift für Literaturwissenschaft und Geistesgeschichte,* XII (1934), 479–503.

Mauriac, Pierre, *Claude Bernard* (Paris, 1954).

‡Mentré, F., *Cournot et la renaissance du probabilisme au xixe siècle* (Paris, 1908).

‡Metz, Rudolf, *A Hundred Years of British Philosophy* (tr. Harvey and others, ed. Muirhead, London and New York, 1938).

‡Mill, John Stuart, *Autobiography* (3rd ed., London, 1874).

‡——, *Essays on Politics and Culture* (ed. and with an Introduction by Himmelfarb, Garden City, N.Y., 1962).

‡Misch, Clara, ed., *Der junge Dilthey: Ein Lebensbild in Briefen und Tagebüchern 1852–1870* (Leipzig and Berlin, 1933).

Misch, Georg, *Vom Lebens- und Gedankenkreis Wilhelm Diltheys* (Frankfurt, 1947).

‡Monod, Gabriel, *Renan, Taine, Michelet* (3rd ed., Paris, 1890).

‡Morley, John, *Recollections* (2 vols., New York, 1917).

‡Morris, Charles, "Scientific Empiricism," *International Encyclopedia of Unified Science,* I (1955), 63–75.

‡——, "The Significance of the Unity of Science Movement," *Philosophy and Phenomenological Research,* VI (1945–46), 508–515.

‡Mueller, Iris Wessel, *John Stuart Mill and French Thought* (Urbana, Ill., 1956).

‡Murray, Gilbert, *An Unfinished Autobiography* (London, 1960).

‡Neff, Emery, *Carlyle and Mill: An Introduction to Victorian Thought* (2nd ed., New York, 1926).

‡Nethercot, Arthur H., *The First Five Lives of Annie Besant* (Chicago, 1960).

‡Neurath, Otto, *Le développement du cercle de Vienne et l'avenir de l'empirisme logique* (tr. Vouillemin, Paris, 1935).

‡Nicard, Pol, *Etude sur la vie et les travaux de M. Ducrotay de Blainville* (Paris, 1890).

‡Nicolson, Harold, *Sainte-Beuve* (London, 1957).

‡Niess, Robert J., *Julien Benda* (Ann Arbor, 1956).

‡Nisbet, Robert A., "Conservatism and Sociology," *American Journal of Sociology,* Vol. 58 (1952–53), pp. 167–175.

‡Nitzschke, Heinz, "Die Geschichtsphilosophie Lorenz von Steins . . . ," Beiheft 26 der *Historischen Zeitschrift* (Munich and Berlin, 1932).

‡Olivier, Louis, "Alexandre Etard, sa vie et ses travaux (1852–1910)," *Revue générale des sciences pures et appliquées,* XXI (1910), 581–605.

Olivier, Sydney, *Letters and Selected Writings* (ed. M. Olivier, London, 1948).

‡Ollivier, Emile, "Lettres d'exil, II," *Revue des deux mondes,* 1 July 1919, pp. 37–61.

‡Olmsted, J. M. D., and E. Harris Olmsted, *Claude Bernard and the Experimental Method in Medicine* (New York, 1952).

Ostwald, Wilhelm, *Lebenslinien: Eine Selbstbiographie* (2 vols., Berlin, 1926–27).

‡Oswald, Eugene, *Reminiscences of a Busy Life* (London, 1911).

‡Packe, Michael St. John, *The Life of John Stuart Mill* (London, 1954).

Pankhurst, Richard K. P., *The Saint-Simonians, Mill and Carlyle: A Preface to Modern Thought* (n.p., n.d.).

‡Parodi, D., *Du positivisme à l'idéalisme: Etudes critiques. Philosophies d'hier et d'aujourd'hui* (Paris, 1930).

‡——, *Du positivisme à l'idéalisme: Philosophies d'hier. Etudes critiques* (Paris, 1930).

——, *En quête d'une philosophie: Essais de philosophie première* (Paris, 1935).

‡——, *La philosophie contemporaine en France: Essai de classification des doctrines* (Paris, 1919).

‡Parsons, Talcott, *The Structure of Social Action: A Study in Social Theory with Special Reference to a Group of Recent European Writers* (Glencoe, Ill., 1949).

Paul, C. Kegan, *Memories* (London, 1899).

‡Pease, Edward R., *The History of the Fabian Society* (London, 1916).

‡Pécaut, Félix, "Un spiritualisme scientifique: La philosophie d'Emile Durkheim," *Revue de l'enseignement français hors de France,* 1920, no. 2, pp. 49–57.

‡Perry, E., "A Morning with Auguste Comte," *Nineteenth Century,* II (1877), 621–631.

‡Petre, M. D., *Autobiography and Life of George Tyrrell* (2 vols., London, 1912).

Petri, Barbara Patricia, *The Historical Thought of P.-J.-B. Buchez* (Washington, D.C., 1958).

‡Petzäll, Åke, "Logistischer Positivismus . . . ," *Göteborgs Högskolas Årsskrift,* XXXVII (1931), No. 3.

Pigou, A. C., ed., *Memorials of Alfred Marshall* (London, 1925).

Pinet, G., *Histoire de l'Ecole Polytechnique* (Paris, 1887).

Pond, E. J., *Les idées morales et religieuses de George Eliot* (Paris, 1927).

Quicherat, J., *Histoire de Sainte-Barbe: Collège, communauté, institution* (3 vols., Paris, 1860–64).

‡Raab, Franz, *Die Fortschrittsidee bei Gustav Schmoller* (Freiburg, 1934).

Rádl, Emanuel, *The History of Biological Theories* (tr. Hatfield, Oxford and London, 1930).

Rambaud, Alfred, *Jules Ferry* (Paris, 1903).

‡Ranulf, Svend, "Methods of Sociology, with an Essay: Remarks on the Epistemology of Sociology," *Acta Jutlandica, Aarskrift for Aarhus Universitet,* XXVII[1] (1955).

‡Ratcliffe, S. K., *The Story of South Place* (London, 1955).

‡Ravaisson, Félix, *La philosophie en France au xixe siècle* (5th ed., Paris, 1904).

‡Rawidowicz, S., *Ludwig Feuerbachs Philosophie: Ursprung und Schicksal* (Berlin, 1931).

‡Reclus, Maurice, *Jules Ferry 1832–1893* (Paris, 1947).

‡*Recueil d'études sociales publié à la mémoire de Frédéric LePlay* (Paris, 1956).

Rees, J. C., *Mill and His Early Critics* (Leicester, 1956).

‡Reid, T. Wemyss, *The Life, Letters, and Friendships of Richard Monckton Milnes, First Lord Houghton* (2 vols., New York, 1891).

Renan, Ernest, *Recollections of My Youth* (tr. Pitman, London, 1883).

‡Rex, John, *Key Problems of Sociological Theory* (London, 1961).

‡Reybekiel-Schapiro, H., "Die introspektive Methode in der modernen Psychologie," *Vierteljahrsschrift für wissenschaftliche Philosophie und Soziologie,* XXX (1906), 73–114.

Rhys, Ernest, *Everyman Remembers* (New York, 1931).

Ribbe, Charles de, *LePlay, d'après sa correspondance* (Paris, 1884).

‡Ribot, Th., *German Psychology of To-day: The Empirical School* (tr. Baldwin, New York, 1886).

Richard, Gaston, *La question sociale et le mouvement philosophique au xixe siècle* (Paris, 1914).

Riehl, Alois, *Der philosophische Kritizismus: Geschichte und System* (2nd ed., 3 vols., Leipzig, 1908–26).

‡Roberts, Morley, *The Private Life of Henry Maitland: A Portrait of George Gissing* (ed. Bishop, London, 1958).

‡Robertson, John Mackinnon, *Buckle and His Critics: A Study in Sociology* (London, 1895).

——, *The Life Pilgrimage of Moncure Daniel Conway* (London, 1914).

‡——, ed., *William Archer as Rationalist* (London, 1925).

‡Rolleston, Sir Humphry Davy, *The Right Honourable Sir Thomas Clifford Allbutt K.C.B.: A Memoir* (London, 1929).

‡Romanell, Patrick, "Romanticism and Croce's Conception of Science," *Review of Metaphysics,* IX (1956), 505–515.

‡Ross, Alf, *Kritik der sogenannten praktischen Erkenntnis: Zugleich Prolegomena zu einer Kritik der Rechtswissenschaft* (Copenhagen and Leipzig, 1933).

‡Rothacker, Erich, *Einleitung in die Geisteswissenschaften* (Tübingen, 1920).

‡Royal Commission on Scientific Instruction and the Advancement of Science, *Reports* (3 vols., London, 1872–75).

Royal Commission on University Education in London, *Final Report of the Commissioners* (London, 1913).

Royer, Clémence, *La vie politique de François Arago* (n.p., n.d.).

‡Russell, Bertrand, "Logical Positivism," *Revue internationale de philosophie,* IV (1950), 3–19.

——, *My Philosophical Development* (London, 1959).

‡—— and Patricia Russell, eds., *The Amberley Papers: The Letters and Diaries of Lord and Lady Amberley* (2 vols., London, 1937).

‡Saenger, Samuel, *John Stuart Mill: Sein Leben und Lebenswerk* (Stuttgart, 1901).

‡St. Aubyn, Giles, *A Victorian Eminence: The Life and Works of Henry Thomas Buckle* (London, 1958).

‡Salverte, Eusèbe, *Des sciences occultes . . .* (3rd ed., Paris, 1856). Preface by Littré.

Scherer, Edmond, "M. Taine ou la critique positiviste," in his *Mélanges de critique religieuse* (Paris, 1860), pp. 451–487.

Schools Inquiry Commission, *Report* (London, 1864).

‡Schulze-Gaevernitz, Gerhart von, *Zum socialen Frieden: Eine Darstellung der socialpolitischen Erziehung des englischen Volkes im neunzehnten Jahrhundert* (2 vols., Leipzig, 1890).

‡Scott, John A., *Republican Ideas and the Liberal Tradition in France, 1870–1914* (New York, 1951).

‡Séailles, Gabriel, *Ernest Renan: Essai de biographie psychologique* (2nd ed., Paris, 1895).

Seifert, Friedrich, *Der Streit um Karl Lamprechts Geschichtsphiloso-phie* (Augsburg, 1925).

‡Select Committee [of the House of Commons] on Scientific Instruction, *Report* (London, 1868).

‡Sertillanges, A.-D., *La philosophie de Claude Bernard* (n.p., n.d.).

‡Shine, Hill, *Carlyle and the Saint-Simonians: The Concept of Historical Periodicity* (Baltimore, 1941).

‡Simey, T. S., and M. B. Simey, *Charles Booth: Social Scientist* (London, 1960).

‡Simon, Walter M., "Herbert Spencer and the 'Social Organism,'" *Journal of the History of Ideas,* XXI (1960), 294–299.

Smith, Goldwin, *Reminiscences* (ed. Haultain, New York, 1910).

Solly, Henry Shaen, *The Life of Henry Morley, LL.D.* (London, 1898).

‡Soltau, Roger Henry, *French Political Thought in the 19th Century* (New York, 1959).

Sorin, Elie, *Histoire du lycée d'Angers* (Angers, 1873).

‡Spaemann, Robert, *Der Ursprung der Soziologie aus dem Geist der Restauration: Studien über L.G.A. de Bonald* (Munich, 1959).

Sparrow Simpson, W. J., *Religious Thought in France in the Nineteenth Century* (London, 1935).

‡Spencer, Herbert, *An Autobiography* (2 vols., New York, 1904).

‡Spiess, Emil Jakob, *Die Geschichtsphilosophie von Karl Lamprecht* (Erlangen, 1921).

Spiller, G., *The Ethical Movement in Great Britain: A Documentary History* (London, n.d.).

‡Srbik, Heinrich Ritter von, *Geist und Geschichte vom deutschen Humanismus bis zur Gegenwart* (2 vols., Munich and Salzburg, 1950–51).

‡Stadler, Peter, *Geschichtschreibung und historisches Denken in Frankreich, 1789–1871* (Zurich, 1958).

‡Stang, Richard, *The Theory of the Novel in England, 1850–1870* (New York and London, 1959).

‡Stephen, Leslie, *The English Utilitarians* (3 vols., London, 1900).

‡——, *George Eliot* (New York and London, 1902).

‡Stevenson, Lionel, *The Ordeal of George Meredith: A Biography* (New York, 1953).

‡Stone, Julius, *The Province and Function of Law: Law as Logic, Jus-

tice and Social Control. A Study in Jurisprudence (Sydney, 1946).

‡Suter, Jean-François, *Philosophie et histoire chez Wilhelm Dilthey: Essai sur le problème de l'historicisme* (Basel, 1960).

‡Swinnerton, Frank, *George Gissing: A Critical Study* (new ed., London, 1924).

Talmon, J. L., *Political Messianism: The Romantic Phase* (New York, 1960).

‡Tarde, Gabriel, "L'accident et le rationnel en histoire d'après Cournot," *Revue de métaphysique et de morale,* XIII (1905), 319–347.

‡Taton, René, "Paul Tannery (1843–1904)," *Revue d'histoire des sciences et de leurs applications,* VII (1954), 303–312.

‡Taylor, A. J. P., *The Trouble Makers: Dissent over Foreign Policy, 1792–1939* (London, 1957).

Thomas, Bernard, ed., *Repton 1557 to 1957* (London, 1957).

‡Thomas, P.-Félix, *Pierre Leroux: Sa vie, son ouvre, sa doctrine. Contribution à l'histoire des idées au xix* *siècle* (Paris, 1904).

Thompson, D., "Science Teaching in Schools during the Second Half of the Nineteenth Century," *School Science Review,* XXXVII (1956), 298–305.

Trevelyan, George Macaulay, *Sir George Otto Trevelyan: A Memoir* (London, etc., 1932).

‡Troeltsch, Ernst, *Der Historismus und seine Probleme. Erstes Buch: Das logische Problem der Geschichtsphilosophie* (Tübingen, 1922).

Tuke, Margaret J., *A History of Bedford College for Women, 1849–1937* (London, etc., 1939).

Turner, D. M., *A History of Science Teaching in England* (London, 1927).

University for London Commission, *Report of the Royal Commissioners* (London, 1889).

‡Urmson, J. O., *Philosophical Analysis: Its Development between the Two World Wars* (Oxford, 1956).

Vallet, P., *Le kantisme et le positivisme: Etude sur les fondements de la connaissance humaine* (Paris, 1887).

‡Vialle, Louis, *Le désir du néant: Contribution à la psychologie du divertissement* (Paris, 1933). Comte interpreted as an escapist.

‡Vier, Jacques, *La comtesse d'Agoult et son temps: Avec des documents inédits* (4 vols., Paris, 1955–61).

——, ed., *Daniel Stern: Lettres républicaines du Second Empire. Documents inédits* (Paris, n.d.).

——, ed., *Marie d'Agoult: Son mari—ses amis. Documents inédits* (Paris, n.d.).

Villèle, comte de, *Mémoires et correspondance* (5 vols., Paris, 1888–90).

‡Virtanen, Reino, *Claude Bernard and His Place in the History of Ideas* (Lincoln, Neb., 1960).

‡Vizetelly, Ernest Alfred, *Emile Zola, Novelist and Reformer: An Account of His Life and Work* (London and New York, 1904).

‡Vossler, Karl, *Positivismus und Idealismus in der Sprachwissenschaft: Eine sprach-philosophische Untersuchung* (Heidelberg, 1904).

‡Wallon, Henri, "Introduction," in *A la lumière du marxisme: Essais,* Vol. II: *Karl Marx et la pensée moderne,* Part I (Paris, 1937), pp. 7–15.

‡Webb, Beatrice, *My Apprenticeship* (London, etc., 1950).

‡Webb, R. K., *Harriet Martineau: A Radical Victorian* (London, etc., 1960).

Webb, Sidney, and Beatrice Webb, *The History of Trade-Unionism* (new ed., London, etc., 1911).

Weill, Georges, *L'école saint-simonienne: Son histoire, son influence jusqu'à nos jours* (Paris, 1896).

——, *Histoire de l'enseignement secondaire en France (1802–1920)* (Paris, 1921).

‡——, *Histoire de l'idée laïque en France au xixᵉ siècle* (Paris, 1925).

Weinberg, Carlton Berenda, *Mach's Empirio-Pragmatism in Physical Science* (n.p., 1937).

‡Weinberg, Julius Rudolph, *An Examination of Logical Positivism* (New York and London, 1936).

Wheatley, Vera, *The Life and Work of Harriet Martineau* (London, 1957).

‡Willey, Basil, *More Nineteenth Century Studies: A Group of Honest Doubters* (London, 1956).

‡——, *Nineteenth Century Studies: Coleridge to Matthew Arnold* (London, 1949).

‡Wilson, David Alec, *Carlyle at His Zenith (1848–1853)* (London and New York, 1927).

Wundt, Wilhelm, *Erlebtes und Erkanntes* (Stuttgart, 1920).

Young, Arthur C., ed., *The Letters of George Gissing to Eduard Bertz, 1887–1903* (London, 1961).

INDEX